Fodor's 07

PUERTO VALLARTA

by Jane Onstott

Where to Stay and Eat for All Budgets

Must-See Sights and Local Secrets

Ratings You Can Trust

S0-BZH-325

Fodor's Travel Publications   New York, Toronto, London, Sydney, Auckland
www.fodors.com

FODOR'S PUERTO VALLARTA 2007
Editor: Shannon Kelly

Editorial Production: Bethany Cassin Beckerlegge
Editorial Contributors: Jane Onstott, Sean Mattson
Maps: David Lindroth, *cartographer,* with additional cartography provided by Henry Columb, Mark Stroud, and Ali Baird, Moon Street Cartography; Rebecca Baer and Bob Blake, *map editors*
Design: Fabrizio La Rocca, *creative director*; Guido Caroti, *art director*; Melanie Marin, *senior picture editor*
Production/Manufacturing: Robert Shields
Cover Photo (Los Arcas ampitheater on the Malecon): Karen Hunt/Corbis

First Edition

ISBN-10: 1-4000-1674-6

ISBN-13: 978-1-4000-1674-7

ISSN: 1558-8718

SPECIAL SALES
This book is available for special discounts for bulk purchases for sales promotions or premiums. Special editions, including personalized covers, excerpts of existing books, and corporate imprints, can be created in large quantities for special needs. For more information, write to Special Markets/Premium Sales, 1745 Broadway, MD 6-2, New York, New York 10019, or e-mail specialmarkets@randomhouse.com.

AN IMPORTANT TIP & AN INVITATION
Although all prices, opening times, and other details in this book are based on information supplied to us at press time, changes occur all the time in the travel world, and Fodor's cannot accept responsibility for facts that become outdated or for inadvertent errors or omissions. So **always confirm information when it matters,** especially if you're making a detour to visit a specific place. Your experiences—positive and negative—matter to us. If we have missed or misstated something, **please write to us.** We follow up on all suggestions. Contact the Puerto Vallarta editor at editors@fodors.com or c/o Fodor's at 1745 Broadway, New York, NY 10019.

PRINTED IN THE UNITED STATES OF AMERICA

10 9 8 7 6 5 4 3 2 1

Be a Fodor's Correspondent

Your opinion matters. It matters to us. It matters to your fellow Fodor's travelers, too. And we'd like to hear it. In fact, we *need* to hear it.

When you share your experiences and opinions, you become an active member of the Fodor's community. That means we'll not only use your feedback to make our books better, but we'll publish your names and comments whenever possible. Throughout our guides, look for "Word of Mouth," excerpts of your unvarnished feedback.

Here's how you can help improve Fodor's for all of us.

Tell us when we're right. We rely on local writers to give you an insider's perspective. But our writers and staff editors—who are the best in the business—depend on you. Your positive feedback is a vote to renew our recommendations for the next edition.

Tell us when we're wrong. We're proud that we update most of our guides every year. But we're not perfect. Things change. Hotels cut services. Museums change hours. Charming cafés lose charm. If our writer didn't quite capture the essence of a place, tell us how you'd do it differently. If any of our descriptions are inaccurate or inadequate, we'll incorporate your changes in the next edition and will correct factual errors at fodors.com *immediately.*

Tell us what to include. You probably have had fantastic travel experiences that aren't yet in Fodor's. Why not share them with a community of like-minded travelers? Maybe you chanced upon a beach or bistro or B&B that you don't want to keep to yourself. Tell us why we should include it. And share your discoveries and experiences with everyone directly at fodors.com. Your input may lead us to add a new listing or highlight a place we cover with a "Highly Recommended" star or with our highest rating, "Fodor's Choice."

Give us your opinion instantly at our feedback center at www.fodors.com/feedback. You may also e-mail editors@fodors.com with the subject line "Puerto Vallarta Editor." Or send your nominations, comments, and complaints by mail to Puerto Vallarta Editor, Fodor's, 1745 Broadway, New York, NY 10019.

You and travelers like you are the heart of the Fodor's community. Make our community richer by sharing your experiences. Be a Fodor's correspondent.

¡Buen Viaje!

Tim Jarrell, Publisher

CONTENTS

PUERTO VALLARTA

1 EXPERIENCE PUERTO VALLARTA 11
Welcome to Puerto Vallarta 12
Puerto Vallarta's Top Experiences 14
Puerto Vallarta Then & Now 16
Great Itineraries 18
When to Go .20

2 WHERE TO STAY 21
Planning 22
Puerto Vallarta 24
North of Puerto Vallarta 39
Costalegre 55

3 WHERE TO EAT 61
Puerto Vallarta 64
North of Puerto Vallarta 79
Costalegre .90

4 BEACHES 93
Puerto Vallarta 95
Nayarit 98
South of Puerto Vallarta 102
The Costalegre 106

5 SHOPPING 109
Puerto Vallarta 114
North & South of Puerto Vallarta 129

6 AFTER DARK 133
Bars & Pubs 134
Live Music .142
Dance Clubs 146
Film 148
More After-Dark Options 148

7 ADVENTURE 151
Outdoor Activities & Sports 152

Other Adventures 169

8 CULTURE 171
Architecture 172
The Arts 172
Classes & Workshops 176
Museums 176
Cultural Centers 177
Festivals & Events 177

9 OVERNIGHT EXCURSIONS 181
Planning 184
San Blas & Environs 186
The Mountain Towns 192
The Guadalajara Region 199

10 GAY PUERTO VALLARTA 229
Daytime Activities 230
After Dark .231
Where to Stay 233

UNDERSTANDING PUERTO VALLARTA

PV at a Glance 238
History 240
Chronology .244
Government & Economy 245
People & Society 248
The Natural World 253
Books & Movies 256
Spanish Vocabulary 257

PLANNING YOUR TRIP

Smart Travel Tips 264
Index 294
About the Writer 304

PUERTO VALLARTA IN FOCUS

CLOSEUPS

Tennis Anyone? 26
Don't Be (Time-Share) Shark Bait . . .38
Buying a Time-Share 48
An Over-the-Top Experience 51
Menu Translator 65
Breakfast of Champions 75
Turtle Rescue 101
Lingering in Yalepa 105
Shopping in Spanish 114
True Mexican Talavera 119
Mexican Rhythm & Roots 144
Multi-Adventure Outfitters 153
Annual Events 157
On the Boardwalk 175
Flight of the Voladores 176
Three Kings Day 178
Public Holidays 179
Live Performance 206
Root for the Home Team 218
Dedicated to its Craft 219
Work up a Sweat 234

MAPS

The Central Pacific Coast 6–7
Puerto Vallarta 8
El Centro & Zona Romántica 9
Where to Stay in Banderas Bay 27
Where to Stay in El Centro 33
Where to Stay in Zona Romántica . . .36
Where to Stay North of the Bay 49
Where to Stay in the Costalegre 57
Where to Eat in Banderas Bay 67
Where to Eat in El Centro 73
Where to Eat in Zona Romántica 76

WHERE TO STAY
Spaaahh 40
WHERE TO EAT
Mexico's Gourmet Town 81
SHOPPING
The Art of the Huichol 122
AFTER DARK
!Tequila! 138
OVERNIGHT EXCURSIONS
Mariachi Born in Jalisco 207

Bandeiras Bay Beaches 97
Shopping in El Centro &
Zona Romántica 112–113
San Blas 189
Inland Mountain Towns 193
Greater Guadalajara 200–201
Historic Guadalajara 205
Tlaquepaque 213

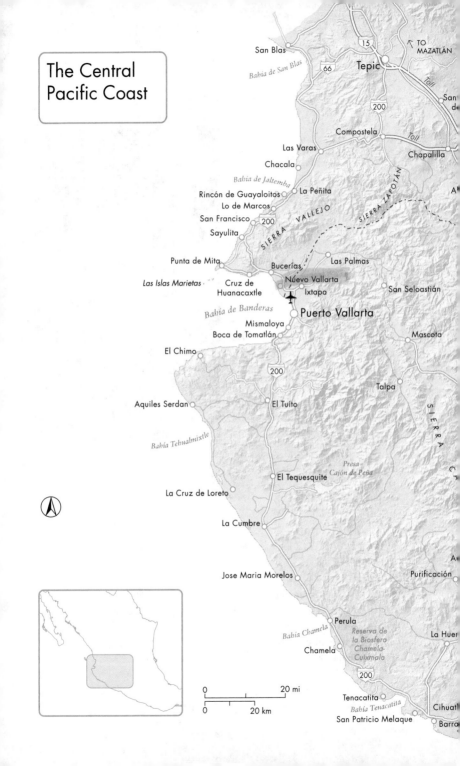

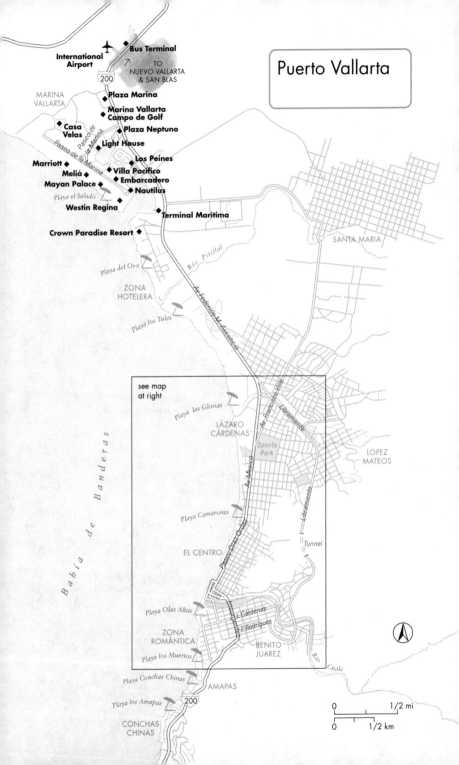

Puerto Vallarta

International Airport

Bus Terminal

TO NUEVO VALLARTA & SAN BLAS

200

MARINA VALLARTA

Plaza Marina

Marina Vallarta Campo de Golf

Casa Velas

Plaza Neptuno

Light House

Los Peines

Marriott

Villa Pacifico

Meliá

Embarcadero

Mayan Palace

Nautilus

Playa el Salado

Westin Regina

Terminal Marítima

Crown Paradise Resort

Paseo de la Marina

Playa del Oro

Río Pitillal

SANTA MARIA

ZONA HOTELERA

Playa los Tules

Av. Federico M. Ascencio

see map at right

Playa las Glorias

LÁZARO CÁRDENAS

Sports Park

LOPEZ MATEOS

Bahía de Banderas

Av. Francisco Villa

Libramiento

Av. México

Playa Camarones

Paseo Díaz Ordaz

EL CENTRO

Libramiento

Tunnel

Playa Olas Altas

L. Cárdenas

F. Rodríguez

ZONA ROMÁNTICA

BENITO JUAREZ

Río Cuale

Playa los Muertos

Playa Conchas Chinas

AMAPAS

200

Playa los Amapas

CONCHAS CHINAS

0   1/2 mi

0   1/2 km

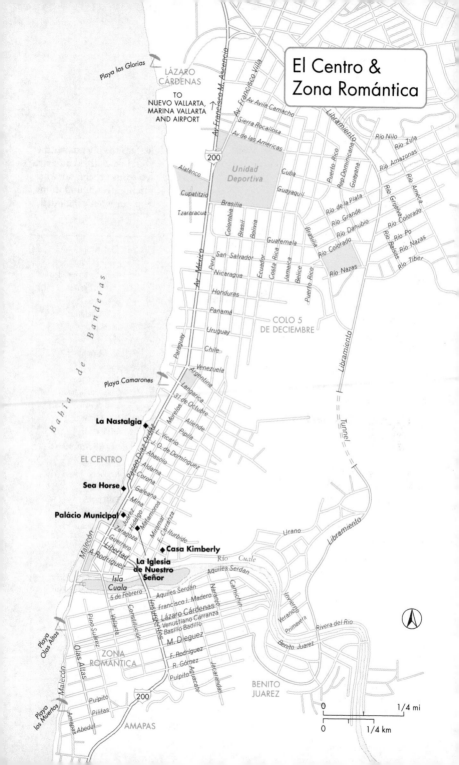

ABOUT THIS BOOK

Our Ratings

Sometimes you find terrific travel experiences and sometimes they just find you. But usually the burden is on you to select the right combination of experiences. That's where our ratings come in.

As travelers we've all discovered a place so wonderful that its worthiness is obvious. And sometimes that place is so experiential that superlatives don't do it justice: you just have to be there to know. These sights, properties, and experiences get our highest rating, **Fodor's Choice**, indicated by orange stars throughout this book.

Black stars highlight sights and properties we deem **Highly Recommended,** places that our writers, editors, and readers praise again and again for consistency and excellence.

By default, there's another category: any place we include in this book is by definition worth your time, unless we say otherwise. And we will.

Disagree with any of our choices? Care to nominate a place or suggest that we rate one more highly? Visit our feedback center at www. fodors.com/feedback.

Budget Well

Hotel and restaurant price categories from ¢ to $$$$ are defined in the opening pages of each chapter. For attractions, we always give standard adult admission fees; reductions are usually available for children, students, and senior citizens. Want to pay with plastic? **AE, D, DC, MC, V** following restaurant and hotel listings indicate if American Express, Discover, Diner's Club, MasterCard, and Visa are accepted.

Restaurants

Unless we state otherwise, restaurants are open for lunch and dinner daily. We mention dress only when there's a specific requirement and reservations only when they're essential or not accepted—it's always best to book ahead.

Hotels

Hotels have private bath, phone, TV, and air-conditioning and operate on the European Plan (a.k.a. EP, meaning without meals), unless we specify that they use the Continental Plan (CP, with a Continental breakfast), Breakfast Plan (BP, with a full breakfast), or Modified American Plan (MAP, with breakfast and dinner) or are all-inclusive (including all meals and most activities). We always list facilities but not whether you'll be charged an extra fee to use them, so when pricing accommodations, find out what's included.

Many Listings

★	Fodor's Choice
★	Highly recommended
⊠	Physical address
⊹	Directions
⌂	Mailing address
☎	Telephone
🖷	Fax
⊕	On the Web
✉	E-mail
🎟	Admission fee
☉	Open/closed times
⌑	Start of walk/itinerary
Ⓜ	Metro stations
⊟	Credit cards

Hotels & Restaurants

🏨	Hotel
⤷	Number of rooms
⌂	Facilities
⧲⧲	Meal plans
✕	Restaurant
⌕	Reservations
🚫	Dress code
⤳	Smoking
ᵇⁱᵖ	BYOB
✕🏨	Hotel with restaurant that warrants a visit

Outdoors

🏌	Golf
⛺	Camping

Other

☾	Family-friendly
🛈	Contact information
⇨	See also
⊠	Branch address
☞	Take note

1

Experience
Puerto Vallarta

Looking out over downtown and the Bay of Banderas

WORD OF MOUTH

"I've been to PV several times now and have loved it every time. It doesn't have the perfect water that Cancún does, but it also doesn't have as many drunk college kids. It's a beautiful village-type town."
—Montanacana

"Spend the day under a *palapa* on Playa Los Muertos, or take a water taxi down to Yelapa. Stroll the *malecón* in the evening, eat an ice cream cone, or get a corn on the cob."

—suze

www.fodors.com/forums

WELCOME TO PUERTO VALLARTA

Huichol Art

TOP REASONS TO GO

★ **Legendary restaurants:** Eat barbecued snapper with your feet in the sand or chateaubriand with a killer ocean view.

★ **Adventure and indulgence:** Ride a horse, mountain bike or go four-wheeling into the mountains, dive into the sea, and relax at an elegant spa—all in one day.

★ **Natural beauty:** Enjoy the physical beauty of Pacific Mexico's prettiest resort town, with cobblestone streets to climb to emerald green hills, and the big, sparkling bay below.

★ **Authentic art:** PV's artists and artisans—from Huichol Indians to expats—produce a huge diversity of exceptional folk treasures and fine art.

★ **Diverse nightlife:** Whether you're old, young, gay, straight, mild, or wild, PV's casual and unpretentious party scene has something to entice you after dark.

1 Old Vallarta. Rising abruptly from the sea are the hilly cobblestoned streets of El Centro (Downtown), lined with white-washed homes and shops. South of the Cuale River, the Zona Romántica (Romantic Zone, or Col. E. Zapata) has PV's highest density of restaurants and shops.

2 North of Downtown. Facing a busy avenue, the Zona Hotelera Norte (Northern Hotel Zone) has malls, businesses, and high-rise hotels. The shopping centers and deluxe hotels of Marina Vallarta are sandwiched between a golf course and the city's main marina.

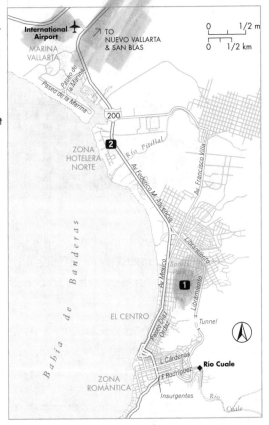

PG 12

3 Nuevo Vallarta. The south-ernmost town in Nayarit State, this planned resort is ideal if you want all-inclusive hotels. It has few restaurants and shops outside the Paradise Plaza mall.

4 The Southern Nayarit Coast. Exclusive Punta de Mita is dominated by the Four Seasons. Sayulita, San Francisco, and La Cruz de Huancaxtle attract visitors with small-town charm. Lovely, un-touristy beaches like Playa Chacala complete the picture.

5 South of Puerto Vallarta. To Mismaloya, the hotels of the Zona Hotelera Sur hug the beach or overlook it from cliff-side aeries. Between La Cruz de Loretos and the Colima State border, the Costalegre is a mixture of luxury resorts and earthy seaside hamlets.

Camino Real Hotel, Puerto Vallarta, Jalisco, Mexico

GETTING ORIENTED

The original town, Old Vallarta, sits at the center of 42-km (26-mi) Bahía de Banderas, Mexico's largest bay, in Jalisco State. From here, the Sierra Madre foothills dive into the sea. Mountain-fed rivers nour-ish tropical deciduous forests as far north as San Blas, in Nayarit State. South of PV the hills re-cede from the coast and the drier tropical thorn forest predominates south to Barra de Navidad.

PUERTO VALLARTA'S TOP EXPERIENCES

The Malecón

Nighttime is the right time for strolling PV's famous *malecón*. Bring your camera to photograph the seawalk's whimsical statues at sunset. Sip a cool drink, buy a caramel-topped crêpe from a vendor, or eat at a restaurant across the street. At the end of your eight-block promenade, take in the near-nightly free evening entertainment—be it a brass band or outdoor dance at the town square or a magician or mime at adjoining Los Arcos outdoor amphitheater, overlooking the sea.

Canopy Tours

Zinging through the treetops makes even a timid traveler feel like a superhero. Canopy tours are action-packed rides, where, fastened to a zip line high off the ground, you fly from tree to tree. Blue sky above, ribbons of river below, and in between: a forest of treetops and a healthy shot of adrenaline. The most highly praised area operators are El Edén and Canopy Tour Los Veranos, both south of PV near Mismaloya.

In, On, Under and Above the Water

Spend a day on the bay. Dive the varied landscape of Las Marietas Islands, angle for giant billfish, or soar above the scene in a colorful parasail. Look for orcas or humpbacks in winter and dolphins year-round. Swim, snorkel, or learn to surf or sail. Perhaps just build a sandcastle with your kids.

What You Want & Where To Get It

This table reflects the atmosphere in high season. In low season, most beaches are uncrowded, activities may decrease, and some shops and restaurants close.

AROUND PV	Peace & Quiet	Luxury Digs	Natural Beauty	Restaurants Nearby	Shopping	Lots of Sports	Low on Tourists
Old Vallarta			✔	✔	✔	✔	
Nuevo Vallarta	✔	✔				✔	
Bucerías	✔			✔			✔
Punta de Mita		✔	✔				
Zona Hotelera Sur	✔	✔	✔				
Costalegre	✔	✔	✔				✔
Barra/Melaque	✔		✔				✔
Rincón de Guayabitos			✔				
Zona Hotelera Norte	✔	✔		✔		✔	
Marina Vallarta	✔	✔				✔	

Late Nights, Latino Style

Much of Vallarta is geared to the gringo palate, however, there's plenty of authentic spice for those who crave it. Stray a bit from the tourist scene for a *mojito*—Cuba's version of the mint julep—at La Bodeguita del Medio, on the malecón. Dine on roast pork, black beans, and fried plantains before heading for the dance floor at around 9, when the house band comes to life. Wednesday through Friday, take a taxi to J.B. Dance Club, in the hotel zone, for $2 dance lessons at 9:30. Otherwise hang at La Bodeguita until around 11, when the Mexican and Latino crowds start to arrive at J.B. for a late night of cumbia, salsa, and hot merengue.

Sensational Sunsets

After a day of activity, you deserve some R, R, and R: rest, relaxation, and rewarding views. Sip a fancy cocktail with a live music accompaniment at busy Los Muertos Beach or indulge in dessert from the crow's nest at Bucerías's The Bar Above. For the most dramatic views from high above the sea head to Barcelona Tapas, Vista Guayabitos, Las Carmelitas, or Le Kliff (⇨ chapter 3). All of them serve dinner and drinks.

20 Minutes to a More Elevated You

Get away from the gringo trail 4,000 feet above sea level in the mountain towns west of PV. Admire the elegant simplicity of tiny San Sebastián; in Talpa, visit the diminutive Virgin of Talpa statue, revered throughout Mexico for petitions granted. Buy keepsakes and mountain-grown coffee in small shops around the square. Or fly to Mascota, where you can sample homemade *raicilla*—second cousin of tequila. Hike into tapestry hills and deep green valleys where, on a good day, you can spy Puerto Vallarta and a ribbon of the Pacific far below.

AUTHENTIC IS KEY

"I love Puerto Vallarta dearly and have been there many times, but I mostly just kick around downtown, lay by the hotel pool, go to the supermercado, have drinks at the beach, enjoy the wonderful restaurants, eat ice cream on the Malecon, and hit the fabric stores. Other fun things to do: hang around Playa los Muertos, go shopping and to the galleries, parasailing, cruises, jungle tours, visiting the cathedral. People in PV are incredibly friendly, welcoming, and proud. The town is authentic, which is important to me."

—suze

"DON'T MISS"

1) Every sunset.
2) Eating out at all the great restaurants. Don't stay in the hotel even if it is all-inclusive. There are too many great places to go.
3) A visit up the coast to Punta Mita
4) Bus rides in town
5) Getting to know the local people
—Anne-Marie

PUERTO VALLARTA THEN AND NOW

People and Culture

Despite its population of 350,000, Puerto Vallarta feels—and thinks—like a small town. People know their neighbors; school chums run the city and the corner taco stand. Although the majority of *vallartenses* (residents of Puerto Vallarta) are far from wealthy, most are middle class, and securely employed; few of the alms-seekers downtown are locals.

Vallartenses value nice things, but much less so than sharing and socializing with family and friends. In her book *The Magic of Puerto Vallarta,* Venezuelan Marilú Suárez-Murias aptly describes Puerto Vallartans as "free, proud, simple, noble, friendly, kind, and never in a hurry."

Like many others from around the world, Ms. Suárez-Murias visited in the 1980s and opted to stay. Vallarta has one of the largest English-speaking expat communities in Mexico consisting of Americans and Canadians especially. Expats tend to settle in Old Vallarta or the condos and private homes climbing the ocean-facing hills south of town. Small towns like Sayulita, north of PV, are also popular.

The Hotel Scene

Choosing where to stay may be half of the equation to having a fabulous vacation. Unfortunately, it's not an easy task since Puerto Vallarta has something for every budget and personality, from cliffside condos with stairs winding down to the sea to classy little cottages surrounded by nature trails. *Gran turismo* (beyond 5-star) hotels and resorts are found up and down the coast; think private beachside villa with a private plunge pool. Some of those on the prettiest beaches are in Punta de Mita and the Costalegre, but you'll find them also in the south and north hotel

zones, Marina Vallarta, and Nuevo Vallarta. Nuevo Vallarta has mainly all-inclusive hotels. Southern Nayarit State, north of PV, has a sprinking of small hotels, guesthouses, private rentals, and B&Bs, many of them popular with honeymooners, families, and anyone looking for more intimate digs away from large crowds.

The Food Scene

First-time travelers come for the sun and sea, but it's PV's wonderful restaurants that create legions of long-term fans. Only a generation ago, much of the best, locally caught fish was shipped to Guadalajara; Vallartans had to buy it back frozen, or overstock and freeze fresh catches for future meals. Likewise, a variety of vegetables was hard to find. But as the destination has grown in popularity and dozens of excellent chefs have opened restaurants, the culinary outlook has improved exponentially. Now those who know where to look can shop locally for designer greens, baby eggplant, and an increasingly sophisticated range of ingredients.

PV's level of culinary chic is reflected in November's International Gourmet Festival, when dozens of guest chefs bring new recipes and ideas from around the globe.

It's not just foreigners and Cordon Bleu-trained chefs, however, that keep the foodies fat and happy. Seaside family-owned eateries grill fish right off the boat, and tiny city cafés have great eats at bargain prices. And a number of streetside stalls are as hygienic as five-star-hotel restaurants.

The Overall Vibe

Mexico's second-most-visited resort after Cancún, Puerto Vallarta is, without a doubt, "touristy." From the clean streets to the English-speaking personnel and

CLEAN STS. & ENGLISH SPEAKING

menus, business owners and tourism officials aim to help you feel at home. But you won't feel like a cipher or, worse, a bothersome intruder. Cancún didn't exist before the 1970s, and employees and business owners are imported from elsewhere. In contrast, the majority of Puerto Vallarta's tour companies, restaurants, and hotels are run by local people—proud of their city and happy to have you. Happy, because tourism is PV's only real industry. And though plenty of twentysomethings party all night at Señor Frogs or Carlos O'Briens, this is not a spring-break destination. A sense of decorum and pride in the city keeps things reasonably restrained.

Thinking Outside the Bay

As numerous as the activities in and around Puerto Vallarta and Banderas Bay are the opportunities beyond its boundaries. Vallarta Adventures and smaller tour operators make things easy with day trips to the mountains, Guadalajara, San Blas, and the nearby estuaries at La Tovara. While tour companies can design individual, overnight tours, most folks heading north or south of Banderas Bay rent a car and go on their own. But there's plenty to keep you busy in and around Puerto Vallarta, so if your time is limited, establishing a base of operations there is usually the most hassle-free way to explore.

A Brief History

Except for small coastal settlements that subsisted on fishing and a small enterprise importing salt (used to separate silver from stone), the first European and mestizo settlers in the region were miners and mine owners far from the coast, in the mineral-laced Sierra Madre. When mining petered out in the early 20th century, many families moved to the band of rich farmland near the coast around present-day Puerto Vallarta. Tourism along the gorgeous, 42-km (26-mi) Bahía Banderas (Bay of Flags), really took off in the '50s and '60s, when a Mexican newsreel showed off its natural beauty and famous lovers Elizabeth Taylor and Richard Burton brought the paparazzi during the filming of *Night of the Iguana,* in 1963.

GREAT ITINERARIES

Each of these fills one day. Together they touch on some of PV's most quintessential experiences, from shopping to getting outdoors for adventure tours or golfing, or just relaxing at the best beaches and spas.

Romancing the Zone

Head south of downtown to the **Zona Romántica** for a day of excellent shopping and dining. Stop at Isla Cuale for trinkets and T-shirts; have an island breakfast overlooking the stream at the River Cafe or an excellent lunch at Le Bistro, where the romantic, neo-Continental décor and monumental architecture produce a flood of endorphins.

■ TIP→ Most of the stores in the neighborhood will either ship your oversized prizes for you or expertly pack them and recommend reputable shipping companies.

Crossing the pedestrian bridge nearest the bay, drop nonshoppers at **Los Muertos Beach.** They can watch the fishermen on the small pier, lie in the sun, sit in the shade with a good book, or walk south to the rocky coves of **Conchas Chinas Beach,** which is good for snorkeling when the water is calm. Meanwhile, the shoppers head to **Calle Basilio Badillo** and surrounding streets for folk art, housewares, antiques, clothing, and accessories. End the day back at Los Muertos with dinner, drinks, and live music.

■ TIP→ Some of the musicians at beachfront restaurants work for the restaurant, others are freelancers. If a roving musician (or six) ask what you'd like to hear, ask the price of a song.

A Different Resort Scene

If you've got wheels, explore a different sort of beach resort. After breakfast, grab beach togs, sunscreen, and other essentials for a day at the beach and head north. Those with a sweet tooth might make a pit stop at Pie in The Sky, with excellent pie, chocolate, and other sugar fixes. About 45 minutes north of PV, join Mexican families on the beach at **Rincón de Guayabitos,** on long Jaltemba Bay. Play in the mild surf; walk the pretty, long beach; or head just a mile south to **Playa Los Ayala,** where you can take a ride in a glass-bottom boat. Vendors on the sand sell chilled coconuts and watermelon from their brightly colored stands. On the way back south, stop in the small town of **San Francisco,** aka San Pancho, for dinner. You can't go wrong at La Ola Rica, Gallo's Pizzeria, or the slightly more sophisticated Cafe del Mar (brush the sand off your feet for that one). In high season and especially on weekend evenings, one of the three will probably have live music, especially Gallo's.

■ TIP→ Take a water taxi out for a look at El Islote island, where with luck you might spot a whale between December and March.

Head for the Hills

For an unforgettable experience (at least for a few days, until your thigh muscles recover), take a horse-riding expedition (⇨ Chapter 7) into Vallarta's verdant tropical forest. Rancho Charro and Rancho Ojo de Agua have full-day excursions; the former has several multiday excursions as well, including tours to the former silver-mining towns of Mascota and San Sebastián. For those who prefer motorized horsepower, Wild Vallarta runs full-day ATV tours to San Sebastián.

■ TIP→ Full-day and overnight trips provide food and refreshments, but if possible bring a day pack with things to make yourself comfortable: bottled water, tissues or handkerchief, bandana, and plenty of sunblock. Don't

pack it so full that it's unpleasantly heavy, however. Wear a hat.

A Day of Golf and Steam

Puerto Vallarta is one of Mexico's best golfing destinations (⇨ chapter 7). And what better way to top off a day of play than with a steam, soak, and massage? At the south end of the Costalegre, Grand Bay Isla Navidad has variety of play (three 9-hole courses) and a spa with massage, facials, and a gym. Above PV, the Four Seasons has 19 holes of good golfing (the optional 19th on its own little island) and an excellent spa, but the latter is for guests only. In between these two extremes are less-exclusive but still great courses. The closest spas to the greens of Marina Vallarta and the excellent Vista Vallarta are those of the Westin Regina and the Casa-Magna Marriott. The El Tigre course is associated with the Paradise Village resort, but this excellent and moderately priced spa is open also to those who golf at Mayan Palace, just up the road and at Flamingos, at the far northern edge of Nuevo Vallarta.

■ TIP➔Ask your concierge (or look online) to find out how far ahead you can reserve, and then try for the earliest possible tee time to beat the heat. If the course you choose doesn't have a club pool, you can have lunch and hang at the pool at the resorts suggested above, or get a massage, facial, or other treatment (always reserve ahead).

Downtown Exploration

Puerto Vallarta hasn't much at all in the way of museums, but with a little legwork, you can get a bit of culture. Learn about the area's first inhabitants at the tiny but tidy **Museo Arqueológico** (closed Sunday), with info in English. Come forward in time more than a millennium to the houses that love built . . . or at least bought. Occupied by lovers Elizabeth Taylor and Richard Burton during their much publicized Vallarta romance, **Casa Kimberly**, and the Burton House across from it, are open to visitors 9–6, except Sunday, for an $8 fee. After seeing the memorabilia, wend through the hilly (and uneven) streets of Gringo Gulch for sea views and a look at homes of various eras en route to Vallarta's **Catedral de La Virgen de Guadalupe,** dedicated to Mexico's most revered icon.

WHEN TO GO

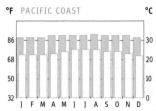

°F PACIFIC COAST   °C

The beach resorts are the most crowded and expensive December through Easter, especially the Christmas/New Year's holiday and the weeks before and after Easter. Despite the humidity, upper-class Mexican families book resort hotels during July and August school vacations while the masses rent bungalows in the smaller beach towns and camp out on popular beaches. Mexicans also travel over extended national holiday weekends, called *puentes* (bridges).

Holy days and cultural festivals play a big role in Mexican life. If you plan to travel during a major national event, reserve lodgings and transportation well in advance. November brings the PV Film Festival of the Americas and International Gourmet Festival.

Climate

On the same latitude as the Hawaiian Islands, Puerto Vallarta is tropical, and can be visited any time of year.

Mid-June through mid-October is the rainy season; afternoon showers clear the air and temporarily reduce humidity. Rainy season temperatures are often in the 80s and 90s and feel hotter due to high humidity. November through May is the dry season. Summer means bathtub-like ocean temperatures, the best diving and snorkeling conditions, and the most surfable waves. December through March bring the coolest temperatures: daytime temps still reach the 80s but at night drop to the 50s or 60s. May, June, August, and September are the hottest months. The proximity of tall mountains to the coast increases humidity: from Puerto Vallarta north to San Blas there's jungly terrain (officially, tropical deciduous forest). South of PV, the mountains recede from the coast, making that area's climate and vegetation drier.

⚑ Forecasts **U.S. National Weather Service** ⊕ http://weather.noaa.gov/weather/current/MMPR.html. **The Weather Channel** ⊕ www.weather.com.

Where to Stay

Massage pavilion at El Tamarindo Golf Resort

WORD OF MOUTH

"In PV I like the Buenaventura, close to town, cheap, great pool, clean. If you are an upscale traveler or need to be out of town, the Velas Vallarta is nice but 15 minutes from the action."

—Montanacana

"We absolutely loved the Presidente Intercontinental. . . . It's a great hotel in a . . . tranquil place where you can enjoy the sounds of waves."

—twinkee

www.fodors.com/forums

When to Go

High season is November through April, but if you don't mind afternoon rain showers and a lot of humidity, late June through October is a great time to visit for lower-priced lodgings (up to 40%) and rental cars and smaller crowds.

By August the entire coast and inland forests are green and bursting with blooms. Afternoon rains clean the streets and houses; waterfalls and rivers outside of town spring into action. On the downside, many restaurants and some other businesses close up shop in the hottest months, August and September, and live performances and nightlife slack off. The humidity is most manageable in May, October, and November, and at its worst in September.

⚠ **Overbooking is a common practice. To protect yourself, get a confirmation in writing, via fax or e-mail.**

Parking Blues

Very few downtown Puerto Vallarta hotels have parking, and there are few pay lots. Most of the condos in the Zona Hotelera Sur have parking, but not necessarily one space per apartment. Virtually all of the hotels outside the city center have free parking for guests.

Choosing a Hotel

If you want to walk everywhere, **Old Vallarta** (downtown, which includes El Centro and the Romantic Zone) is the place to be. El Centro's hilly, cobblestone streets provide excellent views and aerobic workouts. South of the Cuale River, the Romantic Zone has more shops, restaurants, and Los Muertos Beach—and no hills. Most hotels here are inexpensive to moderate.

South of town, the **Zona Hotelera Sur** has mainly condos, with luxury and moderately priced hotels with dramatic ocean views. Downtown is a short cab or bus ride away. The beaches and views aren't as appealing in the **Zona Hotelera Norte.** The long stretch of mid-range chains is interspersed with malls and mega-grocery stores. Relatively car-free **Marina Vallarta,** with its luxury hotels, is close to golf courses and is a good place for biking and strolling.

Nuevo Vallarta is a planned resort on a long, sandy beach about 12 miles north of downtown PV—about 45 minutes by car or bus when traffic cooperates. This is a good place to stay if you're content to stay put and enjoy your all-inclusive, high-rise hotel. Bucerías and the towns of **southern Nayarit** (north of PV) call to adventurous souls. Several hours south of Vallarta, the **Costalegre** is a place of extremes. High-priced hotels on gorgeous beaches attract celebs and honeymooners, while small towns like Barra de Navidad have modest digs and a more authentically Mexican experience.

Gran Turismo

The government's Gran Turismo program categorizes hotels as *superdeluxe* (five-star-plus), of which only about 30 are chosen nationwide each year; five-star to one-star; and economy class. Note that hotels might lose out on a higher rating only because they lack an amenity like air conditioning (which isn't even needed if there are good breezes).

Lodging Alternatives

APARTMENTS & VILLAS

When shared by two couples, a spacious villa can save you a bundle on lodging and on meals. Villas often come with stereo systems, DVD players, a pool, maid service, and air conditioning. Prices range from $100 to $1,000 per night, with 10%–20% discounts off-season.

🏠 **At Home Abroad** ☎ 212/421-9165 ⊕ www. athomeabroadinc.com. **Cochran Real Estate** ☎ 322/228-0419 in PV, 800/603-2959 in U.S. ⊕ www. buyeragentmexico.com. **Hideaways International** ☎ 603/ 430-4433, 800/843-4433 in U.S. ⊕ www.hideaways.com. **Pacific Mexico Real Estate** ☎ 322/298-1644 in PV ⊕ www. pacific mexicorealestate.com. **Villanet** ☎ 206/417-3444, or 800/964-1891 in U.S. ⊕ www.rentavilla.com. **Villas and Apartments Abroad** ☎ 212/213-6435, 800/433-3020 in U.S. ⊕ www.vaanyc.com. **Villas International** ☎ 415/499-9490, 800/221-2260 in U.S. ⊕ www.villasintl.com.

BOUTIQUE HOTELS

Hoteles Boutique de México (☎ 01800/508-7923 in Mexico, 877/278-8018 in U.S., 866/818-8342 in Canada ⊕ www.mexicoboutiquehotels.com) is a private company that represents 26 intimate and unique properties—most with fewer than 50 rooms—
selected for their setting, cuisine, service, and overall allure. Each is inspected annually.

CHAIN HOTELS

Tried-and-true chains may have excellent rates, and can be good last-minute options.

🏨 **Holiday Inn** ☎ 800/465-4329 in U.S. ⊕ www. ichotelsgroup.com. **Howard Johnson** ☎ 800/446-4656 in U.S. ⊕ www.hojo.com. **Inter-Continental** ☎ 800/327-0200 in U.S. ⊕ www.ichotelsgroup.com. **Sheraton** ☎ 800/325-3535 in U.S. ⊕ www.starwood.com/sheraton.

What it Costs In U.S. Dollars

FOR 2 PEOPLE

$$$$	$$$	$$	$	¢
over $250	$150-$250	$75-$150	$50-$75	under $50

For a standard room, generally excluding taxes and service charges.

Our Ratings

The lodgings we list are the cream of the crop in each price category. Hotels have private baths, phone, TV, and a/c, and don't include meals, unless we specify otherwise.

Meal Plans

EP: European Plan; without meals
CP: Continental Plan; continental breakfast
BP: Breakfast Plan; full breakfast
MAP: Modified American Plan; breakfast and dinner
FAP: Full American Plan; breakfast, lunch, and dinner
AI: All-Inclusive; including all meals, drinks, and most activities

Pricing

We give high-season prices before meals or other amenities. Low-season rates usually drop 30%–40%. We always list the available facilities, but we don't specify whether they cost extra.

Less expensive hotels include tax in the quote. Most higher-priced resorts add 17% tax on top of the quoted rate; some add a 5%–10% service charge. Moderately priced hotels swing both ways. You might be charged extra for paying with a credit card. Tax, and often tip, are included with all-inclusive plans, making a $$$$ property affordable.

■ TIP→ An all-inclusive (AI) might make you reluctant to spend money elsewhere. So you don't miss out on area restaurants and activities, stay at more modest digs for part of your trip, and go AI for a day or two. Many AI hotels have day passes ($50–$75).

PUERTO VALLARTA

☽ $$$$ ▦ **Barceló La Jolla de Mismaloya.** Guests consistently give this hotel high marks despite the destruction to the once-pristine beach during Hurricane Kenna. Each of the huge, brightly decorated suites has a separate living area and ample terrace with a table and four chairs; some also have well-equipped kitchens. Most two-bedroom suites have two baths but no kitchen. The pools are surrounded by spacious patios, so there's plenty of room to find the perfect spot in the sun, whether you're on your honeymoon or with the kids. At this writing, the all-inclusive plan costs about the same as the room alone. ⊠ *Zona Hotelera Sur, Km 11.5, Mismaloya, 48300* ☎ *322/226–0660, 877/868–6124 in U.S. and Canada* 🖷 *322/228–0853* ⊕ *www.lajollademismaloya.com* 🗗 *303 suites* ⅋ *5 restaurants, room service, in-room safes, some kitchens, minibars, cable TV, in-room data ports, tennis court, 4 pools, gym, hair salon, hot tub, spa, beach, dive shop, snorkeling, jet skiing, bicycles, volleyball, 4 bars, sports bar, video game room, shops, babysitting, children's programs (ages 5–11), dry cleaning, laundry service, concierge, Internet room, convention center, meeting rooms, car rental, travel services, free parking, no-smoking rooms* ▭ *MC, V* ⭗ *EP, AI.*

☽ ▦ **Dreams.** Dramatic views of the gorgeous, rock-edged beach is just one
Fodor'sChoice reason that this all-inclusive is special. Theme nights go a bit beyond
★ $$$$ the usual Mexican fiestas: there are salsa dancing classes, reggae and circus nights, and for sports night, ball games with hot dogs and beer, and movies on the beach. Instead of buffet restaurants there are four à la carte eateries and one with pizza, taco, pasta, and other stations. All of the charming suites, decorated in aqua and white, have fab views but only the newer ones have balconies, some with a hot tub. There are tons of activities for both kids and adults, and no wristbands to clash with your resort-casual clothes. ⊠ *Carretera a Barra de Navidad (Carretera 200), at Playa Las Estacas Zona Hotelera Sur, 48300* ☎ *322/226– 5000 or 866/237–3267 in U.S. and Canada* 🖷 *322/221–6000* ⊕ *www. dreamsresorts.com* 🗗 *337 suites* ⅋ *5 restaurants, 24-hour room service, in-room safe, some in-room hot tubs, minibars, cable TV, in-room DVDs, 2 tennis courts, 3 pools, gym, sauna, steam room, 3 hot tubs, spa, beach, windsurfing, boating, fishing, bicycles, archery, billiards, Ping-Pong, snorkeling, soccer, recreation room, volleyball, 5 bars, cinema, nightclub, shops, concierge, business center, laundry service, travel service, car rental, children's club (ages 4–17), free parking, no-smoking rooms* ▭ *AE, D, DC, MC, V* ⭗ *AI.*

★ $$$$ ▦ **Hacienda San Angel.** Each room is unique and elegant at this boutique hotel in the hills six blocks above the malecón. Public spaces also exude wealth and privilege: 16th- through 19th-century antiques are placed throughout, water pours from fonts into Talavera tile–lined basins, mammoth tables grace open dining areas. No wonder it was named one of the best new hotels of 2004 by *Condé Nast Traveller*. The Celestial Room has a wondrous view of Bahía de Banderas and the cathedral's tower from its open-air, thatched-roof living room. You can call or e-mail Canada or the U.S. for free; enjoy live music with complimentary cocktails in the early evening. ⊠ *Calle Miramar 336, at Iturbide, Col.*

El Cerro, 48300 ☎ *322/222–2692, 877/278–8018 in U.S., 866/818–8342 in Canada* 🖷 *322/223–1941* ⊕ *www.mexicoboutiquehotels.com/sanangel* ⇨ *14 rooms* ♨ *Restaurant, cable TV, 3 pools, hot tub, laundry service, concierge, Internet room, free airport shuttle, local shuttle* ⊟ *AE, MC, V* ⦿⦿ *CP.*

$$$$ ▦ **Majahuitas.** If travelers were animals, Majahuitas's guests would be bears, not butterflies. Eating well and resting are the two top activities. After a 20-minute boat ride you (and, hopefully, your sweetie, as this intimate place doesn't have a singles scene) arrive at a shell-strewn beach where hermit crabs scuttle about seeking larger accommodations. Eight casitas crouch amid jungly plants (and biting bugs; bring repellent) overlooking the tiny cove. Guest rooms are open to the air and have low-wattage lights and tiny, solar-powered fans. It's a romantic place that also happens to be good for families with tots. Older kids, type-A adults, and anyone who doesn't read will be bored. ⊠ *Playa Majahuitas, Cabo Corrientes Norte* ☎☎ *322/293–4506; 800/728–9098 in U.S. and Canada* ⊕ *www.mexicoboutiquehotels.com/majahuitas* ⇨ *8 rooms* ♨ *Restaurant, fans, massage, beach, snorkeling, fishing, hiking, Ping-Pong, bar; no a/c, no room phones, no room TVs* ⊟ *AE, MC, V* ⦿⦿ *FAP.*

$$$$ ▦ **Presidente InterContinental Puerto Vallarta Resort.** The beautiful aquatone cove the hotel overlooks is the property's best asset. Check-in is handled right in your room, with its white-tile floors and citrus-color fabrics. You'll be asked to choose from among four experiences (Joy of Life, Renewal, Romance, and Peace of Mind) that involve changing the scents, music, stones, flowers, and certain amenities in your room to set the desired tone. Will your choice dictate complimentary red wine or premium tequila? Casablanca lilies or red roses? This marketing gimmick doesn't dramatically enchance the hotel experience, though pillow menus are a nice touch. The long-heralded spa is tiny and has few treatments. ⊠ *Carretera a Barra de Navidad, Km 8.6, Mismaloya, 48300* ☎ *322/228–0191* 🖷 *322/228–0493* ⊕ *www.acquaesencia.com* ⇨ *97 rooms, 23 suites* ♨ *2 restaurants, snack bar, room service, in-room safes, some in-room hot tubs, cable TV with movies, some in-room data ports, tennis court, pool, wading pool, fitness classes, gym, spa, beach, dive shop, 2 bars, shop, dry cleaning, laundry service, babysitting, children's programs (ages 4–12), playground, concierge, Internet room, business services, meeting rooms, travel services, free parking, no-smoking floors* ⊟ *AE, D, MC, V* ⦿⦿ *EP.*

$$$$ ▦ **Sheraton Buganvilias.** Juan Carlos Name, a disciple of modern-minimalist Mexican architect Luis Barragán, designed this looming high-rise near the Hotel Zone's south end and within walking distance of downtown. It's reliable, anonymous, and geared toward conventioneers and other groups. Renovations have modernized rooms after the destruction of Hurricane Kenna in 2002, bringing very snug and comfortable beds with pillow-top mattresses and downy duvets. This is the closest of the Zona Hotelera Norte hotels to downtown PV. ⊠ *Blvd. Francisco Medina Ascencio 999, Zona Hotelera Norte, 48330* ☎ *322/226–0404, 800/325–3535 in the U.S.* 🖷 *322/222–0500* ⊕ *www.sheratonvallarta.com* ⇨ *480 rooms, 120 suites* ♨ *4 restaurants, grocery, room service, in-room safes, cable TV, 2 tennis courts, 2 pools, gym, hair salon, hot*

TENNIS, ANYONE?

Public tennis courts are few and far between in Vallarta, although most hotels have courts for guests. Of the public tennis complexes, **Club de Tenis Canto del Sol** (✉ Hotel Canto del Sol, Local 18, Planta Baja, Zona Comercial Zona Hotelera ☎ 322/226-0123) is the largest, with four clay and four asphalt courts; all but two are lighted. Lessons are $35 per hour, including racquet; court rental is $14 per hour, $22 per hour for night play. Club hours are 7 AM to 10 PM (8–5 on Sunday); fees give you access to showers, lockers, and steam room. The **Holiday Inn** (✉ Blvd. Federico Medina Ascencio, Km. 3.5 Zona Hotelera Norte ☎ 322/226-1700) has two asphalt courts rented out at $8 per hour, and $14 per hour at night. Hours are 8:30 AM-7 PM; make arrangements to stay later. A pro gives lessons. Reservations are essential.

---

tub, sauna, spa, steam room, beach, Ping-Pong, volleyball, bar, lounge, shop, babysitting, children's programs (ages 4–12), laundry service, concierge, concierge floor, business services, meeting rooms, car rental, free parking, no-smoking rooms ▭ *AE, MC, V* ⦿ *EP, CP.*

$$$$ ▦ **Velas Vallarta.** Silky sheets and cozy down comforters, multiple ceiling fans, and large flat-screen TVs are a few of the creature comforts that set Velas apart from the rest. Each large living area has two comfortably wide built-in couches in colorful prints and a round dining table. Huichol cross-stitch and modern Mexican art decorate the walls. Studios and 1-, 2-, and 3-bedroom suites have the same amenities except that the former don't have balconies with a view of the pool and the beach. Tall palms, pink bougainvillea, and wild ginger with brilliant red plumes surround the three enormous pools. ✉ *Av. Costera s/n, Marina Vallarta, 48354* ☎ *322/221-0091 or 800/835-2778* 📠 *322/221-0755* ⊕ *www.velasvallarta.com* ⬒ *339 suites* ⌕ *2 restaurants, grocery, 24-hour room service, fans, in-room safes, some in-room hot tubs, some kitchens, some kitchenettes, some minibars, cable TV, 3 tennis courts, 2 pools, gym, hair salon, sauna, spa, beach, bicycles, 2 bars, shops, babysitting, children's programs (ages 5–12), laundry service, concierge, meeting rooms, car rental, travel services, free parking, no-smoking rooms* ▭ *AE, MC, V* ⦿ *AI.*

$$$$ ▦ **Westin Resort & Spa.** Hot pink! Electric yellow! Color aside, the Westin's buildings evoke ancient temples and are about as mammoth. There's not a bad sightline anywhere—whether you gaze out to the leafy courtyard or down an orange-tiled, brightly painted corridor lined with Mexican art. The jarring echoes here are tempered by the rush of an enormous water feature. In the spacious, balconied rooms concrete-and-stone floors massage bare feet, and top-of-the-line mattresses with whisper-soft duvets make for heavenly siestas. Guest quarters above the sixth floor have ocean views; those below face the 600 palm trees surrounding the four beautiful pools. The Westin's Nikki Beach Club is one of Vallarta's hippest night spots, but time-share touts make some guests

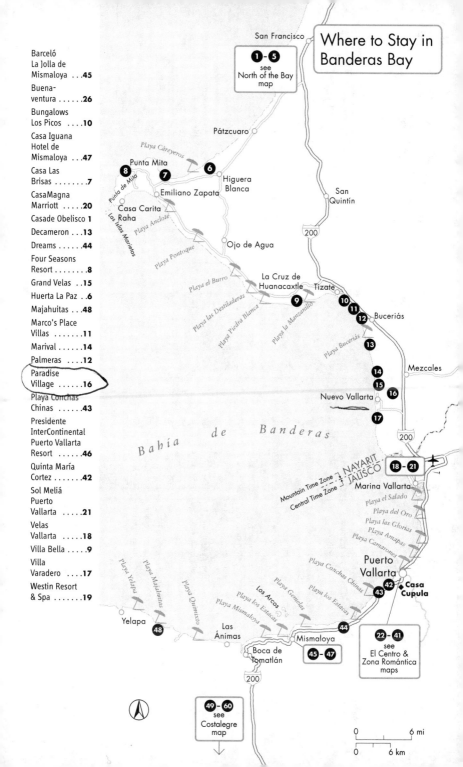

Where to Stay in Banderas Bay

Barceló La Jolla de Mismaloya . . .**45**

Buenaventura **26**

Bungalows Los Picos **10**

Casa Iguana Hotel de Mismaloya . . .**47**

Casa Las Brisas **7**

CasaMagna Marriott **20**

Casade Obelisco **1**

Decameron . . .**13**

Dreams **44**

Four Seasons Resort **8**

Grand Velas . .**15**

Huerta La Paz . .**6**

Marco's Place Villas **11**

Marival **14**

Palmeras **12**

Paradise Village **16**

Playa Conchas Chinas **43**

Presidente InterContinental Puerto Vallarta Resort **46**

Quinta María Cortez **42**

Sol Meliá Puerto Vallarta **21**

Velas Vallarta **18**

Villa Bella **9**

Villa Varadero **17**

Westin Resort & Spa **19**

San Francisco

1 - 5
see North of the Bay map

Pátzcuaro

Playa Careyeros

Punta Mita

6

Higuera Blanca

San Quintín

Punta de Mita

8

7

Emiliano Zapata

Casa Carita Raha

Playa Anclote

Las Islas Marietas

Ojo de Agua

200

Playa Pontoque

Playa el Burro

La Cruz de Huanacaxtle

Tizate

Playa las Destiladeras

9

10

11

12

Bucerías

Playa Piedra Blanca

Playa la Manzanillo

13

Playa Bucerías

14

Mezcales

15

16

Nuevo Vallarta

17

Bahía   de   Banderas

200

Mountain Time Zone

NAYARIT

Central Time Zone

JALISCO

18 - 21

Marina Vallarta

Playa el Salado

Playa del Oro

Playa las Glorias

Playa Amapas

Playa Camarones

Playa Conchas Chinas

Puerto Vallarta

Playa Yelapa

Playa Majahuitas

Playa Quimixto

Playa Gemelas

Los Arcos

Playa los Estacas

42

43

Casa Cupula

Playa Mismaloya

Las Ánimas

Yelapa

48

Playa los Muertos

44

Mismaloya

45 - 47

Boca de Tomatlán

22 - 41
see El Centro & Zona Romántica maps

200

49 - 60
see Costalegre map

0   6 mi

0   6 km

PUERTO VALLARTA HOTELS AT A GLANCE

HOTEL	Worth Noting	Cost	Rooms	Restaurants	On the Beach	Dive Shop	Pools	Spa	Golf Course	Tennis Courts	Health Club/Gym	Children's Program	Location
Puerto Vallarta													
Ana Liz	artsy crowd	$25	23										Col. E. Zapata
Andale	well-known bar-restaurant	$55–$75	10	2			2						Col. E. Zapata
Barceló	all suites; lots to do	$310–$345	303	5	yes	yes	4	yes		yes		5–11	Mismaloy
Buenaventura	ideal location	$120	231	2	yes		2	yes		yes			Centro
Casa Andrea	homey apartments	$600/week	11				1						Centro
Casa Dulce Vida	apartments	$60–$120	6				1						Centro
Casa Iguana	all suites; full kitchens	$115	52	1			1						Mismaloya
CasaMagna Marriott	something for everyone	$229–$309	433	2	yes		2	yes	1	yes		4–12	Marina Vallarta
Los Cuatro Vientos	homey	$59–$74	14	1			1						Centro
Dreams	elaborate theme nights	$438–$544	337	5	yes		3	yes	2	yes		4–12	Zona Hotelera Sur
Eloísa	city and mountain views	$65–$78	74	1			2						Col. E. Zapata
Emperador	viable budget option	$51–$74	69	1	yes		1						Col. E. Zapata
Fiesta Americana	amazing palapa	$229–$298	291	3	yes		1			yes		4–12	Zona Hotelera Norte
Gaviota Vallarta	top location; free parking	$58–$92	84	1			1						Puerto Vallarta
Hacienda San Angel	dripping with antiques	$250–$475	14	1			3						Col. El Cerro
Hotel Molino de Agua	huge pool areas	$97–$132	59	2	yes		2						Col. E. Zapata
Majahuitas	casitas; romantic	$375	8	1	yes								Cabo Corrientes Norte
El Pescador	modest but cheerful	$60	102	1			1						Col. 5 de Diciembre
Playa Conchas Chinas	balconies with great views	$98–$110	22	1	yes		1						Conchas Chinas
Playa Los Arcos	fab location w/rates to match	$84–$130	171	1	yes		1						Col. E. Zapata
Posada de Roger	great location	$55	47	1			1						Col. E. Zapata
Presidente InterContinental	secluded cove	$350–$380	120	2	yes	yes	1	yes	1	yes		4–12	Mismaloya
Quinta María Cortez	warm staff; lots of soul	$100–$195	7		yes		1						Playa Conchas Chinas
Río	well-equipped computer room	$45–$55	47	1			1						Centro
Rosita	great location	$60–$96	115	1			1						Col. 5 de Diciembre
Sheraton Buganvilias	large but reliable	$259–$307	600	4	yes		2	yes	2	yes		4–12	Zona Hotelera Norte
Sol Meliá Puerto Vallarta	great for families	$218–$255	360	3	yes		1		2	yes		4–12	Marina Vallarta

HOTEL	Location	Children's Program	Health Club/Gym	Tennis Courts	Golf Course	Spa	Pools	Dive Shop	On the Beach	Restaurants	Rooms	Cost	Worth Noting
Tropicana	Col. E. Zapata						1			1	160	$75–$91	polite staff
Velas Vallarta	Marina Vallarta	5-12	yes	3		yes	2		yes	2	339	$320	all suites; lots of comforts
Westin Resort & Spa	Marina Vallarta	inf-12	yes	3		yes	3		yes	2	280	$479	great art and architecture
Yasmín	Col. E. Zapata								yes	1	27	$28	budget rooms w/ cable
North of Puerto Vallarta													
Bungalows Los Picos	Bucerías									1	56	35–$57	beautiful beach
Bungalows Tlaquepaque	Lo De Marcos						2		yes	1	67	$87	expansive grounds
Casa Las Brisas	Punta de Mita						1			1	6	$395–$465	cushy hideaway
Casa Obelisco	San Francisco						1				4	$180–$200	romantic and cozy
Costa Azul	Fracc. Costa Azul			3			1		yes	1	27	$140	lots and lots to do
Decameron	Bucerías				yes		4		yes	5	509	$98–137	well-groomed grounds
Four Seasons Resort	Punta de Mita	5-12	yes	4	yes	yes	1			3	140	$495	posh and indulgent
Grand Velas	Nuevo Vallarta	4-12	yes	1		yes	4		yes	4	269	$834	sleek majesty
Huerta La Paz	Higuera Blanca										4	$55–$125	yoga classes; organic food
Marco's Place Villas	Bucerías						1				18	$73–$83	basic but comfortable
Marival	Nuevo Vallarta	4-7	yes	4		yes	4		yes	6	495	$224–$238	lots to do
Palmeras	Bucerías						1			1	11	$63–$78	bright, cheerful rooms
Paradise Village	Nuevo Vallarta	4-11	yes	7	yes	yes	2		yes	8	490	$169–$225	great for families
Villa Amor	Sayulita				yes					1	32	$85–$135	terrific views
Villa Bella	La Cruz de Huanacaxtle						1				6	$80–$190	tranquil
Villa Varadero	Nuevo Vallarta						1		yes	2	58	$96	great for families
Villas Buena Vida	Rincón de Guayabitos						2			1	45	$75–$98	good swimming beach

miserable. ⊠ *Paseo de la Marina Sur 205, Marina Vallarta, 48321* ☎ *322/226–1100, 800/228–3000 in U.S. and Canada* 🖷 *322/226–1131* ⊕ *www.westinvallarta.com* ➳ *266 rooms, 14 suites* ⚷ *2 restaurants, room service, fans, in-room safes, some in-room hot tubs, minibars, cable TV, in-room data ports, 3 tennis courts, 3 pools, wading pool, gym, hair salon, hot tubs, sauna, spa, steam room, beach, Ping-Pong, volleyball, 4 bars, shops, babysitting, children's programs (ages infant–12), playground, dry cleaning, laundry service, concierge, concierge floor, Internet room, business services, meeting rooms, car rental, travel services, free parking, some pets allowed, no-smoking rooms* ⊟ *AE, DC, MC, V* ¶⊙¶ *CP, BP, MAP, FAP, AI.*

★ ⚷ **\$\$\$–\$\$\$\$**   🏨 **CasaMagna Marriott.** Named in *Condé Nast Traveller* magazine's 2005 Gold List of 100 Best Hotels in the World, CasaMagna is hushed and stately in some places, lively and casual in others. Here's a classy property that nonetheless welcomes children. All of the restaurants—including a sleek Asian restaurant serving Thai, sushi, and teppanyaki and a large, pleasant sports bar—have kid's menus. Indicate you are traveling with kids when you book to ensure cookies and milk in your room at bedtime. The meandering grounds boast a large infinity pool as well as indigenous plant and chile gardens. Rooms have an upbeat, classy décor; each has a balcony and most have an ocean view. The cactus garden has 100 varieties, and enough of the blue agave plant to make a small batch of tequila. The Marriott chain requires smoke detectors, sprinklers, thrice-filtered water, and other beyond-the-pale safety features. The spa will get a total facelift in mid-2006. ⊠ *Paseo de la Marina 5, Marina Vallarta, 48354* ☎ *322/226–0000, 888/236–2427 in U.S. and Canada* 🖷 *322/226–0060* ⊕ *www.casamagnapuertovallarta.com* ➳ *404 rooms, 29 suites* ⚷ *2 restaurants, snack bar, 24-hour room service, in-room safes, some in-room hot tubs, minibars, some refrigerators, cable TVs with movies, in-room broadband, Wi-Fi, 2 pools, wading pool, gym, hair salon, hot tub, sauna, spa, beach, billiards, Ping-Pong, soccer, volleyball, 2 bars, sports bar, shop, babysitting, children's programs (ages 4–12), playground, dry cleaning, laundry service, concierge, Internet room, business services, convention center, meeting rooms, car rental, free parking* ⊟ *AE, DC, MC, V* ¶⊙¶ *EP.*

\$\$\$–\$\$\$\$ 🏨 **Fiesta Americana.** The dramatically designed terra-cotta building rises above a deep-blue pool that flows under bridges and beside palm oases; a seven-story palapa (which provides natural air-conditioning) covers the elegant lobby—paved in patterned tile and stone—and a large round bar. The ocean-view rooms have a modern pink and terra-cotta color scheme, beige marble floors, balconies, and tile baths with powerful showers. The beach bustles with activity and equipment rentals. It's about halfway between the Marina Vallarta complex and Downtown PV. ⊠ *Blvd. Federico M. Ascencio, Km 2.5, Zona Hotelera Norte, 48300* ☎ *322/225–2100, 800/343–7821 in the U.S.* 🖷 *322/224–2108* ⊕ *www.fiestaamericana.com* ➳ *288 rooms, 3 suites* ⚷ *3 restaurants, snack bar, room service, IDD phones, in-room safes, minibars, cable TV with movies and video games, in-room data ports, Wi-Fi, pool, gym, hot tub, beach, volleyball, 3 bars, shops, babysitting, children's programs (ages 4–12), laundry service, concierge, business services, meeting rooms, car* *rental, travel services, free parking, no-smoking rooms* ▤ *AE, D, DC, MC, V* ⫶❂⫶ *EP.*

⟲ **$$$–$$$$** ▦ **Sol Meliá Puerto Vallarta.** The sprawling Meliá, on the beach and close to the golf course, is popular with families and hums with activity. An enormous birdcage with several parrots dominates the breezy lobby, which also houses an eclectic collection of Mexican art and memorabilia. The plazas beyond have still more artwork as well as garden areas, fountains, ponds, and such bits of whimsy as a supersize chess board with plastic pieces as big as a toddler. There's a huge pool, an outdoor theater with nightly shows, and elaborate children's programs. Rooms are havens in subdued blues, creams, and sands. Considering it's an all-inclusive only, prices are extremely reasonable. ⊠ *Paseo de la Marina Sur 7, Marina Vallarta, 48300* ☎ *322/226–3000, 800/336–3542 in the U.S.* ⌗ *322/226–3030* ⊕ *www.solmelia.com* ⟿ *356 rooms, 4 suites* ⟐ *3 restaurants, in-room safes, refrigerators, cable TV, 2 tennis courts, pool, gym, hair salon, hot tubs, beach, billiards, 3 bars, video game room, shops, babysitting, children's programs (ages 4–12), laundry service, concierge, Internet room, meeting rooms, car rental, travel services, free parking* ▤ *AE, MC, V* ⫶❂⫶ *AI.*

$$–$$$ ▦ **Quinta María Cortez.** This B&B has soul. Its seven levels ramble up
Fodor'sChoice a steep hill at Playa Conchas Chinas, about a 20-minute walk along the
★ sand to the Romantic Zone (or a short hop in a bus or taxi). Most rooms
have balconies and kitchenettes; all are furnished with antiques and local art. Other draws are the efficient and welcoming staff, the fortifying breakfast (cooked to order) served on a palapa-covered patio, the nearly private beach below, and the views from the rooftop sundeck. It's popular and has few rooms, so make reservations early. Minimum stays are five nights in winter, and three nights in summer. ⊠ *Calle Sagitario 126, Playa Conchas Chinas, 48310* ☎ *322/221–5317, 888/640–8100 reservations* ⌗ *322/221–5327* ⊕ *www.quinta-*

> **WORD OF MOUTH**
>
> "We loved [Quinta María Cortez] so much that the first night we arrived we didn't even venture into town . . . Each morning we woke to the sound of the waves crashing against the rocks and the smell of breakfast . . . The staff was very friendly, we really could not have asked for a better stay."
>
> –travel3773

maria.com ⟿ *7 rooms* ⟐ *Fans, in-room safes, some kitchenettes, refrigerators, pool, beach, Internet room; no a/c in some rooms, no room TVs, no kids under 18* ▤ *AE, MC, V* ⫶❂⫶ *BP.*

$$ ▦ **Buenaventura.** The location is ideal: on downtown's northern edge, just a few blocks from the malecón, shops, hotels, and restaurants. The beach has gentle waves, but with brown sand and rocks, it's not the prettiest beach and attracts few bathers. There's a lively pool scene; the adults-only area facing the sea, always crowded, is a big part of the draw. Some rooms are cheerful, with bright striped textiles and framed tropical prints; the drab ones are undergoing renovation at this writing. Ocean-facing balconies are tiny, and if you sit, you can't see a thing. Still, the sum of the whole makes up for the so-so rooms (with hard beds), and the all-inclusive rate is a good deal, especially for families. ⊠ *Av. México 1301, El Centro, 48350* ☎ *322/226–7000 or 888/859–9439* 🖷 *322/222–3546* ⊕ *www.hotelbuenaventura.com.mx* 🛏 *216 rooms, 15 suites* 🕭 *2 restaurants, room service, cable TV with movies, 2 pools, hot tub, massage, spa, beach, volleyball, 3 bars, babysitting, laundry service, concierge, Internet room, travel services* ▭ *AE, MC, V* ⦿| *EP, AI.*

$$ 🏨 **Casa Iguana Hotel de Mismaloya.** Palms and plants edge walkways that line the swimming pool and goldfish ponds. Balconies look down on this garden scene and on the palapa bar-restaurant. Standard suites have full kitchens, shower-only baths, chunky furniture with cast-iron hardware, and tiles with folkloric patterns. Electric orange and yellow plaids brighten spaces that can be dark at certain times of the day. The hotel is on a cobblestone street off the highway; if you don't want to hoof it into PV, take one of the local buses that pass every 15 minutes. The beach is a five-minute walk away; and the village of Mismaloya, with wandering chickens and even burros, is within braying distance. The all-inclusive plan isn't available during high season. ⊠ *Av. 5 de Mayo 455, Mismaloya, 48394* ☎ *322/228–0186, 877/893–7654 in the U.S., 877/224–5057 in Canada* 🖷 *322/228–0087* ⊕ *www.casaiguanahotel.com* 🛏 *49 2-bedroom suites, 3 3-bedroom suites* 🕭 *Restaurant, grocery, room service, IDD phones, fans, kitchens, refrigerators, cable TV, driving range, pool, pond, outdoor hot tub, massage, bar, babysitting, laundry facilities, Internet room, meeting room, car rental, free parking, no-smoking rooms* ▭ *AE, MC, V* ⦿| *AI, EP.*

★ $$ 🏨 **Hotel Molino de Agua.** This hip spot right next to the bridge on the Río Cuale has a variety of rooms to choose from: all have screened windows and some have small patios looking out on the beach; only a few have bathtubs. Beds are too hard, and what they call suites are just slightly larger rooms, but the beach here is very nice—with chairs and chaises shaded by individual palapas—and the two huge pool areas are great places to meet other guests. Tons of exuberant vegetation give a lost-in-paradise feel to the extensive grounds; the sound of water falling in fountains multiplies that times two. ⊠ *Av. Ignacio L. Vallarta 130, Col. E. Zapata, 48380* ☎ *322/222–1907 or 322/222–1957* 🖷 *322/222–6056* ⊕ *www.molinodeagua.com* 🛏 *24 cabins, 35 rooms* 🕭 *2 restaurants, 2 pools, hot tub, massage, beach, 2 bars, laundry facilities, meeting rooms, free parking; no room phones, no TV in some rooms* ▭ *AE, MC, V* ⦿| *EP.*

$$ 🏨 **Playa Conchas Chinas.** Studios here have functional kitchenettes, basic cookware, and somewhat thin mattresses on wood-frame beds. Each has a small tiled tub as well as a shower. The real pluses of this plain Jane are the balconies with spectacular beach views and the location above Conchas Chinas Beach, about a 20-minute walk to downtown PV along the beach. The three-bedroom presidential suite has a sound system and large-screen TV. ⊠ *Carretera a Barra de Navidad (Carretera 200) Km. 2.5, Conchas Chinas, 48380* ☎ *322/221–5763 or 322/221–5230* ⊕ *www.hotelconchaschinas.com* 🛏 *21 rooms, 1 suite* 🕭 *Restaurant, in-room safe, some kitchens, some refrigerators, cable TV, some in-room DVDs, pool, beach, bar, free parking* ▭ *AE, MC, V* ⦿| *EP.*

Buenaventura .**24**

Casa Dulce
Vida **28**

Los Cuatro
Vientos **27**

Fiesta
Americana **23**

Hacienda San
Angel **29**

El Pescador . . .**25**

Río **30**

Rosita **26**

Sheraton
Buganvilias . . .**22**

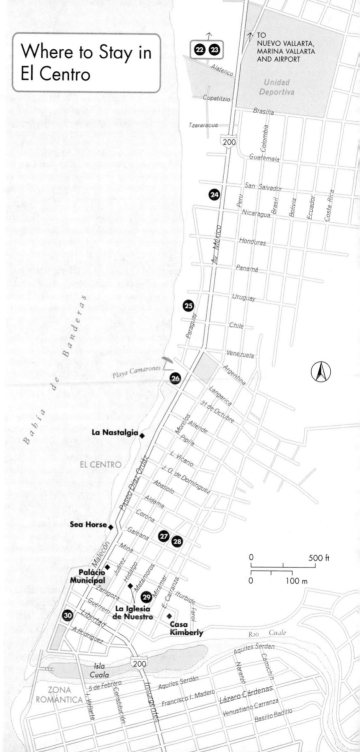

Where to Stay in El Centro

★ **$$** 🖼 **Playa Los Arcos.** This hotel, right on the beach in town, buzzes with a nice mix of guests: Americans, Canadians, Mexicans, and a few Europeans. Though the price is right, not all Los Arcos's guests are budget travelers: some better-heeled guests stay here for the easy-going ambience and the location on the beach near Zona Romántica restaurants, bars, and shops. Furnishings are tired and tour groups abound, but yellow trumpet vines and lacy palms draped in tiny white lights enliven the pool and the bar—restaurant, which has music nightly and a Mexican fiesta on Saturday evening. If you're willing to cross the street, you can get even better deals: Los Arcos Vallarta and Los Arcos Suites have larger rooms with kitchenettes; some have balconies, too. ⊠ *Av. Olas Altas 380, Col. E. Zapata, 48380* 🕾 *322/222–1583, 800/648–2403 in U.S., 888/729–9590 in Canada* 🖷 *322/226–7104* ⊕ *www.playalosarcos. com* ➯ *158 rooms, 13 suites* 🖒 *Restaurant, some in-room safes, some kitchenettes, cable TV, pool, hot tub, beach, bar, babysitting, free parking, no-smoking rooms* ⊟ *MC, V* ⁞○⁞ *EP, AI.*

$–$$ 🖼 **Casa Dulce Vida.** Hidden four blocks off the busy malecón, this '60s-era villa has apartments of various sizes filled with modern Mexican art and comfortable, if well-worn, furniture. All apartments have well-equipped kitchens—again, we're not talking sparkly here (some fridges have rusty faces), but everything works. A few rooms have ocean-view terraces; the largest has three bedrooms, two baths, and a separate dining room. There's a red-tile pool and tropical gardens. In high season the property only accepts weeklong bookings. ⊠ *Calle Aldama 295, El Centro, 48300* 🕾 *322/222–1008, 800/600–6026 in the U.S.* 🖷 *322/222–5815* ⊕ *www.dulcevida.com* ➯ *6 suites* 🖒 *Fans, some in-room safes, kitchens, pool; no a/c in some rooms, no phones in some rooms, no room TVs* ⊟ *V* ⁞○⁞ *EP.*

$–$$ 🖼 **Rosita.** What started as a sleepy 12-room hostelry—one of PV's very first—is now a busy 115-room downtown hotel. It's still a viable budget option, mainly recommended for its location on the north end of the malecón. Rooms are very basic; expect shower-only baths, white-tile floors, and fabrics with floral prints. The cheapest have neither TV nor a/c. Request a room facing the water, as much for the view as for the natural light; rooms facing the street are dark, making them feel cramped. ⊠ *Paseo Díaz Ordaz 901, Col. 5 de Diciembre, 48300* 🕾 *322/223–2000, 877/813–6712 in U.S., 888/242–9587 in Canada* 🖷 *322/223–4393* ⊕ *www.hotelrosita.com* ➯ *115 rooms* 🖒 *Restaurant, fans, pool, bar, shop, laundry service; no a/c in some rooms, no TV in some rooms* ⊟ *AE, MC, V* ⁞○⁞ *BP.*

$ 🖼 **Andale.** Deep in the heart of—no, not Texas, but PV's south side—is a little-known hotel above a well-known restaurant–bar. You'll have to climb loads of steps to get to the brick-lined rooms, which are charming although somewhat stuffy in the hot season. A few lucky rooms and suites have wonderful views of the bay and of the town creeping up the adjoining hills. Only the 2% hotel tax is added to your bill, not the 15% state tax. Ask about the six one-bedroom apartments ($150 per night) down the street, with king bed, two full baths, large living room with sofabed, dining room, balcony, and fully equipped kitchen. ⊠ *Calle Olas Altas 425, Col. E. Zapata, 48380* 🕾 *322/223–2622* ⊕ *www.andales. com* ➯ *8 rooms, 2 suites* 🖒 *2 restaurants, room service, some kitch-*

enettes, some refrigerators, cable TV, bar, travel services; no a/c in some rooms ⊟ *MC, V* ⦿ *EP, BP (high season).*

$ ⊞ **Casa Andrea.** One- and two-bedroom apartments in this spiffy property are truly homey. Each has a different floor plan—some have tiny kitchen—dining areas; others are spacious—but all have ceiling fans and dark-wood beams that contrast with white ceilings and walls. Use the hotel's computers to check your e-mail, or curl up with a book or watch a video in the library. Coffee and pastries are served each morning on the garden patio, where guests (many of them return visitors) sit and chat. The location, a few blocks from Los Arcos and the malecón, is a real plus. With some exceptions, high-season bookings are by the week. Expect some homely but sweet rescued dogs to be wandering about. ⊠ *Calle Francisca Rodríguez 174, El Centro, 48380* ☎ *322/222–1213* ⊕ *www.casa-andrea.com* ⤵ *11 apartments* ⚲ *Fans, kitchens, pool, gym, hot tub, bar, library, laundry facilities, Internet room; no room phones, no room TVs* ⊟ No credit cards ⦿ *CP.*

$ ⊞ **Los Cuatro Vientos.** Gloria Whiting has owned this Old Vallarta original, which opened in 1955, for about 25 years, and some guests have been coming forever. That explains why most of the guests and staff seem like old friends. The restaurant, Chez Elena (⇨ Chapter 3), once the toast of the town, the unadorned rooftop bar, and the best room (3-A) have gorgeous views of the bay and of the city's red rooftops. Come to rub shoulders with Europeans and others who appreciate a bargain and a bit of history. Although it's less common today to hear roosters crowing or see donkeys clomp down the street, it's more likely here than elsewhere in PV. Rooms are plain, yet the traditional brick ceilings give a homey feel. ⊠ *Calle Matamoros 520, El Centro, 48300* ☎ *322/222–0161* 🖷 *322/222–2831* ⊕ *www.cuatrovientos.com* ⤵ *14 rooms* ⚲ *Restaurant, room service (dinner only), pool, bar; no a/c, no room phones, no room TVs* ⊟ *MC, V* ⦿ *CP.*

$ ⊞ **Eloísa.** Despite being a block from the beach, this hotel has more of a downtown feel, and sits on pretty Lázaro Cárdenas Park; rooms 211–216 have the best park views. Rooms are generally plain but clean, and there's a great city-and-mountain view from the rooftop, which has a pool and party area. Bungalows have small kitchenettes in one corner; suites have larger kitchens, separate bedrooms, and two quiet air conditioners. Units with great views cost the same as those without, so ask for one *con vista panorámica* (with a panoramic view). ⊠ *Lázaro Cárdenas 179, Col. E. Zapata, 48380* ☎ *322/222–6465 or 322/222–0286* ⊕ *www.hoteleloisa.com* ⤵ *60 rooms, 6 studios, 8 suites* ⚲ *Restaurant, fans, some kitchenettes, some refrigerators, cable TV, 2 pools, bar, shop; no room phones* ⊟ *MC, V* ⦿ *EP.*

$ ⊞ **Emperador.** Ask for a room on the beach side of the street—those on the other side have no view. In exchange for pressed-wood and faux-bamboo furniture and a tepid-tempered staff, you get an inexpensive lodging overlooking the pier at Playa Los Muertos, and proximity to Old Vallarta. A standard suite for two has a kitchen (with plastic plates, and just the basic, beat-up pots) on a balcony hanging just above the sand. Less than 10 bucks more gets you a junior suite, where the sitting room between the bedroom and outdoor kitchen has two (stiff) couches. The pool and hot tub are down the street. ⊠ *Calle Amapas 114, Col.*

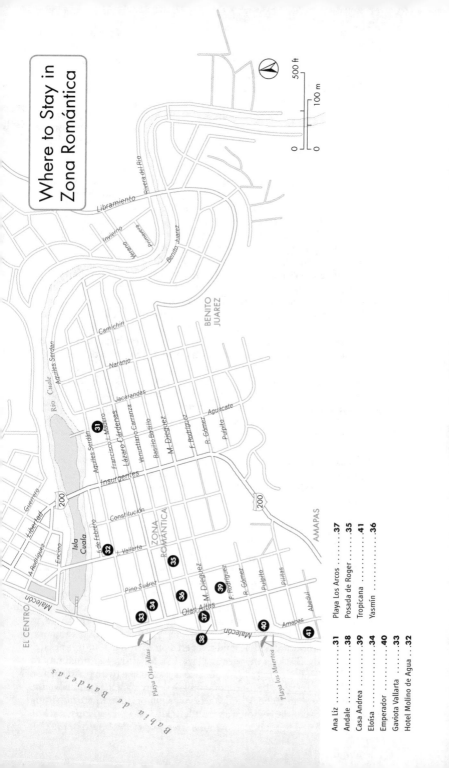

Where to Stay in Zona Romántica

EL CENTRO

Bahía de Banderas

Playa Olas Altas

Playa los Muertos

BENITO JUAREZ

ZONA ROMÁNTICA

AMAPAS

Ana liz **31**
Andale **38**
Casa Andrea **39**
Eloísa **34**
Emperador **40**
Gaviota Vallarta **33**
Hotel Molino de Agua . . .**32**

Playa Los Arcos **37**
Posada de Roger **35**
Tropicana **41**
Yasmín **36**

500 ft

100 m

E. Zapata, 48380 ☎ *322/222–5143 or 322/222–3329* ⚲ *19 rooms, 50 suites* ⚲ *Restaurant, some kitchens, beach, bar* ⊟ *MC, V* ⍦ *EP.*

$ ⬚ **Gaviota Vallarta.** Simple rooms in this six-story low-rise have somewhat battered colonial-style furnishings; some have tiny balconies but only a few on the top floors have a partial ocean view. The small figure-8-shape pool in the middle of the courtyard feels exposed, but still refreshes. The best perks are the location one block from the beach and free parking. Choose air-conditioning or fan, cable TV or no, and a fridge if you like; room costs vary according to these choices.

■ TIP➔ **Don't bother with the two-bedroom apartments; they are poorly designed and not worth $150 a night.** ⊠ *Francisco I. Madero 176, Col. E. Zapata, 48380* ☎ *322/222–1510* ⊞ *322/222–5516* ⊕ *www.hotelgaviota.com* ⚲ *84 rooms* ⚲ *Restaurant, some refrigerators, some cable TV, pool, bar, Internet room, free parking; no room phones* ⊟ *MC, V* ⍦ *EP.*

$ ⬚ **El Pescador.** Fall asleep to the sound of the waves at this modest yet cheerful hotel that's a favorite among Mexican travelers. Balconies are narrow but provide a view of the pool area and beach. The latter has sand but also fist-size rocks in the tidal zone; the curvy, medium-size pool is a nice alternative. Bright white and inexpensive, El Pescador is about five blocks north of the malecón (and a sister property, Hotel Rosita). ⊠ *Calle Paraguay 1117 at Uruguay, Col. 5 de Diciembre, 48350* ☎ *322/222–1884, 888/242–9587 in Canada, 877/813–6712 from U.S.* ⊞ *332/223–4393* ⊕ *www.hotelpescador.com* ⚲ *102 rooms* ⚲ *Restaurant, some fans, bar, pool, laundry service; no a/c in some rooms* ⊟ *MC, V* ⍦ *EP.*

$ ⬚ **Tropicana.** This is a well-groomed, bright-white hotel at the south end of Playa Los Muertos for a reasonable price. Save $15 a night by booking a standard rather than superior room; except for the size of the TV, they're almost the same. Each has several different areas for sitting or playing cards, but the beds are hard. The polite, older staff is a plus; most of these people have worked here for decades. Suites have no separate living area, but are larger than other rooms and each has a four-burner stove, blenders, and fridge. ⊠ *Calle Amapas 214, Col. E. Zapata, 48380* ☎ *322/222–0912* ⊞ *322/222–6737* ⊕ *www.htropicanapv.com* ⚲ *148 rooms, 12 suites* ⚲ *Restaurant, some fans, some in-room safes, cable TV, pool, bar, beach, free parking* ⊟ *MC, V* ⍦ *EP.*

¢–$ ⬚ **Rio.** This budget hotel get points for its location just north of Isla Río Cuale, two blocks from both the beach and the main plaza. It gets even more points for the cheerful, well-air-conditioned little restaurant–bar serving Mexican specials, and for the computer room with many sta-

CAN I DRINK THE WATER?

Most of the fancier hotels have reverse osmosis or other water filtration systems. It's fine for brushing your teeth, but play it safe by drinking bottled water (there might be leaks that let groundwater in). Note that the bottled water in your hotel room may be added to your bill when you leave, even if it appears to be free. It seems that the nicer the hotel, the costlier the water. Buy a few bottles at the corner grocery instead.

2

Don't Be (Time-Share) Shark Bait

In Puerto Vallarta, time-share salespeople are as unavoidable as death and taxes. And almost as dreaded. Although a slim minority of people actually enjoy going to one- to four-hour time-share presentations to get the freebies that range from Kahlua to rounds of golf, car rentals, meals, and shows, most folks find the experience incredibly annoying. For some it even casts a pall over their whole vacation.

The bottom line is, if the sharks smell interest, you're dead in the water. Time-share salespeople occupy tiny booths up and down main streets where tourists and cruise passengers walk. In general, while *vallartenses* are friendly, they don't accost you on the street to start a conversation. Those who do are selling something. Likewise, anyone calling you *amigo* is probably selling. The best solution is to walk by without responding, or say "No thanks" or "I'm not interested" as you continue walking. When they yell after you, don't feel compelled to explain yourself.

Some sly methods of avoidance that have worked for others are telling the tout that you're out of a job but dead interested in attending a presentation. They'll usually back off immediately. Or explaining confidentially that the person you're with is not your spouse. Time-share people are primarily interested in married couples—married to each other, that is! But our advice is still to practice the art of total detachment with a polite rejection and then ignoring the salesperson altogether if he or she persists.

Even some very nice hotels (like the Westin) allow salespeople in their lobbies disguised as the Welcome Wagon or information gurus. Ask the concierge for the scoop on area activities, and avoid the so-called "information desk."

Time-share salespeople often pressure guests to attend time-share presentations, guilt-tripping them ("My family relies on the commissions I get," for example) or offering discounts on the hotel room and services. The latter are sometimes difficult to redeem and cost more time than they're worth. And although it may be the salesperson's livelihood, remember that this is your vacation, and you have every right to use the time as you wish.

tions. On the downside (way down) are visible plastic tubing in the halls, uninspired, older furnishings in most rooms, and rusted fridges in "suites," which are slightly larger than standard rooms and have sinks and microwaves for $10 more. ☒ *Calle Morelos 170, El Centro, 48380* ☏ *322/222–0366* ⊕ *www.hotelrio.com.mx* ➪ *47 rooms* ☖ *Restaurant, fans, some kitchenettes, cable TV, pool, bar, Internet room* ☐ MC, V ❍I *EP.*

¢ ☒ **Ana Liz.** Those who prefer to spend their vacation cash on eating out and shopping might consider this clean, bright, motel-like budget hotel a few blocks south of the Cuale River, behind Cine Bahía. Two floors of rooms face each other across an outdoor corridor and have tiny bathrooms but comfortable beds. Ask for a room away from the noisy street; don't ask to use the lobby phone—it's not allowed. Small TVs (local channels only) are available at an extra charge; a deposit is required for a towel. Artisans stay at this extremely plain place when they come to town, as do small-time businesspeople and backpacking Europeans; they're likely drawn by the substantial discounts for monthly stays. ⊠ *Francisco I. Madero 429, Col. E. Zapata, 48380* ☎ *322/222–1757* ✉ *hotelanaliz@hotmail.com* ⇴ *23 rooms* ⚘ *Some fans; no a/c in some rooms, no room phones* ⊟ *No credit cards* ⎟⚭⎟ *EP.*

¢ ⊞ **Posada de Roger.** If you hang around the pool or the small shared balcony overlooking the street and the bay beyond, it's not hard to get to know the other guests—many of them savvy budget travelers from Europe and Canada. A shared, open-air kitchen on the fourth floor has a great view, too. Rooms are spare and vaultlike, the showers are hot, and the beds comfortable—if you like a very firm mattress. Freddy's Tucan, the indoor-outdoor bar-restaurant (no dinner; $) is popular with locals—mainly for breakfast. The hotel is in a prime part of the Zona Romántica known for its restaurants and shops; Playa los Muertos is a few blocks away. ⊠ *Calle Basilio Badillo 237, Col. E. Zapata, 48380* ☎ *322/222–0836 or 322/222–0639* 🖷 *322/223–0482* ⊕ *www.hotelposadaderoger.com* ⇴ *47 rooms* ⚘ *Restaurant, fans, cable TV, pool, bar* ⊟ *AE, MC, V* ⎟⚭⎟ *EP.*

¢ ⊞ **Yasmín.** Two-story and L-shape, this budget baby has no pool, but it's just a block from the beach and joined at the hip to Café de Olla (⇨ Chapter 3), the extremely popular Mexican restaurant. Small, ho-hum rooms have low ceilings, firm beds, and open closets but also floor fans and cable TV: not a bad deal for the price. ⊠ *Calle Basilio Badillo, Col. E. Zapata, 48380* ☎ *322/222–0087* ⇴ *27 rooms* ⚘ *Restaurant, fans, cable TV; no room phones* ⊟ *No credit cards* ⎟⚭⎟ *EP.*

NORTH OF PUERTO VALLARTA

★ **$$$$** ⊞ **Casa Las Brisas.** Architect–owner Marc Lindskogh has created a nook of nonchalant elegance, with updated country furnishings of wicker, leather, and wood; rock-floor showers without curtains or doors; and cheerful Pacific Coast architectural details. Mosquito netting lends romance to cozy, quilt-covered beds. Waves crashing onshore, their sound somehow magnified, create white noise that lulls you to sleep. In the morning, settle into a cushy chaise on your private patio to watch seabirds swim; at night watch the sun set behind Punta de Mita. These simple pleasures make this hideaway a winner. It doesn't hurt that the food is truly delicious, the bar is well-stocked with international labels, and it's all included in the room price. You can avoid the 10% surcharge for credit cards by using PayPal. ⊠ *Playa Careyeros, Punta de Mita, Nayarit, 63734* ☎ *329/298–4114* 🖷 *329/298–4112* ⊕ *www.casalasbrisas.com* ⇴ *6 rooms* ⚘ *Restaurant, fans, in-room safes, refrigerators, pool, bar, windsurfing, library, concierge, travel services, free parking; no room phones, no TV in some rooms* ⎟⚭⎟ *AI.*

$$$$ ⊞ **Four Seasons Resort.** The hotel and its fabulous spa perch above a lovely
FodorsChoice   beach at the northern extreme of Bahía de Banderas, about 45 minutes
★   from the PV airport and an hour north of downtown Puerto Vallarta. Spacious rooms occupy Mexican-style casitas of one, two, and three sto-

Continued on page 47

SPAAAHH

The trend of luxury spas in Mexico, and particularly in vacation hot spots like Puerto Vallarta, shows no signs of slowing. From elegant resort spas scented with essence of orange and bergamot to Aztec-inspired day spas, each has its own personality and signature treatments. Competition keeps creativity high, with an ever-changing menu of new treatments, many using native products like sage, aloe vera, and even tequila.

Four Seasons Resort, Punta Mita

Spa Savvy

All of the spas listed here are open to nonguests, but reservations are essential. Guests of the hotel may get discounts. Spa customers can sometimes use other facilities at a resort, such as the restaurant, beach, pool, or gym. Ask when you book. Prices are generally on par with those of resort spas worldwide, but some deals are to be had, if you go with the less-expensive but still high-quality spas we lists. Or scout out hotel-spa packages and specials.

RESORT NAME	BODY TREATMENTS	SEASIDE TREATMENTS	TREATMENTS FOR TWO	FITNESS DAY PASS	HOT TUB	TEMAZCAL
Four Seasons	$80–$188	yes	yes	no*	yes	yes
Gran Velas	$58–$178	yes	yes	$40	yes	no
Paradise Village	$69–$104	no	no	$15	yes	no
El Tamarindo	$48–$152	yes	yes	no	no	yes
Terra Noble	$50–$130	yes	yes	no	yes	yes

* a fitness day pass is free for Four Seasons guests

TOP SPOTS

Organically Yours

EL TAMARINDO

This *Gilligan's Island*–style spa has no sauna, whirlpool, or fancy extras. But it does have some of the best treatments and staff in Pacific Mexico, and one of the most authentic *temazcals* (*See* Glossary, *p. 46*) around. The vibe is more convivial warmth than nonchalant New Age. Products are often made with lemongrass, aloe vera, fresh coconut, and mineral-laced mud. Try the Tonameyotl Teocuitlatic facial, which employs a mixture of champagne and real gold. A new facility, halfway up the adjacent cliff will be done by early 2007.

Body Treatments & Services: Exfoliation; massage; wraps, scrubs and body treatments (11 types); temazcal sweat lodge; yoga and Chi-Kung classes; meditation.

Beauty Treatments: Facials, manicure, pedicure

Prices: Body treatments $67–$152; facials $86–$95; manicure/pedicure $38–$48

Carretera Malaque–*Puerto Vallarta (Carretera 200) km. 7.5, Cihuatlán. Tel. 315/351-5032* ⊕ *www.mexicoboutiquehotels.com/thetamerindo* ▭ *AE, MC, V.*

El Careyes Beach Resort

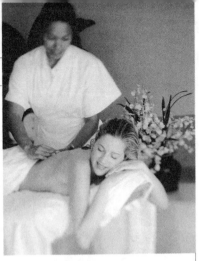

A Spa for All Seasons

FOUR SEASONS PUNTA MITA APUANE SPA

Professional service is the hallmark of this exclusive spa. An excellent kid's club allows you to enjoy spa treatments, knowing that your children are thoroughly engaged. The gym is first rate. An inspirational experience is a traditional temazcal ceremony, which takes place in a little building on knoll near the sea.

Treatments are among the most expensive in the area, but everything is top drawer. Native products are used almost exclusively; the Punta Mita massage combines tequila and locally grown sage. And refreshing lime is mixed with tequila and salt for a margarita body scrub.

Body Treatments: Aromatherapy; facials; exfoliation; massage (12 types); Vichy hydrotherapy; wraps and scrubs (5 types); temazcal sweat lodge.

Beauty Treatments: Facials (7 types); manicure; pedicure; hair/scalp treatment.

Prices: Body treatments $80–$188; facials $94–$206; hair: $44–$95; manicure or pedicure $30–$95; waxing $25–$70.

Packages: Standard treatment combinations, such as the Day of Beauty, with deep-cleansing facial, manicure, pedicure, and Swedish massage. *Punta de Mita, Bahía de Banderas. Tel. 329/291-6000* ⊕ *www.fourseasons.com/puntamita.* ▭ *AE, DC, MC, V.*

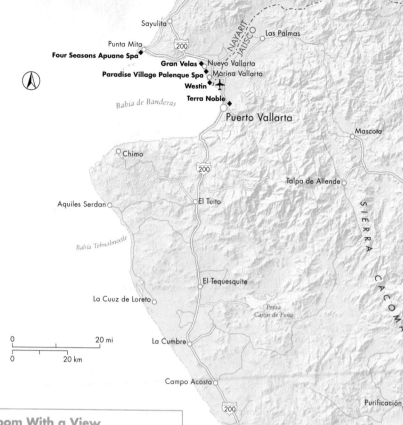

Room With a View

TERRA NOBLE

Your cares begin to melt away as soon as you enter the rustic, garden-surrounded property of this day-spa aerie overlooking Banderas Bay. Familiar and unpretentious, Terra Noble is more accessible pricewise than some of the area's more elegant spas. After-treatment teas are served on an outdoor patio with a great sea view. Two-hour temazcal sweat lodge rituals cleanse on three levels: physically, mentally, and spiritually. Or recharge with clay and painting classes, and Tarot readings.

Body Treatments: Reflexology; massage; several wraps and scrubs; temazcal sweat lodge; yoga/meditation.

Beauty Treatments: Facials; manicure; pedicure.

Packages: A few economical packages such as the Stress Recovery (a sea-salt body scrub, a massage, and a facial), for $138.

Prices: Body treatments $50–$130; facials $65–$85; manicure/pedicure $20–$25.
Av. Tulipanes 595, at Fracc. Lomas de Terra Noble, Col. 5 de Diciembre. Tel. 322/223-3530
🌐 *www.terranoble.com.* ▭ *MC, V.*

MORE TOP SPOTS

Something for Every Body

PARADISE VILLAGE PALENQUE SPA

On a peninsula between the beach and marina, this modern Maya temple of glass and marble is a cool, sweet-smelling oasis with separate wings for men and women; each is equipped with private hydrotherapy tubs, whirlpools, saunas, and steam rooms. The coed gym has state-of-the-art equipment and views of the ocean, plus aerobics classes in a separate studio and an indoor lap pool.

Spa designer Diana Mestre, an old hand in these parts, brings together ancient healing arts and the latest technologies. The reasonably priced therapy selections are extensive, from an anti-cellulite seaweed wrap to milk baths with honey, amaranth, and orange oil or the raindrop aromatherapy massage, employing clove, sage, bergamot, and other essential oils.

Body Treatments: Aromatherapy; facials; electro-acuscope anti-pain & stress therapy; Reiki; exfoliation; hot-stone massage; hydrotherapy; wraps, scrubs, and body treatments (14 types); reflexology; shiatsu.

Beauty Treatments: Facials (10 types), manicure, pedicure.

Prices: Body treatments $36–$104; facials $36–$104; manicure/pedicure $20–$60; hair $36–$80; waxing $8–$55.

Packages: A wide variety of packages that allow switching treatments in an equivalent price bracket. The basic plan combines three 50-minute treatments: marine body scrub, holistic massage, and hydrating facial.
Paseo de los Cocoteros 1 Nuevo Vallarta.
Tel. 322/226-6770 ⊕ *www.paradisevillage.com.*
▱ *AE, MC, V.*

Drama Queen

GRAN VELAS

The spa at Nuevo Vallarta's most elegant all-inclusive has the same dramatic architectural lines and artful use of marble, stone, teak, and tile. The 16,500-square-foot facility has 23 treatment rooms, and ample steam, sauna, and whirlpools. Lounge in the comfortable chaises in the "plunge lagoon" (with warm and cold pools) between or after treatments, with a cup of hot tea or cold chlorophyll water.

Reading the extensive menu of treatments can take hours—highlights are the chocolate, gold, or avocado wraps, Thai massage, European facial, cinnamon-sage foot scrub, and the challenging buttocks sculpt-lift. Adjoining the spa is an impressive fitness facility.

Body Treatments: Reflexology; massage (18 types); shiatsu; Vichy shower; exfoliation; wraps, scrubs, baths, and body treatments (32 types).

Beauty Treatments: Facials (12+); manicure/pedicure; hair care; waxing; makeup.

Prices: Body treatments: $58–$178; facials: $89–$148; manicure/pedicure: $20–$89; hair care: $29–$89; waxing: $29–$58; makeup: $78.

Packages: 10% discount for three or more treatments; otherwise, no packages.
Av. de los Cocoteros 98 Sur, Nuevo Vallarta.
Tel. 322/226-8000 ⊕ *www.grandvelas.com.*
▱ *AE, MC, V.*

HONORABLE MENTIONS

EL CAREYES

As it's secluded on a bay-front, palm tree–studded fringe between ocean and jungle, El Careyes Beach Resort lets you get in touch with nature while still enjoying your creature comforts. Eucalyptus, rose, and ylang-ylang perfume the spa, which sits on the edge of a private golden beach. You can sweat in style at the fully equipped gym, overlooking the ocean. No chlorine is used in the 3-meter indoor plunge pool, where the water is scented, filtered, and changed daily.

Services: Aromatherapy; reflexology; exfoliation; facials; mud wrap; clay wrap; seaweed wrap; body scrubs; body masks; Swedish massage; polarity massage.

Packages: Spa & Room Package includes room, breakfast, one stress-reducing massage, and one facial (per person), use of tennis courts, spa, and gym.

Carretera Barra de Navidad–Puerto Vallarta Carretera 200, Km 53. Tel. 5888/433-3989 ⊕ *www.elcareyesresort.com.* ▭ *AE, MC, V.*

■ TIP→On the day of your treatment, it's wise to call and ask the spa staff to crank up the heat in the whirlpool, sauna and/or steam rooms, which are sometimes left to chill until you arrive. Leave jewelry and watches in your room, but take tip money with you so you can tip the technician in person.

WESTIN

The concept at the Westin's spa involves the "seven pillars of well-being." Although this is basically a marketing strategy, the "aqua" pillar is a nod to the many water-related therapies as well as the fact that treatments are often performed in cabanas facing the ocean.

The hotel's grounds, with acres of royal palms surrounding the pool, are lovely. Popular with locals and visitors, the excellent fitness facility has a good selection of top-notch equipment.

Services: Exfoliation; wraps, scrubs, and body treaments (10 types); herbal mud; massage; reflexology, Reiki, shiatsu; facials; pedicures; manicures; waxing; hair salon.

Packages: A variety of packages are available, from the basic spa plan (exfoliation, sports massage, facial) to the pricey "spa day" (gym class, sauna, Swedish massage, breakfast, pedicure/manicure, and facial for $330).

Paseo de la Marina Sur 205, Marina Vallarta. Tel. 322/226-1100 ⊕ *www.westinvallarta.com.* ▭ *AE, MC, V.*

Junior suite at Careyes

GLOSSARY

acupuncture. Painless Chinese medicine during which needles are inserted into key spots on the body to restore the flow of *qi* and allow the body to heal itself.

aromatherapy. Massage and other treatments using plant-derived essential oils intended to relax the skin's connective tissues and stimulate the flow of lymph fluid.

ayurveda. An Indian philosophy that uses oils, massage, herbs, and diet and lifestyle modification to restore perfect balance to a body.

body brushing. Dry brushing of the skin to remove dead cells and stimulate circulation.

body polish. Use of scrubs, loofahs, and other exfoliants to remove dead skin cells.

hot-stone massage. Massage using smooth stones heated in water and applied to the skin with pressure or strokes or simply rested on the body.

hydrotherapy. Underwater massage, alternating hot and cold showers, and other water-oriented treatments.

reflexology. Massage on the pressure points of feet, hands, and ears.

reiki. A Japanese healing method involving universal life energy, the laying on of hands, and mental and spiritual balancing. It's intended to relieve acute emotional and physical conditions. Also called radiance technique.

salt glow. Rubbing the body with coarse salt to remove dead skin.

shiatsu. Japanese massage that uses pressure applied with fingers, hands, elbows, and feet.

shirodhara. Ayurvedic massage in which warm herbalized oil is trickled onto the center of the forehead, then gently rubbed into the hair and scalp.

sports massage. A deep-tissue massage to relieve muscle tension and residual pain from workouts.

Swedish massage. Stroking, kneading, and tapping to relax muscles. It was devised at the University of Stockholm in the 19th century by Per Henrik Ling.

Swiss shower. A multijet bath that alternates hot and cold water, often used after mud wraps and other body treatments.

Temazcal. Maya meditation in a sauna heated with volcanic rocks.

THE TEMAZCAL TRADITION

Increasingly popular at Mexico spas is the traditional sweat lodge, or *temazcalli*. Herb-scented water sizzles on heated lava rocks, filling the intimate space with purifying steam. Rituals blend indigenous and New Age practices, attempting to stimulate you emotionally, spiritually, and physically. For the sake of others, it's best to take a temazcal only if you're committed to the ceremony, or at least open-minded, and not claustrophobic.

Thai massage. Deep-tissue massage and passive stretching to ease stiff, tense, or short muscles.

thalassotherapy. Water-based treatments that incorporate seawater, seaweed, and algae.

Vichy shower. Treatment in which a person lies on a cushioned, waterproof mat and is showered by overhead water jets.

Watsu. A blend of shiatsu and deep-tissue massage with gentle stretches—all conducted in a warm pool.

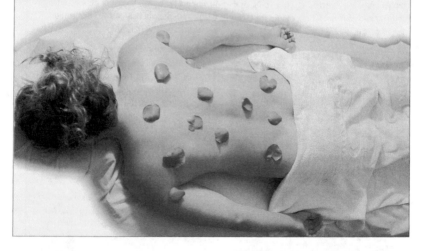

ries. Each room has elegant yet earthy furnishings and a private terrace or balcony—many with a sweeping sea view. The Jack Nicklaus–designed championship golf course has a challenging, optional 19th-island hole; the gym is first rate; and a good variety of sporting and beach equipment is on hand. Just offshore, the Marietas Islands are great for snorkeling, diving, whale watching, and fishing. This is the place for indulging golf and spa fantasies, exploring beaches and small towns to the north and south, or doing absolutely nothing. ⊠ *Bahía de Banderas, Punta de Mita, 63734, Nayarit* ☎ *329/291–6000, 800/322–3442 in U.S., 800/ 268–6282 in Canada* 🖷 *329/291–6060* ⊕ *www.fshr.com* 📞 *114 rooms, 26 suites* ☼ *3 restaurants, room service, fans, in-room safes, minibars, cable TV, in-room DVDs, in-room broadband, 19-hole golf course, 4 tennis courts, pool, wading pool, gym, sauna, hair salon, spa, steam room, beach, snorkeling, volleyball, 2 bars, library, shops, babysitting, children's programs (ages 5–12), dry cleaning, laundry service, concierge, Internet room, convention center, meeting room, car rental, free parking, no-smoking rooms* ▤ *AE, DC, MC, V* ⦿ *EP, MAP, FAP.*

> **WORD OF MOUTH**
>
> "Aside from the big pain-in-the-tookus factor, Nuevo tends to be more ho-hum: all-inclusive time-share resorts with no really top-notch hotels and no real boutique properties. The more interesting places to stay are in Puerto Vallarta." —TioGringo
>
> "I'd recommend Nuevo is for a family or couple who just want a decent resort on a beach to kick back and relax for a week, maybe take an organized tour or two." —suze

$$$$ ⊡ **Grand Velas.** In scale and majesty, the public areas of this luxury brand compare to other Nuevo Vallarta all-inclusives like the Taj Majal to a roadside taco stand. Ceilings soar overhead, and the structure and furnishings are simultaneously minimalist and modern, yet earthy, incorporating stucco, rock, polished teak, and gleaming ecru marble. The spa is excellent, and the views—with the garden-shrouded pool in the foreground and the beach beyond—are striking. Rooms are sleek, with elegant furnishings and appointments. In terms of food and drink, the high price entitles you to top-of-the-line spirits in minibars and restaurants, but the food, in our experience, is not exceptional. ⊠ *Paseo de los Cocoteros 98 Sur, Nuevo Vallarta, Jalisco, 63735* ☎ *322/226–8000, 877/ 398–2784 in U.S., 866/355–3359 in Canada* 🖷 *322/297–2005* ⊕ *www. grandvelas.com* 📞 *269 suites* ☼ *4 restaurants, snack bar, room service, fans, in-room safes, some in-room hot tubs, minibars, cable TV, in-room DVDs, Wi-Fi, tennis court, 4 pools, wading pool, gym, hair salon, hot tub, spa, steam room, beach, bicycles, Ping-Pong, 2 bars, lobby lounge, shops, babysitting, children's programs (ages 4–12), dry cleaning, laundry service, Internet room, business services, convention center, car rental, travel services, free parking, some pets allowed (fee)* ▤ *AE, MC, V* ⦿ *AI.*

$$$ ⊡ **Marival.** Rooms have strong air-conditioning and amenities like hair dryers, iron and ironing boards, and small tubs but also has an uninspired attempt at modern decor, as well as cheap doors. There's an extra

Buying a Time-Share

If you return to PV frequently, a time-share might make sense. Here are some tips for navigating the shark-infested waters:

■ Cruise the Internet before your vacation. Check out resale time-shares in the area, which makes it easier to determine the value of what's offered.

■ Worthwhile time-shares come with the option of trading for a room in another destination. Ask what other resorts are available.

■ Time-share salespeople get great commissions and are very good at their jobs. Be brave, be strong, and only sign on the dotted line if it's what you really want. Remember there are plenty of good vacation deals out there that require no long-term commitment.

Buyer's Remorse? If you buy a time-share and get buyers' remorse, be aware that most contracts have a five-day "cooling off period." Ask to see this in writing before you sign the contract; then you can get a full refund if you change your mind.

charge for room service and, inexplicably, the use of in-room safes. Only a few units have ocean views, but there are plenty of individual palapas and lounge chairs at the beach. Come here for the relatively inexpensive all-inclusive price and the wealth of activities. ⊠ *Paseo Cocoteros s/n at Blvd., Nuevo Vallarta, Jalisco, 63735* ☎ *322/226–8200* 🖷 *322/ 297–0160* ⊕ *www.gomarival.com* ⤳ *373 rooms, 122 suites* ⚓ *6 restaurants, room service, some fans, some kitchenettes, cable TV, 4 tennis courts, 4 pools, gym, hair salon, spa, beach, bicycles, archery, basketball, boccie, pool tables, volleyball, children's programs (ages 4–17), shops, 7 bars, convention center, business center, free parking* ▤ *MC, V* ⫶⊙⫶ *AI.*

☋ **$$$** 🔲 **Paradise Village.** Built like a Maya pyramid, this Nuevo Vallarta hotel and time-share property is perfect for families, with lots of activities geared to children. Many people love it, others complain of the overzealous time-share pitch and poor service. All suites have balconies with either marina or ocean views; the smallest, a junior suite, is 700 square feet. Furnishings are attractive as well as functional, with pretty cane sofa beds in a soothing palette and well-equipped kitchens. Locals like to visit the clean, well-organized spa, which smells divine, and is noted for its massages and facials. The beach here is tranquil enough for swimming, although some small waves are suitable for bodysurfing. ⊠ *Paseo de los Cocoteros 1, Nuevo Vallarta, Jalisco, 63732* ☎ *322/ 226–6770, 800/995–5714 Ext. 111 in U.S. and Canada* 🖷 *322/226– 6752* ⊕ *www.paradisevillage.com* ⤳ *490 suites* ⚓ *8 restaurants, room service, fans, in-room safes, kitchens, microwaves, refrigerators, cable TV, 18-hole golf course, 7 tennis courts, 2 pools, gym, hair salon, hot tub, sauna, spa, steam room, beach, boating, jet skiing, marina, basketball, volleyball, 3 bars, dance club, shops, babysitting, children's programs (ages 4–11), concierge, convention center, car rental, travel services, free parking* ▤ *AE, MC, V* ⫶⊙⫶ *EP, AI.*

$–$$$ 🔲 **Casa Obelisco.** The vibe is warm and romantic, the cozy-chic rooms—

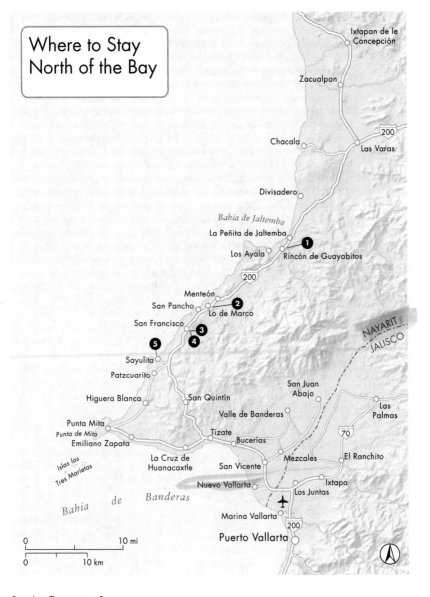

Where to Stay North of the Bay

Bungalows Tlaquepaque . . **2**
Casa Obelisco **4**
Costa Azul **3**
Villa Amor **5**
Villas Buena Vida **1**

endowed with original paintings, folk art, and super-comfortable king beds with pillowtop mattresses and mosquito nets—are perfect for spooning and honeymooning. Drinks by the pool, walks on the beach, and trips into town or down to Sayulita (5 km [3 mi] south) are about as ambitious as most guests get. Each ocean-facing patio (some private, some shared) has either a hammock or table with *equipale* (pigskin) chairs. American owners provide opinions and information about the area. Breakfasts are expansive. Kahlua, the well-behaved doodle dog, is a boon to pet-starved guests. ⊠ *Calle Palmas 115, Fracc. Costa Azul, San Francisco Nayarit, 63732* ☎ *311/258–4316* ⊕ *www.casaobelisco.com* ⤴ *4 rooms* ⚤ *Dining room, fans, pool, bar; no room TVs, no room phones, no kids under 16* ⊟ *No credit cards* ❍⎮ *BP* ❂ *Closed Aug. and Sept.*

$–$$$ ☷ **Villa Bella.** Tranquility reigns, and tropical plants give character to this privately owned property on a hill above quiet La Cruz, just north of Bucerías. Choose a garden-view room or ocean-facing suite in one of two villas that share common rooms—with TV, telephone, computer with Internet access, DVD and CD players—as well as a swimming pool and gardens. Other pretty shared spaces include a dining area and kitchen in the guest villa, and second-story terraces off some of the suites. A very Mexican village with a growing number of foreign residents and snowbirds, Villa Bella is the perfect place to enjoy the simple charms of earthy La Cruz. Payment is accepted only via PayPal. ⊠ *Calle del Monte Calvario 12 La Cruz de Huanacaxtle, Nayarit, 63732* ☎ *329/295–5161 or 329/295–5154, 877/273–6244 toll-free in U.S. or in Canada 877/513–1662* ☎ *329/295–5305* ⊕ *www.villabella-lacruz.com* ⤴ *2 rooms, 4 suites* ⚤ *Dining room, fans, some kitchens, some cable TV, pool, bar; no a/c in some rooms, no TV in some rooms, no room phones, no smoking* ⊟ *MC, V* ❍⎮ *CP.*

☾ **$$** ☷ **Costa Azul.** What makes this place attractive are the many activities offered: horseback riding, kayaking, hiking, surfing (with lessons), and excursions to the Marietas Islands or La Tobara mangroves near San Blas. The all-inclusive plan includes activities, but since the food is mainly mediocre and San Pancho has a few excellent restaurants, the European Plan is recommended. Although the sandy beach faces the open ocean, it curves around to a spot that's safer for swimming. Some guests have complained of disorganized and unhelpful staff members, and hotel maintenance has declined in recent years. ⊠ *Carretera 200 Km 118, Fracc. Costa Azul, San Francisco, Nayarit, 63732* ☎ *311/258–4210, 800/365–7613 in U.S.* ☎ *949/498–6300 in U.S.* ⊕ *www.costaazul.com* ⤴ *24 rooms, 3 villas* ⚤ *Restaurant, fans, some kitchenettes, some refrigerators, pool, beach, snorkeling, fish-*

PILLOW TALK

If you're picky about your pillow, Gran Velas, Presidente Intercontinental, Four Seasons, or another top-drawer accommodation might prove to be the hotel of your dreams. Some of the swankiest hotels in the area have pillow menus with a half-dozen or more styles to choose from. Go with whisper-soft eider-down or, if you're allergic to farm animals, 100% man-made materials.

An Over-the-Top Experience

YOU DON'T HAVE TO BE A ROCK star to rent one of Vallarta's most beautiful homes, but a similar income or a never-ending trust fund might help.

Just beyond Destiladeras Beach at the north end of Banderas Bay, **Casa Canta Rana** ⊕ www.casacantarana. com provides stunning views of the coast from inside a gated community. Indoor—outdoor living and dining spaces have bay and island views. Decorated with tasteful, seductively subdued furnishings, two of the three bedroom suites share a tall palapa roof; the master suite has an indoor—outdoor shower and private patio. A maid, gardener, and pool boy are included. Additional staff, airport transfer, and other services are provided at additional cost. For the nanny, pilot, or bodyguard on your payroll, there's a separate apartment with bedroom, kitchen, and bath. High season (November 1–April 30) rate is $1,350 per night.

What could be better than a former president's home, the site hand-picked for its almost incomprehensibly beautiful vistas of the sea? President Luis Echevarrí's mansion, **Villa Vista Mágica,** is on a highly forested point between Sayulita and San Francisco, Nayarit. The circular, 10-bedroom property comes with a cook who will

prepare three meals a day (Mexican food from a Mexican cook). The waverunners and two Suburbans are also at your disposal. This fabulous place costs a mere $31,250 a week (much more during holidays). To rent this—or a less-pricey property where you'll feel equally special and pampered—contact **Boutique Villas** (866/823–9739 ⊕ www. boutiquevillas.com).

Twenty years ago the private heaven of simple fisherfolk and their families, the spearhead-shape point at the northern point of Banderas Bay is today home to the gated, low-density community **Punta Mita** (888/647-0979 in U.S. and Canada ⊕ www. puntamita.com.mx). Here you find the Four Seasons (and soon the Rosewood and St. Regis resorts), as well as multiple golf courses, beach clubs, spas, and shops. Within the 1,500-acre retreat, the Four Seasons and other brands rent luxury villas whose high-season rates range from $4,000 to $10,000 per night. Floor plans vary but there's consistency in the large outdoor living spaces; air-conditioned common areas and bedrooms with natural-hue, high-quality furnishings; and attentive staff members, including your own full-time chef.

---

ing, hiking, horseback riding, 2 bars, shop, laundry service, travel services, free parking; no room phones, no room TVs ▭ *AE, D, DC, MC, V* ¶⊙¶ *EP, FAP, AI.*

$$ ▣ **Decameron.** This high-volume hotel is at the south end of long and lovely Bucerías Beach and has beautifully manicured grounds. It also has quality entertainment, activities, and food, and strives to maintain high sanitary standards. Rooms are plain and not particularly modern or appealing, with laminate bathroom counters and textured stucco interior walls that have been painted over many times. Those in the older section have the best views since they were built along the water. Reservations must be made online (Expedia.com, Travelocity.com, etc.) or through FunJet Travel. ✉ *Calle Lázaro Cárdenas, Bucerías, Nayarit, 63732* ☎ *FunJet: 329/298–0226 or 888/558–6654* 🖷 *329/298–0333* ⊕ *www.decameron.com* 🛏 *509 rooms* ⌂ *5 restaurants, pizzeria, in-room safes, cable TV, 3 tennis courts, 4 pools, hair salon, massage, sailing, bicycles, basketball, soccer, volleyball, 3 bars, car rental, Internet room, disco, free parking* ⊟ *MC, V* 🍽 *AI.*

★ **$$** ▦ **Villa Amor.** What began as a hilltop home has slowly become an amalgam of unusual, rustic-but-luxurious suites with indoor and outdoor living spaces. The higher up your room, the more beautiful the view of Sayulita's coast. The trade-off for such beauty? A long walk up a seemingly endless staircase, and the dearth of room phones that make contacting the front desk frustrating. Accommodations, managed by different owners, range from basic to honeymoon suites with terraces and plunge pools. Details like recessed colored-glass light fixtures, talavera sinks in bathrooms, brick ceilings, wrought-iron table lamps, art in wall niches, and colorful cement floors add a lot of class. The property overlooks a rocky cove where you can fish from shore; a beautiful sandy beach is a few minutes' walk. The staff lends out bikes, kayaks, boogie boards, and snorkeling gear. The restaurant is closed in low season unless occupancy is unusually high. ✉ *Playa Sayulita, Sayulita, Nayarit, 63842* ☎ *329/291–3010* 🖷 *329/291–3018* ⊕ *www.villaamor.com* 🛏 *32 villas* ⌂ *Restaurant, fans, some kitchenettes, some microwaves, some refrigerators, massage, snorkeling, bicycles, horseback riding, volleyball, bar, laundry service, free parking; no a/c in some rooms, no room phones, no room TVs* ⊟ *No credit cards* 🍽 *EP.*

> **OM AWAY FROM HOME**
>
> **Via Yoga** (⊕ www.viayoga.com), based in Seattle, WA, offers week-long packages at Villa Amor that include twice-daily yoga classes with group activities, various disciplines of yoga, and if you like, surfing classes and excursions.

$–$$ ▦ **Villas Buena Vida.** On beautiful Rincón de Guayabitos Beach, this property has three-story units, breeze-ruffled palms, swimming pools, and manicured walkways. Four guests are allowed in even the smallest rooms (which have two double beds and run-of-the-mill hotel furnishings), making this a deal for bargain hunters. Guayabitos is a Mexican resort town that's recently begun attracting snowbirds and travelers looking for less-touristy digs. The town has calm surf that's good for swimming, a long flat beach embraced by twin headlands (great for walking), and skiffs on the sand for boat trips to the quiet coves and solitary beaches along Jaltemba Bay. ✉ *Retorno Laureles 2, Rincón de Guayabitos, Nayarit, 63727* ☎ *327/274–0231* 🖷 *327/274–0756* ⊕ *www.villasbuenavida.com* 🛏 *36 rooms, 9 suites* ⌂ *Restaurant, kitchens, refrigerators, cable TV, 2 pools, Wi-Fi, laundry facilities* ⊟ *MC, V* 🍽 *EP, FAP.*

¢–$$ ▦ **Huerta La Paz.** A few miles from the beach at Punta de Mita, this small ecoretreat has yoga classes and massage. Each of the cozy furnished bungalows is decorated with original art and artifacts. Its name means "the Orchard of Peace," and the 8-acre ranch serves mainly organic,

2

vegetarian food; as much as possible is grown on the grounds. Fish and chicken are served on request. ⊠ *Carretera a Sayulita, Km 4, Punta de Mita, 63734* ☎ *No phone* ⊕ *www.huertalapaz.com* ↩ *4 bungalows* ⚘ *Dining room, massage, hiking, mountain bikes* ☰ *No credit cards* ⏐⚬⏐ *CP* ⊙ *Closed June 15–Nov. 15.*

$ 🏠 **Bungalows Tlaquepaque.** Like a little village, the white-washed cement-block bungalows on the extensive grounds here are lined with tropical almond trees and surrounded by grassy lawns. Rooms are rather dark, beds are hard, and some rooms have hideously faux-finished furniture. On the plus side, the grassy grounds, sports areas, beach (not visible from rooms), and pool (sometimes murky in off-season) with giant slides provide lots of places for kids to play. The price is a bit steep for the quality of rooms, unless divided among four or more people; some rooms presumably house up to 10 adults and kids. ⊠ *Av. Luis Echeverría 44, Lo De Marcos, Nayarit, 63726* ☎ *327/275–0800* 🖷 *327/275–0097* ↩ *67 bungalows* ⚘ *Restaurant, fans, some kitchens, some refrigerators, cable TV, 2 pools, beach, basketball, soccer, volleyball, free parking; no room phones* ☰ *No credit cards* ⏐⚬⏐ *EP.*

$ 🏠 **Marco's Place Villas.** Despite its name, this is a motel-like three-story property, and one of the few standard hotels in Bucerías, which is filled with apartment and condo rentals. Rooms are on the small side, with tiny baths, but beds are comfortable. Junior suites are slightly larger, with a tiled breakfast counter. The property is a block from the beach. ⊠ *Calle Juventino Espinoza 6–A, Bucerías, Nayarit, 63732* ☎ *329/298–0865* ⊕ *www.marcosplacevillas.com* ↩ *15 rooms, 3 suites* ⚘ *Pool* ☰ *No credit cards* ⏐⚬⏐ *EP.*

★ ☾ **$** 🏠 **Villa Varadero.** The all-inclusive price at this small, friendly, four-story hotel in Nuevo Vallarta is only slightly higher than the cost of the room alone. Other pluses are the wide beach with gentle surf; the free use of bikes, kayaks, and boogie boards; and the chummy bar with its billiards salon, dart boards, dominoes, chess, and other games. Only a few of the compact, well-maintained units have tubs, and decor is standard, although walls are painted in cheerful hues. Kids under 10 stay and eat for free. ⊠ *Retorno Nayarit, Lotes 83 and 84, Manzana XIII, Nuevo Vallarta, Jalisco, 63732* ☎ *322/297–0430* 🖷 *322/ 297–0506, 800/238–9996 in U.S., 877/742–6323 in Canada* ⊕ *www. villavaradero.com.mx* ↩ *29 rooms, 29 suites* ⚘ *2 restaurants, in-room safes, some kitchenettes, refrigerators, cable TV, pool, hot tub, massage, beach, bicycles, billiards, 2 bars, recreation room, laundry service, free parking* ☰ *AE, MC, V* ⏐⚬⏐ *EP, AI.*

¢–$ 🏠 **Bungalows Los Picos.** Deep ochre walls are trimmed in cobalt blue and brick archways at this warm, two-story property. The value is even greater if you put several families

> **GET YOUR ZZZ'S**
>
> Some accommodations in coastal Nayarit and Jalisco are along the main highway and experience heavy traffic. And resort hotels often have lobby bars in the middle of an open-air atrium leading directly to rooms, or rooftop discoteques, or outdoor theme nights with live music. When you book, request a room far from the noisiest part of the hotel.

COSTALEGRE HOTELS AT A GLANCE

HOTEL	Worth Noting	Cost	Rooms	Restaurants	On the Beach	Dive Shop	Pools	Spa	Golf Course	Tennis Courts	Health Club/Gym	Children's Program	Location
Las Alamandas	ultra-exclusive	$430–$810	14	2	yes		1	yes		1	yes		Quemaro
El Careyes Beach Resort	impeccable decor	$345–$425	80	1	yes		1	yes	priv.	2	yes		Careyes
Coconuts By the Sea	stylish but homey	$95	4				1						Bahia Tenacatita
Grand Bay Isla Navidad	elegant architecture	$365–$390	199	3	yes		3	yes	yes	3	yes	4–12	Barra de Navidad
Hotelito Desconocido	bright, idyllic escape	$385–$468	29	2	yes		1	yes					Cruz de Loreto
La Paloma Oceanfront	well-equipped studios	$89–$119	11	1	yes		1						San Patricio--Melaque
Punta Serena	adults-only oasis	$360	24	1	yes		1	yes		yes	yes		Tenacatita
Rancho de Cuixmala	to-die-for views	$59	3										Emiliano Zapata
El Tamarindo	stunning location	$515	29	1	yes	yes	1		yes	1			Chihuatlán
Vagabundo	peaceful	$49–$68	21	1	yes		1						Punta Perula
Las Villas	comfy beds	$59–$78	8	1	yes								Barra de Navidad
Las Vilitas	lovely bay	$78–$117	10	1	yes		1						Bahia Tenacatita

in the two- and three-bedroom bungalows. Don't expect to be in town: this enclave of about a half dozen hotels is on Playa del Beso at the north end of Bucerías. You'll need a car or a taxi if you plan on straying from the pool or the beautiful beach for grocery shopping, sightseeing, or dining out. Bungalow-style motels and related trailer parks fill up with Canadian and American snowbirds in winter, and with large Mexican families during school vacations. The restaurant is closed in low season. ⊠ *Carretera Tepic–Puerto Vallarta (Carretera 200), Km 140, Playa del Beso, Bucerías, Nayarit, 63732* ☎ *329/298–0470* 🖶 *329/298–0131* ⊕ *www.lospicos.com.mx* 🛏 *56 bungalows for 4, 6, or 8 people* ⚫ *Restaurant, some fans, some kitchenettes, some refrigerators, cable TV; no a/c in some rooms* ▭ *No credit cards* ⦿ *EP.*

¢–$ 🏨 **Palmeras.** A block from the beach, in an area with lots of good restaurants, Palmeras has small rooms with brightly painted interior walls and modeled-stucco sunflowers serving as a kind of headboard behind the bed. Rooms on the second floor have a partial ocean view. There's plenty of space to socialize around the pool, basketball court, outdoor grill, and grassy picnic area, and a TV with satellite in the lounge for essential programs in English. ⊠ *Lázaro Cárdenas 35, Bucerías, Nayarit, 63732* ☎ *329/298–1288* ⊕ *www.hotelpalmeras.com* 🛏 *11 rooms* ⚫ *Picnic area, kitchenettes, refrigerators, pool, basketball, Wi-Fi; no room phones, no room TVs, no smoking* ▭ *MC, V* ⦿ *EP.*

COSTALEGRE

$$$$ 🏨 **Las Alamandas.** Personal service and exclusivity lure movie stars and royalty to this low-key resort in a nature preserve about 1½ hours from both PV and Manzanillo. Suites are filled with folk art; their indoor-outdoor living rooms have modern furnishings with deliciously nubby fabrics in bright, bold colors and Guatemalan-cloth throw pillows. Request a TV, VCR, and movie from the library for an evening in; there's little else to do at night except socialize. There's lots more to do in the daytime, however, including picnics anywhere on the property (the thorn forest here is scrubby and dry rather than tropical and green) and boat rides on the Río San Nicolás. There's a two-night minimum; the average stay is seven nights. If you have to ask the price, you can't afford it. ⊠ *Carretera 200, Km 85, Quemaro, 83 km (52 mi) south of PV, 133 km (83 mi) north of Barra de Navidad* ☎ *322/285–5500 or 888/882–9616* 🖶 *322/285–5027* ⊕ *www.alamandas.com* 🛏 *14 suites* ⚫ *2 restaurants, room service, fans, in-room DVDs, in-room VCRs, minibars, tennis court, pool, gym, spa, beach, snorkeling, fishing, mountain bikes, croquet, horseback riding, Ping-Pong, volleyball, 2 bars, shops, laundry service, concierge, Internet room, meeting room, airstrip, car rental, free parking* ▭ *D, DC, MC, V* ⦿ *EP, FAP.*

★ $$$$ 🏨 **El Careyes Beach Resort.** On a gorgeous bay framed by flowering vegetation, El Careyes is a boldly painted village of a resort. Guest rooms have large windows and private patios or balconies; suites have outdoor hot tubs. Colorful furnishings and artwork create a sophisticated Mexican palette. The full-service spa has fine European beauty and body treatments; a deli sells fine wines, prosciutto, and other necessities of the good life. A full range of water-sports equipment awaits you at the beach, and there are dune buggies and kayaks, too. There are more dining options in the area than at other Costalegre resorts, making a rental car a plus. It's a short walk to pretty Playa Rosa and a short drive to Bahía Tenacatita. ⊠ *Carretera a Barra de Navidad (Carretera 200), Km 53.5, Careyes, Jalisco, 48983, 161 km (100 mi) south of PV, 55 km (34 mi) north of Barra de Navidad* ☎ *315/351–0000, 888/433–3989 in U.S.* 🖷 *315/351–0100* ⊕ *www.elcareyesresort.com* ⤳ *51 rooms, 29 suites* ⚐ *Restaurant, grocery, room service, some fans, in-room safes, some in-room hot tubs, some kitchenettes, minibars, some refrigerators, cable TV with movies, some in-room DVDs, in-room broadband, Wi-Fi, golf privileges, putting green, 2 tennis courts, pool, gym, hot tub, sauna, spa, steam room, beach, snorkeling, windsurfing, boating, fishing, mountain bikes, horseback riding, Ping-Pong, volleyball, bar, cinema, recreation room, shops, babysitting, laundry service, business services, Internet room, meeting rooms, car rental, free parking* ▤ *AE, MC, V* ⦿ *EP.*

> ### TURTLES 911
>
> Releasing tiny turtles into the sea, done in the evening when there are fewer predators, is a real thrill for kids, and for many adults as well. The Westin, Marriott CasaMagna, Fiesta Americana, Velas Vallarta, and Dreams Resort in Puerto Vallarta; Las Alamandas, Hotelito Desconocido, and El Tamarindo on the Costalegre have marine turtle conservation programs. They employ biologists to collect eggs from nests on nearby beaches, incubate them in protected sand pits, and help guests repatriate them into the wild blue sea.

$$$$ 🏨 **Grand Bay Isla Navidad.** On a 1,200-acre peninsula between the Pacific and the Navidad Lagoon, this no-holds-barred resort cascades down to a private, though not terribly scenic, beach. An island unto itself, the lovely and rather snooty Grand Bay faces humble Barra de Navidad across the lagoon. Spanish arches, shady patios, cool fountains, and lush gardens contribute to the elegant architecture; tiered swimming pools are connected by slides and waterfalls. ⊠ *Isla Navidad, Barra de Navidad, Jalisco, 48987* ☎ *315/331–0500, 800/996–3426 in U.S.* 🖷 *315/355–6071* ⊕ *www.islaresort.com.mx* ⤳ *158 rooms, 41 suites* ⚐ *3 restaurants, room service, fans, in-rooom safes, some in-room hot tubs, some kitchenettes, minibars, cable TV, 27-hole golf course, 3 tennis courts, 3 pools, gym, beach, spa, jet skiing, marina, waterskiing, fishing, volleyball, 3 bars, shops, babysitting, children's programs (ages 4–12), laundry service, concierge, business services, convention center, airport shuttle, car rental, free parking* ▤ *AE, MC, V* ⦿ *EP.*

★ **$$$$** 🏨 **Hotelito Desconocido.** Although every inch of the place is painted, tiled, or otherwise decorated with bright Mexican colors and handicrafts, the effect is distinctive rather than fussy. Perhaps that's because rooms and suites incorporate local building styles and materials, including plank floors, reed mats, bamboo walls, and palm-frond roofs. They're cooled by battery-powered fans and lighted by lanterns, candles, and low-wattage lamps. Rustic but lovely bathrooms bring the outdoors in through large open windows. Signal for morning coffee by running up

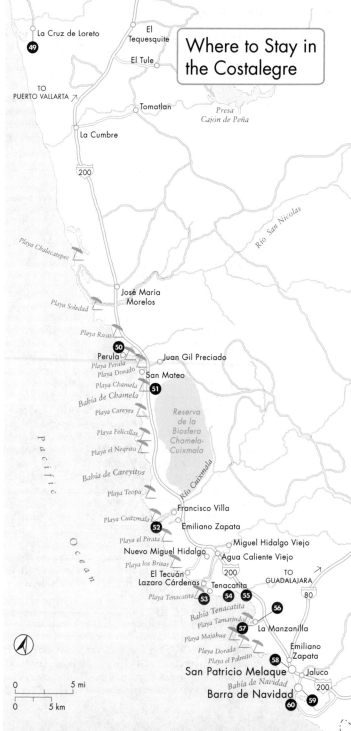

Las Alamandas .**50**

El Careyes
Beach Resort . .**51**

Coconuts By
the Sea **54**

Grand Bay
Isla Navidad . . .**60**

Hotelito
Desconocido . .**49**

La Paloma
Oceanfront
Retreat **58**

Punta Serena . .**55**

Rancho de
Cuixmala **52**

El Tamarindo
Golf Resort **57**

Vagabundo . . .**56**

Las Villas **59**

Las Villitas Club
& Marina **53**

Where to Stay in
the Costalegre

La Cruz de Loreto

El
Tequesquite

El Tule

TO
PUERTO VALLARTA

Tomatlan

Presa
Cajón de Peña

La Cumbre

200

Río San Nicolas

Playa Chalacatepec

José María
Morelos

Playa Soledad

Playa Rivas

Perula

Juan Gil Preciado

Playa Perula
Playa Dorado
San Mateo

Playa Chamela

Bahía de Chamela

Playa Careyes

Reserva
de la
Biosfera
Chamela-
Cuixmala

Playa Felicillas

Playa el Negrito

Bahía de Careyitos

Río Cuixmala

Playa Teopa

Francisco Villa

Playa Cuitzmala

Emiliano Zapata

Playa el Pirata

Miguel Hidalgo Viejo

Nuevo Miguel Hidalgo

Agua Caliente Viejo

Playa los Brisas

El Tecuán
Lazaro Cárdenas

200

TO
GUADALAJARA

80

Tenacatita

Playa Tenacatita

Bahía Tenacatita

Playa Tamarindo

La Manzanilla

Playa Majahua

Emiliano
Zapata

Playa Dorada

Playa el Palmito

San Patricio Melaque

Jaluco

Bahía de Navidad

200

Barra de Navidad

P a c i f i c

O c e a n

0   5 mi

0   5 km

the red flag. On a long stretch of beach, this isolated hotel is an idyllic escape for its clientele: about 60% American, 25% European, and 100% laid-back. ⊠ *Playón de Mismaloya s/n, Cruz de Loreto, Jalisco, 97 km (60 mi) south of PV, 119 km (74 mi) north of Barra de Navidad* ☎ *322/281–4010, 800/851–1143 in U.S.* ☎ *322/281–4010, 01800/013–1313 toll-free in Mexico* 🖷 *322/281–4130* ⊕ *www.*

hotelito.com 🛏 *16 rooms, 13 suites* ⚒ *2 restaurants, fans, saltwater pool, sauna, spa, steam room, beach, windsurfing, bicycles, billiards, hiking, horseback riding, volleyball, bar, concierge, airport shuttle, free parking; no a/c, no room phones, no room TVs* ☰ *AE, MC, V* ⭐ *BP, FAP.*

★ **$$$$** 🏨 **Punta Serena.** Guests come from New York and Italy to this adults-only oasis of calm. Perched on a beautiful headland, "Point Serene" enjoys balmy breezes and life-changing views from the infinity hot tub; the beach far below and pool are clothing optional. Spa treatments are inventive: roses and red wine promote moisturizing; carotene and honey contribute to a glowing tan; and the "Mayan Wrap" connects you herbally to the glowing god within. Shamans lead healing steam ceremonies on weekends; mud-and-music therapies are on the beach, and activities like horseback riding and nonmotorized water sports at the adjacent Blue Bay hotel are included in the price. Additionally, rooms have lovely furnishings and decor, and shared or private terraces, some with fab beach views. ⊠ *Carretera Barra de Navidad–Puerto Vallarta (Carretera 200), Km 20, Tenacatita, Jalisco, 48989, 196 km (122 mi) south of PV, 20 km (12 mi) north of Barra de Navidad* ☎ *315/351–5427 or 315/351–5020* 🖷 *315/351–5412* ⊕ *www.puntaserena.com* 🛏 *12 rooms, 12 suites* ⚒ *Restaurant, fans, in-room safes, cable TV, pool, gym, 2 hot tubs, massage, spa, beauty salon, steam room, beach, bar, recreation room, laundry service, meeting room, free parking; no kids under 18* ☰ *AE, MC, V* ⭐ *AI.*

$$$$ 🏨 **El Tamarindo Golf Resort.** More than 2,000 acres of ecological reserve and jungle surround this magical resort along 16 km (10 mi) of private coast. The architecture utilizes simple design elements (with a Mediterranean flavor) and local building materials; world-renowned Ricardo Legorreta was one of the architects. Many villas have outdoor living rooms. All have dark, wood floors, king-size beds, wet bars, ample bathrooms, and patios with plunge pools, hammocks, and chaise lounges. Sofas are upholstered in rich textured fabrics, and all furnishings and details are spare and classy. At night the staff lights more than 1,500 candles around the villas to create a truly enchanting setting. The hotel receives our highest accolade, Fodor's Choice, for its stunning location, gorgeous rooms, and excellent golf course. ⊠ *Carretera Melaque–Puerto Vallarta (Carretera 200), Km 7.5, Cihuatlán, Jalisco, 48970, 204 km (127 mi) south of PV, 12 km (7 mi) north of Barra de Navidad* ☎ *315/351–5032, 888/625–5144*

Fodor'sChoice
★

*in U.S. or Canada ☎315/351–5070 ⊕ www.mexicoboutiquehotels.com/
thetamarindo/ ⇘29 villas ⬧Restaurant, room service, fans, in-room safes,
some in-room hot tubs, minibars, 18-hole golf course, tennis court, pool,
massage, beach, dive shop, dock, snorkeling, windsurfing, boating, jet skiing, fishing, mountain bikes, bar, shop, babysitting, laundry service,
concierge, business services, Internet room, car rental, travel services,
free parking; no room TVs ⊟ AE, MC, V* ⦿| *EP.*

★ **$$** 🏨 **Coconuts By the Sea.** A friendly couple of American expats (he's a for-
mer Eastern Airlines pilot) own and run this charming cliff-top hide-
away with a drop-dead gorgeous view of the ocean and Boca de Iguana
Beach below. The furniture is stylish, and homey touches like lamps and
fish-theme wall decorations make the snug apartments just right for hol-
ing up for a week or even a month. The two apartments upstairs, with
thatched roofs and kitchen and living room open to the elements, are
not usually available in summer due to the rain; the rest of the year they're
highly coveted. One has an outdoor shower with a view. ⊠ *Playa Boca
de Iguanas, 6 Dolphin Way, Bahía Tenacatita, Jalisco, 48987, 195 km
(121 mi) south of PV, 21 km (13 mi) north of Barra de Navidad* ☎ 315/
351–5232 ⊕ *www.coconutsbythesea.com* ⇘ 4 *rooms* ⬧ *Fans, BBQ,
kitchens, refrigerator, microwaves, cable TV with movies, WiFi, pool,
free parking; no room phones* ⊟ *No credit cards* ⦿| *EP.*

$–$$ 🏨 **La Paloma Oceanfront Retreat.** Room prices are reasonable consider-
ing the small studio apartments have almost everything home does, and
four of them face the beach (where the waves are often good for boogie boarding, and always great for long walks along the bay). Each room
is configured differently, but all are uniformly bright and cheerful, with
private patios and paintings by the owner (she gives lessons in high season). There's a large pool and patio for outdoor barbecuing facing the
ocean. Unlike most hotels, La Paloma does not have off-season discounts.
⊠ *Las Cabañas 13, San Patricio–Melaque, 48980, 6 km (4 mi) north
of Barra de Navidad* ☎🏨 315/355–5345 ⊕ *www.lapalomamexico.
com* ⇘ 11 *studio apartments* ⬧ *Dining room, BBQs, fans, kitchens,
refrigerators, some microwaves, some cable TV, some in-room DVDs,
pool, hot tub, Internet room, free parking; no a/c in some rooms, no
room phones* ⊟ *No credit cards* ⦿| *CP.*

$–$$ 🏨 **Las Villitas Club & Marina.** Each of the small bungalows on the beach
at Tenacatita has a small sitting room with two single beds doubling as
couches, and a king-size bed in the separate bedroom. Cheerfully painted
rooms have beach views and bathtubs as well as *equipale* (pigskin) tables and chairs for lounging outside; doors and windows are screened.
Ask to borrow the kayak; sometimes there are bikes to lend, too. This
is a wonderful place to kick back on one of Pacific Mexico's most beautiful bays. ⊠ *Playa Tenacatita, Calle Bahía de Tenacatita 376, Bahía
Tenacatita, Jalisco, 183 km (114 mi) south of PV, 37 km (23 mi) north
of Barra de Navidad* ☎ *No phone* ⇘ 10 *bungalows* ⬧ *Cable TV,
kitchenettes, refrigerators, pool, beach; no room phones* ⊟ *No credit
cards* ⦿| *EP.*

$ 🏨 **Rancho de Cuixmala.** This ecologically inspired ranch has views to die
for, plus horseback riding, massage, yoga, and birding. Relaxation and
communing with nature are what this 12-acre, thorn-forest retreat (in

owner Mercedes Gargallo Chavez' family since the 19th century) is all about; cell phones don't work and there's no TV. The luxurious indoor-outdoor complex on a cliff overlooking the ocean is lovely and belies the modest price. ⊠ *Carretera a Barra de Navidad (Carretera 200), Km 44.5, Emiliano Zapata (Municipio La Huerta), Jalisco, 48943, 171 km (106 mi) south of PV, 45 km (28 mi) north of Barra de Navidad* ☎ *315/ 351–0272* 🖷 *315/351–0398* ⊕ *www.cuixmala.com* 🛏 *3 rooms, 3-bedroom house* △ *Dining room, fans, horseback riding, mountain bikes; no a/c, no room phones, no room TVs* ▭ *No credit cards* ❙◯❙ *BP.*

$ ▦ **Las Villas.** Aside from the luxurious and costly Grand Bay Isla Navidad and the behemoth Hotel Alondra, Barra de Navidad has only basic hotels with few rooms, and not a particularly good value compared to similar hotels elsewhere. This hotel with a domed brick ceiling, comfortable beds, and remote control air-conditioning is among the best choices. Ask for a 25% discount between Easter and New Year's, and a free cot anytime for an additional guest. ⊠ *Calle López de Legazpi 127, Barra de Navidad, Jalisco, 48987* ☎ *315/355–5354* 🛏 *8 rooms* △ *Restaurant, cable TV, beach; no room phones* ▭ *No credit cards* ❙◯❙ *EP.*

¢–$ ▦ **Vagabundo.** This humble beach town on Chamela Bay is an excellent place off the gringo trail for swimming, fishing, or exploring the offshore islands. Simple hotel rooms surround a swimming pool in this motel-like, quiet, two-story hotel a block from the beach at Punta Perula. Bungalows have tiny but well-equipped kitchens; the restaurant serves breakfast and dinner. The hotel owner spent many years in the U.S. and speaks excellent English. ⊠ *Calle Independencia 100, Punta Pérula, Chamela Bay, Punta Perula, Jalisco, 79 km (49 mi) south of PV, 137 km (85 mi) north of Barra de Navidad* ☎ *315/333–9736* ⊕ *www. hotelvagabundo.com* 🛏 *21 rooms* △ *Restaurant, some kitchenettes, some refrigerators, cable TV, pool, laundry service; no room phones* ▭ *No credit cards* ❙◯❙ *EP.*

Where to Eat

61

3

Food with a view.

WORD OF MOUTH

"There are so many great restaurants you won't have time to get to them all on your trip. Once you get to PV just ask around; you'll have umpteen recommendations."

–blondlady

"Each night we went to dinner at great restaurants like De Santos and Centro. The last night we went to Café des Artistes. Beautiful! The bistro menu included wine, an appetizer, a main course, and dessert for 395 pesos."

–Linda

DINING PLANNER

Quick Take

Puerto Vallarta's restaurants are to die for, but what a misuse of earthly delights that would be. Variety, quality, and innovation are the norm whether you dine in a beachfront café or a swanky candlelighted restaurant. The best restaurants buy fresh fish and shellfish daily—and it's a great bargain. Vallarta's already superior restaurants really overachieve during the 10-day Festival Gourmet International in mid-November. More than three dozen establishments invite guest chefs to prepare special menus, some of which influence restaurant menus the following year.

Meals

PV restaurants cater to tourists with multicourse dinners, but traditionally, *comida* (lunch) is the big meal of the day, usually consisting of soup and/or salad, bread or tortillas, a main dish, side dishes, and dessert. Traditional *cena* (dinner) is lighter; in fact, many people just have milk or hot chocolate and a sweet roll, or *tamales*.

Desayuno (breakfast) is served in *cafeterías* (coffee shops) and small restaurants. Choices might be hefty egg-and-chorizo or -ham dishes, enchiladas, or *chilaquiles* (fried tortilla strips covered in tomato sauce, shredded cheese, and meat or eggs). Tacos and quesadillas are delicious for breakfast; some of Vallarta's best taco stands set up shop by 9 AM.

Foodie Hot Spots

PV's biggest concentration of restaurants is the south side (aka Zona Romántica, mostly in Colonia Emiliano Zapata). Once called Restaurant Row, Calle Basilio Badillo now has as many shops as restaurants, but on the surrounding streets eateries continue to crop up. Downtown has its fair share of choice places, too. All in all, gourmets will be happiest here in Old Vallarta, where an appetizer, sunset cocktail, or espresso and dessert isn't more than a $3 cab ride away.

Bucerías has good restaurants in the center of town. Marina Vallarta's worthwhile eateries are mainly in the resorts and surrounding the marina. Punta de Mita's restaurant scene is diversifying to include more than the palapas at El Anclote.

Beer & Spirits

Jalisco is far and away Mexico's most important tequila producing state. Mexican beers range from light beers like Corona and Sol to medium-bodied, golden beers like Pacífico and the more robust Bohemia, to dark beauties Negra Modelo and Indio.

Mealtimes

Mexican mealtimes are generally as follows. Upon rising: coffee, and perhaps *pan dulce* (sweet breads). Schedule permitting, Mexicans love to eat a hearty *almuerzo*, a full breakfast, at about 10. *Comida*, typically between 2 and 5 PM, is the main meal. *Cena* is between 8 PM and 9 PM.

Restaurants have long hours in PV, though seafood "shacks" on the beach often close by late afternoon or sunset. Outside PV and the southern Nayarit and the Costalegre, lunch is served from 1 PM to 4 PM, and dinner is rarely served before 8 PM. Unless otherwise noted, the restaurants listed in this guide are open daily for lunch and dinner.

Taco Primer

In this region, a taco is generally a diminutive corn tortilla heated on an oiled grill and filled with one of many meats, shrimp, or batter-fried fish.

If your server asks *"Preparadita?"*, he or she is asking if you want cilantro and onions. Then add your own condiments: salsa mexicana (chopped raw onions, tomatoes, and green chilies), guacamole, and pickled jalapeño peppers. Some restaurants go further with chopped nopal cactus and other items.

Reservations

Reservations are always a good idea. During low season, getting a table is usually a snap. But it's always wise to call ahead and make sure the place hasn't been reserved for a party.

What to Wear

We'd love to suggest resort casual or at least grunge chic, but it's not that easy.

The Mexicans are usually the best dressed, but even they forego jacket and tie for a nice button-down and slacks. The most elegant restaurants, like Café des Artistes, simply request that men wear T-shirts with sleeves.

If you enjoy dressing up, don't despair: looking good is always in style. The maitre d' *will* take notice.

What it Costs In U.S. Dollars

AT DINNER

$$$$	$$$	$$	$	¢
over $25	$18-$25	$12-$17	$5-$11	under $5

The restaurants we list are the cream of the crop in each category. Prices are for a main course at dinner, excluding tax and tip

Pricing

PV's extremely high number of excellent eateries—from corner taco stands to 5-star Diamond-Award winners—means competition is high, and that keeps prices reasonable. While some restaurants do charge as much as those in New York or L.A., there are tons of wonderful places ranging from moderate to downright cheap. To really experience Puerto Vallarta, try both ends of the spectrum, and everything in between.

Paying

Credit cards are widely accepted at pricier restaurants, especially MasterCard and Visa, and to a lesser extent American Express. More modest restaurants might accept cash only, and are leery of traveler's checks. Small eateries that do accept credit cards sometimes give a "discount" for cash (i.e., they charge a small fee for credit card use).

Tips on Tipping

Twenty years ago, leaving a tip in Puerto Vallarta meant pocketing the bills and leaving the loose change. Today, influenced by big tippers from the U.S., servers count on 10%-15%. In more humble establishments, where the bill is often shockingly low, tips are taken more casually than in the more prestigious restaurants. But in any case, we suggest tipping 15% for good service, a bit less for a seriously flawed performance, and a bit more if the tab is ridiculously low.

PUERTO VALLARTA

American-Casual

$–$$ ✕ **Andale.** Although many have been drinking, rather than eating, at this local hangout for years, the restaurant serves great burgers, fries, herb-garlic bread, black-bean soup, and jumbo shrimp, as well as daily lunch and nightly drink specials at the chummy bar. The interior is cool, dark, and informal; two rows of mini-tables line the sidewalk outside. Service is generally attentive, although that doesn't mean the food will arrive promptly. Plus-size patrons should beware the munchkin-size toilet stalls. ⊠ *Av. Olas Altas 425, Col. E. Zapata* ☎ *322/222–1054* ☐ *MC, V.*

☺ **¢–$** ✕ **Memo's Pancake House.** If your child can't find something he or she likes on the Pancake House menu, you might have an alien on your hands. There are 12 kinds of pancakes—including the Oh Henry, with chocolate bits and peanut butter—and 8 kinds of waffles. Other breakfast items include machaca burritos, *chilaquiles,* and eggs Florentine, but these tend to be perfunctory: pancakes and waffles are your best bet. Waiters bustle around the large, fairly noisy dining room, which is bursting with local families on weekends and homesick travelers daily. The back patio—draped in pothos and serenaded by birds—experiences a greenhouse effect when the day heats up. ⊠ *Calle Basilio Badillo 289, Col. E. Zapata* ☎ *322/222–6272* ⟡ *Reservations not accepted* ☐ *No credit cards* ☉ *No dinner.*

> Plus-size patrons should beware the munchkin-size toilet stalls [at Andale].

Barbecue

¢–$ ✕ **Chiles.** Local people wait all summer for their favorite barbecue chicken and burger place to reopen. The menu's straightforward, chock-full of mouthwatering hot dogs, burgers, and fried potatoes. The back patio is shaded with lovely old trees, the owners wait tables, and the place is "straight friendly." It's a relaxing place to eat a satisfying meal, but many call ahead and order food to go. ⊠ *Calle Pulpito 122, Col. E. Zapata* ☎ *322/223–0373* ☐ *No credit cards* ☉ *Closed Sun. and May–mid-Oct. No dinner.*

Cafés

¢–$ ✕ **A Page in the Sun.** This corner café in the middle of Olas Altas is always full of coffee drinkers reading newspapers and paperback books purchased here, or playing chess. The salads, sandwiches, and desserts on the menu are almost an afterthought. It's the location and the opportunity to hang out with one's friends that really count, plus the good coffee. ⊠ *Olas Altas 399, Col. E. Zapata* ☎ *322/222–3608* ☐ *No credit cards.*

¢–$ ✕ **The Coffee Cup.** Coffee is sold in all its various presentations, including freshly ground by the kilo. You can munch on pastries, sandwiches, wraps, and breakfast breads, or get a fresh fruit smoothie. A chit gets

MENU TRANSLATOR

Because eating is such an integral part of a Puerto Vallarta vacation, we've described here some of the dishes you're likely to find on area menus or in our reviews below. *Buen provecho!*

arrachera: skirt steak

carne asada: thin cut of flank or tenderloin (sometimes not *that* tender), grilled or broiled and usually served with beans, rice, and guacamole

carnitas: bites of steamed, fried pork served with tortillas and a variety of condiments

chilaquiles: pieces of corn tortillas fried and served with red or green sauce; good ones are crispy, not soggy, and topped with chopped onions and *queso cotija:* a crumbly white cheese

chile en nogada: a green poblano chili stuffed with a semi-sweet meat mixture and topped with walnut sauce and pomegranate seeds; the Mexican national dish, it's often served in September in honor of Independence Day

chile relleno: batter-fried green chili (mild to hot) stuffed with cheese, seafood, or a sweetish meat mixture; served in a mild red sauce

menudo: tripe stew

pozole: a rich pork- or chicken-based soup with hominy; a plate of accompanying condiments usually includes raw onions, radishes, cilantro, oregano, sliced cabbage, and tostadas

tostada: a crispy fried tortilla topped with beans and/or meat, cheese, and finely chopped lettuce or cabbage; or, the corn tortilla by itself, which is served with foods like ceviche and pozole

you 10 minutes of free Internet around the corner, ostensibly to be used the same day. It's no relation to the Coffee Cup in Marina Vallarta. ⊠ *Calle Rodolfo Gómez 146-A, Col. E. Zapata* ☎ *322/222–8584* ▭ *No credit cards* ◐ *No dinner Sun. Nov.–Apr.*

Contemporary

★ **$$–$$$$** ✕ **Café des Artistes.** Several sleek dining spaces make up Café des Artistes, the liveliest of which is the courtyard garden with modern sculpture. The main restaurant achieves a modern Casablanca feel with glass rain-drops and tranquil music. Thierry Blouet's Cocina de Autor (closed Sunday and September) is the restaurant's latest innovation, and it was listed in Conde Nast's 2005 "80 hottest new restaurants in the world." The limited seating restaurant pairs 4- to 6-course tasting menus with appropriate wines. Décor is restrained, with a waterfall garden behind plate glass taking center stage. The clubby cigar bar has one of the structure's few original adobe walls; the Constantini Wine Bar has some 50 vintages by the glass as well as distilled spirits, appetizers, and live music Monday through Saturday nights. ⊠ *Av. Guadalupe Sánchez 740, Centro* ☎ *322/222–3229* ▭ *AE, MC, V* ◐ *No lunch.*

★ **$–$$$$** ✕ **Vitea.** When chefs Bernhard Güth and Ulf Henriksson, of Trio, needed a challenge they cooked up this delightful seaside bistro. So what if your legs bump your partner's at the small tables? This will only make it easier to steal bites off her plate. The decor of the open, casual venue is as fresh as the food. Appetizers include the smoked salmon roll with crème fraiche and the spicy shrimp tempura; crab manicotti and other entrées are light and delicious. Half portions are available, or make a meal of the bistro's soups, sandwiches, and appetizers. ⊠ *Libertad 2, near south end of Malecón, Centro* ☎ *322/222–8703* ▭ *AE, MC, V* ⊘ *Closed 1 wk in late Sept.*

$$$ ✕ **Trio.** Conviviality, hominess, and dedication on the parts of chef-owners Bernhard Güth and Ulf Henriksson have made Trio one of Puerto Vallarta's best restaurants—hands-down. Fans, many of them members of PV's artsy crowd, marvel at the kitchen's ability to deliver perfect meal after perfect meal. Popular demand guarantees rack of lamb with fresh mint and for dessert, the warm chocolate cake. The kitchen often stays open until nearly midnight, and there's a back patio and rooftop terrace on which to dine in fair weather. Waiters are professional yet unpretentious; sommelier Cesar Porras can help you with the wine. But the main reason to dine here is the consistently fabulous food at great value. ⊠ *Calle Guerrero 264, Centro* ☎ *322/222–2196* ▭ *AE, MC, V* ⊘ *No lunch.*

■ TIP→ **A waiter would never consider bringing you your check before you ask for it; that would be rude. However, it's also considered rude to dally in bringing that check once you do ask for it.**

Fodor'sChoice
★

$$–$$$ ✕ **Boca Bento.** Rated as one of the top "new" restaurants in Puerto Vallarta (it opened in 2004), this restaurant in the heart of the Romantic Zone represents fusion of Latin American, Mediterranean, and Caribbean elements. The feeling is simultaneously Eastern and modern, with contemporary music and artwork. Small plates permit sampling; or order an entrée such as pork ribs with a honey–chili glaze, or the cross-cultural mu shu carnitas with hoisin sauce. ⊠ *Calle Basilio Badillo 180, Col. E. Zapata* ☎ *322/222–9108* ⊕ *www.bocabento.com* ▭ *MC, V* ⊘ *No lunch.*

$$–$$$ ✕ **Le Kliff.** From a table on one of four tiers you can watch for whales in season or boats heading to the docks as the sun sets. Asian and Mediterranean flavors have been added to the recipes without great success. This open-air restaurant with an enormous palapa roof is best for sunset hors d'oeuvres and cocktails, as the food is not worth the inflated prices. Or come during the day to use the beach club (still not finished, but on its way), down hundreds of stairs on the sand. Weddings are a big part of the business, so call ahead to make sure it's not booked, and to reserve a table on the lowest deck, closest to the water. ⊠ *Carretera a Barra de Navidad, Km 17.5, just north of Boca de Tomatlán, Zona Hotelera Sur* ☎ *322/224–0975* ▭ *AE, MC, V.*

$$–$$$ ✕ **River Cafe.** At night, candles flicker at white-skirted tables with comfortable cushioned chairs, and tiny white lights sparkle in palm trees surrounding the multilevel terrace. This riverside restaurant is recommended for breakfast and for the evening ambience. Attentive waiters serve such international dishes as chicken stuffed with wild mushrooms and spinach or rack of lamb with polenta; the fish and shrimp combo with

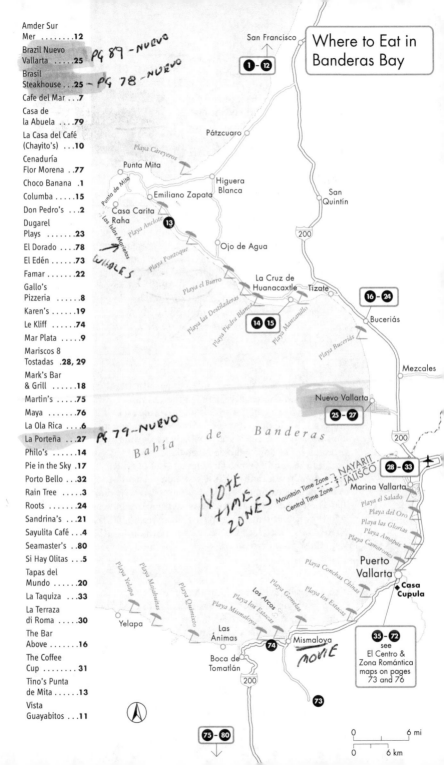

Amder Sur Mer **12**

Brazil Nuevo Vallarta .....**25** PG 89 - NUEVO

Brasil Steakhouse . . .**25** PG 78 - NUEVO

Cafe del Mar . . .**7**

Casa de la Abuela **79**

La Casa del Café (Chayito's) . . .**10**

Cenaduría Flor Morena . .**77**

Choco Banana .**1**

Columba **15**

Don Pedro's . . .**2**

Dugarel Plays **23**

El Dorado **78**

El Edén **73**

Famar **22**

Gallo's Pizzeria **8**

Karen's **19**

Le Kliff **74**

Mar Plata **9**

Mariscos 8 Tostadas .**28, 29**

Mark's Bar & Grill **18**

Martin's **75**

Maya **76**

La Ola Rica . .**6** PG 79 - NUEVO

La Porteña ..**27**

Philo's **14**

Pie in the Sky .**17**

Porto Bello . . .**32**

Rain Tree **3**

Roots **24**

Sandrina's . . .**21**

Sayulita Café . .**4**

Seamaster's ..**80**

Si Hay Olitas . . .**5**

Tapas del Mundo **20**

La Taquiza . . .**33**

La Terraza di Roma ...**30**

The Bar Above **16**

The Coffee Cup **31**

Tino's Punta de Mita **13**

Vista Guayabitos . . .**11**

Where to Eat in Banderas Bay

San Francisco

1 - **12**

Pátzcuaro

Playa Careyeros

Punta Mita

Higuera Blanca

Emiliano Zapata

San Quintín

200

Casa Carita Raha **13**

Playa Anclote

Ojo de Agua

WHALES

Playa Pontoque

La Cruz de Huanacaxtle   Tizate

16 - **24**

Playa el Burro

Buceriás

Playa las Destiladeras

14 **15**

Playa Piedra Blanca

Playa Manzanillo

Playa Bucerías

Mezcales

Nuevo Vallarta

25 - **27**

Bahía   de   Banderas

NOTE TIME ZONES

Mountain Time Zone ─ NAYARIT
Central Time Zone ─ JALISCO

200

28 - **33**

Marina Vallarta

Playa el Salado
Playa del Oro
Playa las Glorias
Playa Amapas
Playa Camarones

Puerto Vallarta

Casa Cupula

Playa Conchas Chinas

Playa Yelapa

Playa Majahuitas

Playa Quimixto

Los Arcos

Playa Gemelas
Playa los Estacas

Playa Mismaloya

Playa los Estacas

35 - **72**
see El Centro & Zona Romántica maps on pages 73 and 76

Yelapa

Las Ánimas

74

Mismaloya

MOVIE

Boca de Tomatlán

200

73

75 - **80**

0   6 mi

0   6 km

lobster sauce is especially recommended. If you're not into a romantic (some say overpriced) dinner, belly up to the intimate bar for a drink and—Friday through Sunday evenings—a listen to the live jazz. ⊠ *Isla Río Cuale, Local 4, Centro* ☎ *322/223–0788* ▭ *AE, MC, V.*

★ **$–$$$** ✕ **La Palapa.** This large, welcoming, thatch-roof place is open to the breezes of Playa los Muertos and filled with wicker chandeliers, art-

> ### WORD OF MOUTH
>
> "La Palapa is the epitome of Mexican romantic restaurants. On the beach, excellent food and service, very good margaritas, and a little combo playing soft Mexican jazz. This is my idea of heaven, palapa style."
>
> –Bill

glass fixtures, and lazily rotating ceiling fans. The menu meanders among international dishes in modern presentation: roasted stuffed chicken breast, pork loin, or seared yellowfin tuna drizzled in cacao sauce. The seafood enchilada plate is divine. For a pricey but romantic evening, enjoy one of several set menus ($170–$240 for two; reserve in advance) at a table right on the sand. There's a good breakfast daily after 8 AM, and a guitarist or Latin jazz combo nightly between 9 and 11. ⊠ *Calle Púlpito 103, Playa Los Muertos, Col. E. Zapata* ☎ *322/222–5225* ▭ *AE, D, DC, MC, V.*

Continental

★ **$$$** ✕ **Kaiser Maximilian.** Viennese and Continental entrées dominate the menu, which is modified each year when the restaurant participates in PV's culinary festival. One favorite is herb-crusted rack of lamb served with horseradish and pureed vegetables au gratin; another is venison medallions with chestnut sauce served with braised white cabbage and steamed vegetables. The adjacent café (open 8 AM–noon) has sandwiches, excellent desserts, and 20 specialty coffees—all of which are also available at the main restaurant. Because a stream of street peddlers is anathema to fine dining, eat in the charming, European-style dining room, where handsome black-and-white-clad waiters look right at home amid dark-wood framed mirrors, brightly polished brass, and lace café curtains. ⊠ *Av. Olas Altas 380, Col. E. Zapata* ☎ *322/223–0760* ▭ *AE, MC, V* ☉ *Closed Sun. No lunch.*

Cuban

$–$$ ✕ **La Bodeguita del Medio.** Near the malecón's north end, this restaurant with a fun-loving atmosphere has a bit of a sea view from its second-floor dining room, and a Caribbean flavor. Specials vary by season; if possible, try the roast pork, the Cuban-style paella, or the pork loin in tamarind sauce; order rice, salad, or fried plantains separately. Like its Havana namesake, La Bodeguita sells Cuban rum and cigars, and the live music—like the cuisine—is pure *cubano*. A sextet performs most nights until past midnight. Try the Havana specialty drink *mojito*: a blend of lime juice, sugar, mineral water, white rum, and crushed fresh mint leaves. ⊠ *Paseo Díaz Ordáz 858, Centro* ☎ *322/223–1585* ▭ *AE, MC, V.*

Delicatessens

¢–$ ✕ **The Coffee Cup.** Early-risers will appreciate the 5:30 opening (you might come at 6 just in case). There are fruit smoothies, and coffee in many manifestations, including frappés of Oreo cookie and German chocolate cake. Have a breakfast bagel (all day), wrap, deli sandwich, or homemade dessert. Located right on the marina, the café is filled with wonderful art for sale, and is open daily until 10 PM. ⊠ *Condominios Puesto del Sol, Local 14–A, at marina, Marina Vallarta* ☎ *322/221–2517* ⊟ *MC, V.*

Eclectic

★ $$$–$$$$ ✕ **Le Bistro.** Start off with hummus with toasted pita before moving to a soup of Mexican or Cuban origin and then on to one of the international main dishes, like the Mediterranean-style pasta on a bed of fresh spinach, herbed Cornish hen, or sea scallops with jicama coleslaw. The restaurant overlooks the Cuale River and its eclectic decor draped in ferns and tropical plants is a knockout. ⊠ *Isla Río Cuale 16–A* ☎ *322/222–0283* ⊕ *www.lebistro.com.mx* ⊟ *AE, MC, V* ⊘ *Closed Sun. and Aug. and Sept.*

$$$ ✕ **Daiquiri Dick's.** Locals come for the reasonably priced breakfasts (the

Fodor'sChoice homemade orange-almond granola is great); visitors come (often more

★ than once during a vacation) for the good service and consistent Mexican and world cuisine. The lunch-dinner menu has fabulous appetizers, including superb lobster tacos with a drizzle of béchamel sauce and perfect, tangy jumbo-shrimp wontons. On the menu since the restaurant opened almost 30 years ago is Pescado Vallarta, or grilled fish on a stick. Start with a signature daiquiri; move to the extensive wine list. The tortilla soup is popular, too. The very plain patio dining room frames a view of Playa Los Muertos. ⊠ *Av. Olas Altas 314, Col. E. Zapata* ☎ *322/222–0566* ⊟ *MC, V* ⊘ *Closed Sept. and Wed. May–Oct.*

$$–$$$ ✕ **Chez Elena.** Frequented in its heyday by Hollywood luminaries and the who's who of PV, this downtown restaurant still has a loyal following. The patio ambience is simple, but the wholesome food is satisfying. House specialties include fajitas, Yucatan-style pork, and mixed satay of pork, beef, and shrimp served with steamed vegetables, rice, and peanut sauce. Elena's is known for its martinis and the killer, handcrafted margaritas. ⊠ *Calle Matamoros 520, Centro* ☎ *322/222–0161* ⊟ *MC, V* ⊘ *Closed Tues. May–Oct. No lunch.*

$–$$$ ✕ **La Playita de Lindo Mar.** A favorite breakfast spot any day, or for Sunday brunch, this restaurant has a wonderful view of the waves crashing on or lapping at Conchas Chinas Beach. The breakfast menu wanders among savory crèpes, fritatta, omelets, and the tasty *huevos Felix:* eggs scrambled with fried corn tortillas, served with a grilled cactus pad, beans, and grilled serrano chilies. The multitude of lunch and dinner choices includes grilled burgers and chicken, shrimp fajitas, and lobster thermador. Open to the ocean air, the wood-and-palm front building looks right at home here. See the sign on Carretera a Mismaloya or follow your nose on the beach at Conchas Chinas. ⊠ *Conchas Chinas* ☎ *322/221–5511* ⊟ *MC, V.*

LIKE THIS ONE

$–$$ ✕ **El Repollo Rojo.** Better known as the Red Cabbage (its English name), this restaurant is by—but doesn't overlook—the Cuale River. It's hard to find the first time out, but it's the best place in town for international comfort food. Homesick Canadians fill up on chicken with mashed potatoes, gravy, and cranberry sauce, while Italians indulge in pasta with

WORD OF MOUTH

How about rather than getting tolerable food at a posh hotel restaurant, walking to Red Cabbage? Dirt cheap, but waaay better.
                                              –Carolred

fresh tomatoes; there are even a few Russian dishes. Frida's Dinner includes an aperitif of tequila followed by cream of peanut soup, white or red wine, *chile en nogada* (a mild chili decorated with colors of the Mexican flag), a main dish from the Yucatán or Puebla, and flan for dessert. Romantic ballads fill the small space, and the walls are crowded with movie posters and head shots of international stars. ⊠ *Calle Rivera del Río 204–A, El Remance* ☎ *322/223–0411* ▬ No *credit cards* ☾ *Closed Sept. and Sun. May–Oct. No lunch.*

ON BEACH

¢–$ ✕ **Fidensio's.** Let the tide lick your toes and the sand caress shoeless feet as simple yet tasty food is brought to your comfortable cloth, palapa-shaded chair right at the ocean's edge. Made when you order them, the shrimp enchiladas—served with rice, a small handful of piping hot fries, and a miniature salad—are simply delicious. Many expats come for breakfast, or before 6 PM for burgers, nachos, club or tuna sandwiches, or a fresh fish filet. Service is relaxed and friendly, not overbearing or phony; the only soundtrack is the sound of the waves. ⊠*Pilitas 90, Los Muerto Beach, Col. E. Zapata* ☎ *322/222–5457* ▬ No *credit cards* ☾ *No dinner.*

Italian

$$–$$$$ ✕ **Porto Bello.** Yachties, locals, and other return visitors attest that everything on the menu is good here. And if you're not satisfied, the kitchen will give you something else without quibbling. Undoubtedly that's what makes Marina Vallarta's veteran restaurant its most popular as well. The dining room is diminutive and air-conditioned; the outdoor patio overlooking the marina is more elegant, with a white chiffon ceiling drape and white ceiling fans. Since there are no lunch specials and the Italian menu is the same then as at dinner, most folks come in the evening. ⊠*Marina del Sol, Local 7, Marina Vallarta* ☎ *322/221–0003* ▬ *MC, V.*

$–$$$ ✕ **La Piazzeta.** Locals come for the delicious Naples-style pizza (the crust not too thick, not too thin, and cooked in a brick oven), but there's also great pasta and a good variety of entrées, like the cream-based salmon with caviar and lemon. For appetizers try the top-heavy (*con molto tomate*) bruschetta or steamed mussels with lemon, parsley, and butter. Most folks choose to sit on the open patio, but La Piazzeta also has an intimate dining room. The personal attention of the owner, Mimmo, guarantees repeat business. It's open 4 to midnight. ⊠ *Calle Rodolfo Gómez 143, Col. E. Zapata* ☎ *322/222–0650* ▬ *MC, V* ☾ *Closed Sun. No lunch.*

$–$$ ✕ **La Terraza di Roma.** The small dining room is nondescript, although a pianist most evenings adds a bit of panache. The food is fine, with homemade pasta and individual pizzas as well as the usual Italian nosh. It's the square patio hanging right above the marina, amid the boats, that brings most people back. Breakfast is also served. ⊠ *Condominios Puesta del Sol, Local 2, at marina, Marina Vallarta* ☎ *322/221–0560* ▤ *AE, MC, V.*

Mexican

★ **$–$$$** ✕ **Las Carmelitas.** Hawks soar on updrafts above lumpy, jungle-draped hills. The town and the big blue bay are spread out below in a breathtaking, 200-degree tableau. Under the palapa roof of this small, open restaurant romantic ballads play as waiters start you off with guacamole, fresh and cooked salsas, chopped cactus pad salad, and tostadas. Seared meats—served with grilled green onions and tortillas made on the spot—are the specialty, but you can also order seafood stew or soups. The restaurant opens at 1 PM. Don't despair about the $5 per person fee you pay to enter (apparently to discourage lookie-loos); it will be deducted from your tab. ⊠ *Camino a la Aguacatera, Km 1.2, Fracc. Lomas de Terra Noble* ☎ *322/303–2104* ▤ *No credit cards.*

$–$$$ ✕ **Los Xitomates.** Both fun and modern, Los Zitomates has bright white tablecloths and oxidized, cutout-figure wall sconces. This hip, tranquil place in the heart of downtown is worth a try if you want an upscale ambience and variations on traditional Mexican dishes. Some recipes, like the tomato soup, leave a little to be desired. Winners include the tortilla soup (a classic) and the rib-eye steak sautéed with wild mushrooms and seasoned with the distinctive herb *epazote*. Chef-owner Luis Fitch, of Oaxaca, is amenable to fixing meals for Rastafarians, Orthodox Jews, or others with specific dietary requirements, preferably with advance notice. ⊠ *Calle Morelos 571, Centro* ☎ *322/222–1695* ▤ *AE, MC, V* ⊗ *No lunch.*

> **DAILY SPECIALS**
>
> To save money, **look for the fixed-menu lunch** called either a *comida corrida* or a *menú del día,* served from about 1 to 4 almost everywhere in Mexico.

$–$$ ✕ **Los Alcatraces.** For a breakfast of chilaquiles that are crisp, not soggy, come to "The Calla Lily." *Café de olla,* real Mexican coffee simmered with cinnamon and *panela,* (unrefined brown sugar), is served in a keep-warm carafe; crumbly white cheese is brought from a ranch in the nearby hills. All meals are economical, especially the combo plate: a quesadilla, chile relleno, arrachera beef, rice, beans, and a taco. The only downside is traffic noise from the busy highway. The newer three-level location on a side street in the Romantic Zone is quieter, and has charming ranch-style decor. ⊠ *Blvd. Federico M. Ascencio 1808, Col. Olímpica* ☎ *322/222–1182* ▤ *No credit cards* ⊠ *Pulpito 220, Col. E. Zapata* ☎ *322/222–4420* ▤ *No credit cards* ⊗ *Closed Mon.*

$–$$ ✕ **El Andariego.** A few blocks past the north end of the malecón is this lively Mexican restaurant. Lovely paintings of the city brighten the walls, lighting is subdued, and the mood is romantic Mexico. The large menu includes numerous salads, pasta dishes, lots of variety in chicken and beef, and seafood and lobster prepared to your taste. You're allowed to choose your poison (beef, cheese, or chicken fillings) for the tacos and enchiladas on the combo plates. Enjoy live music (electric guitar versions of "My Way," or mariachi music) nightly between 3 and 11 PM. Breakfast is served. ⊠ *Av. México 1358, at El Salvador, Col. 5 de Diciembre* ☎ *322/222–0916* ⊕ *www. elandariego.com* ▤ *MC, V.*

★ **$–$$** ✕ **El Arrayán.** The oilcloth table covers, enameled tin plates, exposed rafters, and red roof tiles of this patio-restaurant conjure up nostalgia for the quaint Mexican home of less frenetic times. Carmen Porras, the hip, cute co-owner (with her parents) masquerades as your waitress, dispensing interesting info about the origins of chiles en nogada (first prepared for Emperor Agustín Iturbide—who knew?) and the other Mexican comfort foods on her menu. Here you'll find the things *grandmamá* still loves to cook, with a few subtle variations. Maximize your culinary experience by sharing starter plates: steak tacos, pickled duck tostadas, plantain fritters, or crab-filled chiles rellenos. ⊠ *Calle Allende 344, at Calle Miramar, Centro* ☎ *322/222–7195* ▤ *MC, V Tues. and Aug.* ☉ *Closed Tues. and Aug. No lunch.*

$–$$ ✕ **El Brujo.** The street corner on which the small restaurant is tucked means noise on either side. Service is reasonably attentive, although it sometimes seems grudging. Still, this is an expat favorite, and no wonder: the food is seriously good and portions generous. The *molcajete*—a sizzling black pot of tender flank steak, grilled green onion, and soft white cheese in a delicious homemade sauce of dried red peppers—is served with a big plate of guacamole, refried beans, and made-at-the-moment corn or flour tortillas. ⊠ *Venustiano Carranza 510, at Naranjo, Col. Remance* ☎ *No phone* ⌲ *Reservations not accepted* ▤ *No credit cards* ☉ *Closed Mon., 2 wks in late Sept., and early Oct.*

$–$$ ✕ **Café de Olla.** This close-ceiling, earthy restaurant fills up as soon as it reopens for the season. Repeat visitors swear by the enchiladas and carne asadas. As reservations are not accepted, you may need to wait for a table, especially at breakfast and dinner. A large tree extends from the dining-room floor through the roof, local artwork adorns the walls, and salsa music often plays in the background. ⊠ *Calle Basilio Badillo 168–A, Col. E. Zapata* ☎ *322/223–1626* ⌲ *Reservations not accepted* ▤ *No credit cards* ☉ *Closed Tues. and Sept. and Oct.*

$ ✕ **Tía Catarina.** Co-owner Erin Gulliver used her interior decorator skills to create this beautiful, bright gem with an exhibition kitchen. Candles in blue glasses light tables, and reliquaries hang on vividly painted walls. Designed with the local's palate and budget in mind, the restaurant has some interesting vegetarian appetizers in addition to traditional dishes

---

WHERE DOGS HAVE THEIR DAY

If you travel with a lapdog instead of a laptop, PV is the place for you. Small breeds, like the universally popular chihuahua, are escorted into upscale restaurants on their own little pillows; big dogs accompany their owners to beachfront bistros. A few restaurants take issue; if you and Fifi are going to an unfamiliar eatery, call ahead.

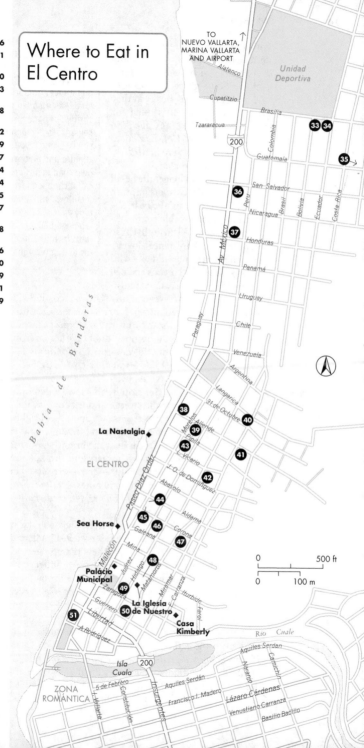

Where to Eat in El Centro

El Andariego .. **36**
El Arrayán **41**
Barcelona
Tapas Bar **40**
Blue Shrimp .. **43**
La Bodeguita
del Medio **38**
Café des
Artistes **42**
El Campanario .**49**
Chez Elena **47**
Cueto's **34**
Jumaica **44**
Las Carmelitas .**35**
Pepe's Tacos ..**37**
Planeta
Vegetariana ...**48**
Taberna
San Pascual ...**46**
Trio **50**
Tutifruti **39**
Vitea **51**
Los Xitomates .**49**

with a twist: beet soup with tequila, chile relleno stuffed with shrimp and cheese, ceviche, and tacos de arrachera. Some guests complain of uneven food service, but even they go back for more. It's open for breakfast after 9 AM. ✉ *Calle Pino Suárez at Madero, Col. E. Zapata* ☎ *No phone* ⊟ *No credit cards* ☉ *Closed Sun. No lunch.*

¢–$ ✕ **Pepe's Tacos.** No longer the be-all and end-all of taco consumption in PV, Pepe's still can't be beat at 4 AM, when most sensible taco-makers are asleep. Although these diminutive tacos are a meat-lover's treat, there are quesadillas—and one taco with grilled onions and bell peppers, cheese, and canned mushrooms—for wayward vegetarians. Order tacos individually for about 70¢ each to try different types, or by the set. Or order one of several plates for two with a stack of tortillas. Expect plastic tablecloths and sports on several TVs at this open-door dive across from the Pemex station at the north end of Old Vallarta. ✉ *Honduras 173, between Avs. Peru and Mexico, Col. 5 de Diciembre* ☎ *322/223–1703* ⊟ *No credit cards* ☉ *Closed Tues. No lunch.*

★ ¢–$ ✕ **La Taquiza.** Here's a tip: stop by this local's den on your way to the airport (it's just across the street), and get food to go. Dollar, Budget, and Thrifty rental car storefronts surround this bright and shiny hole-in-the-wall. You can order food, drop off your rental car, and then get a shuttle to the airport. Or eat in at the brightly polished green formica tables (with matching chairs). The tasty lime drink, lunch specials, pinto bean soup, and the house specialty—tacos—are served in or on old-fashioned red pottery plates, bowls, and mugs. ✉ *Blvd. Federico M. Ascencio s/n, Col. Las Flores* ☎ *No phone* ⊟ *No credit cards* ☉. *Closed Sun. No dinner*

¢ ✕ **El Campanario.** This little jewel is increasingly popular with budget travelers. Egg dishes and chilaquiles are served 9–11 AM, and an inexpensive daily lunch menu is served 2–5 PM. Less than $5 gets you soup, a main dish, drink, homemade tortillas, and dessert. Office workers come in for takeout, or drift in between 6 and 10:30 PM for tacos, *tortas* (Mexican-style sandwiches on crispy white rolls), or pozole. A recipe for the latter is given—along with a positive dining review—in a framed *Los Angeles Times* article from the 1980s. Fans swirl the air, doors are open to the street, and cheerful oilcloths cover wooden tables at this no-frills spot across from the cathedral. ✉ *Calle Hidalgo 339, Centro* ☎ *322/223–1509* ⊟ *No credit cards* ☉ *Closed Sun., and often between 5 and 6 PM.*

¢ ✕ **Tutifruti.** If you find yourself near the main square at lunchtime, consider having a taco at this little stand. While we can't exactly call this *fast* food, the quesadillas and machaca (shredded beef) burritos are de-

---

TACO PRIMER

In this region, a taco is generally a diminutive corn tortilla heated on an oiled grill filled with meat, shrimp, or batter-fried fish. If your server asks *"Preparadita?"*, he or she is asking if you want it with cilantro and onions. Add-your-own condiments are salsa mexicana (chopped raw onions, tomatoes, and green chilies), liquidy guacamole, and pickled jalapeño peppers. Some restaurants include chopped nopal cactus and other signature items.

> ## BREAKFASTS OF CHAMPIONS
>
> **IN PUERTO VALLARTA, Memo's Pancake House** is the favorite for hotcakes, while ritzier **La Palapa** and **Dacquiri Dick's** are popular for breakfast at the beach. **Langostino's** and **Playita de Lindo Mar** have more casual, oceanside morning fare. In **Bucerías,** head to
>
> **Famar** for an excellent Mexican breakfast or **Chayito's,** in **San Francisco,** for good coffee, fruit smoothies, and eggs. In the **Costalegre,** our picks are **Casa de la Abuela** for excellent coffee and jazzy tunes and **El Dorado** for a full breakfast overlooking the beach.

licious; you can also get a sandwich or burger. Consider sharing, because the portions are large. For breakfast, order up a *licuado* (smoothie) made from fresh fruit and milk. If you're lucky, you might get one of the few stools at the tiled counter. ⊠ *Calle Allende, between Av. Juaréz and Av. Guadalupe Sánchez, Centro* ☎ *322/222–1068* ▭ *No credit cards* ⊙ *Closed Sun. No dinner.*

Pan-Asian

★ **$–$$$** ✕ **Archie's Wok.** This extremely popular South Side restaurant has a variety of Asian cuisines and dishes such as Thai garlic shrimp, *pancit* (Filipino stir-fry with pasta), and Singapore-style (lightly battered) fish, plus lots of vegetarian dishes. Thursday through Saturday after 7:30 PM the soothing harp music of well-known local musican D'Rachel is the perfect accompaniment to your meal. It opens for lunch only after 2 PM. ⊠ *Calle Francisca Rodríguez 130, Col. E. Zapata* ☎ *322/222–0411* ▭ *MC, V* ⊙ *Closed Sun.*

Seafood

$$–$$$$ ✕ **Blue Shrimp.** The lighting, table and window dressings, and other details are on the blue side, making you feel as if you're under water. Cushioned booths encourage cozy conversation. Choose your shrimp by size and weight and the chef prepares it to order, most likely with rice and steamed veggies. Lobster and a variety of fish plates are also available, or dive into the salad bar (more impressive at night), which costs just a couple of bucks. ⊠ *Calle Morelos 779, Centro* ☎ *322/222–4246* ▭ *MC, V.*

★ **$–$$$** ✕ **Cueto's.** Teams of engaging waiters, all family members, nudge aside mariachi duos to refill beer glasses, remove empty plates, or bring more fresh tostadas and hot, crusty garlic bread. But don't fill up on nonessentials, as the recommended cream-based and mild-chili casseroles—with crab, clams, fish, shrimp, or mixed seafood—are so delicious you won't want to leave even one bite. You can have a complimentary margarita with dinner or a free digestif later on. Cueto's is a few blocks behind the Unidad Deportivo sports complex. Don't confuse this fabulous seafood restaurant with Cuates y Cuetes, on the beach at Los Muertos. ⊠ *Calle Brasilia 469, Col. 5 de Diciembre (Zona Hotelera)* ☎ *322/223–0363* ⊠ *Hidalgo 102, Bucerís* ☎ *329/298–2410* ▭ *No credit cards.*

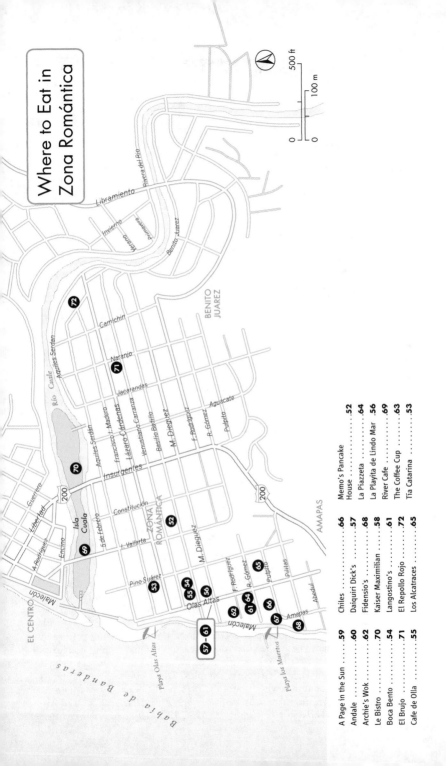

Where to Eat in Zona Romántica

500 ft

100 m

A Page in the Sun **59**
Andale **60**
Archie's Wok **62**
Le Bistro **70**
Boca Bento **54**
El Brujo **71**
Cafe de Olla **55**

Chiles **66**
Daiquiri Dick's **57**
Fidensio's **68**
Kaiser Maximilian **58**
Langostino's **61**
El Repollo Rojo **72**
Los Alcatraces **65**

Memo's Pancake
House **52**
La Piazzeta **64**
La Playita de Lindo Mar .**56**
River Cafe **69**
The Coffee Cup **63**
Tía Catarina **53**

☺ **$–$$$** ✕ **El Edén.** The location, a jungly riverside place where the movie Predator was filmed, is as much of a draw as the mainly seafood fare. This is a place to spend time, splashing in the river or zinging through the air on a canopy tour. Not on the menu but worth asking about is the Festival de Camarones: shrimp is prepared breaded, butterflied, sautéed in garlic, and several other styles, and served with rice, tortillas, homemade chips, and various salsas. You might catch a ride at El Edén's downtown PV office, when they transport their canopy tour patrons; otherwise plan to drive or take a cab. If it's not too busy, the restaurant will sometimes return patrons on the highway, where buses frequently pass. ⊠ *Carr. al Edén, Predio el Venado, 10 min east of Mismaloya* ☎ *No phone* ▭ *No credit cards* ☽ *No dinner.*

$–$$$ ✕ **Langostino's.** Right on the beach just north of the pier at Playa Los Muertos, Langostino's is a great place to start the day with a heaping helping of Mexican rock, cranked up to a respectable volume. The house favorite at this professional and pleasant place is surf and turf, and the three seafood combos are a good value. ⊠ *Los Muertos Beach at Calle Manuel M. Dieguez, Col. E. Zapata* ☎ *322/222–0894* ▭ *No credit cards* ☽ *No breakfast or lunch for 2 wks in Sept. (wks vary).*

> **WORD OF MOUTH**
>
> "Re: mango margaritas, my favorite fun place was Langostino's. Happy hour is 5–7 and you get two for US$3.50."
>
> –baglady

★ **$–$$$** ✕ **Tino's.** Vine-covered trees poke through the roof of the breeze-blessed, covered outdoor eatery overlooking the Río Ameca. The Carvajal family has worked hard to make this a favorite Nuevo Vallarta restaurant, though the Punta de Mita branch is also nice, on a pretty beach. Tino's is full even midweek, mainly with groups of friends or businesspeople leisurely discussing deals. A multitude of solicitous, efficient waiters proffer green-lipped mussels meunière, crab enchiladas, oysters, and the regional specialty, fish *sarandeado* (rubbed with herbs and cooked over coals). Concha de Tino is a dish with seafood, bacon, mushrooms, and spinach prettily presented in three seashells. ⊠ *2a Entrada a Nuevo Vallarta, Km 1.2, Las Jarretaderas* ☎ *322/297–0221* ▭ *MC, V* ⊠ *Av. El Anclote 64, l Anclote Punta de Mita* ☎ *322/224–5584.*

★ **$–$$** ✕ **Mariscos 8 Tostadas.** Extremely popular with locals, this large restaurant hums with activity and a varied, upbeat soundtrack with tunes by icons such as Bob Marley and Frank Sinatra. The menu is oddly translated—tuna sashimi appears as *atun fresco con salsa rasurada,* or "tuna cut thick with shaved sauce, alone if there was fishing" (the latter meaning that it's only available if the fish was caught that day)—indicating that this is a spot geared to locals, not tourists. The freshly caught, raw tuna, which is thicker than in U.S. sushi houses, but not too thick, is served in a shallow dish with soy sauce, micro-thin cucumber slices, sesame seeds, green onions, chili powder, and lime. Eat with tostadas until fit to burst. Avoid the scallop tostadas, as the shellfish is virtually raw. The ceviche, however, couldn't be better—or fresher. There's a small storefront subsidiary in the parking lot at Plaza Marina; the charming orig inal venue is behind Blockbuster Video in the Hotel Zone. ☒ *Calle Quilla at Calle Proa, Local 28–29, Marina Vallarta* ☎ *322/221-3124* ☱ *No credit cards* ☉ *No dinner* ☒ *Calle Niza 132 at Lucerna, Col. Versalles (Zona Hotelera), behind Blockbuster Video store* ☎ *No phone* ☱ *No credit cards* ☉ *Closed Sun. No dinner.*

Spanish

★ **$-$$** ✕ **Barcelona Tapas Bar.** One of the few places in town with both great food and an excellent bay view, Barcelona has traditional Spanish tapas like *patatas alioli* (garlic potatoes), spicy garlic shrimp, and grilled mushrooms. Full entrées are available, too, like the beef ribs with potatoes and steamed spinach. To start you off, attentive waiters bring a free appetizer, served with delicious homemade bread. In addition to traditional paella, the restaurant serves veggie and other versions. Choose the small, highly air-conditioned room or the expansive, open-air patio. You'll have to pay for the patio view by walking up a few dozen stairs. ☒ *Matamoros at 31 de Octubre, Centro* ☎ *322/222-0510* ☖ *Reservations essential* ☱ *AE.*

> ### STREET-FOOD SMARTS
>
> Many think it's madness to eat "street food," but when you see professionals in pinstripes thronging to roadside stands, you've got to wonder why. Stands can be just as hygienic as restaurants, as they are actually tiny exhibition kitchens. Make sure the cook doesn't handle cash, or takes your money with a gloved hand. Ask locals for recommendations, or look for a stand bustling with trade.

$-$$ ✕ **Taberna San Pascual.** This snug little tapas bar really feels like Spain. The co-owner Lorenzo Ballesteros Gil (with Luis Fitch, of Los Xitomates) presides over the diminutive, brightly polished bar dispensing *rioja* and other Iberian wines. The chef peeks in to make sure all is well. All is well: the snack-size portions of garlicky potatoes, Manchego cheese, or Spanish potato-and-egg tortilla, perfect for sharing, are a nice break from Mexican or seafood. It opens at 3 PM. ☒ *Corona 176, Centro* ☎ *322/223-9371* ☱ *No credit cards* ☉ *Closed Tues.*

Steak

NUEVO

$$ ✕ **Brasil Steakhouse.** Vallarta's most popular venue for grilled meat is this all-you-can-eat place, where you're treated to excellent barbecue, steak, pork, BBQ ribs, and grilled chicken. Waiters first bring soup and chicken wings, a shared plate of three different chopped salads, and then platters of meat of your choosing. Lunch begins after 2 PM. ☒ *Venustiano Carranza 210, Col. E. Zapata* ☎ *322/222-2909* ☱ *AE, MC, V.*

Vegetarian

★ ☕ **$** ✕ **Planeta Vegetariana.** Those who stumble upon this hog-less heaven can partake of the tasty meatless carne asada and a selection of main dishes that change daily. Choose from at least three delicious main dishes, plus beans, several types of rice, and a daily soup at this buffet-only place. Though the selection of overdressed salads is good, the greens tend to get wilted or soggy. A healthful fruit drink, coffee, or tea, and dessert is included in the reasonable price. Eggs are not used; items containing milk products are labeled as such. It's about a block north of the Church of Guadalupe. ⊠ *Iturbide 270, Centro* ☎ *322/ 222–3073* ▭ *No credit cards.*

HANGOVER CURES
For a hangover, menudo (tripe stew) and pozole are recommended, both with the addition of chopped fresh onions and cilantro, a generous squeeze of lime and as much chili as one can handle. Ceviche is another popular cure, with the same key ingredients: lime and chili.

¢ ✕ **Jumaica.** Salads win high marks for meticulous construction, if not artistic presentation, and for $1 extra you get organic lettuce. Young servers in the sweet-scented, small restaurant—which sprouts a good number of convincing plastic flowers, plants, and fruit trees—are accommodating and attentive. In addition to pancakes and bagels, deli sandwiches, and fruit salads there's a large juice menu and smoothies made with milk, yogurt, bottled water, or ice cream. Delivery is available to downtown Vallarta. ⊠ *Calle Aldama 162, Centro* ☎ *322/ 222–9393* ▭ *No credit cards.*

NORTH OF PUERTO VALLARTA

American-Casual

☾ ¢ ✕ **Choco Banana.** BLTs and burgers, omelets and bagels, and chicken with rice and chai tea are some of what you'll find here. Service isn't fast and the setting is beyond casual, in keeping with laid-back Sayulita's surfer attitude. This perennial favorite is almost always full of young people eating and loafing; there's a kid's menu for the truly young. ⊠ *Calle Revolución at Calle Delfin, on plaza, Sayulita* ☎ *329/291–3051* ☉ *No dinner Sun.*

Argentine

$–$$$ ✕ **La Porteña.** Restaurants are a hard sell in all-inclusive-dominated Nuevo Vallarta. Hopefully this one will break the mold. Every cut of meat is grilled over mesquite, from the steaks to Angus prime rib (both imported from Texas). The adventurous yet tasty *chinculinas* (tender tripe appetizers) and chorizo turnovers certainly are authentic. Rice, veggies, and other sides must be ordered separately. The setting, an L-shape covered patio with kids' play equipment in the center, is Mexican, but the food is pure Argentine. It opens for lunch only after 2 PM. ⊠ *Blvd. Nayarit Pte. 250, Nuevo Vallarta, between highway to Bucerías and El Tigre golf course* ☎ *322/297–4950* ▭ *MC, V* ☉ *Closed Mon.*

Cafés

¢ ✕ **The Bar Above.** This little place above Tapas del Mundo defies categorization. It's a martini bar without a bar (the owner, Buddy, prefers that people come to converse with friends rather than hang out at a bar) that also serves dessert. Order from the day's offerings, maybe molten chocolate soufflé—the signature dish—or a charred pineapple bourbon shortcake. Lights are dim, the music is romantic, and there's an eagle's view of the ocean from the rooftop nest. ⊠ *Corner of Av. Mexico and Av. Hidalgo, 2 blocks north of central plaza, Bucerías* ☎ *329/298–1194* ▭ *No credit cards* ⊘ *Closed Sun.,Aug., Sept., and Mon. in June, July, Oct. No lunch.*

★ ¢ ✕ **Pie in the Sky.** Although the cars on the highway can be noisy, the lure of deliciously decadent mini-cheesecakes and fruit pies, pecan tarts, and crunchy chocolate cookies exerts a strong gravitational pull. The signature dessert here is the *beso,* a deep chocolate, soft-center brownie. Cakes, including gorgeous wedding cakes, are decorated by Zulem, a fine artist who excels with frosting as her medium. In addition to iced coffee and gourmet ice cream, Pie in the Sky has chicken pot pie, spinach empanadas, and a spinach-and-cheese pizza. ⊠ *Héroes de Nacozari 202, Bucerías* ☎ *329/298–0838* ⊠ *Lázaro Cárdenas 247, at I. Vallarta, Col. E. Zapata* ☎ *322/223–8183* ▭ *No credit cards* ⊘ *Closed Wed.*

Contemporary

★ $–$$ ✕ **Mark's Bar & Grill.** You can dine alone at the polished black-granite bar without feeling too lonely, or catch an important ball game. But seemingly a world away from the bar and TV is the charming restaurant known for its delightful decor and excellent cuisine. Both are best appreciated on the back patio, open to the stars. Standouts include the homemade bread and pizza, the salads, and the macadamia-crusted fresh fish fillets with mushroom ragout. The owners travel in the summer, shopping for objets d'art to add to the stylish mix of glassware from Tonalá, special-order lamps from Guadalajara, rocks from the local beach, and shells from New Zealand. ⊠ *Av. Lázaro Cárdenas 56, Bucerías* ☎ *329/298–0303* ▭ *MC, V* ⊘ *Closed Tues. May–Oct. No lunch.*

$–$$ ✕ **La Ola Rica.** Oh. My. God. The food is good. *Really* good. Somehow chef and co-owner Gloria Honan (with Triny Palomera Gil) makes garlic-sautéed mushrooms (a huge portion) into a minor miracle on toast. The cream of poblano-chili soup is simply to die for: not too spicy, but wonderfully flavorful. And these are just the starters. The restaurant is understandably popular, and reservations are encouraged when there's live music, often jazz or Cuban. Locals come for the medium-crust pizzas; everyone laps up the lovely margaritas. ⊠ *Av. Tercer Mundo s/n, San*

Fodor'sChoice
★

> ### TIME IS OF THE ESSENCE
>
> The state of Nayarit (Nuevo Vallarta and points north) is in the Mountain Standard Time zone, while Jalisco (Marina Vallarta to Barra de Navidad) is on Central Standard Time. But because tourism in Bucerías and Nuevo Vallarta has always been linked to that of Puerto Vallarta, many Nayarit businesses run on Jalisco time. When making dinner reservations or checking restaurant hours, ask whether the place runs on *hora de Jalisco* (Jalisco time) or *hora de Nayarit.*

MEXICO'S GOURMET TOWN

Mar Plata restaurant

PV merges cooking styles and ingredients from all over the world

After Mexico City, Puerto Vallarta beats anywhere in the country for sheer number of excellent restaurants. Many talented chefs are drawn to this area by its natural beauty, aspiring chefs have fallen in love with the place and opened restaurants, contributing to the varied world cuisine. The chefs duke it out, creating confits, reductions, tapanades, and tempuras. You, the visitor, are the clear winner, able to indulge in spring rolls or Filipino pancit, great pizza, melt-in-your-mouth beef carpaccio, and wonderful seafood dishes made with sea bass and tuna, shrimp, and shellfish plucked from local waters.

Competition creates excellence. "The high season is only five months long," says chef Bernhard Güth. "You have to be creative and good year-round to survive." PV doesn't have a signature cuisine—instead, it merges cooking styles and ingredients from all over the world. Traditional Mexican dishes are plentiful, but more often upscale restaurants use these as a springboard for their own specialties, infusing European techniques and classical recipes with new life. The most elegant restaurants present dishes so beautifully that you might dread the thought of disassembling these works of art.

TOP RESTAURANTS AND CHEFS

Stars among Puerto Vallarta's many fine chefs and restaurants, these trailblazers march to a different drummer.

Trio

Conviviality, hominess, and dedication on the parts of the chef-owners have made Trio one of Puerto Vallarta's best restaurants, hands-down. Fans, many of them members of PV's artsy crowd, marvel at the kitchen's ability to deliver perfect meal after perfect meal. Popular demand guarantees rack of lamb with fresh mint and for dessert, the warm chocolate cake.

Vitea

The chefs at Trio, opened this oceanfront bistro in 2005— which all but guaranteed its success. In addition to the great oceanfront location and upbeat Caribbean soundtrack, Vitea charms with its wide range of Mediterranean-inspired, contemporary sandwiches, soups, small plates, and full entrées—all at accessible prices.

THE DUO AT TRIO AND VITEA When you ask patrons why they love Trio, they almost universally mention the personal attention of high-energy but low-key owner–chef **Bernhard Güth** and his colleague, **Ulf Henriksson**. Güth says "Our mission here is to hug all of our clients, mentally, to make them feel more than welcome."

TOP: Fish Dish from Trio
ABOVE: Bernhard Guth &
Ulf Henriksson

Daiquiri Dick's

Visitors come often more than once during a vacation for the excellent service and consistent and innovative Mexican and world cuisine. The menu has fabulous appetizers and fish. Start with a signature daiquiri; move to the lingering wine list. Twin patios face the sea—one covered, one not.

THE COLLABORATORS The fish on a stick has been around since Dick's was a palapa on the beach. But most of the stellar recipes originated with departed chef Rafael Nazario, and are now expertly executed by talented Mexican chef **Ignacio Uribe.** During high season, Seattle chef **Hnoi Latthitham** joins Uribe, adding sizzle and spice from her native Thailand.

Daquiri Dick's fish on a stick

La Ola Rica

Presentation is artful, portions generous, and the decor—a cross between whimsical and chic—is as yummy as the food. Owners Gloria Honan and Triny Palomera Gil scour the coast each day for fresh ingredients, fish, and bread, and preside over the restaurant each night to make sure the food's as good as it can be.

SELF-MADE CHEF In 1996 **Gloria Honan** and her partner were selling espresso from a lopsided wooden table inviting potential clients to sign up for a meal. But when the pasta primavera proved wildly successful, they opened La Ola Rica in Triny's family home. Their expertise is self-taught. "I've got to learn the names of the fish," Gloria laughs, "and then I can expand my repertoire."

Gloria Honan (chef-owner) and her partner Triny Palomero Gil (co-owner)

Mark's Bar & Grill

Standout dishes at this Bucerías restaurant include the homemade bread and pizza, great salads, and such entrées as macadamia-crusted fish fillets and lobster ravioli. The restaurant cozy but chic, with glassware from Tonalá, special-order lamps from Guadalajara, and rocks from the local beach. Vie for the back patio, open to the stars.

NATURAL TALENT Creative New Zealand transplant **Jan Benton** spent happy childhood hours digging potatoes, shaking walnuts from trees, and roaming for wild mushrooms. Her appreciation for wholesome, natural foods shows in her cuisine, of which Jan says: "Everything has its own reason to be on the plate. You'll not find a repeat flavor."

Still Life No. 1: Mussels

Café Des Artistes

In Thierry Blouet's kitchen Mexican ingredients and European techniques produce such stellar dishes as cream of prawn and pumpkin soup, artichoke-and-potato terrine, and grilled tenderloin served with Camembert and smoky chipotle chile sauce.

THE MASTER Given the title of Master Chef of France in 2000, **Thierry Blouet** is well-spoken and confident, piling up the accolades and awards. Born in the Philippines to French parents, Chef Blouet describes his cooking as French cuisine with Mexican—and to a lesser extent, Asian—ingredients and spices. He is also president and co-founder of PV's Gourmet Festival.

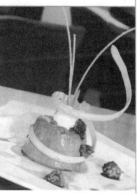

Dessert as sculpture

THE DISH ON THE DISHES

Lobster Taco, Daquiri Dick's

Puerto Vallarta has dozens of wonderful restaurants, and diligent research has produced the following list of some of the most exciting plates this gourmet town has to offer.

AMAZING APPETIZERS

Daiquiri Dick's **lobster tacos** are divine and its shrimp wonton's wonderful, melange of flavors dance a merengue in your mouth. At Trio, try the **anise-infused Portobello mushrooms** with vegetable vinaigrette. La Ola Rica has delightful **garlic mushrooms** and the sweetest **coconut shrimp** around.

SEAFOOD, MEXICAN-STYLE

The **mixed-seafood enchiladas** at La Palapa are wonderful, the best thing on the menu. Daiquiri Dick's **fish on a stick**, called Pescado Vallarta, has been pleasing crowds for nearly 30 years.

A-LIST ASIAN

Archie's Wok is the best place on the bay for multi-ethnic Asian cuisine, including Filipino, Thai, and Chinese. Favorite dishes are the **spicy Thai noodles** and **pancit** (Filipino noodle stir-fry). It's also great for vegetarians, with several wonderful stir-fried veggie dishes.

CHOCOLATE A-GO-GO

Indulge in a delicious **chocolate fondue** served with nutmeg ice cream at Café des Artistes. For special occasions, it's prepared on an creatively decorated tray with spun sugar and a liquid chocolate greeting. Trio's **warm chocolate cake** is legendary in PV. Make a pit stop at Pie in the Sky, in Bucerías, for a bag of crunchy **chocolate chip cookies** for the road, or sit down for an addictive **chocolate brownie** *beso* (kiss), so rich it goes best with strong, black coffee.

IT'S ALL IN THE ATMOSPHERE

FOOD WITH A VIEW

Get a magnificent view of the city and bay, and a varied menu of excellent Spanish tapas at **Barcelona Tapas.**

DECADENT DECOR

Greco-Roman meets modern at **Le Bistro,** one of Vallarta's original gourmet restaurants, recently revitalized, has river-view dining among stone pillars and stands of towering bamboo. **Café des Artistes**

has a magical, multilevel garden of ferns and figs, mangos and palms. Open to the ocean, **Vitea** is a casually hip bistro with

Boca Bento

clever and chic glass-and-metal furnishings. **Boca Bento** is serene, sensual, and open, with modern and elegant artwork, a soothing waterfall, and lots of candles. Grandiose yet romantic, **Mar Plata** is saved from looking industrial by innovative installations, fixtures, and antiques.

EPICUREAN EVENTS

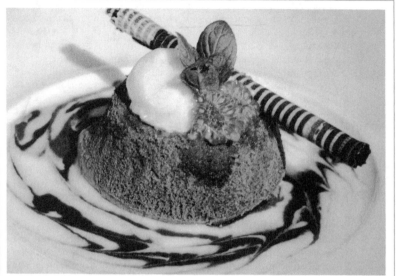

Chocolate fondant with tomato and basil sorbet and white chocolate and raspberry sauce, Café Des Artistes

INTERNATIONAL GOURMET FESTIVAL

The success of Puerto Vallarta's dining scene owes its thanks in part to its annual gourmet festival, which has brought international attention to PV since 1994. During the eight-day food fling each November, chefs from Africa, Europe, South America, and the United States bring new twists on timeless classics. Starting with an elegant chef's cocktail reception, the festival continues with a full table of events. Each of the more than two dozen participating restaurants invites a guest chef to create special menus with wine pairings. Local and guest chefs teach cooking classes and seminars. The culmination is a gala dinner with live music, fireworks, and naturally, an over-the-top gourmet meal. ☎ 322/222–3229 *Café des Artistes,* ⊕ *www.festivalgourmet.com.*

RESTAURANT WEEK (The May Food Festival)

Most everyone in Vallarta works his or her tail off during the December to Easter high season. When *vallartenses* can finally take a breath—and then give a collective sigh of relief—they reward themselves with some reasonably priced nights out at the destination's best restaurants during this two-week (despite its name) event. In 2005 more than 30 restaurants participated, each offering prix-fixe meals (with choices among appetizers, entrées, and desserts) for either 159 or 259 pesos. ☎ 322/221–0106.

FOOD FOR A CAUSE

As if our clothes weren't already bursting at the seams, some of PV's most benevolent gastronomes began teaming up at fundraising events for local charities in 2005. Local chefs now produce Palomazo Gastronómico, or the "Culinary Jam Session," several times a year. Along with four courses of haute cuisine, they serve up wine, song, and a warm and fuzzy feeling to boot. Cost is about $60 per person. ☎ 322/226–0000 or 322/222–1695.

Francisco ☎ *311/258–4123* ▭ *MC, V* ☉ *Closed Sun. and Aug.–Oct. Closed weekends June and July. No lunch.*

$ ✕ **Karen's.** Karen, a displaced Brit from Manchester, can really cook. Her simple outdoor beachfront eatery has innovative and predictably good contemporary dishes. Locals come for Sunday brunch. The rest of the time there's pork cutlet with garlic mashed potatoes and green beans, steak chimichangas with cheese and potatoes, jumbo coconut-encrusted shrimp, and chicken breast sandwiches. If you dare, try the Full Monty: a typical Manchester breakfast. ⊠ *Av. Lázaro Cárdenas s/n at Suites Costa Dorada, Bucerías* ☎ *329/229–6892* ▭ *No credit cards.*

Continental

$–$$ ✕ **Amber Sur Mer.** A French woman from Provence brings a welcome addition to Barra's circumspect culinary scene, along with good thin-crust pizzas, escargot, crepes, and other tasty French and Italian fare. The restaurant's compact size and good tunes, along with the small bar in the middle and the few tables out on the street, give it a bistro feel. ⊠ *Calle López de Legazpi 160, across from Hotel Alondra, Barra de Navidad* ☎ *315/355–8169* ▭ *No credit cards* ☉ *No lunch.*

$–$$ ✕ **Don Pedro's.** Sayulita institution Don Pedro's has pizzas baked in a wood-fire oven, prepared by European-trained chef and co-owner Nicholas Parrillo. Also on the menu are reliable seafood dishes and mesquite-grilled filet mignon—served with baby vegetables and mashed potatoes accompanied by crusty, home-baked bread—which is just about the best around. The pretty second-floor dining room, with the better view, is open when the bottom floor fills up, usually during the high season (December–Easter). ⊠ *Calle Marlin 2, at beach, Sayulita* ☎ *329/291–3090* ▭ *MC, V* ☉ *Closed Aug. 15–Oct. 15.*

Eclectic

$–$$$ ✕ **Cafe del Mar.** Chefs Eugene of Singapore and Amandine, a Belgian–Mexican, collaborate to create beautiful food focusing on seafood and chicken; the varied and excellent appetizers and desserts are especially recommended. The dishes blend Asian, Mediterranean, and haute Mexican cuisine in simple yet successful dishes. The setting itself is romantic and sophisticated. Tiny white lights and soft music accompany individual tables down the side of a hill to a vine-drenched tressis at the bottom. There's live music on Tuesday. ⊠ *Av. China 9, San Francisco* ☎ *311/258–4251* ▭ *MC, V* ☉ *Closed Wed. and Aug.–Nov. No lunch.*

$–$$ ✕ **Gallo's Pizzeria.** If a hole in the wall could be out of doors, this would be it. Frankly, it looks best by candlelight. But folks don't come for the decor; they come for the fab filet mignon, great fish and shrimp, and good pizza. The affable owner, Gallo, is also a musician who presents tunes (often blues or acoustic guitar) whenever possible, usually Friday through Sunday after 7:30 PM. Nightlife being the exception rather than the rule in San Pancho, this is a great locals' after-dark hangout. ⊠ *Av. Tercer Mundo 7, San Francisco* ☎ *298/258–4135* ▭ *No credit cards* ☉ *Closed Tues. No lunch.*

$–$$ ✕ **Mar Plata.** Grandiose yet romantic, these impressive second-story digs have a celestial seasoning of stars on the ceiling in the form of tin lamps from Guadalajara. Dark-blue and deep terra-cotta walls juxtapose nicely; the huge space is saved from looking industrial by innovative installations and fixtures. Co-owner and chef Amadine's recipes wed traditional Argentine meats with updated Continental cuisine in a happy transcontinental marriage. Portions are smallish, and entrées exclude sides. There's live music Sunday and occasional flamenco shows or tango classes. ✉ *Calle de Palmas 30, Col. Costa Azul, San Francisco* ☎ *311/258–4424* ▭ *MC, V* ⊗ *Closed Mon. and Aug. and Sept. No lunch.*

$–$$ ✕ **Philo's.** Ambitious Philo does it all: breakfast, lunch, dinner. It's a bar with live music, a meeting place for local fundraisers and events and a community center (there are computers, yoga, and Spanish classes). There's even a pool table in the back and a small swimming pool. And if you were wondering, the food is good, too. Choose among barbecue, veggie fajitas, tacos, and inexpensive salads, but pizza is the specialty. Philo's special pizza has goat cheese, sundried tomatoes, onion, and pineapple. ✉ *Calle Delfín 16, La Cruz de Huanacaxtle* ☎ *329/295–5068* ▭ *No credit cards.*

$–$$ ✕ **Tapas del Mundo.** Here, worldy recipes of this and that are served in small plates perfect for sharing. Sit at one of three long bars around the open kitchen, soaking in the ambience created by the colorful American owners. Nosh on a hot pot of shrimp with guajillo chilies served with homemade tortillas, breaded olives, Anaheim chilies stuffed with goat cheese, or Oriental beef strips. Be apprised of the wonderful margaritas. The owners plan to open a new restaurant in San Sebastian: check it out. The Bar Above, upstairs(⇨ *above*) sells desserts, coffee, and mixed drinks. ✉ *Corner of Av. Mexico and Av. Hidalgo, 2 blocks north of central plaza, Bucerías* ☎ *329/298–1194* ▭ *No credit cards* ⊗ *Closed Sun. No lunch.*

Mediterranean

☕ **$–$$** ✕ **Sandrina's.** Canadian owner Sandy is as colorful as her wonderful art, which graces this locals' favorite. Dine on the back patio at night amid dozens of candles and tiny lights. The varied menu has plenty of salads as well as Greek and Italian dishes like falafels with *tzatziki* (yogurt, cucumber, garlic, and salt) and pita bread with hummus. The kids can text-message their friends in the computer room while you dine in peace, listening to cool, contemporary music. Order an espresso, delicious doctored coffee, or dessert from the bakery counter. ✉ *Av. Lázaro Cárdenas 33, Bucerías* ☎ *329/298–0273* ⊕ *www.sandrinas.com* ▭ *MC, V* ⊗ *Closed Tues. and 2 wks in Sept.*

Mexican

$–$$$ ✕ **Rain Tree.** Newish at this writing, Rain Tree is a spacious art gallery and outdoor garden restaurant surrounded by trees that shows great promise but is still being tested by locals and visitors. The interesting menu includes tequila-flamed shrimp served with nopal cactus, grilled rib eye with achiote demi-glace, and faji-tas of U.S.-certified Angus beef. Breakfast is served. ✉ *Calle Revolución 21, entrance to town, Sayulita* ☎ *329/291–3523* ▭ *MC, V* ☉ *Closed Sun.*

$–$$ ✕ **Vista Guayabitos.** Portions are large but the cooking is predictable at best. This newish restaurant's beauty lies in the setting, which couldn't be more dramatic. Enjoy lovely views of a solitary beach, an unattended island, and the beaches of Guayabitos. The hawk's-eye ocean view is especially wonderful around sunset. ✉ *Carretera a Los Ayala, Km 1.5, Rincón de Guayabitos* ☎ *327/274–2580* ▭ *MC, V.*

$ ✕ **Sayulita Café.** The restaurant bills itself as "home of the perfect chile relleno," but it also serves other Mexican plates from Puebla and Oaxaca as well as Continental dishes like rib eye with baked potato. The decor's looking a bit worn these days, but the restaurant and small bar in this small, rather dark converted home look good by candlelight. From the sound system emerge jazz, classic, and Latin tunes; waiters with perfect English are the rule. ✉ *Av. Revolución 37, Sayulita* ☎ *329/291–3511* ▭ *No credit cards* ☉ *Closed Sept. No lunch.*

$ ✕ **Si Hay Olitas.** This simply decorated, open-fronted Mexican restaurant is the one most often recommended by locals for dependable Mexican and American fare. Order a giant burrito, vegetarian platter, burger or grilled chicken, or a seafood combo. There's a little of everything to choose from, and it's open for breakfast. ✉ *Av. Revolución 33, Sayulita* ☎ *329/291–3203* ▭ *No credit cards.*

¢–$ ✕ **Famar.** This unassuming restaurant gets the vote of just about everyone we queried in Bucerías: expats and locals alike. Breakfast in the noisy front room includes chilaquiles, waffles, and omelettes. It's more peaceful on the back patio where the top picks are beef fajitas and shrimp Famar: the chef's secret recipe, containing shrimp, bacon, cheese, and salsa. Consistency and friendly, familial service is the name of the game. ✉ *Héroes de Nacozari 105, Bucerías* ☎ *329/298–0113* ▭ *No credit cards* ☉ *Closed Wed.*

¢ ✕ **La Casa del Café (aka Chayito's).** Breakfast is the name of the game at this casual little place next to La Ola Rica. Service inside or on the street-facing patio is easygoing but attentive. Between 8 and noon or 1 PM you can get the house favorites: huevos rancheros y chilaquiles as well as freshly squeezed orange juice, a banana strawberry smoothie, or an excellent fruit plate. ✉ *Av. Tercer Mundo s/n at Calle Mexico San Francisco* ☎ *329/258–4126* ▭ *No credit cards* ☉ *Closed Tues. and Aug.–Oct. No lunch or dinner.*

TACO NIGHTS

Weekend nights in La Cruz de Huanacaxtle are Taco Nights (6 to 10 or 11). At the home of the Diaz Gómez family (Calle Huachinango, 2 blocks north of traffic circle) locals and travelers socialize over delicious carne asada tacos, or quesadillas with freshly made flour or corn tortillas, excellent homemade salsas, and homemade flan for dessert. Bring your own beer or indulge in *horchata* or *agua de jamaica*, made, respectively, of rice and hibiscus plant.

Seafood

$–$$ ✕ **Dugarel Plays.** Do they mean "Dugarel's Place"? No matter, of Bucerías' many beachfront eateries, this one gets extra points for longevity, attentive service, good views north and south along the bay, and the best breezes. The menu is not extensive: there are several beef plates and Mexican dishes, and a larger assortment of fresh fish and seafood served with the usual rice and toasted bread, as well as some underdone veggies. ⊠ *Av. del Pacífico s/n, Bucerías* ☎ *329/298–1757* ▭ *No credit cards.*

> **NATURAL THIRST BUSTER**
>
> The guy on the malecón or in the main plaza with a giant gourd and a handful of plastic cups is selling *agua de tuba*, a refreshing, pleasant, yet innocuous drink made from the heart of the coconut palm. It's stored in a gourd container called a *huaje*, and served garnished with chopped walnuts and apples.

$ ✕ **Columba.** Yearn for manta ray stew? Crave fresh tuna balls? Simply must have shark soup? The recipes here are geared to the local palate; if you're an adventurous eater with a hankering for fresh, strangely prepared (a lot of things are minced beyond recognition) seafood dishes, give Columba a try. It's on the road to the fishermen's beach in Cruz de Huanacaxtle. As a backup plan, have an appetizer here, then head for one of the other picks in Bucerías. This restaurant closes at 7 PM, and serves only beer and sodas as beverages. It has the least expensive lobster around. ⊠ *Calle Marlin 14, at Calle Coral, Cruz de Huanacaxtle* ☎ *329/295–5055* ▭ *No credit cards* ⊘ *Closed Mon. and wk after Easter.*

Steak

$$ ✕ **Brasil Nuevo Vallarta.** Although the food and presentation is the same as the steak house restaurant in downtown Vallarta (⇨ *above*), this venue in Nuevo Vallarta's large, comprehensive mall has café seating on the corridor. Lunch is served only after 2 PM. ⊠ *Paradise Village Mall, 2nd fl., Nuevo Vallarta* ☎ *322/297–1164* ▭ *AE, MC, V.*

Vegetarian

$ ✕ **Roots.** Young owner–chef Andrew Field apprenticed for two years at Fressen in Toronto. A vegan himself, he uses cheese and other lacto-ovo products with a light hand, and all of the basic sauces and stocks are vegan. Try the fresh daily soup or pasta, small starter plates (like tomato crostini or roasted potatoes with herbs and garlic), Lebanese dishes (tabouli or hummus), eggplant ravioli, or veggie stir fry. During high season (late November–April), the lounge at the back sometimes has live music. It opens at 4:30 PM. ⊠ *Lazaro Cardenas 40, Bucerías* ☎ *329/298–2504* ▭ *No credit cards* ⊘ *Closed Thurs. and Aug., Sept. No lunch.*

COSTALEGRE

American-Casual

¢–$ ✕ **Casa de la Abuela.** The amiable and service-oriented owner, Miguel, makes this one of the town's top choices for breakfast, snacks, or a light lunch. Listen to rock and jazz on the great sound system as you sip cappuccino and munch on the assortment of Mexican cookies that comes with it. Refills of the good American-style coffee are a given. Besides omelets, chilaquiles, fresh juices, and other breakfast food, Miguel and his family serve snacks like guacamole and chips, and burgers and fries for lunch. ⊠ *Av. Miguel López de Legazpi 150, Barra de Navidad* ☎ *No phone* 🚫 *No credit cards* 🕐 *Closed Mon. No dinner.*

Eclectic

★ $–$$ ✕ **Maya.** Two Canadian women have teamed up to bring sophistication to San Patricio–Melaque's dining scene. East meets West in contemporary dishes such as tequila-lime prawns and grilled eggplant rollups. Favorite entrées include Szechuan prawns and prosciutto-wrapped chicken stuffed with spinach and goat cheese. Their hours of operation are complex and subject to change; it's best to check their Web site or confirm by phone. ⊠ *Calle Alvaro Obregón 1, Villa Obregón, San Patricio–Melaque* ☎ *315/355–6764* 🕐 *Closed Mon., Tues. in Nov.; mid-May–Oct. No lunch.* 🚫 *No credit cards.*

> **KNOW YOUR TORTILLAS**
>
> In PV, tortillas are made of boiled and milled corn, griddle cooked, and served with just about every traditional dish. Butter to accompany tortillas is offered to *gringos* only. Foreigners also are given their choice of corn or flour tortillas, the latter native to northern Mexico and typically offered only with certain dishes, like *queso fundido* (cheese fondue).

Mexican

$–$$ ✕ **Martin's.** This second-floor, palapa-roofed restaurant is the most reliable in town for food and good cheer, and for hours of operation, too, as it's open year-round. There are Mexican- and American-style breakfasts, fajitas and shrimp for lunch and dinner, and guitar music most nights after 8 PM. This is as much a place for socializing as for eating; at the bar you can quaff champagne, cognac, martinis, and wine. ⊠ *Calle Playa Blanco 70, La Manzanilla* ☎ *315/351–5106* 🚫 *No credit cards* 🕐 *Closed Tues.*

★ ¢ ✕ **Cenaduría Flor Morena.** Some folks say these are the best enchiladas they've ever eaten; others call it a "local institution." Locals and foreigners all pretty much agree that this hole in the wall on the main square is the best place around to get good, inexpensive Mexican favorites like pozole, tamales, and tacos. ⊠ *Facing main plaza below Catscan bar, San Patricio–Melaque* ☎ *No phone* 🕐 *Closed Mon. and Tues. No lunch.* 🚫 *No credit cards.*

Seafood

$–$$ ✕ **El Dorado.** Also called El Piramide, this is the best place in town for seafood with an ocean view under a tall, peaked palapa roof. Besides seafood there's grilled chicken with baked potato, beef tips with rice and beans, soups, quesadillas, great guacamole, and fries. It's open all day (8 AM until 10 PM) and serves everyone from white-collar business types to families and friends meeting for lunch, to tourists cleaned up for an evening out. ⊠ *Calle Gómez Farias 1, San Patricio–Melaque* ☎ *315/ 355–5239 or 315/355–5770* ⊟ *MC, V.*

$–$$ ✕ **Seamaster's.** Although most of the ocean-facing restaurants in Barra have a similar menu, this friendly family favorite is often recommended above the others. Have a shrimp or fish burger, the catch of the day bathed in garlic cream, or the house special: shrimp flambéed in brandy and Kahlua served in a nubby pineapple. The bar sometimes stays open late in high season, keeping clients around after the kitchen has shut down. ⊠ *Av. Miguel López de Legaspi 146, Barra de Navidad* ☎ *315/355– 5119* ⊟ *No credit cards.*

Beaches

Ixtapa

WORD OF MOUTH

"Yelapa is gorgeous. It's in a cove, protected from wind and waves . . . with a small village all around the cove and climbing part way up the mountains. We passed Las Animas, Quimixto, Las Caletas, and Mahajuitas beaches on the way—Yelapa was the prettiest."

–balasteve

Puerto Vallarta sits at the center of horseshoe-shape Bahía de Banderas (Banderas Bay), the second largest bay in North America (after the Hudson). While Pacific Mexico's beaches are not the sugar-sand, crystal-water variety of the Caribbean, the beaches are lovely, the water unpolluted, and the coastline itself among the most majestic in Mexico.

Accounting for much of its beauty are the foothills that race down to meet the sea. Crowded with palms and cedars, the jungle's blue-green canopy forms a highly textured background to the deep blue ocean and creamy sand. Dozens of creeks and rivers follow the contours of these hills, creating estuaries, mangrove swamps, and other habitats for exploration. Exquisitely visible from cliff-side hotels and restaurants, the scalloped coast holds myriad coves and small bays perfect for shelling, sunning, swimming, and more strenuous activities.

At crowded Hotel Zone beaches and a few of the more popular stretches of sand north and south of town you can parasail, take boat rides, jet ski, kayak, boogie board, snorkel, and dive. If you want to explore the coast, some of the isolated beaches accessible by boat offer some of the above activities. Accessible by both land and sea are untouristy hideaways where there's little to distract you beyond the waves lapping at the shore. Almost any beach has at least one low-key seafood restaurant to provide simple fish lunches, cold beer, and warm pink sunsets.

Getting Oriented

The mountainous backdrop of the beaches in Puerto Vallarta and to the north makes them beautiful—even though the water isn't translucent and the sand is grainy and brown, rather than powdery white. South of PV the mountains recede from the coast. The lovely yet loney beaches and bay are fringed by dry tropical thorn forest with a wonderful variety of plant species. Several species of whales cruise down in winter and turtles spawn on the beaches. Throughout the region from southern Nayarit to the Costalegre, long, flat beaches invite walking and reefs and offshore breaks draw surfers; the omnipresent seafood shanties are perfect vantage points for sunsets on the sand.

Beach Regions

Puerto Vallarta

Paralleling the Romantic Zone, Playa los Muertos is PV's most popular beach, with restaurants and bars with music; vendors selling barbecued fish on a stick; and people cruising the boardwalk. The beaches in the Hotel Zone and Marina Vallarta are a bit dull by comparison. At the south end of the bay are beautiful mountain-backed *playas* accessible only by boat.

Nuevo Vallarta

WHERE WE ARE

One wide, flat, sandy beach stretches north of the Ameca River mouth for miles into the town of Bucerías. The generally calm water is good for swimming and, when conditions are right, bodysurfing or boogie boarding. Activities are geared to all-inclusive hotel guests north of

Paradise Village marina. Guys on the beach rent water-sports equipment, and most of the hotels rent equipment, too.

Southern Nayarit

Rocky headlands sandwich scallops of sand from Bucerías to Chacala. These beaches attract boogie boarders, beachcombers, and those who make their own fun, as there are fewer services than in Vallarta. Surfing is big at Punta de Mita. Guayabitos, with its offshore island, is a vacation mecca for Mexican families and a refuge for (mainly) Canadian snowbirds. Off the main highway, long, sandy roads lead to more isolated beaches.

The Costalegre

This is the domain of the independent traveler and the well-heeled recluse. High-end hotels on picturesque, rock-framed beaches arrange fishing and other pastimes. Other long, sandy beaches—many on large, semi-protected bays—are frequented by fishermen and local people relaxing at seafood shanties, and allow shelling, snorkeling, fishing, and trips to offshore islands. Having a car is almost required, and services are negotiated directly with locals on the beach.

PUERTO VALLARTA

PV beaches include those between Marina Vallarta in the north and those accessible by boat only, south of Vallarta proper from Las Animas to Yelapa. The wild beaches on Cabo Corriente, which didn't have electricity until the 1970s, tend to fill up with day-trippers between December and April. Downtown Vallarta's main beach, Los Muertos, is a fun scene, with shoulder-to-shoulder establishments for drinking and eating under the shade, and year-round action. The itinerant vendors can be annoying, however. At Los Muertos as well as the Hotel Zone and Marina Vallarta, beaches have Jet Skis, parasailing, and banana-boat rides in high season (December–April) and on weekends year-round.

Getting There

The only public beach access (with on-street parking) at Marina Vallarta is between the airport and Condominios Grand Bay. There's little to stop you from walking through the major hotels, though, if you take a bus or cab to the area. The Hotel Zone and Centro beaches are easily accessed from the street. Take a bus, a cab, or drive your car; there's curbside parking but no parking lots to speak of.

Downtown Puerto Vallarta

Playa los Muertos is PV's original happenin' downtown beach. Facing Vallarta's South Side (south of the Río Cuale), this flat beach runs about 1 ½ km (1 mi) south to a rocky point called El Púlpito. Joggers cruise the cement boardwalk (interrupted by sandy areas) early morning and after sunset; vendors stalk the beach nonstop, hawking kites, jewelry, and sarapes as well as hair-braiding and alfresco massage. Their parade can range from entertaining (good bargainers can get excellent deals) to downright maddening. Restaurant-bars run the length of the beach;

the bright blue umbrellas near the south end of the beach belong to the Blue Chairs resort, the hub of PV's effervescent gay scene.

The surf ranges from mild to choppy with an undertow; the small waves crunching the shore usually discourage mindless paddling. Strapping young men occasionally occupy the lifeguard tower, and local people fish from the small pier at the foot of Calle Francisca Rodríguez or cast nets from waist-deep water near the south end of the beach. Jet Skis zip around, but stay out beyond the small breakers, and are not too distracting to bathers and sunbathers. Guys on the beach offer banana-boat and parasailing rides. ■ TIP→ The steps (more than 100) at Calle Púlpito lead to a lookout with a great view of the beach and the bay.

> **BEACH OF THE DEAD**
>
> There are several versions of how Playa los Muertos got its name. One says that around the time it was founded, Indians attacked a mule train laden with silver and gold from the mountain towns, leaving the dead bodies of the muleters on the beach. A version crediting pirates with the same deed seems more plausible. In 1935, anthropologist Dr. Isabel Kelly postulated that the place was an Indian cemetery.

Playa Olas Altas means High Waves Beach, but the only waves suitable for body surfing or boogie boarding are near the Cuale River, at the north end of this small beach. Although Olas Altas more often refers to the neighborhood of bars and businesses near the ocean south of the Río Cuale, it is also the name of a few blocks of sand between Daiquiri Dick's restaurant and the Río Cuale. It attracts fewer families than Los Muertos, but is otherwise an extension of that beach. Olas Altas Beach has open-air stands selling beach accessories, small grocery stores, leafy Lázaro Cárdenas Plaza, and easy access to beach-facing bars and restaurants.

The rock-strewn beach paralleling the malecón and the beach hotels like Rosita and El Pescador just north of it is **Playa Camarones**. Hurricane Kenna (2003) stole *mucho arena* (a lot of sand), however, and most people prefer to walk along the cement boardwalk than the beach here. Likewise, although the waves are gentle, the ocean floor is rocky and most bathers opt for the hotel pool. What you see here most often are small groups of men and boys surf casting, more for diversion than for hopes of great catches.

North of Downtown

The high-rise-backed **Zona Hotelera and Marina Vallarta beaches** have several names—**Playa las Glorias** to the south, **Playa los Tules** in the middle (around the Holiday Inn and Fiesta Americana), and **Playa El Salado** to the north. Most people, however, just refer to each beach by the hotel that it faces. These gray-beige, coarse-sand beaches are generally flat with a slope down to the water. Major winds and tides sometimes strew them with stones that make it less pleasant. The Sheraton and its beachfront, at the south end of the strip, were hit hard by Hurricane Kenna in 2003, and tons of sand was trucked in, in 2005. The beach in front of it is

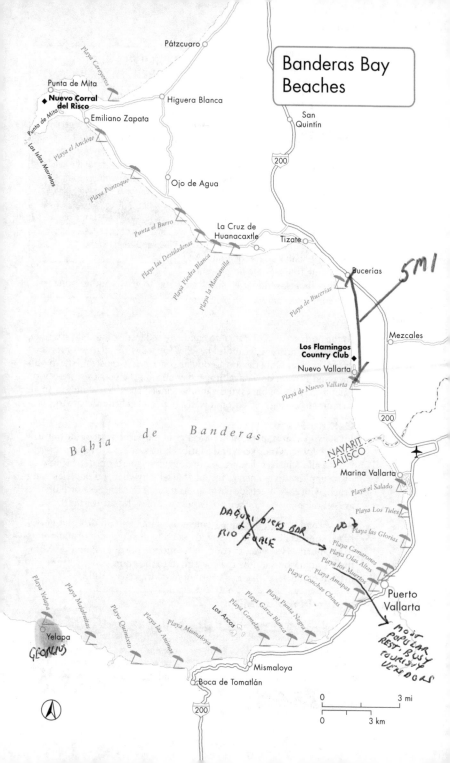

Banderas Bay Beaches

Pátzcuaro

Punta de Mita
Nuevo Corral del Risco
Playa Careyeros
Punta de Mita
Las Islas Marietas
Emiliano Zapata
Playa el Anclote
Higuera Blanca
San Quintín
200
Playa Pontoque
Ojo de Agua
Punta el Burro
La Cruz de Huanacaxtle
Tizate
Playa las Destiladeras
Playa Piedra Blanca
Playa la Manzanilla
Bucerías
5 MI
Playa de Bucerías
Mezcales
Los Flamingos Country Club
Nuevo Vallarta
Playa de Nuevo Vallarta
200

Bahía de Banderas

NAYARIT
JALISCO

Marina Vallarta
Playa el Salado
Playa Los Tules
Playa las Glorias
DAQURI DICKS BAR
RIO QUALE
NO ?
Playa Camarones
Playa Olas Altas
Playa los Muertos
Playa Conchas Chinas
Playa Amapas
Puerto Vallarta

Playa Yelapa
Playa Majahuitas
Playa Quimixto
Playa las Ánimas
Playa Mismaloya
Los Arcos
Playa Gemelas
Playa Garza Blanca
Playa Punta Negra
MOST POPULAR REST, BUSY TOURISTY VENDORS

Yelapa
GEORGES

Mismaloya
Boca de Tomatlán
200

0   3 mi
0   3 km

therefore sandier than its neighbors, although still pocked with smooth egg-size rocks.) At Marina Vallarta, Playa El Salado—facing the Grand Velas, Meliá, Marriott, Mayan Palace, and the Westin—is pleasantly sandy.

Colorful in high season with parasailers and with windsurfers rented or lent at area hotels, these beaches are actually more fun when crowded than when solitary. During fine weather and on weekends, and daily during high season, you can rent Jet Skis and pack onto colorful banana boats for bouncy 10-minute tours. Some hotels rent small sailboats, sailboards, and sea kayaks to guests and to nonguests.

BEACH BLANKET BOTHER

Although it might feel rude, it's culturally permissible to simply ignore itinerant vendors, especially if you're in the middle of a conversation. However, being blatantly impolite (i.e., shouting at the vendor to take a hike) *is* rude—no matter where you're from. A wide grin and a firm *"No, gracias,"* with no further eye contact, is the best response—apart from "Yes, please, I'll take it," that is!

NAYARIT

At the northern end of Bahía de Banderas and farther into Nayarit state, to the north, are long, beautiful beaches fringed with tall trees or scrubby tropical forest. Only the most popular beaches like those of Nuevo Vallarta and Rincón de Guayabitos have much in the way of water-sports equipment rentals, but even the more secluded ones have stands or small restaurants serving cold coconut water, beer, and grilled fish with tortillas.

Getting There

In Nuevo Vallarta, park on the street or in the parking lot of the tourism office, between Gran Velas and Maribal hotels. Buses arrive here as well, but the all-inclusives that predominate cater to guests only, so bring your own supplies. It's a cinch to install yourself anywhere on Bucerías' long beach, with easy streetside parking. As most of the beaches north of here are off the main road, they are easiest to access by car (or taxi).

A new road (rather, the improvement of an old, narrow dirt-and-gravel road) connects Punta de Mita with Sayulita, San Francisco, and points to the north. However, if your destination is north of Punta de Mita, there's no need to follow the coast road to the point. Simply bear right instead of left after Bucerís, continuing on Carretera 200.

Nuevo Vallarta to Punta de Mita

Several kilometers of pristine, if plain, beach face the hotels of **Playa Nuevo Vallarta.** The wide, flat, sandy beach is perfect for long walks: in fact, you could walk all the way to Bucerías, some 8 km (5 mi) to the north. Most of the hotels here are all-inclusives, so guests generally move between their hotel pool, bar, restaurant, and the beach in front. The same all-inclusive program means that nonguests are generally barred from the bars and restaurants.

Bucerías Eighteen kilometers (11 mi) north of Nuevo Vallarta, the substantial town of Bucerías attracts a loyal flock of snowbirds, which has encouraged the establishment of small hotels, apartments for rent, and good restaurants. The beach here is endless: you could easily walk along its medium-coarse beige sands all the way south to Nuevo Vallarta. The surf is gentle enough for swimming, but also has body-surfable waves, and beginning surfers occasionally arrive with their longboards.

> ### A SHADY DEAL
>
> You can spread a blanket on the sand, but because the strong sun can burn you to a crisp or even cause sunstroke, it's a better idea to rent a *palapa* (typical shade structure of wood and palm thatch) for shade. These generally cost around $5 a day, with no deals for shorter stays. Beachfront hotels and restaurants have their own tables and chairs on or near the sand for those who order at least a soda.

Just north of Bucerías, **La Cruz de Huanacaxtle,** better known as simply "La Cruz," has a fishing fleet but not much of a beach. Like other Vallarta–Nayarit beaches, homey La Cruz is growing and becoming somewhat more sophisticated. On the north side of La Cruz, **Playa la Manzanilla** is a crescent of soft, gold sand where kids play in the shallow water while their parents sip cold drinks at one of several seafood shacks. It's somewhat protected by the Piedra Blanca headland to the north.

A few miles north of Piedra Blanca headland, **Destiladeras** is a 1 ½-km-long (1-mi-long) beach with white sand and good waves for bodysurfers and boogie-boarders. There's nothing much here except for a couple of seaside *enramadas* (thatch-roof shelters) serving filets of fish and ceviche. **Punta el Burro,** at the north end of the beach, is a popular surf spot often accessed by boat from Punta de Mita.

Punta de Mita, about 40 km (25 mi) north of Puerto Vallarta, is home to the posh Four Seasons and the boutique resort Casa Las Brisas; other exclusive developments, including a number of private villas, are under construction. Just a few minutes past the entrance to the Four Seasons, the popular beach at **El Anclote** has a string of restaurants of increasing sophistication. This is a primo spot for viewing a sunset. Artificially calmed by several rock jetties and shallow for quite a ways out, it's also a good spot for children and average to not-strong swimmers to paddle and play, but there's a long slow wave for surfing, too. Under an improvised palm-thatch shelter, jewelry and sarape sellers play cards with fishermen as both wait patiently for customers.

Accessible from El Anclote or the adjacent town of **Nuevo Corral del Risco,** Punta de Mita has the most surf spots in the region, nearly a dozen, and the long swells here pump year-round.

Divers favor the fairly clear waters and abundance of fish and coral on the bay side of the **Islas Marietas** about a half-hour offshore from El Anclote. In winter, especially January through March, these same islands are also a good place to spot orcas and humpback whales, which come to mate and give birth. Las Marietas is the destination for fishing, diving, and snorkeling; in addition, sealife viewing expeditions set out from El Anclote and Nuevo Corral de Risco as well as from points up and down Banderas Bay.

North of Banderas Bay

As is happening up and down the Pacific Riviera, real estate north of the bay is booming. Mexicans are selling family holdings, jaded gringos are building private homes, and speculators from around the globe are grabbing what land they can, on and off the beach. For now, however, the Nayarit coast continues to enchant, with miles of lovely beaches bordered by arching headlands and Pacific hamlets drowsing in the tropical sun.

> **WATER-TOY PRICES**
>
> Prices for water toys in and around Vallarta are fairly consistent:
>
> ■ wave runners:$45–50 per half hour (one or two riders)
> ■ parasailing:$35 for a 10-minute ride
> ■ banana-boat rides: $15 for 10-minute ride (usually 4 people minimum)
> ■ Hobie Cat or small sailboat: $30–$45 per hour

★ The increasingly popular town and beach of **Sayulita** is about 45 minutes north of PV on Carretera 200, just about 19 km (12 mi) north of Bucerías, and 35 km (22 mi) north of the airport. Some say it's like PV was 40 years ago, apart from the sounds of construction ringing through the sandy streets. Despite the growth, the small-town vibe is still generous and laid-back. Fringed in lanky palms, Sayulita's heavenly beach curves along its small bay. A decent shore break here is good for beginning or novice surfers; the left point break is a bit more challenging. Skiffs on the beach have good rates for surfing or fishing safaris in area waters.

★ Ten minutes north of Sayulita, **San Francisco** is known to most people by its nickname: San Pancho. Barely developed, it stretches between headlands to the north and south, and is accessed at the end of the town's main road: Avenida Tercer Mundo. You'll see men fishing from shore with nets as you walk the 1½-km-long (1-mi-long) beach of coarse beige sand. There's an undertow sometimes, but otherwise nothing to discourage strong swimmers. Its small waves occasionally support longboard surfing (especially in September), but this isn't a surf spot. In fact its small waves—too big for family splashing and too small for surfing—have probably maintained its innocence . . . until now. Popular with a hip crowd of European artists and intellectuals, San Pancho has just a few hotels but a growing number of good restaurants. Of the few beachfront restaurants in San Pancho, **La Perla**—serving burgers, tacos, fish filets, and lobster—is the most dependable.

About 8 km (5 mi) north of San Pancho, **Lo de Marcos** is a humble town of quiet, wide streets that sometimes fill up on weekends and holidays with Mexican families renting the nondescript, bungalow-style motel rooms that predominate. After entering town on the main street, head left on the last road before the beach to reach **Playa las Minitas**, a small brown-sand beach on a pretty little cove framed by rocks. When not camped out at a half-dozen seafood shanties specializing in barbecued fish, local people bob in the super-tranquil surf. Continue another ½ km (¼ mi) along the road to **Playa los Venados,** which like Las Minitas, is a good spot for both swimming and snorkeling.

From south to north, the main beaches of **Bahía de Jaltemba** are: Los Ayala, Rincón de Guayabitos, and La Peñita.

A mini version of Guayabitos (⇨ *below*), **Playa los Ayala** has a level beach, mild surf, and an excellent view of **Isla del Coral,** to which glass-bottom boats ferry passengers for about $6 per person. On weekends, holidays, and in high season take a ride on a banana boat; most any time you can find a skiff owner to take you to **Playa Fidrieras** or **Playa del Toro,** two pretty beaches for bathing that lie around the headland to the south, accessible only by boat. You can walk, however, over the hill at the south end of the beach to a seafood restaurant on a small scallop of beach.

★ A couple of kilometers north of Ayala along the highway, **Rincón de Guayabitos** bustles with legions of Mexican families on weekends and holidays; less visible are the foreigners who take up residence here during the winter months. Streets house modest hotels and identical shops selling cheap bathing suits and plastic beach toys. Colorfully painted stands on the sand sell fresh chilled fruit and coconuts; oceanfront *enramadas* serve up fresh seafood. This lovely beach bounded by headlands and the ocean is tranquil and perfectly suited for swimming.

Contiguous with Guayabitos, **La Peñita,** at the north end of the bay, has fewer hotels and the beach is often nearly abandoned. Its name means "little rock." The center for area business, La Peñita has banks, shoe stores, and ice-cream shops; a typical market held each Thursday offers knock-off CDs, polyester clothing, and fresh fruits and vegetables.

A few kilometers north of Peñita, a dusty road leads to **Boca de Naranjo,** a long, secluded sandy beach with excellent swimming. The rutted dirt road from the highway, although only about 4 km (2½ mi) long, takes almost a half hour to negotiate in most passenger cars. Enjoy great views of the coastline from one of nearly a dozen seafood shanties. Turtles nest here in August and September.

TURTLE RESCUE

In San Pancho, **Grupo Ecológico de la Costa Verde** (Green Coast Ecological Group; ✉ Av. Latino América 102, San Pancho ☎ 311/258-4100 or 311/258-4135 🌐 www.project-tortuga.org) works to save the olive ridley, leatherback, and eastern Pacific green turtles that once swamped area beaches.

Encouraged to dedicate two to six months to the cause, volunteers patrol beaches, collect eggs, maintain the nursery, tabulate data, and educate the public about their program. The group has helped increase the number of nesting females in the area from 72 in 1991 to 641 in 2004.

Some 30 km (19 mi) north north of Rincón de Guayabitos, **Chacala** is another 9 km (5 mi) from the highway through exuberant vegetation. Although most people are content to dine or drink at the handful of eateries right on the beach while imbibing the soft-scented sea air and the sight of the green-blue sea, you can bodysurf and boogie board here, too. Swimming is safest under the protective headland to the north of the cove; surfing is often very good, but you have to hire a boat to access the point break.

GO FOR:	IN PV	NORTH OR SOUTH OF PV
WILDLIFE	Los Arcos	Kayak adventures from La Manzanilla (Bahía Tenacatita); Islas Marietas (Punta de Mita)
SNORKELING	Los Arcos; Playa Conchas Chinas	Islas Marietas; Playa Mora
WALKING OR JOGGING	Playa los Muertos	Nuevo Vallarta; Bucerís; Barra de Navidad and San Patricio Melaque (Bahía de Navidad)
CALM, SWIMMABLE WATERS	Hotel pool	Los Ayala, Rincón de Guayabitos (Bahía de Jaltemba); Playa Las Minitas; Boca de Naranjo; Playa Chalacatepec
SURFING	N/A	El Anclote (Punta de Mita); Sayulita; Quimixto; Barra de Navidad
EATING/DRINKING WITH LOCALS	Boca de Tomatlán	Chacala; Rincón de Guayabitos (Bahía de Jaltemba); Playa Tenacatita; Colimilla (Bahía de Navidad)

SOUTH OF PUERTO VALLARTA

While coastal Nayarit is jumping on the development bandwagon, the isolated beaches of Cabo Corriente and those of southern Jalisco—some surrounded by ecological reserves—continue to languish for the time being in peaceful abandon. Things here are still less formal, and aside from the super-posh resorts like El Tamarindo, the Careyes, and Las Alamandas, whose beaches are off-limits to nonguests, words like "laid-back" and "run-down" or "very basic" still apply, much to the delight of adventurous types.

Getting There

Catch a green bus to Conchas Chinas, Mismaloya, or Boca de Tomatlán from the southwest corner of Calle Basilio Badillo and Constitución, Col. E. Zapata in Puerto Vallarta. Give the driver sufficient notice when you want to get off; pulling over along the narrow highway is challenging.

There are several ways to reach the beaches of southern Banderas Bay. Party boats (aka booze cruises) and privately chartered boats leave from Marina Vallarta's cruise-ship terminal (⇨ Chapter 7) and generally hit Las Animas, Quimixto, Majahuitas, and/or Yelapa. You can also hire a water taxi from Boca de Tomatlán ($6 one-way, usually on the hour 9 AM through noon, and again in early afternoon), from the pier at Los Muertos ($20 round-trip, 11 AM and in high season at 10:15 AM), or from the tiny pier next to Hotel Rosita ($20 round-trip, 11:30 AM).

■ TIP➜ **If not full, the water taxi from Hotel Rosita will stop at Los Muertos to pick up passengers.** You can catch the 4 PM taxi from Los Muertos to Yelapa if you're planning to spend the night; it will not return until the next day. Pangas (skiffs) can be hired at Boca, Mismaloya, or Los Muertos. The price depends on starting and ending points, but runs about $35 per hour for up to eight passengers.

It's best to have your own car for exploring the Costalegre, as many beaches are a few kilometers—down rutted dirt roads—from the highway. However, if you want to hang out in the small but tourist-oriented towns of San Patricio–Melaque and Barra de Navidad, you may not need wheels.

Southern Banderas Bay & Cabo Corrientes

★ Frequented mainly by visitors staying in the area, **Playa Conchas Chinas** is a series of rocky coves with crystalline water. Millions of tiny white shells, broken and polished by the waves, form the sand; rocks that resemble petrified cowpies jut into the sea, separating one patch of beach from the next. These individual coves are perfect for reclusive sunbathing and, when the surf is mild, for snorkeling around the rocks; bring your own equipment. It's accessible from Calle Santa Barbara, the continuation of the cobblestone coast road originating at the south end of Los Muertos Beach, and also from Carretera 200 near El Set restaurant. Swimming is best at the cove just north of La Playita de Lindo Mar, below the Hotel Conchas Chinas (where the beach ends), as there are fewer rocks in the water. You can walk—be it on the sand, over the rocks, or on paths or steps built for this purpose—from Playa Los Muertos all the way to Conchas Chinas. The beach does not have services.

Though **Punta Negra,** about a mile south of Conchas Chinas, lost a lot of sand and allure during Hurricane Kenna, waves usually break gently on shore and the water is usually glassy and nice for swimming. It is accessible from Carretera a Mismaloya (Carretera 200) down a somewhat steep stone-and-cement path. Park off the highway at the north end of Condominios Jalisco Vacactional, near the blue Playa Punta Negra sign. The beach is mainly big round rocks, with little sand. There's shade under several tall trees sprouting from an old foundation, but there's sometimes trash from previous picnics. The beach has no facilities.

Playa Garza Blanca, or "White Heron Beach," is a mirror image of Punta Negra Beach about half a

> **WORD OF MOUTH**
>
> "Mismaloya Beach is a great spot if you want to hang out with the locals away from the tourists. Restaurants line the beach and you can have lunch with your feet in the sand as the waves come right up to your table. We even got massages on the beach after lunch for a great deal . . . two one-hour massages for 500 pesos."
>
> –twinkee

mile away at the opposite end of the narrow cove. It's also signed, and accessible on foot by a dirt path. The beach does not have facilities.

Playa Mismaloya is the cove where *The Night of the Iguana* was made. Unfortunately, Hurricane Kenna stole much of Mismaloya's white sand. A half-dozen full-service seafood restaurants crouch above what's left of the beach on the south side of a wooden bridge over the mouth of Río Mismaloya. The place retains a certain *caché,* and a pretty view of the famous cove. The tiny village of Mismaloya is on the east side of Carretera 200, about 13 km (8 mi) south of PV.

Boca de Tomatlán is both the name of a small village and a rocky cove that lie at the mouth of the Río Tomatlán, about 5 km (3 mi) south of Mismaloya and 17 km (10½ mi) south of PV. Water taxis leave from Boca to the southern beaches; you can arrange snorkeling trips to Los Arcos. Five seaside cafés cluster at the water's edge.

There's lots to do besides sunbathe at **Playa las Ánimas,** a largish beach 15 minutes south of Boca de Tomatlán by boat, so it tends to fill up with families on weekends and holidays. The usual seafood eateries line the sand, and you can also rent Jet Skis, ride a banana boat, or soar up into the sky behind a speedboat while dangling from a colorful parachute.

Between the sandy stretches of Las Animas and Majahuitas, and about 20 minutes by boat from Boca de Tomatlán, rocky **Quimixto** has calm, clear waters that attract boatloads of snorkelers. There's just a narrow beach here, with a few seafood eateries. Day-trippers routinely rent horses ($15 round-trip; ask at the restaurants) for the 25-minute ride—or only slightly longer walk—to a large, clear pool under a waterfall. You can bathe at the fall's base, and then have a cool drink at the casual restaurant. There's a fun, fast wave at the reef here, popular with surfers but because of its inaccessibility, rarely crowded.

Majahuitas—between the beaches of Quimixto and Yelapa and about 35 minutes by boat from Boca de Tomatlán—is the playground of people on day tours and guests of the exclusive Majahuitas Resort. The beach has no services for the average José; the lounge chairs and bathrooms are for hotel guests only. Palm trees shade the white beach of broken, sea-buffed shells. The blue-green water is clear, but tends to break right on shore.

The secluded village and ½-km-long (¼-mi-long) beach of **Yelapa** is about an hour southeast of downtown or a half hour from Boca de Tomatlán. Several seafood *enramadas* (thatch-roof huts) edge its fine, clean, grainy sand. During

> ## SNORKELING SANCTUARY
>
> Protected area **Los Arcos** is an offshore group of giant rocks rising some 65 feet above the water, making the area great for snorkeling and diving. For reasonable fees, local men along the road to Mismaloya Beach run diving, snorkeling, fishing, and boat trips here and as far north as Punta de Mita and Las Marietas or the beach villages of Cabo Corrientes. Restaurants at Playa Mismaloya can also set you up.

Lingering in Yelapa

If you can't tear yourself away at the end of the day (or you miss the last water taxi), consider renting one of the locally run rustic accommodations near the beach. Modest but charming, Hotel La Lagunita (closed in the rainy season) has rooms right over the water; "rustic chic" describes La Verana hotel, a five-star property represented by Mexico Boutique Hotels.

If you're lucky enough to be staying in Yelapa, ask around for Oscar "Burrito" (everyone here knows everyone else), a young local man who leads inexpensive tours to the Los Veranos canopy zip line with lunch afterward at Las Animas beach. Rudolfo Garcia (322/209–5064, 044–322/107–4642

cell) leads trips to a secluded southern beach for swimming and a trek to a clandestine waterfall.

Back in Yelapa, check out the candle-lighted Club Yates disco on the south side of the estuary (Wednesday and Saturday nights during high season, December through Easter week) and holidays. Or ask around for one of several yoga classes, or schedule a therapeutic massage with Claudia (322/209–508; $50).

But the best part of staying in Yelapa is that after the booze cruises decamp and the water taxis put in for the night, you'll have the cool and groovy place to yourself.

4

---

high season, parasailers float high above it all. From here you can hike 20 minutes into the jungle to see the small Cascada Cola del Caballo (Horse's Tail Waterfall), with a pool at its base for swimming. (The falls are often dry near the end of the dry season, especially April–early June.) A more ambitious expedition of several hours brings you to less-visited, very beautiful Cascada del Catedral (Cathedral Falls).

But, for the most part, Yelapa is *tranquilisimo:* a place to just kick back in a chair on the beach and sip something cold. Seemingly right when you really need her, Cheggy the pie lady will show up with her fantastic homemade pies.

Phones and electricity arrived in Yelapa around the turn of the 21st century. ■ TIP➔ But bring all the money you'll need, as there is nothing as formal as a bank.

Just south of the end of Banderas Bay are the lovely beaches of pristine, wonderful, fairly inaccessible **Cabo Corrientes.** These take an effort to visit, and preferably, a four-wheel-drive vehicle, although a sturdy, high-clearance vehicle will do. Public transportation goes there and back once a day from the small town of El Tuito (40 km/[25 mi] south of Puerto Vallarta) along a rutted dirt road.

A somewhat difficult 40 km (25 mi) from the highway, the tiny town of **Aquiles Serdán** lies between the ocean and a river-fed lagoon. Boats hired here give access to miles of solitary, sandy beaches where primitive camping is permitted—providing you bring all of your own supplies and clean up after yourself. To get to Aquiles Serdán, bear right at the fork just past the village of Los Conejos.

Bearing left (and then right) just past Los Conejos brings you to bucolic **Tehualmixtle**, a sheltered cove that has, in addition to several restaurants, places to camp and basic rooms to rent. The pristine beach invites snorkeling and diving (bring your own equipment). Or you can explore the inland area with the help of an experienced guide at CandelaRío's palapa (no phone).

THE COSTALEGRE

Most people come to the Costalegre (www.costalegre.ca)—dubbed "The Happy Coast" by Jalisco's tourism authorities—to stay at luxury accommodations on lovely, clean beaches: Hotelito Desconocido, Las Alamandas, the Careyes, and El Tamarindo. Others head to southern Jalisco state without reservations to explore the coast at their leisure. Whether you kick back at an elegant resort or explore the wild side, the area between Cabo Corrientes and Barra de Navidad, at the southern extreme of the state, will undoubtedly delight.

Getting There

It's optimum to explore the beaches of southern Jalisco by car, SUV, or small RV. Camping is permitted on most beaches, and these are most often down a long dirt road from the highway. Fill up with gas at every opportunity, as gas stations are numbered. If you're in a rental car, reset the odometer and look for the kilometer signs at the side of the road. If you're driving a car marked in miles, not kilometers, the road signs are still useful, as many addresses are simply "Carretera 200" or "Carretera a Barra de Navidad" along with the number of kilometers the place is from Puerto Vallarta. Buses leave from the **Central Camionero** (⊠ Carretera Puerto Vallarta, Tepic [Carretera 200], Km 9, Col. Las Mojoneras ☏ 322/290–1009) in Puerto Vallarta.

Costalegre

The nicest beaches, with services, are now the private domain of Gran Turismo (5-star-plus) hotels. However, there are some delightful, pristine, and mainly isolated beaches along the Costalegre, most with few services aside from the ubiquitous seafood enramadas serving fish filets and fresh ceviche.

A sylvan beach with no services, **Playa Chalacatepec** lies down a packed dirt road about 82 km (50 mi) south of El Tuito and 115 km (70 mi) south of Puerto Vallarta. The road to the beach is rutted and negotiable only by high-clearance passenger cars and smallish RVs. The reward for 8 km (5 mi) of bone-jarring travel is a beautiful rocky point, Punta Chalacatepec, with a sweep of protected white-sand beach to the north perfect for swimming, bodysurfing, and hunting for shells. Admire the tidepools at the point during low tide; take a walk of several kilometers along the open-ocean beach south of the point, where waves crash more dramatically, discouraging swimming. To get here, turn right into the town of José María Morelos (at Km 88). Just after 8 km (5 mi), leave the main road (which bears right) and head to the beach over a smaller track. From there it's less than a 1½ km (1 mi) to the beach.

The handful of islands just offshore of lovely **Bahía de Chamela**, about 131 km (81 mi) south of PV, protect the beaches from strong surf. The best place on the bay for swimming is **Playa Perula** (turnoff at Km 76, then 3 km/[2 mi] on dirt road), in the protective embrace of a cove just below the Punta Perula headland. Fishermen there take visitors out to snorkel around the islands or to hunt for dorado, tuna, and mackerel; restaurants sitting on the coarse beige sand sell the same as fresh filets and ceviche. The sand curves the length of the 8-km-long (5-mi-long) bay to **Playa Negrita**, with camping and RV accommodations and plenty of opportunities for shore fishing, swimming, and snorkeling. Almost every pretty beach in Mexico has its own humble restaurant; this one is no exception.

About 11 km (6½ mi) south of Bahía Chamela, **Playa Careyes** is a lovely soft-sand beach framed by headlands. When the water's not too rough, snorkeling is good around the rocks, where you can also fish.

You can walk south from Playa Careyes along the dunes to **Playa Teopa**, although guards protect sea turtle nests by barring visitors without written permission during the summer and fall nesting seasons. A road from the highway at Km 49.5 gains access to Playa Teopa by car; ask for written permission at Hotel El Careyes, a few kilometers to the north, or just roll up in your car and try your luck.

★ Named for the bay on which it lies, **Playa Tenacatita** is a lovely beach of soft sand about 34 km (20 mi) north of San Patricio Melaque and 172 km (106 mi) south of Puerto Vallarta. Dozens of identical seafood shacks line the shore; birds cruise the miles of beach, searching for their own fish. Waves crash against clumps of jagged rocks at the north end of the beach, which curves gracefully around to a headland. The water is sparkling blue. There's camping for RVs and tents at Punta Hermanos, where the water is calm, and local men offer fishing excursions. ■ TIP→ Of the string of restaurants on the beach, La Fiesta Mexicana is especially recommended.

★ On the north end of Playa Tenacatita, **Playa Mora** has a coral reef close to the beach, making it an excellent place to snorkel.

A little more than 6 km (4 mi) south of Bahía de Tenacatita at Km 20, is the entrance to down-at-the-heels **Bahía de los Angeles Locos** all-inclusive hotel; the buffed-out naturalistic resort at **Punta Serena**; and **Coconuts by the Sea** guesthouse, all of which enjoy lovely breezes from their hilltop aeries.

Farther south along Tenacatita Bay, **Playa Boca de Iguanas** is a wide, flat beach of fine gray-blond sand that stretches for several kilometers north of Playa Tenacatita. Gentle waves make it great for swimming, boogie boarding, and snorkeling, but beware the undertow. There are two RV parks here, and a couple of beach restaurants. The entrance is at Km 17.

Two-kilometer-long (1-mi-long) **Playa la Manzanilla** is little more than a kilometer in from the highway, on the southern edge of Bahía de Tenacatita, 193 km (120 mi) south of Puerto Vallarta and 25 km (15½ mi) north of Barra de Navidad (at Km 14). Informal hotels and restaurants are interspersed with small businesses and modest houses along the main street of the town. Rocks dot the gray-gold sands and edge both ends of the wide beach. The bay is calm. At the beach road's north end, gigantic, rubbery-looking crocodiles lie heaped together just out of harm's way in a mangrove swamp. The fishing here is excellent; boat owners on the beach can take you fishing for snapper, sea bass, and others for $20–$25 an hour.

Twenty-one kilometers (13 mi) south of La Manzanilla, **Bahía de Navidad** represents the end of the Costalegre at the border with Colima State. First up (from north to south) is **San Patricio–Melaque,** the most populous town on the Costalegre, with about 12,000 people. (The town is actually two towns that have now met in the middle.) While parts of town look dilapidated or abandoned, its long, coarse-white-sand beach is rather beautiful, with gentle waves. ■ TIP→ The best swimming and boogie boarding is about half the length of town, in front of El Dorado restaurant.

Fishermen congregate at the west end of San Patricio–Melaque, but it's most common to hire a panga for fishing at **Barra de Navidad** (usually called just "Barra"), a laid-back little town with sandy streets. At any time but at high tide you can walk between San Patricio and Barra, a distance of about 6 km (4 mi). It's about 4.5 km (3 mi) on the highway from one town to the other.

Most of Barra is comprised of two streets on a long sand bar. Calle Veracruz faces the vast lagoon and **Isla Navidad,** now home to the posh Gran Bay resort. Water taxis take folks to the Gran Bay's golf course or marina, or to the seafood restaurants of Colimilla, on the lagoon's opposite shore. Avenida Miguel de Legazpi faces Barra's sloping brown-sand beach and the ocean. These and connecting streets have small shops, simple but charming restaurants, and—like everywhere along Mexico's Pacific coast—a host of friendly townspeople. ■ TIP→ Surfers look for swells near the jetty, where the sea enters the lagoon.

Shopping

Huichol bowls

WORD OF MOUTH

"PV has lots to choose from. Nice, expensive stores to booths along the river to guys strolling the beaches. A popular craft is the Huichol bead or yarn art. I also try to look for local artisan goods. Jewelry, particularly silver, is common. You will have no trouble finding places to shop."

—MichelleY

It's hard to decide which is more satisfying: shopping in Puerto Vallarta, or feasting at its glorious restaurants. There's enough of both to keep a dedicated bon vivant busy for weeks. But while gourmands undoubtedly return home with enlarged waistlines or thighs, gluttonous shoppers need an extra suitcase or duffel for the material booty they bring home.

Puerto Vallarta's highest concentration of shops and restaurants share the same prime real estate: Old Vallarta. But as construction of hotels, time-shares, condos, and private mansions marches implacably north up the bay, new specialty stores and gourmet groceries follow the gravy train. To the south, the Costalegre is made up primarily of modest seaside towns and self-contained luxury resorts, and shopping opportunities are rare.

In Puerto Vallarta, more than a half dozen malls line "the airport road," Francisco M. Ascencio, which connects downtown with the hotel zone, the marina area, Nuevo Vallarta, and towns to the north. There you'll find folk art, comfortable resort clothing, and home furnishing stores tucked in amid supermarkets, and in some cases bars, movie theaters, and banks.

A 10%–15% value added tax, locally called IVA, officially the *impuesto al valor agregado* (*see* Taxes), is levied on most purchases, though it's often included in the price; it may be disregarded entirely by market vendors.

Smart Souvenirs

Arts & Crafts

Puerto Vallarta is an arts and crafts paradise, particularly if you're fond of ceramics, masks, fine art, and Huichol folk art ("The Art of the Huichol," *below*). Occasionally you'll find vivid handwoven and embroidered textiles from Oaxaca and Chiapas, and comfortable, family-size hammocks from Yucatán State. Handmade or silkscreened, blank greeting cards make inexpensive and lovely framed prints.

Glass & Pewter

Glassblowing and pewter were introduced by the Spanish. A wide range of decorative and utilitarian pewter items are produced in the area, as well as distinctive deep blue goblets, emerald-rimmed, chunky drinking glasses, and other glassware. All are excellent buys today.

Jewelry

Many PV shop owners travel extensively during the summer months to procure silver jewelry from Taxco, south of Mexico City.

Pottery

After Guadalajara and its satellite towns Tlaquepaque and Tonalá— which produce ceramics made using patterns and colors hundreds of years old— Puerto Vallarta is the best place in the region to buy pottery, and at reasonable prices. PV shops also sell Talavera (majolica or maiolica) pottery from Puebla.

Unusual Gifts

For less-than-obvious souvenirs, go traditional and consider a *molinillo,* a carved wooden beater for frothing hot chocolate; you can find these at street vendors or traditional markets for about $1.50. A set of 10 or so *tiras de papel* (string of colored tissue-paper cuts) in a gift shop will only set you back about $2. Handmade huaraches (traditional sandals) are hard to break in (get them wet and let them dry on your feet), but last for years.

Tips & Tricks

Better deals are often given to cash customers—even though credit cards are nearly always accepted—because stores must pay a commission to the credit-card companies. U.S. dollars are almost universally accepted, although most shops pay a lower exchange rate than a bank (or ATM) or *casa de cambio* (money exchange). You may have to pay 5% to 10% more on credit-card purchases.

Bargaining is expected in markets and by beach vendors, who may ask as much as two or three times their bottom line. Occasionally an itinerant vendor will ask for the real value of the item, putting the energetic haggler into the awkward position of offering far too little. One vendor says he asks *norteamericanos* "for twice the asking price, since they always want to haggle." The trick is to **know an item's true worth** by comparison shopping. It's not common to bargain for already inexpensive trinkets like key chains or quartz-and-bead necklaces or bracelets.

Shop early. Though prices in shops are fixed, smaller shops may be willing to bargain if they're really keen to make a sale. Anyone even slightly superstitious considers the first sale of the day to be good luck, an auspicious start to the day. If your purchase would get the seller's day started on the right foot, you might just get a super deal.

Hours of Operation

Most stores are open daily 10–8 or even later in high season. A few close for siesta at 1 PM or 2 PM, then reopen at 4 PM. Perhaps half of PV's shops close on Sunday; those that do open usually close up by 2 or 3 in the afternoon. Many shops close altogether during the low season (August or September through mid-October). We've noted this whenever possible; however, some shops simply close up for several weeks if things get excruciatingly slow. In any case, low season hours are usually reduced, so call ahead during that time of year.

WATCH OUT Watch that your credit card goes through the machine only once, so that no duplicates of your slip are made. If there's an error and a new slip needs to be drawn up, make sure the original is destroyed before your eyes. Another scam is to ask you to wait while the clerk runs next door ostensibly to use another business's phone or to verify your number—but really to make extra copies. Don't let your card leave a store without you. While these scams are not common in Puerto Vallarta and we don't advocate excessive mistrust, taking certain precautions doesn't hurt.

Don't buy items made from tortoiseshell or any sea turtle products: it's illegal and many of Mexico's turtle species are endangered or threatened. These items are also not allowed into the U.S., Canada, or the U.K. Cowboy boots, hats, and sandals made from the leather of endangered

Shopping in El Centro & Zona Romántica

A Page in the Sun **79**
AgroGourmet **75**
Alas de Aguila **38**
Alberto's **42**
Alfarería Tlaquepque **1**
Anfitrión de México **47**
Banderas Bay **71**
Boutique Osiris **4**
Caprichoso **5**
D'Paola **66**

El Instituto de la
Artesanía Jalisciense **45**
Etnica Boutique **80**
Galería 8 y Más **50**
Galería Arte
Latinoamericano **29**
Galería Corona **39**
Galería de Ollas **53**
Galería Em **6**
Galería Gradiva **72**
Galería Huichol **21**

Galería Indígena **31**
Galería Octavio **2**
Galería Pacífico **33**
Galería Uno **36**
Galería Vallarta **46**
Gallería Dante **69**
Gecko **7**
Gúeros **48**
Gutiérrez Rizo **56**
Huarachería Fabiola **55**

Jades Maya **25**
Joyas Finas Suneson **35**
Joyería El Opalo **22**
Joyería Yoler **78**
La Aldaba **52**
La Bohemia **8**
La Brisa **9**
La Casa del Habano **32**
La Cava **10**
La Piedra **76**

La Playa **11**	Mar de Sueños **26**	Olinalá **70**	Serafina **65**
La Surtidora **49**	María de Guadalajara . . .**14**	Peyote People **44**	Sergio Bustamante **28**
LANS **12**	México Místico **77**	Plaza Caracol **15**	Seven Deli **19**
Leornardo Galerías **30**	Mercado de Artesanías . .**51**	Plaza Genovesa **16**	Sirenas **68**
Ley **3**	Mercado Isla Río Cuale . .**54**	Plaza Marina **17**	Talavera Etc. **73**
Librería Guadalajara **13**	Mundo de Azulejos **57**	Plaza Neptuno **18**	The Book Store **60**
Libros Libros Books Books **23**	Mundo de Cristal **59**	Ponciana **67**	The Huichol Collection . .**27**
Lucy's CuCú Cabana **61**	Mundo de Pewter **58**	Querubines **41**	Ucho Bali **27**
Majolica Antica **37**	Myskova Beachwear Boutique **63**	Rebeca's **81**	Viva **64**
Manta Maya **62**	Oahu **43**	Rolling Stones **24**	Wild West **74**

SHOPPING IN SPANISH	
bakery: *panadería*	**jewelry store:** *joyería*
bookseller: *librería*	**market:** *mercado*
candy store: *dulcería* (sometimes sells piñatas)	**notions store:** *mercería*
	stationery store: *papelería*
florist: *florería*	**tobacconist:** *tabaquería*
furniture store: *mueblería*	**toy store:** *juguetería*
grocery store: *abarrotes*	**undergarment store:** *bonetería*
hardware store: *ferretería*	
health-food store: *tienda naturista*	

species such as crocodiles may also be taken from you at customs, as will birds, or stuffed iguanas or parrots. Both the U.S. and Mexican governments also have strict laws and guidelines about the import-export of antiquities. Check with customs beforehand if you plan to buy anything unusual or particularly valuable.

Although Cuban cigars are readily available, American visitors aren't allowed to bring them into the U.S. and will have to enjoy them while in Mexico. However, Mexico produces some fine cigars from tobacco grown in Veracruz. Mexican cigars without the correct Mexican seals on the individual cigars and on the box may be confiscated.

PUERTO VALLARTA

Department Stores

LANS (✉ Calle Juárez 867, at Pípila Centro ☎ 322/226–9100 ✉ Plaza Caracol, near Gigante supermarket, Blvd. Francisco M. Ascencio 2216, Zona Hotelera ☎ 322/226–0204) is a multilevel department store with clothing for men, women, and children: look for Perry Ellis khakis, Levi's, Lee, and Dockers shirts and trousers, and jeans from Colombia. The store also sells housewares; purses and Swatch watches; Samsonite luggage; ladies' perfume and makeup (Chanel, Gucci, Estée Lauder); and men's undies.

Groceries

If you crave country-style Texas sausage and other comfort foods from north of the border, try **AgroGourmet** (✉ Calle Basilio Badillo 222, Col. E. Zapata ☎ 322/222–5357). You can find oils (sesame, grapeseed, nut, virgin olive), locally made pastas, homemade spaghetti sauce, lox, real maple syrup, and agave "honey." A nice gift is the Mexican vanilla, in blown-glass containers. **Don Chuy's Wine & Deli** (✉ Calle Tercer Mundo s/n, San Pancho ☎ No phone) started out as a branch of AgroGourmet, and has the same eclectic assortment of food, condiments, and wines.

The most convenient market to the Romantic Zone, **Gutiérrez Rizo** (✉ Av. Constitución 136, between 5 de Febrero and Aquiles Serdan, Col. E Zapata ☎ 322/222–1367) has an ample liquor section, American-brand cereals, canned food, condiments, good produce, and ground-to-order coffee. **Ley** (✉ Av. México 1150, at Veracruz, Col. 5 de Diciembre ☎ 322/223–2878), a small standard grocery store with the usual supplies, is convenient to Colonia 5 de Diciembre and downtown Vallarta.

Malls

PV's most popular mall with locals, **Plaza Caracol** (✉ Blvd. Federico M. Ascencio, Km 2.5, Zona Hotelera, across from Fiesta Americana hotel ☎ 322/224–3239), aka Gigante Plaza, is lively and full on weekends and evenings, even when others are dead. Its anchors are the Gigante supermarket and the adjacent LANS department store. Surrounding these are tiny stores dispensing electronics and ice cream, fresh flowers, manicures, and inexpensive haircuts. Adding to the commercial center's appeal is the sixplex movie theater.

A few worthwhile jewelry shops still reside at **Plaza Genovesa** (✉ Blvd. Federico M. Ascencio s/n Zona Hotelera ☎ 322/224–4763), though the mall has suffered since Hurricane Kenna in 2002, and many shops are empty. A string of beachwear, curio, and jewelry shops face the mall on the south side.

Plaza Marina (✉ Carretera al Aeropuerto, Km 8, Marina Vallarta ☎ 322/221–0490), one long block north of Plaza Neptuno, has ATMs, dry cleaning, photo developing, a pharmacy, a café, and several bars. In the parking lot is a cupcake-size branch of the 8 Tostadas Restaurant (⇨ Chapter 3). The mall is anchored by the Comercial Mexicana supermarket. **Plaza Neptuno** (✉ Carretera al Aeropuerto, Km 7.5, Marina Vallarta ☎ No phone) is a small mall in the heart of the marina district with a number of fine-home-furnishing shops, several classy clothing boutiques, and just behind it, a few good, casual restaurants.

Markets

In the **Mercado de Artesanías** (✉ Calle Francisca Rodríguez, between Calles Matamoros and Miramar, at base of bridge ☎ No phone), flowers, piñatas, produce, and plastics share space in indoor and outdoor stands with souvenirs and lesser-quality crafts. Upstairs, locals eat at long-established, family-run restaurants. Small shops and outdoor market stalls sell an interesting mix of wares at the informal and fun **Mercado Isla Río Cuale** (✉ Dividing El Centro from Colonia E. Zapata: access at Calle Morales, Calle I. Vallarta, Calle Matamoros, Calle Constitución, and Calle Libertad, Av. Insurgentes ☎ No phone). Harley-Davidson kerchiefs, Che paintings on velvet, and Madonna icons compete with the usual synthetic lace tablecloths, shell and quartz necklaces, and silver jewelry amid postcards and key chains. The market is partially shaded by enormous fig and rubber trees and serenaded by the rushing river; a half dozen cafés and restaurants provide sustenance.

Specialty Stores

Art

Galería 8 y Más (✉ Calle Miramar 237, Centro ☎ 322/222–7971 ⊕ www.artismexico.com) started with eight Guadalajara artists and has expanded under new ownership to almost 50 artists from or residing in Jalisco. The large old building (which lacks air-conditioning) has glass, bronze, chalk, and oil paintings. **Galería Arte Latinoamericano** (✉ Calle Josefa O. de Domínguez 155, Centro ☎ 322/222–4406) sells contemporary art, primarily paintings. There are representative Indian portraits by Marta Gilbert and chunky village scenes—a cross between the Flintstones and Chagall—by Celeste Acevedo.

Galería Corona (✉ Calle Corona 164, Centro ☎ 322/222–4210 ⊕ www.galeria-corona.com) is a small shop with some sculpture and art jewelry as well as etherial and painterly portraits and landscapes in various genres. **Galería Em** (✉ Blvd. Francisco M. Ascencio 2758 Marina Vallarta ☎ 322/221–1728 ✉ Las Palmas II, Local 17, Marina Vallarta ☎ 322/221–2856) sells art glass, stained glass, glass sculpture, and jewelry made of glass. You can commission a piece, or watch the artisans work, at the Las Palmas workshop.

Contemporary painters based in Oaxaca are represented by **Galería Gradiva** (✉ Av. Ignacio L. Vallarta 179, Centro ☎ 322/222–1681), which is open by appointment only in September and October. The artist who created the whale sculpture at the entrance to Marina Vallarta produces the ocean-theme, more portable pieces shown in **Galería Octavio** (✉ Av. México 1115, Col. 5 de Diciembre ☎ 322/223–3492 ⊕ www.octavioarteenbronce.com). The lifelike bronze whales, dolphins, sea turtles, and sea lions range from table or desk size, on a wooden base, to larger, free-standing garden or patio models. The gallery is closed Sunday and often from August through October; call ahead.

★ **Galleria Dante** (✉ Calle Basilio Badillo 269, Col. E. Zapata ☎ 322/222–2477) is a 6,000-square-foot gallery (PV's largest) and sculpture garden with classical, contemporary, and abstract works by more than 50 Latin American artists. A pioneer in Puerto Vallarta, **Galería Pacífico** (✉ Calle Aldama 174, Centro ☎ 322/222–1982 ⊕ www.galeriapacifico.net), open since 1987, features the sculpture of Ramiz Barquet, who created the bronze *Nostalgia* piece on the malecón. Patrick Denoun is among the representational portrait artists; Brewster Brockmann paints contemporary abstracts. The gift shop sells less expensive items, including art books, figurines, and posters. You'll find wonderful, varied art in many mediums at **Galería Uno** (✉ Calle Morelos 561,

> ### WALKING AND GAWKING
>
> On Wednesday evenings during high season (late October–end of April), the PV art community hosts Old Town artWalk (⇨ Chapter 8). Participating galleries welcome lookie loos as well as serious browsers between 6 PM and 10 PM; most provide at least a cocktail. Look for signs in the windows of participating galleries, or pick up a map at any of them ahead of time.

Centro ☎ 322/222–0908). Owners Jan Lavender and Martina Gold-berg love to showcase local talent, and during the season host individ-ual shows that change up to three times a month. National and international artists represented include João Rodriguez, Esaú Andrade, and Daniel Palmer. **Galería Vallarta** (✉ Av. Juárez 263, Centro ☎ 322/222–0290 ⊕ www.gaeriavallarta.com) is notable since, in addition to a large cadre of fine artists showing watercolors, oils, mixed media, and sculptures of bronze, wood, and ceramics, it has a comprehensive col-lection of lithographs and art prints, from the likes of Frida Kahlo and Diego Rivera to contemporaries such as Marta Gilbert.

Tiny **Leonnardo Galerías** (✉ Calle Morelos 664–A, Centro ☎ 322/223–4755) showcases newer talent and is correspondingly less expensive than some of PV's other galleries. Internationally known **Sergio Bustamante** (✉ Av. Juárez 275, Centro ☎ 322/222–5480 ✉ Paseo Díaz Ordáz 716, Centro ☎ 322/223–1407 ✉ Paseo Díaz Ordáz 542, Centro ☎ 322/222–5480 ⊕ www.sergiobustamante.com.mx)—the creator of life-size brass, copper, and ceramic animals, mermaids, suns, and moons—has a team of artisans to execute his neverending pantheon of creative and quirky objets d'art, such as pots shaped like human torsos that sell for more than US$1,000. Paintings and jewelry are sold here as well.

Books & Periodicals

English-language books and magazines are found at **The Book Store** (✉ V. Carranza 334–A at Av. Insurgentes, Col. E. Zapata ☎ 322/322–3608). Owner Tom Barret stocks a little of everything in his diminutive storefront, mainly "beach reads" in the fiction department and books of self-discovery in the nonfiction arena. Some 200 books are special-ordered each week. **Librería Guadalajara** (✉ Plaza Genovesa, Av. Fran-cisco M. Ascencio s/n, Zona Hotelera ☎ 332/224–9084) sells books in English and Spanish, and educational toys. It's closed Sunday.

Libros Libros Books Books (✉ 31 de Octubre 127, Centro ☎ 322/222–7105) has more than 50 magazine titles in English, plus a small but respectable selection of English-language nonfiction and fiction. Folks read books they've bought or traded at outdoor café **A Page in the Sun** (✉ Calle Olas Altas 399, Col. E. Zapata ☎ 322/222–3608). The shelves tend to be full of romance novels and other light reading. **Seven Deli** (✉ Plaza Marina, 2 doors down from McDonald's, Marina Vallarta ☎ 322/221–0177) has the *Miami Herald* as well as *Cosmo, GQ, Vogue, People,* and *Marie Claire* in English, along with many Spanish-language magazines.

Ceramics, Pottery & Tile

Alfarería Tlaquepaque (✉ Av. México 1100, Centro ☎ 322/223–2121) is a large store with a ton of red-clay items traditional to the area—in fact, their predecessors were crafted before the 1st century AD. Talav-era and Talavera-style pottery are available at good prices. The 300 or so potters from the village of Juan Mata Ortiz add their touches to the intensely—sometimes hypnotically—geometric designs of their ances-tors from Paquimé. The place to buy this wondrous pottery is **Galería de Ollas** (✉ Calle Morelos 101, Local 3–B, Centro ☎ 322/223–1045).

Pieces range from about $60 to $10,000, with an average of about $400. Stop in during artWalk, or at the branch in Paradise Plaza if you're based in Nuevo Vallarta.

⚠ **Before you buy rustic ceramic plates, bowls, and cups, ask if there's lead in the glaze, unless you plan to use them for decoration only and not for food service.**

Majolica Antica (✉ Calle Corona 191, Centro ☎ 322/222–5118) sells just that, which, according to knowledgeable shop owner Antonio Cordero, is also called Talavera or tin-glazed pottery. You get a certificate of origin with each piece of beautiful ornamental tile, utilitarian pitcher, plate, or place setting. Buy machine-made tiles from Monterrey, painted locally, for about 60¢ each at **Mundo de Azulejos** (✉ Av. Venustiano Carranza 374, Col. E. Zapata ☎ 322/222–3292 ⊕ www.talavera-tile.com). Slightly sturdier at about $1 each are the handmade tiles. You can get mosaic tile scenes (or order your own design), a place setting for eight, hand-painted sinks, or any number of soap dishes, cups, saucers, plates, or doodads. Around the corner and run by family members, Mundo de Cristal (⇨ *below*) has more plates and tableware in the same genre.

★ Jackie Kilpatrick, who owns **Talavera Etc.** (✉ Av. Ignacio L. Vallarta 266, Col. E. Zapata ☎ 322/222–4100), is happy to share her knowlege of Talavera pottery. She sells the exclusive Uriarte line, the oldest maker of Talavera in Mexico (est. 1805), as well as reproductions of tiles from Puebla churches and small gift items. Look in the book to choose made-to-order pieces. The shop is closed Sunday, during lunch, and for two weeks in September.

Cigars

Guantanamera (✉ Calle Corona 186B, Centro ☎ 322/223–3513) sells Mexican and Cuban cigars. The Mexican tobacco, from Veracruz, is hand-rolled here in Vallarta. Drinks and coffee are served in the small bar. It's closed Sunday. At **La Casa del Habano** (✉ Aldama 170, Centro ☎ 322/223–2758) sells only Cuban cigars, starting at $3.50 each and topping out at $44 for a Cohiba Millenium 2000. You can smoke your stogey downstairs in the casual lounge while sipping coffee or a shot of liquor.

■ TIP→ **If you're bringing any Mexican cigars back to the States, make sure they have the correct Mexican seals on both the individual cigars and on the box. Otherwise they may be confiscated.**

Clothing

La Bohemia (✉ Calle Constitución, at Calle Basilio Badillo, Col. E. Zapata ☎ 322/222–3164 ✉ Plaza Neptuno, Av. Francisco M. Ascencio, Km 7.5, Plaza, Marina Vallarta ☎ 322/221–2160) sells elegant clothing, some of it designed by the equally elegant owner, Toody. You'll find unique jewelry, accessories, and the San Miguel shoe—the elegant yet comfortable footwear designed for walking on cobblestone streets like those of San Miguel and Puerto Vallarta. It's closed Sunday. **Boutique Osiris** (✉ Plaza Marina, Local F–6, Marina Vallarta ☎ 322/221–0732) has simple gauze, cotton, and linen clothing for day or evening wear, although it's more practical than formal or fancy. The specialty is plus sizes.

TRUE MEXICAN TALAVERA

Talavera, the style of blue-on-white or multicolor pieces—from tiles to plates and platters—is named for the Spanish town where it originated. Authentic Mexican Talavera (aka majolica or maiolica) is produced almost exclusively in Puebla and parts of Tlaxcala and Guanajuato. The process follows centuries-old "recipes" dictating the type and proportion of minerals used and the number of glazes applied. Look on the back or bottom of the piece for the factory name and state of origin. Manufacturers throughout Mexico use similar styles and colors to produce Talavera-style pieces, which should sell for much less.

La Bohemia sells the popular San Miguel shoe, which combines comfort and elegance in many styles and colors. **Caprichoso** (⊠ Plaza Neptuno, Av. Federico M. Ascencio, Km 7.5, Marina Vallarta ☎ 322/221–3067) sells sizes from XS to 2X. This is the only store in PV to stock the Oh My Gauze line of women's resortwear, and also sells Dunes, Juanita Banana, and unusual clothing by Chalí, with cut-out, painted flowers. Most of the inventory is cotton, including a smaller selection of clothing for men. **D'Paola** (⊠ Calle Basilio Badillo 258, Col. E. Zapata ☎ 322/223–2742) has a large and somewhat unusual selection of pashmina, purses, shawls, and lots of muslin (some painted or otherwise decorated) clothing. It's surrounded by other interesting shops. It's closed Sunday. Diminutive **Etnica Boutique** (⊠ Av. Olas Altas 388, Col. E. Zapata ☎ 322/222–6763) has a well-edited collection of cotton and linen dresses, shawls, purses, hats, sandals, and jewelry. A few items from Indonesia are mixed in with things from different regions of Mexico and Central America.

☾ **Gecko** (⊠ Condominios Puesto del Sol, Marina Vallarta ☎ 322/221–2165) is the place to go for beach togs for kids and teens. The selection of any one type of item isn't large, but there are bikinis, sunglasses, flip-flops, nice ball caps, and T-shirts. Board shorts and rash guards are stocked for surfers and wannabes. Facing the city hall across the main square, **Güeros** (⊠ Calle Zaragoza 160, Centro ☎ 322/222–0633) sells contemporary clothing with Huichol designs executed in subtle cross-stitch. All of the shirts, vests, and unstructured trousers for men and women are

★ 100% prewashed cotton; there's a small kids' clothing selection. **Mar de Sueños** (⊠ Leona Vicario 230–C, Centro ☎ 322/222–2662) carries classy Italian threads, including the stylish La Perla brand. The selection of linen blouses and exquisitely cut linen pants is perfect for PV's sultry climate. Or choose from Lycra™ tops, sexy silk lingerie, and several lines of bathing suits. Everything is top-notch and priced accordingly. It's closed Sunday.

★ **María de Guadalajara** (⊠ Puesta del Sol condominiums, Local 15–A, Marina, Marina Vallarta ☎ 322/221–2566 ⊠ Calle Morelos 550, Centro ☎ 322/222–2387 ⊕ www.mariaguadalajara.com) has inspired jewelry and a fabulous line of women's cotton clothing. It's DIY chic here: you choose the colorful triangular sash of your liking, miraculously transforming pretty-but-baggy dresses into flattering and stylish frocks. The color palette is truly inspired. The selection for men is limited. **Manta Maya** (⊠ Basilio Badillo 300 at Av. Constitución, Col. E. Zapata ☎ 322/223–5915) has mainly white- and cream-color women's and men's clothing, with the occasional brightly colored blouse or skirt tossed in for contrast. Like its sister stores in other resort cities, this small shop has smart clothes at reasonable prices.

Myskova Beachwear Boutique (⊠ Calle Basilio Badillo 278, Col. E. Zapata ☎ 322/222–6091) has its own line of bikinis, plus cover-ups, nylon slacks, and some items for children (sunglasses, bathing suits, flip-flops). There's a small line of jewelry, and Brazilian flip-flops for adults in a rainbow of colors. **Oahu** (⊠ Calle Juárez 314, Centro ☎ 322/223–1058) has men's surf and casual wear, including well-made flip-flops, high-quality T-shirts, as well as pint-size Hawaiian shirts for children. In fact, this is one of the best places to shop for children's casual wear and for water gear like board shorts and rash guards.

Rebeca's (⊠ Olas Altas 403, Col. E. Zapata ☎ 322/222–2320), open daily, has a large selection of beachwear, including shorts, pseudo-Speedos, and bathing trunks for men; and sandals and fashionable flip-flops, attractive tankinis, lots of bikinis, and a few one-piece suits for women. Most of the goods are manufactured in Mexico. For over-the-top ethnic clothing, stamped leather purses from Guadalajara and belt buckles from San Miguel, as well as clunky necklaces and bracelets of quartz, amber, and turquoise, head to **Serafina** (⊠ Calle Basilio Badillo 260, Col. E. Zapata ☎ 322/223–4594), which also sells wonderful tchotchkes. Worth a look for women with eclectic tastes is **Sirenas** (⊠ Basilio Badillo 252B, Col. E. Zapata ☎ 322/223–1925), a sister store to Serafina. Here, creative sisters from Tamaulipas State create chic and unusual, exuberant fantasy jewelry. Colorful clutches and makeup bags made from recycled packaging are an innovation from Mexico City. At this writing, the shop is filled with tight-fitting ribbed T-shirts edged in sequins and an assortment of ethnically inspired yet edgy and contemporary blouses and skirts from Indonesia and elsewhere. It's closed Sunday. Long-established **La Surtidora** (⊠ Morelos 256 at Guerrero, Centro ☎ 322/222–1439) may not have the most trendy clothes, but it does have men's guayabera shirts and ladies cotton and muslin blouses in a wide range of styles. **Ucho Bali** (⊠ Calle Lázaro Cárdenas 330, Col. E. Zapata ☎ 322/222–7175 ✉ Plaza Marina, Local 119, Marina Vallarta ☎ 322/209–0800) is a great place to purchase inexpensive, cool, beachy clothing for women, imported from Indonesia. There's an extensive collection of Bali batiks made into dresses of all lengths, long straight skirts, and sexy top-and-trouser outfits. The lightweight cotton shawls come in an array of colors, with same-color embroidery and sequins. There are outfits in sheer material and stacks of lovely sarongs. Most items are $20 or less.

Folk Art & Crafts

In addition to pewter, **Alas de Aguila** (⊠ Av. Juárez 547, at Calle Corona, Centro ☎ 322/222–4039 ⊙ Closed Sunday) has a wide selection of Talavera-style objects—from soap holders and liquid soap dispensers to pitchers, platters, and picture frames—in a variety of patterns. Quality is middle-of-the-road; prices are excellent. **El Instituto de la Artesanía Jalisciense** (⊠ Calle Juárez 284, Centro ☎ 322/222–1301) promotes Jalisco State's handicrafts, selling burnished clay bowls signed by the artist, blown glass, plates and bowls from Tonalá, and other items at fair prices. That said, Bustamante knockoffs and Huichol pieces in less-than-traditional themes (smiley faces not being one of the Huichols' typical motifs) are indications that quality is slipping. Still, there's a representative sampling of the state's ceramics, blue-and-red glassware, and *barro bruñido*: clay pieces finished by burnishing only. It's catercorner from La Plaza de Armas, and is open 9 to 9 daily.

Expansive **Galería Indígena** (⊠ Av. Juárez 628, Centro ☎ 322/223-0800) has an assortment of handicrafts: Huichol yarn paintings and beaded bowls and statuettes, real Talavera ceramics from Puebla, decorative pieces in painted wood, and many other items. Small, sweet-smelling **La Aldaba** (⊠ Isla Río Cuale, Local 23, Isla Río Cuale ☎ 322/223–3060), just east of the Avenida Insurgentes bridge, sells unique glass vases, metal wall sculptures, and small housewares.

★ Shop for inexpensive, one-of-a-kind folk art from Guerrero, Michoacán, Oaxaca, and elsewhere at **Lucy's CuCú Cabana** (⊠ Calle Basilio Badillo 259, Col. E. Zapata ☎ 322/222–1220). Note that Lucy closes during lunch, on Sunday, and in low season (mid-May through mid-October). Young artist Diego Mateos Gamboa, of Tonalá, creates hand-painted scenes using multiple tiles for **México Místico** (⊠ Lazaro Cardenas 175, Col. E. Zapata ☎ 322/223–1021), across from Plaza Lázaro Cárdenas. Themes are traditional, like pastoral scenes with donkeys and whitewashed villages. Stained glass can be custom ordered, or purchased ready-made with traditional motifs such as hummingbirds, bearded irises, lighthouses, and angelfish; or less-traditional motifs, such as the Harley-Davidson logo.

Purchase glassware from Jalisco and Guanajuato states in sets or individually at **Mundo de Cristal** (⊠ Av. Insurgentes 333, at Calle Basilio Badillo, Col. E. Zapata ☎ 322/222–1426). Also available are Talavera place settings and individual platters, pitchers, and decorative pieces. Look in the back of the store for high-quality ceramics with realistic portrayals of fruits and flowers. You can have your purchase packed, but shipping is left to you. It's closed Sunday and

> **EXPAT HUMOR**
>
> The co-owner of Lucy's CuCú Cabana is Gil Gevens, who writes quirky epistles, often at his own expense, or the expense of other expats, about life in Puerto Vallarta. Gil writes regularly for the weekly English-language paper *Puerto Vallarta Tribune,* and you can buy his tongue-in-cheek books around town, at Lucy's, or through the Web site ⊕ www.gilgevens.com.

Continued on page 127

The intricately woven and beaded designs of the Huichols' art are as vibrant and fascinating as the traditions of its people, best known as the "Peyote People" for their traditional and cermonial use of the hallucinigenic drug. Peyote-inspired visions are thought to be messages from God, and are reflected in the art.

THE ART OF THE HUICHOL

Like the Lacandon Maya, the Huichol resisted assimilation by Spanish invaders, fleeing to inhospitable mountains and remote valleys. There they retained their pantheistic religion in which shamans lead the community in spiritual matters and the use of peyote facilitates communication directly with God.

Huichol is pronounced wee-CHOL; the people's name for themselves, however, is Wirarika (we-RAH-ri-ka), which means "healer."

Roads didn't reach larger Huichol communities until the mid-20th century, bringing electricity and other modern distractions. The collision with the outside world has had pros and cons, but art lovers have only benefited from the Huichols' centuries-long mastery of intricately patterned woven and beaded goods. Today the traditional souls that remain on the land— a significant population of perhaps 6,000 to 8,000—still create votive bowls, prayer arrows, jewelry, and bags, and sell them to finance elaborate religious ceremonies. The pieces go for as little as $5 or as much as $5,000, depending on the skill and fame of the artist and quality of materials.

Bead-covered wooden statuette

UNDERSTANDING THE HUICHOL

When Spanish conquistadors arrived in the early 16th century, the Huichol, unwilling to work as slaves on the haciendas of the Spanish or to adopt their religion, fled to hard-to reach mountains and valleys of the Sierra Madre. They lived there, disconnected from society, for nearly 500 years. Beginning in the1970s, roads and electricity made their way to tiny Huichol towns. The reintroduction to society has come at a high price: at least one ill-advised government project encouraged Huichol farmers to sell their land, and with it, their traditional lifestyle, in favor of a city existence. Today, about half of the population of perhaps 12,000 continues to live in ancestral villages and *rancheritas* (tiny individual farms).

THE POWER OF PRAYER

Spirituality and prayer infuse every aspect of Huichol life. They believe that without their prayers and offerings the sun wouldn't rise, the earth would cease spinning. It is hard, then, for them to reconcile their poverty with the relative easy living of "free-riders" (Huichol term for nonspiritual freeloaders) who enjoy fine cars and expensive houses thanks to the Huichols efforts to sustain the planet. But rather than hold our reckless materialism against us, the Huichol add us to their prayers.

Huichol yarn artist at work

THE PEYOTE PEOPLE

Visions inspired by the hallucinogenic peyote plant are considered by the Huichol to be messages from God, and to help in solving personal and communal problems. Indirectly, they provide inspiration for their almost psychedelic art. Just a generation or two ago, annual peyote-gathering pilgrimages were done on foot. Today the journey is still a man's chief obligation, but they now drive to the holy site at Wiricuta, in San Luis Potosi State. Peyote collected is used by the entire community—men, women, and children—throughout the year.

SHAMANISM

A Huichol man has a lifelong calling as a shaman. There are two shamanic paths for the Huichol: the path of the wolf, which is more aggressive, demanding, and powerful (wolf shamans profess the ability to morph into wolves); and the path of the deer, which is playful—even clownish—and less inclined to prove his power. A shaman chooses his own path.

Huichol craftsmen, Cabo San Lucas

SMART SHOPPING TIPS

Huichol Art, Sun Face

of color. Beads should fit together tightly in straight lines, with no gaps.

YARN "PAINTINGS": Symmetry is not necessary, although there should be an overall sense of unity. Thinner thread results in finer, more costly work. Look for tightness, with no visible gaps or broken threads. Paintings should have a stamp of authenticity on the back, including artist's name and tribal affiliation.

BEADED ITEMS: The smaller the beads, the more delicate and expensive the piece. Beads with larger holes are fine for stringed work, but if used in bowls and statuettes cheapen the piece. Items made with iridescent beads from Japan are the priciest. Look for good-quality glass beads, definition, symmetry, and artful use

PRAYER ARROWS: Collectors and purists should look for the traditionally made arrows of brazilwood inserted into a bamboo shaft. The most interesting ones contain embroidery work, or tiny carved icons, or are painted with copal symbols indicative of their original, intended purpose, for example protecting a child or ensuring a successful corn crop.

WHERE TO SHOP

SUPPORTING HUICHOL TRADITIONS

Families that continue to work the land may dedicate a few hours a day to crafts production, working to maintain their ceremonies, not to pay the cable bill. Buying directly from them can ensure a higher degree of artistry: the Huichol who make art to supplement farming work more slowly and with less pressure than their city-dwelling brethren. Shopping at stores like Peyote People and Hikuri supports artisans who live in their ancestral villages and practice the ancient traditions.

Peyote People treats the Huichol as a people, not a product. At their downtown Vallarta shop, the owners—a Mexican-Canadian couple—are happy to share with cus-

tomers their wealth of info about Huichol art and culture. They work with just a few farming families, providing all the materials and then paying for the finished product. ✉ Calle Juárez 222, Centro ☎ 322/222-2303.

Hikuri At the north end of Banderas Bay, is run by a British couple that pays asking prices to their Huichol suppliers and employs indigenous men in the adjoining carpentry and screen-printing shops. The men initially have little or no experience, and the jobs give them a leg up to move on to more profitable work. The excellent inventory includes fine yarn paintings. ✉ Calle Coral 66A, La Cruz de Huanacaxtle ☎ 329/295-5071.

The Huichol Collection
Native artisans working on crafts and wearing their stunning and colorful clothing draw customers in. The shop has an excellent inventory, with some museum-quality pieces. Though the merchandise is genuine, the shop is also venue for time-share sales—albeit with a soft sales pitch. ✉ Paseo Diaz Ordaz 732, Centro ☎ 322/223-0661b ✉ Morelos 490, Centro ☎ 322/223-2141.

Galería Huichol sells yarn paintings, beaded bowls and statuettes, and some smaller items like beaded jewelry and Christmas ornaments. ✉ Paradise Plaza, 2nd fl., Nuevo Vallarta ☎ 322/297-0342

TRADITION TRANSFORMED

The art of the Huichol was, for centuries, made from undyed wool, shells, stones, and other natural materials. It was not until the 1970s that the Huichol began incorporating bright, zingy colors, without sacrificing the intricate patterns and symbols used for centuries. The result is strenuously colorful, yet dignified.

YARN PAINTINGS
Dramatic and vivid yarn paintings are highly symbolic, stylized visions of life.

MASKS AND ANIMAL STATUETTES
Bead-covered wooden or ceramic masks and animal statuettes are other adaptations made for outsiders.

PRAYER ARROWS
Made for every ceremony, prayer arrows send petitions winging to God.

VOTIVE BOWLS
Ceremonious votive bowls, made from gourds, are decorated with bright, stylized beadwork.

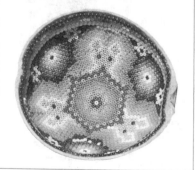

WOVEN SHOULDER BAGS
Carried by men, the bags are decorated with traditional Huichol icons.

For centuries, Huichol women have worn BEADED BRACELETS; today earrings and necklaces are also made.

Diamond-shape GOD'S EYES of sticks and yarn protect children from harm.

5

THE ART OF HUICHOL

HOW TO READ THE SYMBOLS

Spiders that come out at dawn are thought to welcome the rising sun.

The deer is the animal manifestation of the god Kahumari, who intercedes in heaven on earthlings' behalf.

Anything with horns or antlers symbolizes communion and oneness with God.

Yarn painting

■ The trilogy of corn, peyote, and deer represent three aspects of God. According to Huichol mythology, peyote sprang up in the footprints of the deer. Depicted like stylized flowers, peyote represents communication with God. Corn, the Huichol's staple

Corn symbol

food, symbolizes health and prosperity. An image drawn inside the root ball depicts the essence of god within it.

■ The double-headed eagle is the emblem of the omnipresent sky god.

Peyote

■ A nierika is a portal between the spirit world and our own. Often in the form of a yarn painting, a nierika can be round or square.

■ Salamanders and turtles are associated with rain; the former provoke the clouds. Turtles maintain underground springs, and purify water.

■ A scorpion is the soldier of the sun.

Scorpion

■ The Huichol depict raindrops as tiny snakes; in yarn paintings they descend to enrich the fields.

Snakes

Jose Beníctez Sánchez, (1938–) may be the elder statesman of yarn painters, and has shown in Japan, Spain, the U.S., and at the Museum of Modern Art in Mexico City. His paintings sell for upward of $3,000 a piece.

after 2 PM Saturday. Relatives of the owners of Mundo de Cristal and Mundo de Azulejos (⇨ *above*) own **Mundo de Pewter** (⊠ Av. Venustiano Carranza 358, Col. E. Zapata ☎ 322/222–2675 ⊕ www.mundodepewter. com), which is wedged in between the other two stores. Attractive, lead-free items in modern and traditional designs are sold here at reasonable prices. The practical, tarnish-free pieces can go from stovetop or oven to the dining table and be no worse for wear.

Olinalá (⊠ Av. Lázaro Cárdenas 274, Col. E. Zapata ☎ 322/222–4995 or 322/228–0659) sells mainly painted ceremonial masks and a limited selection of other folk art from throughout Mexico. It's closed Sunday and September and October. **Querubines** (⊠ Av. Juárez 501–A, at Calle Galeana, Centro ☎ 322/223–1727) has woven goods from Guatemala and southern Mexico, including tablecloths, napkins, placemats, and *rebozos* (stoles) made of rayon, silk, and cotton. The shop is in an old house that once belonged to Jesús Langarica, PV's first mayor. The structure's stone, cement, and brick floors make interesting backdrops for painted gourds from Michoacán and carved gourds from the Costa Chica (northern Oaxaca coast), and Talavera pottery.

Home Furnishings

Also *see* Folk Art & Craft, *above*.

★ The American owners of **Banderas Bay** (⊠ Lázaro Cárdenas 263, Col. E. Zapata ☎ 322/223–4352), who also own Daiquiri Dick's restaurant (⇨ Chapter 3), travel around the country for months in search of antiques, collectibles, handicrafts, and unique household items. About two-thirds of the merchandise is new. The shop, which will pack and ship your purchases, is closed Sunday. **Ponciana** (⊠ Basilio Badillo 252–A, Col. E. Zapata ☎ 322/222–2988) has things you won't find at all the other stores, like porcelain replicas of antique dolls. The "antique" cupboards may have only original doors, but that's a common practice. Other antiques, perhaps an old reliquary, are transformed into wall art. You can also find tablecloths and placemats from Michoacán, place settings, arty statuettes, matchboxes decorated with Frida Kahlo and Mexican movie themes, and other decorative items.

Jewelry

The jewelers at **Alberto's** (⊠ Av. Juárez 479, Centro ☎ 322/222–1690), family to jewelers of the same surname in Zihuatanejo, are happy to explain, in English, which pieces carry authentic stones and which are composites or synthetics. Prices are reasonable and the selection is impressive. It's closed Sunday. **La Brisa** (⊠ Condominios Puesta del Sol, Local 11–B, Marina Vallarta ☎ 322/221–2516) is one of several silver stores owned by the same family. All have fair prices and no pressure; this one also has Talavera pottery for sale.

La Piedra (⊠ Av. Mexico 1087, Centro ☎ 322/223–2242) has fine stones and beads for jewelry makers as well as findings and other bits needed for jewelry-making. Spend as little as $5 or as much as $5,000 on anything and everything jade at **Jades Maya** (⊠ Leona Vicario 226–A, Centro ☎ 322/222–0371 ⊕ www.jademaya.com). The shop is open daily until 10 PM in high season. In addition to jewelry made from the

20 different colors of jade, there are replicas of ancient Mayan masks.

Joyería El Opalo (✉ Local 13–A, Plaza Genovesa, Col. Las Glorias ☎ 322/224–6584), a bright spot in a nearly abandoned mall, has managed to remain afloat through its cruise ship contacts. Silver jewelry ranges in price from $1.50 per gram for simpler pieces to $6 a gram for the lighter, finer quality and more complex pieces. There's high-grade "950" silver jewelry in addition to the usual 0.925 sterling silver), and gold settings as well. Most of the semi-precious stones—amethyst, topaz, malachite, black onyx, and opal in 28 colors—are of Mexican origin. The diamond-cut necklaces are magnificent.

> ### ALL THAT GLITTERS ISN'T SILVER
>
> There's a great selection of Mexican silver in PV, but watch out for "German silver," (aka *alpaca* or *chapa*): an alloy of iron, zinc, and nickel. Real silver is weightier, and is marked "925" (indicating a silver content of at least 92.5%) for sterling and "950" (at least 95% silver content) for finer pieces. When size permits, the manufacturor's name and the word "Mexico" should also appear.

Joyas Finas Suneson (✉ Calle Morelos 593, Centro ☎ 322/222–5715) specializes in silver jewelry and objets d'art by some of Mexico's finest designers. Most pieces have modern rather than traditional motifs, and designs are creative and unusual. It's closed Sunday.

★ Manager Ramon Cruz of **Joyería Yoler** (✉ Calle Olas Altas 391, Col. E. Zapata ☎ 322/222–8713 or 322/222–9051) proudly shows off the store's collection of the Los Castillo family's silver jewelry made with lost-wax casting as well as hammering and burnishing techniques, small silver pitchers with lapis lazuli dragonfly handles, napkin rings, abalone pill boxes, and other lovely utilitarian pieces. The merchandise—which includes an extensive yet not overwhelming array of silver and semi-precious-stone jewelry—is nicely arranged in the ample shop. The worldly

Fodor$Choice **Viva** (✉ Calle Basilio Badillo 274, Col. E. Zapata ☎ 322/222–
★ 4078 ⊕ www.vivacollection.com) represents hundreds of jewelry designers from around the globe, and so achieves an impressive diversity. The store also sells unique espadrilles, flats, and sandals as well as beach clothing, magnifying sun glasses, and accessories for men and women.

Leather, Shoes & Handbags

Aranpelli (✉ Morelos 600–A, between Calles Aldama and Corona, Centro ☎ 322/223–2854) is a small shop with a classy selection of handbags, day packs, valises, wallets, and other leather goods (but no shoes). The fun, stamped-leather purses come in various colors and modern designs from Spain; other handbags hail from Italy and Colombia. The shop also has coin purses, penknife cases, and other small gift items. It's closed Sunday. Longtime visitors to Puerto Vallarta will remember **Huarachería Fabiola** (✉ Av. Ignacio L. Vallarta 145, Col. E. Zapata ☎ 322/222–9154). Buy huaraches off the rack (literally) or order custom sandals (and a few styles of closed shoes in softer leather) for men or women. Most styles can be made in one to three days. Credit cards are not accepted. Guys, did you leave your ostrich-leather sandals at home? Ladies, want manta ray boots that look like no leather you've seen before? Then come to **Rolling Stones** (⊠ Paseo Diaz Ordáz 802, Centro ☎ 322/223–1769) for custom-made boots, sandals, and shoes (or off the rack). There's a less impressive line of handbags and wallets, and upstairs, leather jackets. Though the selection is limited and quality average, the best things about **Wild West** (⊠ Av. Ignacio L. Vallarta 174, Col. E. Zapata ☎ 322/222–9766) are the accessible prices of handbags, wallets, belts, and jackets.

> ## DO WEAR THEM OUT
>
> *Huaraches* are woven leather sandals that seem to last several lifetimes. Traditionally worn by peasants, they're now sold by fewer shops, but in a slightly larger assortment of styles. Once broken in—and that takes a while—this classic, sturdy footwear will be a worthwhile addition to your closet.

Wine, Beer & Spirits

Run by the sommelier at Trio, **Anfitrión de México** (⊠ Calle Guerrero 278–A, Centro ☎ 322/222–8130) sells imported wine at a reasonable markup. Near the south end of the marina, **La Cava** (⊠ Condominios Marina del Sol, Local L–2B, Marina Vallarta ☎ 322/209–0787) delivers. The selection of liquor isn't huge, but fair enough, and you can pick up olives, beer, champagne, and some gourmet food items. No credit cards.

La Playa (⊠ Constitución 136, Col. E. Zapata ☎ 322/223–1818 ⊠ Olas Altas 246, Col. E. Zapata ☎ 322/222–5304 ⊠ Av. Francisco M. Ascencio, Km 2.5, Zona Hotelera, across from IMSS [Mexican Social Security Agency] ☎ 322/224–7130 ⊠ Av. Francisco M. Ascencio, Km 1.5, Col. Olímpica ☎ 322/223–3645) has tequila, wines from Chile, California (Gallo), and Spain, imported vodka and other spirits, and the cheapest beer around.

NORTH & SOUTH OF PUERTO VALLARTA

Groceries

With a walk-in cold storage, **Frutería Chabacano** (⊠ Calle Hidalgo 16, Bucerías ☎ 329/298–0692) has the freshest fruits and vegetables in town, and a good variety. **El Indio** (⊠ Av. América Latina 23 at Av. Mexico, San Pancho ☎ 311/258–4010) is the most convenient place in San Pancho to get liquor, wine, milk, water, and Mexican brands of condiments and other necessities. Facing the main plaza, **Mi Tiendita** (⊠ Calle Marlin 44–A, Sayulita ☎ 329/291–3145) sells Häagen-Dazs ice cream, deli sandwiches, and some groceries, as well as wine and national beer brands. Grocery-hodgepodge store **Super La Peque** (⊠ Morelos 7, Bucerías ☎ 329/298–0598) has wine, liquor, cleaning supplies, junk food, and some fresh fruit, as well as a nice assortment of rustic red-clay pottery typical of the state.

Malls

Paradise Plaza (⊠ Paseo de los Cocoteros 85 Sur, Nuevo Vallarta ☎ 322/ 226–6770) is the most comprehensive plaza north of Marina Vallarta, with a food court, ice-cream and coffee shops, hair salon, video arcade, Internet café, clothing and handcraft boutiques, and a bank, but no movie theater.

Specialty Stores

Art

Galería La Manzanilla (⊠ Calle Playa Perula 83, La Manzanilla ☎ 315/ 351–7099 ⊕ www.artinmexico.com) has a cadre of more than a dozen fine artists from Mexico, Canada, and the U.S. Their work ranges from photography and portraiture to lovely landscapes and other paintings in various media to pottery and jewelry. It's closed September through mid-October.

Books & Periodicals

Try **Gringo's Books & Coffee** (⊠ Calle Morelos 7–A Bucerías ☎ 329/298– 1767) for novels a-go-go, including lots of beach reading, that is, romance novels and other light fiction. **Librería Sayulita** (⊠ Calle Manuel Navarrete 3, Sayulita ☎ 329/291–3382) has new books in Spanish, used paperbacks in English (mainly quick fiction reads), and a small selection of magazines like *Runner's World* and *Surfer.*

Clothing

Shop for dressier dresses and casual, unique resort wear in linen and cotton at **D'Paola** (⊠ Paradise Plaza, Local 11 ☎ 322/297–1030). **Ruly's Boutique** (⊠ Paradise Plaza, Local 10, Paseo de los Cocoteros 85 Sur, Nuevo Vallarta ☎ 322/297–1724) has the choicest men's clothing around. They have nice trousers, shirts, and shorts in a wide selection of handsome yet vibrant colors, as well as accessories, underwear, hats, and so on. The owner of Ruly's designs the clothing sold here and supervises their construction. The color palette and fabrics—blends, linens, cottons, and some synthetics—are superb.

The owner of Ruly's designs the clothing sold here and supervises their construction. The color palette and fabrics—blends, linens, cottons, and some synthetics—are superb.

Folk Art

Galería Corazón (⊠ Av. América Latina 1, at Av. Tercer Mundo, San Pancho ☎ 311/258–4170) specializes in high-end arts and crafts from Michoacán as well as jewelry, paintings, sculpture, and traditional ceramics. Take note of the "beyond bankers" hours: Thursday, Friday, and Saturday noon to 4 and Tuesday 3–7. It's closed mid-May through October, however. **La Hamaca** (⊠ Calle Revolución 110, Sayulita ☎ 329/291– 3039) has a wonderful inventory of folk art and utilitarian handicrafts; each piece is unique. Scoop up masks and pottery from Michoacán, textiles, and shawls from Guatemala, hammocks from the Yucatán, and lacquered boxes from Olinalá. The items aren't cheap, but the store is wonderful.

Shop for pottery, small housewares, tin frames sporting Botero-style fat ladies, and other gifts at **Jan Marie's Boutique** (✉ Lázaro Cárdenas 56, Bucerías ☎ 329/298–0303). The Talavera pottery is both decorative and utilitarian. This is not the place for bargain hunters. **La Aldaba** (✉ Paradise Plaza, 2nd fl., Nuevo Vallarta ☎ 322/297–0903) has an interesting collection of gifts and small decorative items and housewares: Bustamante-inspired cat and moon candles, subtly painted sheet metal candleholders and wall art, and glass vases.

CERAMICS, POTTERY & TILE **Galería de Ollas** (✉ Paradise Plaza, Local J12, 2nd fl., Nuevo Vallarta ☎ 329/297–1200) is a small shop selling museum-class Mata Ortiz pottery. It's much the same as its El Centro branch (⇨ *above*).

Home Furnishings

The flamboyant, displaced Brit and owner of **Anthony Chetwynd Collection** (✉ Calle Las Palmas 30, Col. Costa Azul, San Francisco ☎ 311/158–4373) travels to estates and villages all over Mexico to stock his antiques shop. About half the inventory is antique masks, chandeliers, reliquaries . . . whatever he can get his hands on. The rest are copies of the same, and some furnishings and housewares imported from Asia.

5

After Dark

Mariachi

6

WORD OF MOUTH

"I merrily ate and drank my week away [in PV]! Oh, how I miss those mango margaritas at 5:30 PM!"

—baglady

"There is definitely some fun nightlife [in PV] without being quite so spring breakish [as Cancún.] People tend to be a little older than in Cancún (when I was there I think the average age was 17 at most clubs)."

—Bain05

Organic, outdoorsy Vallarta switches gears after dark and rocks into the wee hours. After the beachgoers and sightseers have been showered and fed, Vallarta kicks up its heels and puts the baby to bed. Happy hour in martini lounges sets the stage for evening entertainment that might include a show, live music, or just hobnobbing under the heavens at a rooftop bar.

Many hotels have Mexican fiesta dinner shows, which can be lavish affairs with buffet dinners, folk dances, and even fireworks. Tour groups and individuals—mainly middle-age and older Americans and Canadians—make up the audience at the Saturday night buffet dinner show at Playa Los Arcos and other hotels. *Vaqueros* (cowboys) do rope tricks and dancers perform Mexican regional or pseudo-Aztec dances. The late-late crowd gets down after midnight at dance clubs, some of which stay open until 6 AM.

The scene mellows as you head north and south of Puerto Vallarta. In Punta de Mita, Bucerías, Sayulita, and San Francisco (aka San Pancho), local restaurants provide live music; the owners usually scare up someone good once or twice a week in high season. Along the Costalegre, tranquillity reigns. Most people head here for relaxation, and nightlife most often takes the form of stargazing, drink in hand. If you're visiting June through October (low season), attend live performances whenever offered, as they are few and far between.

Although there's definitely crossover, many Mexicans favor the upscale bars and clubs of the Hotel Zone and Marina Vallarta hotels, while foreigners tend to like the Mexican flavor of places downtown and the south side (the Zona Romántica), where dress is decidedly more casual.

⇨ For more nightlife options, *see* "Gay Puerto Vallarta" (Chapter 10).

BARS & PUBS

Like any resort destination worth its salt—the salt on the rim of the margarita glass, that is—PV has an enormous variety of watering holes. Bars on or overlooking the beach sell the view along with buckets of beer. Martini bars go to great lengths to impress with signature drinks, and sports bars serve up Canadian hockey and Monday-night football. Hotels have swim-up bars and lobby lounges, and these, as well as restaurant bars, are the main options in places like Nuevo Vallarta, Marina Vallarta, and most of the small towns to the north and south. ⇨ For gay bars, *see* Chapter 10.

All-Purpose Bars

★ **Andale** (⊠ Av. Olas Altas 425, Col. E. Zapata ☎ 322/222–1054) fills up most nights. Crowds spill out onto the sidewalk as party-hearty men and women shimmy out of the narrow saloon, drinks in hand, to the strains of Chubby Checker and other vintage tunes. For a laugh, intoxicated or less inhibited patrons sometimes take a bumpy but safe ride on the burro just outside Andale's door (a handler escorts the burro).

It's difficult to categorize **The Bar Above** (⊠ Av. México at Av. Hidalgo, 2 blocks north of central plaza, Bucerías ☎ 329/298–1194), a little place above Tapas del Mundo. It's a martini bar without a bar (the owner, Buddy, prefers that people come to converse with friends at tables rather than "hang out" at a bar), that also serves dessert. Molten chocolate soufflé—

> ## COCKTAILS TO GO
>
> Stop-and-go bars, where you get your drink in a cardboard cup, are mainly geared toward teens. But it can be fun to sip a cocktail while drinking in the sights along the malecón.

the signature dish—or charred pineapple bourbon shortcake may be on the menu. Lights are dim, the music is romantic, and there's an eagle's view of the ocean from the rooftop crow's nest. It's closed every Sunday; in August and September; and Monday in June, July, and October. At other times, it's open 6 PM–midnight.

Right on the sand across from Parque Lázaro Cárdenas, restaurant–bar **Burro's Bar** (⊠ Av. Olas Altas at Calle Lázaro Cárdenas, Col. E. Zapata ☎ No phone ⊕ www.burrosbar.com) has bargain brewskis (three beers for three bucks) and equally inexpensive fruity margaritas by the pitcher. The seafood is less than inspired, but nachos and other munchies are good accompaniments to the drinks. Watch the waves and listen to Bob Marley and the Gypsy Kings among lots of gringo couples and a few middle-age Mexican vacationers. It opens daily at 10 AM.

Second-floor **La Cantina** (⊠ Morelos 709, at J.O. de Dominguez, Centro ☎ 322/222–1734), while not especially hip, has a good view of Banderas Bay and the boardwalk as well as canned Mexican tunes, especially *ranchera, grupera,* and *cumbia.*

The rooftop bar of **Chez Elena** (⊠ Hotel Los Cuatro Vientos, Matamoros 520, Centro ☎ 322/222–0161) is plain as can be, but the margaritas are first rate and the bay view expansive.

Geckos Pub (⊠ Calle Morelos between Calles Madero and Av. Cárdenas Bucerías ☎ 322/298–1861) is an unassuming local watering hole with a billiards table. It's the kind of place a single woman can enter without feeling weird or being hassled as bartenders tend to keep an eye out for them in the small venue. The tallest building around, **Hotel Alondra** (⊠ Calle Sinaloa 16, Barra de Navidad ☎ 315/355–8372), has a rooftop bar that's great for sunset cocktails.

Fodor'sChoice ★ **Memories** (⊠ Av. Juárez, at Calle Mina 207, Centro ☎ 322/205–7906) is a wonderful little second-story nightspot. Right in downtown PV near the main plaza, it is frequented mainly by locals. The space is darkly romantic and a great place for a date, but still ideal for groups of friends, or for singles with a book. The extensive drink list includes "hair of the squirrel," with Frangelica, and lots of specialty alcoholic and nonalcoholic coffees. The classic-rock soundtrack pays homage to John Lennon, the Eagles, and Bob Marley; black-and-white posters and photos honor other rock and rollers.

Called simply "Frog's" by the locals, **Señor Frog's** (✉ V. Carranza 218, at Ignacio I. Vallarta, Col. E. Zapata ☎ 322/222–5171) is a good old-fashioned free-for-all for the young and the restless. There's sawdust on the floor, black lights on the walls, and a giant-screen TV above the tiny dance floor. Expect a foam party at least once a week, and other shenanigans.

> **WORD OF MOUTH**
>
> "Around 2 AM, they held the requisite wet t-shirt contest. It was really gross and if you're easily offended, you should look away or relocate like I did. Otherwise, Señor Frog's was a good time."
> —lfalcone

Although primarily a gay bar, **The Palm** (✉ Olas Altas 508, Col. E. Zapata ☎ No phone) has a straight following as well. Patrons love the imported drag queens like the Kingsey Sicks and Acapella ("America's only drag-apella beauty shop quartet") that perform several times a week in high season. Everyone in town gets excited about the occasional theater performances—it was *The Vagina Monologues* in 2005. The Palm is closed Monday and Tuesday May–October.

Party Lounge (✉ Av. Mexico 993, across from Parque Hidalgo, Centro ☎ No phone) is open daily after 1 PM for stop-and-go drinks: mainly *litros,* that is, 32-ouncers of tequila sunrise, Long Island ice tea, piña colada, and the like. Because they have '70s, '80s, and lounge music rather than electronic music, the upstairs bar, open 8 PM to 4 AM, is popular with the middle-age and older set, foreign and domestic, as well as with the younger crowd.

We Be Sausage Roadhouse Bar & Grill (✉ Av. de los Picos 102, Bucerías ☎ 329/298–0954 ⊕ www.webesausage.com) is a pub owned by a Canadian sausage lover; have one of their excellent Italian-sausage sandwiches with your suds. Ball games are usually on the tube. It's closed Monday.

Karaoke Bar

There's no cover at **La Regadera** (✉ Morelos 666, Centro ☎ 322/222–3970), where you can dazzle or frazzle your fellow karaoke fans with songs in English or Spanish. It's open daily between 8 PM and 4 AM, but things don't begin to bounce until around midnight.

Martini Bars

★ **Apaches** (✉ Olas Altas 439, Col. E. Zapata ☎ 322/222–4004) is gay friendly, lesbian friendly, *people* friendly. Heck, superwomen Mariann and her partner Endra would probably welcome you and your pet python with open arms, give you both a squeeze. PV's original martini bar, Apaches is the landing zone for expats reconnoitering after a long day, and a warm-up for late-night types. When the outside tables get jam packed in high season, the overflow heads into the narrow bar and the adjacent, equally narrow bistro. It opens after 5 PM; happy hour is 5 to 7. If you're alone, this is the place to make friends of all ages.

Garbo (✉ Pulpito 142, Olas Altas, Col. E. Zapata ☎ 322/229–7309) is open nightly after 6. This is not the kind of place where you'll strike up a conversation; rather it's an upscale place to go with friends for a sophisticated, air-conditioned drink or two. Cigarette smoke perfumes the air, and a musician plays gentle electric guitar music Thursday through Saturday evenings 7 to 10.

The cozy **Kit Kat Club** (✉ Calle Púlpito 120, Col. E. Zapata ☎ 322/223–0093) has great martinis and a retro feel. Both straights and gays are drawn to this elegant lounge, which has full meals as well as millions of $6 martinis. Most popular include the Peggy Lee (vodka, orange and cranberry juices, and banana liqueur) and the Queen of Hearts (vodka, amaretto, cranberry juice, and 7UP).

Piano Bars

Bon vivants should head for **Constantini Wine Bar** (✉ Café des Artistes, Av. Guadalupe Sánchez 740, Centro ☎ 322/222–3229), the latest innovation of hot-shot restaurant Café des Artistes. Order one of 50 wines by the glass (more than 300 by the bottle, from 10 countries) and snack on caviar, bruschetta, and carpaccio—or go directly to dessert. On Thursday, area wine distributors host wine tastings between 6 and 7 PM. There's live music Monday through Saturday. Weekdays it's piano music from 7:30 to 11:30 PM; Friday and Saturday nights there's jazz and blues between 8:30 and midnight.

At romantic **El Faro** (✉ Royal Pacific Yacht Club, Marina Vallarta ☎ 322/221–0541) you can admire the bay and marina from atop a 110-foot lighthouse. There's often live guitar or other music in the evening, and happy hour is from 6 to 7 PM. It's mainly a baby-boomer crowd.

Restaurant Bars

Right in the heart of old Vallarta near the Insurgentes street bridge, pretty **Bianco** (✉ Calle Insurgente 109, Centro ☎ 322/222–2177) is a lounge known for its martinis. With its curvaceous glass bar and undulating white-on-white banquettes, it seems straight from the hippest part of Miami. The bar has an excellent sound system, and there's usually live salsa (with lessons beforehand) several days a week; otherwise tap your foot or dance among the tables to pop and a mix of other genres from the '80s and and '90s. It's closed Monday.

A classy and modern lounge, **Citrus** (✉ Plaza Villas Vallarta, Calle José Clemente Orozco C–46, Zona Hotelera ☎ 322/293–6381 ⊕ www.citruscafepv.com) attracts an upscale crowd. It's a fashionable place for a drink while listening to contemporary music, be it Mexican pop, international house, or electronic.

★ Soon after its 2004 inauguration, the sophisticated **Nikki Beach** (✉ Westin hotel, Paseo de la Marina Sur 205, Marina Vallarta ☎ 322/226–1150) hosted several events during the *Maxim* magazine model competition, guaranteeing instant fame and a clientele of beautiful people. Just about everything under the palapa roof is white, and hanging beds and furnishings encourage lounging. In the restaurant, hard-body waiters in sarongs deliver dishes from Continental to Mediterranean to Asian, including sushi. It's closed Monday and Tuesday.

Continued on page 142

A cross-section of la piña (the heart) of the blue agave plant

¡TEQUILA!

If God were Mexican, tequila would surely be our heavenly reward, flowing in lieu of milk and honey. Local lore asserts that it was born when lightning hit a tall blue agave cooking its heart.

Historians maintain that, following Spanish conquest and the introduction of the distillation process, tequila was developed from the ancient Aztec drink *pulque*. Whatever the true origin, Mexico's national drink long predated the Spanish, and is considered North America's oldest intoxicating spirit.

Conjuring up tequila, what might come to mind is late-night teary-eyed confessions or spaghetti-Western-style bar brawls. But tequila is more complex and worldly than many presume. By some accounts it's a digestive that reduces cholesterol and stress. Shots of the finest tequilas can cost upward of $100 each, and are meant to be savored as ardently as fine cognacs or single-malt scotches.

Just one of several agaves fermented and bottled in Mexico, tequila rose to fame during the Mexican Revolution when it became synonymous with national heritage and pride. Since the 1990s tequila has enjoyed a soaring popularity around the globe, and people the world over are starting to realize that tequila is more than a one-way ticket to a hangover.

The Blue Agave

Tequila is made from the blue agave plant (not from a cactus, as is commonly thought), a member of the lily family. Nearly 100,000 acres of blue agave are grown in Mexico today; the plant is native to Sierra Madre region, still the center for agave fields and tequila production.

After the blue agave plant matures (which takes 8–12 years), its spiky leaves are removed and the hearts cooked up to three days in a traditional pit oven (or convection oven) to concentrate the sugars. Seeping blood-red juice, the hearts are then ground and strained, then fermented and distilled at least two or three times.

Workers harvest *Agave tequilana Weber azul*

Mezcal

Liquor distilled from any maguey (agave) plant is called mezcal, so technically, tequila is a type of mezcal. But mezcal is usually used to describe a liquor made from any agave *except* the blue agave from which tequila is made. Originally hailing from Oaxaca, mezcal is as popular as tequila in Mexico, if not more so. Like tequila, quality varies widely from cheap firewater to smooth (and expensive) varieties with complex flavors. The type of maguey used influences the quality greatly.

At the fermentation stage, the agave is added to water.

Effortless Education

You can chat with your local bartender about the blue agave revolution, but the information you get may be flawed. Close to *casa*, you can learn a lot at **La Casa del Tequila** (⊠ Calle Morelos 589, Centro ☎322/222–2000 ☉ Closed Sun.) Ask the owner to educate you as you taste a few of the 150 tequilas on hand.

An assembly-line worker fills tequila bottles

TEQUILA TOURS

Near Boca de Tomatlán, **Agave Don Crispín** (⊠ Las Juntas y Los Veranos, 10 mi south of PV ☎322/223–6002) is a small but proud producer of 100% agave tequila that also sells *raicilla*, an unsophisticated liquor made from green agave. Learn the basics of tequila production, and see the pit ovens and old-fashioned stills. If you're serious about tequila, you must go to tequila country. One of the most complete tours is with **Hacienda San José del Refugio** (⊠ Amatitán, about 400 km [250 mi] east of PV, ☎33/3613–9585), producer of the Herradura brand. On the two-hour **Tequila Express** (☎ 33/3880–9099 or 33/3122–7920) train ride, blue agave fields zip by as you sip tequila and listen to roving mariachis. After a distillery tour, there's lunch, folk dancing, and *charro* (cowboy) demonstrations.

José Cuervo is Mexico's largest tequila maker

CHOOSING A TEQUILA

Line 'em up!

Connoisseurs recommend imbibing nothing but 100% pure agave—with no added sugar or chemicals—even for mixed drinks. A tequila's quality is most directly related to the concentration of blue agave, and a higher agave content adds significantly to the price. The cheapest varieties have 49% of their alcohol derived from sugars other than blue agave. (The max allowed by law.) This fact will be clearly marked on the label as TEQUILA 100% DE AGAVE or TEQUILA 100% PURO DE AGAVE.

Aging tequila changes the flavor, but doesn't necessarily improve it. Whiskey and scotch inspired the aging process in oak barrels, which instills a smoky taste or imparts one of many other subtle bouquets. Some experts consider the unmitigated flavor of *blanco* (silver) superior to, or at least less influenced by Yankee and European tastes than that of *reposado* (aged) or *añejo* (mature).

Distinctions you should know (from—generally speaking—least to most expensive) are:

BLANCO (SILVER): Also known as white tequila (though "silver" is the official name), tequila blanco is clear as water. It is unaged—bottled immediately after distillation—and therefore has the purest agave taste of the tequila varieties.

ORO (GOLD): Also called *joven* (young) tequila, this is tequila blanco to which colorants or flavorings have been added, or that has been mixed with tequila aged in oak barrels, giving it a golden hue. Additives (all strictly regulated) such as caramel, oak tree extract, glycerin, and sugar syrup simulate the flavor of tequila aged in oak barrels.

REPOSADO (AGED): Aged in oak barrels 2 to 11 months, reposado; smoother and more flavorful than blanco, as it has acquired some of the oak flavor.

AÑEJO (EXTRA-AGED): Tequila aged more than one year in oak barrels; may also be called "mature tequila." This is the smoothest tequila variety, and the one that most resembles cognac or whiskey—ideal for sipping. Some feel that the agave taste is watered down.

CREAM OF THE CROP

In the tequila business, innovation and young energy aren't as successful as age and experience. Traditional *tequilera* families like those behind Don Julio, Sauza, and José Cuervo tend to get the most outstanding results, having pursued perfection for generations. All of our top picks are 100% blue agave.

El Tesoro de Don Felipe Platinum: Triple distilled, and produced the old-fashioned way, the agave hearts crushed with a stone grinder and baked in a brick oven

Three faces of tequila. . .

Don Eduardo: Youthful, crisp, and jubilant, with herby notes; triple distilled

Sauza's Tres Generaciones Blanco: Clean and balanced with hints of cinnamon

Chinaco Blanco: International World Spirits Competition judges proclaimed it "the epitome of tequila character, ... with a lively finish"

Amatitlán Reposado: A complex spirit with a suggestion of nutmeg and spice; awarded best in class at the 2005 International World Spirits Competition

Penacho Azteca Reposado: Another award winner by the same distillery as Amatitlán Reposado

Chinaco Reposado: Medium-dry rested tequila with an oak-spice bite and subtle fruit and flower aromas

Don Julio 1942: Exquisite, complex tequila with the aroma of toffee and vanilla

José Cuervo's Reserva de la Familia: Aged for three years in new oak barrels; rich flavor with touches of vanilla and herbs, and a long, graceful finish

Arette Gran Clase: Ultrasmooth, one of the suavest tequilas anywhere; aged for a full three years, it goes for nearly $200 a bottle

A TEQUILA BY ANY OTHER NAME ISN'T TEQUILA

To be called "tequila" a drink must meet the following strict requirements, as put forth by Consejo Regulador de Tequila (Tequila Regulatory Council; CRT):

- made entirely in Mexico, and from blue agave grown in Mexico (though it can be bottled elsewhere)

- distilled twice; some varieties are distilled three times

- contains at least 51% alcohol derived from Weber blue agave plant

- bears the official stamp of the CRT on the label

- if it is 100% blue agave, it must be bottled in Mexico at the plant at which it was made

Marina 220, Mayan Palace Ma-
...000) is a dark and atmospheric
...music pulses house, lounge, techno
... the crowd demands. It's open 6
...sday, when a $5 cover gets you a
...cktail) to put you in the mood for
... the tiny, improvised dance floor.

...ominios Las Palmas, Local 9, Ma-
...n excellent, inexpensive restaurant
...d by the owner. Beer for a buck and
...ers are practically a house rule.

...ng, NFL on Monday night, hockey,
...elterweight fights, **Steve's Sports Bar**
(✉ Basilio .... Zapata ☎ 322/222-0256) is a sports
mecca. It looks like it belongs in Anytown, North America, with a shiny
wood bar and multiple TVs. There are piles of board games, too, and
the burgers and crinkle fries couldn't be better.

LIVE MUSIC

Most of Puerto Vallarta's live music is performed in restaurants and bars,
often on or overlooking the beach. Musical events happening anywhere
in Vallarta are listed in *Bay Vallarta*. This twice-monthly rag is an excellent source of detailed information for who's playing around Old Vallarta, the Zona Hotelera Norte, Marina Vallarta, and even as far north
as Bucerías. More detail-oriented than most similar publications, *Bay
Vallarta* lists showtimes, venues, genres, and cover charges. Live music
is much less frequent in the smaller towns to the north and south of PV;
to find out what's happening there, ask in tourist-oriented bars, restaurants, or hotels.

Latino

Blanco y Negro (✉ Calle Lucerna at Calle Niza, behind Blockbuster
Video store, Zona Hotelera ☎ 322/293-2556) is a wonderful place to
have a drink with friends. The intimate café–bar is comfortable yet rustic, with *equipale* (leather-and-wood) love seats and traditional round cocktail tables. The music, which begins at 10:30, is *trova* (think Mexican
Cat Stevens) by Latino legends Silvio Rodríguez and Pablo Milanés;
some songs composed and sung by the owner are thrown in. There's never
★ a cover. It's closed Sunday. **La Bodeguita del Medio** (✉ Paseo Díaz Ordaz
858, Centro ☎ 322/223-1585) is a wonderful Cuban bar and restaurant with a friendly vibe. People of all ages come to dance salsa (and drink
mojitos made with Cuban rum), so the small dance floor fills up as soon
as the house sextet starts playing around 9 PM. There's no cover.

Claudio's Meson Bay (✉ Lázaro Cárdenas 17, by footbridge, Bucerías
☎ 329/298-1634) is a casual, open-sided, ocean-facing restaurant

NOT TO FAR NORTH OF N.V.

with live music (usually marimba). The current schedule for these light-hearted melodies—which coincide with excellent all-you-can-eat buffets—is Monday, Wednesday, Friday, and Sunday. Start off with a happy-hour drink between 5 and 6 PM.

Cuates y Cuetos (✉ Francisca Rodriguez 101, Playa los Muertos ☎ 322/223–2724) is a great out-

> ## MUSIC ALFRESCO
>
> The outdoor Los Arcos amphithe-ater frequently has some sort of live entertainment on weekends and evenings. It's as likely to be mimes or magicians as musicians, but always worth stopping for the camaraderie with local people.

door venue where you can have a drink while watching the sun set and the people promenade. After 8 PM listen to live music, usually a seductive guitarist, romantic trio, or more lively version of folk music, like trova or samba rhythms.

An institution for Mexican breakfast, **La Paloma** (✉ Paseo Diaz Ordaz, at Aldama, Centro ☎ 322/222–3675), has otherwise average food but is recommended for sunset cocktails with live marimba and, later, mariachi music.

The privileged location overlooking the malecón and the sea is reserved for dining, but **Tequila's** (✉ Paseo Diaz Ordaz at Galeana, Centro ☎ 322/222–5725) is still a good place to sip a hand-crafted margarita made with your favorite brand. Sit in the second-floor cantina to absorb the full flavor of mariachis nightly (except Monday, their day off) between 8 and 10 PM. There's no cover.

Rock, Jazz & Blues

Cactus (✉ Ignacio L. Vallarta, Col. E. Zapata ☎ 322/222–4060) attracts a mixed crowd of locals and visitors when live rock is played, Wednesday through Sunday after 10:30 PM in high season, less often in low season. But it's a fun place for drinks at other times, too.

Philo's (✉ Calle Delfin 15, La Cruz de Huanacaxtle ☎ 329/295–5068 ⊕ www.philohayward.com) is the unofficial cultural center and meeting place of La Cruz, with music, food, a large-screen TV, a diminutive swimming pool, and pool table. The namesake owner, a former record producer, also has a small recording studio here. The space is plain but there's excellent live music after 9 PM Thursday through Saturday in low season (plus Tuesday and Wednesday late November through Easter). Get down with rhythm and blues, country, and rock; or chow down on good pizza and barbecue.

Qué Pasa (✉ Olas Altas 351, Col. E. Zapata ☎ No phone) means "What's Happening." What's happening is that when it's hot—especially Tuesday and Thursday nights, when there's good live music, usually rock or country—it's hot, but when it's not—mainly low season—it's dead. The vibe is 100% American. Some call it a baby boomer pickup spot; others call it a casual spot for a drink with friends. In addition to live

CLOSE UP

Mexican Rhythms & Roots

SALSA, MERENGUE, *CUMBIA* . . . do they leave you spinning, even off the dance floor? This primer is designed to help you wrap your mind around Latin beats popular in Pacific Mexico. Unfortunately, it can't cure two left feet.

These and other popular Latin dance rhythms were born of African drumming brought to the Caribbean by slaves. Dancing was vital to West African religious ceremonies; these rhythms spread with importation of slaves to the New World. Evolving regional tastes and additional instruments have produced the Latin music enjoyed today from Tierra del Fuego to Toronto, and beyond.

While the steps in most dances can be reduced to some basics, these flat-footed styles of dancing are completely foreign to most non-Latins. Dance classes can definitely help your self-esteem as well as your performance. In Puerto Vallarta, the dance club J.B. (⇨ *below*) is the place to go for lessons.

From Colombia, wildly popular **cumbia** combines vocals, wind, and percussion instruments. With a marked rhythm (usually 4/4 time), the sensual music is *relatively* easy to dance to. Hip-hop and reggae influences have produced urban cumbia, with up-tempo, accordion-driven melodies. Listen to Kumbia Kings, La Onda, Control, and Big Circo to get into the cumbia groove.

Fast-paced and with short, precise rhythms, **merengue** originated in the Dominican Republic. Although the music sounds almost frantic, the feet aren't meant to keep pace with the melody. Check out Elvis Crespo's 2004 album *Saboréalo.*

Born in Cuba of Spanish and African antecedents, **son** is played on accordion, guitar, and drums. The folkloric music was translated to various dialects in different parts of Mexico. "La Bamba" is a good example of *son jarrocho* (from Veracruz).

American Prohibition sent high-rollers sailing down Cuba way, and they came back swinging to son, mambo, and rumba played by full orchestras—think Dezi Arnaz and his famous song "Babalou." In New York these styles morphed into **salsa,** popularized by such luminaries as Tito Puente and Celia Cruz and carried on today by superstars like Marc Anthony. Wind instruments (trumpet, trombone), piano, guitar, and plenty of percussion make up this highly-spiced music.

Mexicans love these African-inspired beats, but are especially proud of homegrown genres, like **música norteña,** which has its roots in rural, northern Mexico (in Texas, it's called *conjunto*). The traditional instruments are the *bajo sexto* (a 12-string guitar), bass, and accordion; modern groups add the trap drums for a distinctive rhythmic pulse. It's danced like a very lively polka, which is one of its main influences. Norteña is the music of choice for working-class Mexicans and Mexican-Americans in the United States.

A subset of música norteña is the **corrido,** popularized during the Mexican Revolution. Like the ballads sung by wandering European minstrels, corridos informed isolated Mexican communities of the adventures of Emiliano Zapata, Pancho Villa, and their compatriots. Today's "narco-corridos" portray dubious characters: the drug lords who run Mexico's infamous cartels. Popular norteño artists include Michael Salgado and the pioneering Los Tigres del Norte, whose album "Americas Sin Fronteras" was terrifically popular way back in 1987.

But the quintessential Mexican music is **mariachi,** a marriage of European instruments and native sensibilities born right here in Jalisco, Mexico. Guitars, violins, and trumpets are accompanied by the vihuela (a small, round-backed guitar) and the larger, deep-throated *guitarrón*. Professional mariachis perform at birthdays and funerals, engagements, anniversaries, and life's other milestones. You won't find mariachi music at nightclubs, however; the *huapango, jarocho,* and other dances the music accompanies are folk dances. ⇨ For more about mariachi, *see* "Mariachi: Born in Jalisco" *in* Chapter 11. For concerts, clubbing, and dancing, Mexicans look to the contemporary music scene. **Latin jazz** was born when legendary Cuban musician Chano Pozo teamed up with the great bebop trumpeter Dizzy Gillespie. Current Latin jazz acts worth applauding are Puerto Ricans Eddie Palmieri and David Sanchez; representing pop, Obie Bermúdez also hails from that Caribbean mecca of music. Check out **Latin pop** by Cuba's Bebo Valdez, and **rock *en español***by Colombian-born Juanes as well as Mexico's own los Jaguares, El Tri, Ely Guerra, Molotov, and the veteran band Maná.

music at least three nights a week, the bar has open mike and movie nights, great BBQ, and dance classes. Check out the whiteboard downstairs for weekly events.

With the ambience (or lack thereof) of a small auditorium, **Route 66** (✉ Av. Ignacio L. Vallarta 217, Col. E. Zapata ☎ 322/223–2404) is a hit with locals and foreigners who like live blues, rock, reggae, and a little pop, mostly played by cover bands. The club, formerly known as Roxy, doesn't begin to rock until around 10 PM, when the variable—but always small—cover charge begins. It's closed Sunday.

At the malecón in the heart of downtown, second-floor **Viejo Vallarta** (✉ Morelos 484, Centro ☎ 322/222–0589), open nightly in high season, is popular with locals for live blues, rock, and reggae from 11 PM to 4 AM.

DANCE CLUBS

You can dance salsa with the locals, groove to rock in English or *en español*, or try your hand at *banda* or even tango. Things slow down substantially in the off-season, but during school vacations and the winter season clubs stay open until 3, 5, or even 6 AM. Except those that double as restaurants, clubs don't open until 10 PM. Don't arrive at a club before midnight—it will most likely be dead. Have a late and leisurely dinner, take a walk on the beach and get some coffee, then stroll into the club cool as a cucumber at 12:30 AM or so.

Carlos O'Brien's (✉ Paseo Diaz Ordaz 796, Centro ☎ 322/222–1444) is the destination of choice for Vallarta's very young people—a mix of local teens and foreigners come after midnight to mingle and party, especially on weekends. Music is a bit of everything: rock, house, techno, banda, hip-hop, disco, you name it. The ground floor fills up from early afternoon, however, with cruise-shippers and other travelers seeking food and drinks in a relatively familiar atmosphere. There's an $8 cover on weekend nights and also during the week during high season. When the place is hopping it stays open until dawn.

★ **Christine** (✉ Krystal Vallarta, Av. de las Garzas s/n, Zona Hotelera ☎ 322/224–6990 or 322/224–0202) has spectacular light shows set to bass-thumping music that ranges from techno and house to disco, rock, and Mexican pop. Most people (young boomers and Gen-Xers) come for the duration (it doesn't close until 6 AM), as this is the top of the food chain for the PV dancing experience. Cover is usually $10 for women and $20 for men, except on Thursday and Sunday, when it's $40 per person for open bar until 4 AM. It's closed Monday and Tuesday, and opens at around 10 PM other nights.

ROCK ON

The sound system at de Santos is top-notch, not surprising since one of the principal partners is Alex González, the drummer from Mexico's venerable rock band Maná.

Although no longer fashionable, **Collage** (✉ Blvd. Federico M. Ascencio s/n, Marina Vallarta ☎ 322/221–0505) is convenient to Marina Vallarta hotels. There's a $40 cover for all-you-can-drink on Tuesday (foam party night) and during Friday's "Brazilian Carnaval," but since these are sometimes dead, it's better to come on Saturday night, when there's no cover and you can move on if no one else shows up. The exception to the no-cover rule is during the Saturday boxing matches, when there's a $10 cover. It's closed Monday, Wednesday, Thursday, and Sunday.

★ In addition to pretty good Mediterranean dinners in the ground-floor restaurant, **de Santos** (✉ Calle Morelos 771, Centro ☎ 322/223–3052) has flamenco, Brazilian, jazz, and lounge music that appeals to a mixed, though slightly older, crowd in the evening. Later, local and guest DJs spin the more danceable, beat-driven disco and house tunes that appeal to slightly younger folk. If the smoke and noise get to you, head upstairs to the rooftop bar, where you and your friends can fling yourselves on the giant futons for some stargazing. This is a see-and-be-seen place for locals.

Popular with young, hip *vallartenses*, **Hilo** (✉ Paseo Díaz Ordaz 588, Centro ☎ 322/223–5361) attracts a mix of locals and visitors. It's mainly, but not exclusively, young (as in late teens to early thirties) and serves up anything from house and techno to hip-hop, electronic, and Top 40. The ceiling is several stories high, and enormous bronze-colored statues give an epic yet modern feeling. It's open from 10 PM to 4 or 6 AM, but doesn't get rolling until around midnight. The cover is $7–$10, or $30 with open bar.

★ **J.B.** (✉ Blvd. Francisco M. Ascencio 2043, Zona Hotelera ☎ 322/224–4616), pronounced "Hota Bay," is the best club in town for salsa. The age of the crowd varies, but tends toward thirty- and fortysomethings—definitely not teenyboppers. J.B. is serious about dancing, so it feels young at heart. There's usually a band Thursday through Saturday nights, DJ music the rest of the week. Those with *dos patas zurdas* (two left feet), or who simply don't know the steps, can attend salsa lessons Wednesday through Friday 9:30–10:30 PM; cost is $2 with no additional cover; otherwise, the cover is $9 after 10:30 PM.

Ready to party? Then head to **The Zoo** (✉ Paseo Díaz Ordaz 630, Centro ☎ 322/222–4945) for DJ-spun techno, dance, disco, Latin, reggae, and hip-hop. The adventurous can dance in the cage. It attracts a mixed crowd of mainly young (teenagers to thirtysomething) locals and travelers, though after midnight the median age plunges. It's open until 6 AM when things are hopping. The downstairs restaurant is often full in the early evening with cruise-ship passengers.

> ## LET'S GET PHYSICAL
>
> Tango aficionados since 1985, **Al and Barbara Garvey** (☎ 322/222–8895 ⊕ www.tangobar-productions) of San Francisco teach the Argentine dance for beginner through advanced levels. They also give private lessons and meet up with fellow dancers for practice at Vallarta's Latin dance club, J.B. The Garveys are usually only around during the winter season; call or check their Web site for schedules.

FILM

Movie tickets here are less than half what they are in the U.S. and Canada. Many theaters have discounted prices on Wednesday. For showtimes, see the theater's Web site or www.vallartaonline.com/cinema.

Cine Bahía (⊠ Insurgentes 63, Centro ☎ 322/222–1717 ≌ $4) is no spring chicken, but it's right in Old Puerto Vallarta. It still has an intermission, a boon to some, a source of irritation for others. It has five screens and numerous English-language choices.

Cineápolis (⊠ Plaza Soriana, Av. Francisco Villa 1642–A, Pitillal ☎ 322/225–1251 ⊕ www.cinepolis.com.mx) was, until Cinemark showed up, PV's newest theater. Next to Soriana department stores at the south entrance to El Pitillal, it has 14 screens and shows in English and Spanish. Tickets are $4.

Easy to access in the heart of the Hotel Zone, **Cinemark** (⊠ Plaza Caracol, Zona Hotelera ☎ 322/224–8927) is on the second floor at the south end of Plaza Caracol (aka Plaza Comercial Gigante). The latest films are shown on its 10 screens, with plenty in English. Tickets are $3.

Versalles (⊠ Av. Francisco Villa 799, Col. Versalles ☎ 322/225–8766) has five screens. Tickets are $4.

> **DRINKS ON THE BEACH**
>
> Playa Los Muertos is the destination of choice for a sunset cocktail and dinner on the beach. Strolling mariachi bands serenade diners overlooking the sand; at some tables the waves kiss your toes under the table. Candles and torches light the scene, along with the moon. After dinner you can take a stroll or sit on the beach, or head to another restaurant bar for a coffee or after-dinner *digestif* to the tunes of marimba, folk music, or jazz.

MORE AFTER-DARK OPTIONS

Enjoy a dinner show or sunset cruise or see silver-studded mariachis in their elegant, fancy dress uniforms and boots. Most of the large hotels have live lounge music, especially on weekends, holidays, and during the winter high season. Drag shows (⇨ chapter 10) are crowd pleasers— whether the crowd is straight or gay; they usually take place on the south side of downtown.

Coffeehouses

⇨ For more coffeehouses, *see* "Where to Eat" in Chapter 3.

Beanz (⊠ Olas Altas 490, Local 7, Col. E. Zapata ☎ 322/222–0324) serves excellent coffee. It's an Internet hot-spot, and access is free for customers.

Dark and romantic, albeit open to the four winds, **Café San Angel** (⊠ Av. Olas Altas 449, at Calle Francisca Rodriguez, Col. E. Zapata ☎ 322/223–1273) is always pleasantly crowded. It has tables along the sidewalk and comfortable couches and chairs within. The menu holds soups, sandwiches, salads, and a great frappuccino.

Dinner Cruises

⇨ *See* "Cruises" *in* Chapter 7.

Shows

In addition to those listed here, many hotels have buffet dinners with mariachis, charros, and folkloric dancers. All-inclusive hotels generally include nightly entertainment in the room price. ⇨ For more dinner shows, *see* "Theater" *in* Chapter 8.

Enjoy Vallarta's original dinner show Thursday or Sunday at **La Iguana** (⊠ Calle Lázaro Cárdenas 311, Col. E. Zapata ☎ 322/222–0105). Large troops of professional mariachis entertain, beautiful women dance in colorful costumes, couples dance, kids whack piñatas, and fireworks light up the sky. The simulated cockfight is supposed to be painless for the roosters, and nearly so for alarmed foreign visitors. There's an open bar, and the buffet has 40 different dishes to choose from. Cockfights notwithstanding, most folks deem this party well worth the price of $50 per person.

El Mariachi Loco is the place to see silver-studded mariachi musicians.

El Mariachi Loco (⊠ Lázaro Cárdenas 254, Centro ☎ 322/223–2205) is the place to see silver-studded mariachi musicians. The mariachis begin at 10:30 PM Monday through Wednesday; the rest of the week an organ player and drummer warm up the crowd before the mariachis come on-stage at around 11:30 PM. On weekends, a comedian and ranchera group are added to the mix at around 1 AM. Cover is $5.

Playa Los Arcos (⊠ Av. Olas Altas 380, Col. E. Zapata ☎ 322/222–1583) has a theme dinner show most nights 6:30–10:30 PM. The show, which costs $15, includes a buffet and Mexican beer and spirits. The most popular theme night is Saturday's Mexico Night, with mariachis, a charro doing rope tricks, and folkloric dance.

Adventure

Snorkeling

WORD OF MOUTH

"I can recommend an activity I participated in. It was a canopy tour. You ride on zip lines from treetop to treetop through the jungle. So thrilling, scary and just fun!!!! I had such a blast on this—I am definitely going to do it again when I go back."

–lvitaly

"Great whale watching, mellow atmosphere, amazing snorkeling [at Marietas Islands]. I highly recommend it."

–dabblingman

Puerto Vallarta is the best adventure-vacation destination on Mexico's Pacific Coast, at least for the sheer variety of activities. The water's warm and swimmable year-round, although downright bathlike July through September. The big blue bay attracts sea turtles, humpback whales, several species of dolphins, and a growing number of snorkelers and divers. The fishing is excellent—from deep sea angling for gigantic marlin and sailfish to trolling near shore for roosters and red snapper. Banderas Bay and the beaches to the north and south have waves for surfing as well as plenty of calm bays and inlets for swimming.

Among the lush subtropical mountains—so close to the coast and laced with streams and rivers rushing to the ocean—are challenging mountain biking trails for the fit, and, for those who prefer gas-driven excitement, dune and ATV safaris into the hills. Many family-owned ranches have horse-riding tours at reasonable prices—lasting from an hour or two to overnight forays into the Sierra.

Most tour operators provide transportation from strategic pick-up points, usually in downtown Puerto Vallarta, Marina Vallarta, and Nuevo Vallarta and sometimes in Conchas Chinas, but you'll save traveling from one end of the bay to the other by choosing an outfitter near your neck of the woods. Party boats and private yachts are great for accessing gorgeous and hard-to-reach beaches, primarily south of Vallarta along Cabo Corrientes.

Most of the tour operators are in Puerto Vallarta, but whenever possible we've listed some of the companies springing up to meet the needs of visitors staying north and south of town.

OUTDOOR ACTIVITIES & SPORTS

ATV & Dune-Buggy Tours

There's an increasing number of ATV, dune buggy, and jeep tours heading to the hills around Puerto Vallarta. Sharing a vehicle with a partner means a significant savings. Also take into consideration location; some head south of PV proper, others to the north. Most rides are to small communities, ranches, and rivers north, south, and east of Puerto Vallarta.

Logistics

A valid driver's license and a major credit card are required. Wear lightweight long pants, sturdy shoes, bandanna (some operators provide one as a keepsake) and/or tight-fitting hat, sunglasses, and both sunscreen and mosquito repellent. In rainy season (July–October) it's hotter and wetter—ideal for splashing through puddles and streams; the rest of the year is cooler but dusty. In either season, prepare to get dirty. Four-hour tours go for $75–$120; full-day trips to San Sebastián cost about $165 for one or $175 for two riders.

Outfitters

Adventure ATV Jungle Treks (✉ Basilio Badillo 400, Col. E. Zapata ☎ 322/ 223–0392) rents dirt bikes by the hour ($15 for one or two passengers)

MULTI-ADVENTURE OUTFITTERS

Don't see what you want here? Try one of these outfitters, whose multitude of tours include bird-watching, ATV tours, whale-watching, biking, hot-air ballooning, sailing, and much, much more.

Ecotours (☎ 322/223–3130 or 322/222–6606 ⊕ www.ecotoursvallarta.com). **Immersion Adventures** (⊠ La Manzanilla ☎ 315/351–5341 ⊕ www.immersionadventures.com).

Tours Soltero (⊠ San Patricio Melaque ☎ 315/355–6777).
Vallarta Adventures (☎ 322/297–1212 Nuevo Vallarta, 322/221–0657 Marina Vallarta, 888/303–2653 from U.S. and Canada ⊕ www.vallarta-adventures.com). **Wild Vallarta** (☎ 322/224–2118 or 322/225–6105 ⊕ www.wildpv.com).

and leads four-hour dune buggy tours and three-hour ATV tours that head into the hills behind Vallarta, daily. Convenient to Marina Vallarta and Nuevo Vallarta, **Best Ride** (⊠ Orquidia 117, Col. Villa Las Flores ☎ 322/221–3066 ⊕ www.magiic.com) runs custom tours in addition to twice-daily, three-hour ATV and dune buggy tours; kids under 11 ride free with a parent. **Wild Vallarta** (⊠ Calle Cardenal 160, Col. Los Sauces ☎ 322/224–2118 or 322/225–6105 ⊕ www.wildpv.com) has full-day and half-day tours in Honda four-wheel ATVs and open-frame, five-speed buggies with VW engines. The long and rugged ATV tour to San Sebastián, high in the Sierra, requires some experience, but four-hour trips to the beach at Sayulita or the tequila-producing factory Hacienda Doña Engracia are fine for beginners. (Consider riding two per ATV for the tequila tasting, solving the drinking-and-driving conundrum.) Based in the north part of the bay, the company has a pickup point in Conchas Chinas too, but it's a longish ride through Vallarta.

Canopy Tours

Puerto Vallarta's newest thrill is canopy tours, which are better described as high-octane thrill rides. On a canopy tour you'll "fly" from treetop to treetop (or in some cases, between steel rods), securely fastened to a zip line. Despite the inherent danger of dangling from a cable hundreds of feet off the ground, the operators we list have excellent safety records. It's permissible to take photos while zipping along so if you're brave, bring your camera along, with a neck strap to leave hands free.

Logistics

Even during the rainy season, however, mornings and *early* afternoons are generally sunny. Check with each operator regarding maximum weight (usually 250 pounds) and minimum ages for kids.

■ TIP→ Since a thunderstorm isn't the time to hang out near trees attached to metal cables, and rain makes the activity scary to say the least, don't take a tour when rain threatens.

Outfitters

★ **Canopy El Edén** (⊠ Office: Basilio Badillo 370, Col. E. Zapata ☎ 322/222–2516 ⊕ www.canopyeleden.com) has daily trips to the spirited Mismaloya River and adjacent restaurant. During the 3½-hour adventure ($66), which departs from the downtown office, you zip along 10 lines through the trees and above the river. To take full advantage of the lovely setting (bring your swimsuit) and good restaurant, take the first tour (they depart at 9, 11, and 1 daily); if there's room, you can return with a later group. Otherwise you can return to Vallarta by taxi, or ask the restaurant staff for a lift to the highway, where buses frequently pass.

★ Vallarta's top canopy tour is **Canopy Tour de Los Veranos** (⊠ Office: Calle Francisca Rodríguez 336, Centro ☎ 322/223-6060 ⊕ www.canopytours-vallarta.com). Slightly more expensive than its competitors ($78), Los Veranos also has the most zip lines (16), the longest zip line (600 feet), the highest zip line (500 feet off the ground), and the most impressive scenery: crossing the Rio Los Horcones half a dozen times on several miles of cables. Departures are from the office, across from the Pemex station at the south side of Puerto Vallarta, on the hour between 9 and 2, with reduced hours in low season (June through November). It's the only PV tour company that doesn't require helmets. After your canopy tour, there's time to scale the climbing wall, play in the Los Horcones River, eat at the restaurant, or hang out at the bar overlooking the river, but check to make sure that a ride back to town is available.

Luis Verdin of **Rancho Mi Chaparrita** (⊠ Manuel Rodriguez Sanchez 14, Sayulita ☎ 329/291-3112 ⊕ www.ranchomichapatrita.com) runs a 10-zip-line tour on his family ranch. Access the ranch on his lively, healthy horses via the beach and backcountry for a complete adventure. Canopy tours are $40; a canopy tour plus the horseback ride is $60. The most convenient canopy tour if you're staying in Nuevo Vallarta is **Vallarta Adventures** (⊠ Paseo de las Palmas 39–A, Nuevo Vallarta ☎ 322/297-1212, 888/303-2653 in U.S. and Canada ⊠ Edifício Marina Golf, Local 13–C, Calle Mástil, Marina Vallarta ☎ 322/221-0657 ⊕ www.vallarta-adventures.com), although it's not the best show in town. Participants use gloved hands rather than a braking device to slow down or stop, and must return to town right after their zip line canopy adventure with no time for other activities. It's $70 per person.

Fishing

Sportfishing is excellent off Puerto Vallarta, and fisherfolk have landed monster marlin well over 500

SEASONAL CATCHES

Sailfish and dorado are abundant practically year-round. (Though dorado drop out a bit in early summer and sailfish dip slightly in spring.)

Winter: bonito, dorado, jack crevalle, sailfish, striped marlin, wahoo

Spring: amberjack, jack crevalle, grouper, mackerel, red snapper

Summer: grouper, roosterfish, yellowfin tuna

Fall: black marlin, blue marlin, sailfish, striped marlin, yellowfin tuna, wahoo pounds. Surf casting from shore nets snook, roosters, and jack crevalles. Hire a *panga* (skiff) to hunt for Spanish mackerel, sea bass, amberjack, snapper, bonito, and roosterfish on full- or half-day trips within the bay. Yachts are best for big-game fishing: yellowfin tuna, blue, striped, and black marlin, and dorado. Hire them for 4 to 10 hours, or overnight. Catch-and-release of billfish is encouraged. If you don't want to charter a boat, you can also join a "party" boat.

Most sportfishing yachts are based at Marina Vallarta; only a few call "home" the marina at Paradise Village, in Nuevo Vallarta. Pangas can be hired in the traditional fishing villages of Mismaloya and Boca de Tomatlán, just south of town; in the Costalegre towns of La Manzanilla and Barra de Navidad; and in the north, La Cruz de Huanacaxtle, but more commonly at El Anclote and Nuevo Corral del Risco, Punta de Mita. The resort hotels of the Costalegre and Punta de Mita arrange fishing excursions for their guests. Bass fishing at Cajón de Peña, about 1 ½ hours south of Vallarta, nets 10-pounders on a good day.

Logistics

Most captains and crews are thoroughly bilingual, at least when it comes to boating and fishing.

LICENSES Licenses are necessary, but don't worry about procuring yours on your own. If the captain hasn't arranged it ahead of time, he will make sure that a SEMARNAP official is on-hand to sell you one before the boat departs. Cost is $13 per day; there are no weekly rates.

PRICES Prices generally range $300–$400 for four hours on a yacht to $600–$1,050 for a 10-hour cruise for four to eight anglers. A longer trip is recommended for chasing the big guys, as it takes you to prime fishing grounds like Los Bancos and Cobeteña.

Party boats range from $100 to $140 per person for an eight-hour day. Drinking water is generally included in the price; box lunches and beer or soda may be sold separately or included, or sometimes it's BYOB. Pangas and superpangas, the latter with shade and a head of some sort, charge $150 to $400 for four to eight hours and generally accommodate one to three anglers. For a boat and round-trip transportation to Cajón de Peña, an all-day affair, expect to pay $150 to $600 per person.

Outfitters

CharterDreams (✉ Marina Vallarta, Dock C–5, Puerto Vallarta ☎ 322/221–0690 ⊕ www.charterdreams.com) has a variety of excursions, from trips with one to three people in *pangas* (skiffs) for bass fishing to cruises with up to eight people aboard luxury yachts. Although most fisherfolk choose to leave around the smack of dawn, you set your own itinerary. The same rates apply for whale-watching or private sightseeing or snorkeling tours. Aboard group boats—aka "party boats"—belonging to **Cruceros Princesa** (✉ Terminal Marítima, Marina Vallarta ☎ 322/224–4777) you'll get a reliable boat, knowledgeable crew, and a box lunch to boot. Equipment, live bait, and an ice chest with ice are included; bring your own drinks. The eight-hour tour departs from the maritime pier. Yachts from 38 to 46 feet are available for individual charter as well.

Reliable for sportfishing (as well as sightseeing, surfing, or snorkeling tours) at Punta de Mita is Don Félix of **Félix Ocean Tours** (⊠ Mini-Super Las Palmeras Av. El Anclote 20, Punta de Mita ☎ 329/291–6342). He and his son Javier are local fishermen who know all the hot spots—in fact, they guarantee their services. They charge $47 per hour, four hour minimum, for fishing (with live bait) for up to four persons. A new boat with twin motors, sonar, and GPS is an additional $10 per hour. In Barra de Navidad, Costalegre, contact **Gerardo Kosonoy** (☎ 044 315/354–2251 cell) for honest fishing excursions. You can easily round up a fisherman with a panga from one of the two large fishing co-ops on the lagoon side of town. There's usually at least one representative hoping for clients at the water taxi dock.

Master Baiter (⊠ Puesto del Sol Condominiums, near lighthouse, Marina Vallarta ☎ 322/209–0498 or 322/209–0499 ⊕ www.mbsportfishing. com ⊠ Calle 31 de Octubre 107, across from McDonald's, Centro ☎ 322/222–4043) is a comprehensive fishing outfitter with a proven track record. Its superpanga fleet consists of 26-foot skiffs with shade and bathroom; some have GPS. The eight-hour yacht charter is one of the most expensive in town, but you're guaranteed to catch something or you get a third of your money back. An overnight trip ($2,500) allows further exploration, and includes meals and drinks. Both storefronts (downtown Vallarta and Marina Vallarta) sell fishing tackle, although there's a better selection at the Marina store.

Do you remember the seductive-looking divers in *Night of the Iguana?* Well, their progeny might be among the local guys of **Mismaloya Divers** (⊠ Road to Mismaloya Beach, Mismaloya ☎ 322/228–0020). Panga trips here are comparatively inexpensive. Local fishermen at Punta de Mita have formed the **Sociedad Cooperativa de Servicios Turísticos** (Tourist Services Cooperative ⊠ Av. El Anclote 1, Manz. 17, Nuevo Corral del Risco ☎ 329/291–6298 ⊕ www.prodigyweb.net.mx/cooperativapuntamita), whose are competitive with Mismaloya Divers. The families who run this co-op were forcibly relocated from their original town of Corral del Risco due to the development of luxurious digs like the Four Seasons. The guides may not speak English as fluently as the more polished PV operators, but they know the local waters, and the fees go directly to them and their families. Sportfishing costs about $44 per hour, with a four-hour minimum, for up to five people. Two hours of whale-watching or snorkeling around the Marietas Islands, for up to eight people, costs $81.

Captain Peter Vines of **Vallarta Tour and Travel** (⊠ Marina Los Palmas Local 4, in front of Dock B, Marina Vallarta ☎ 322/209–0005, 866/682–1971 in U.S. and Canada) can accommodate eight fisherfolk with top-of-the-line equipment, including the latest electronics, sonar, radar, and two radios. Rates are very reasonable, especially because they include lunch, beer, soda, and fish-cleaning service at the end of the day. Transportation from your hotel is included in the full-day bass-fishing expedition to Cajón de Peña.

ANNUAL EVENTS

FEBRUARY

Hundreds of bikes roar into PV for **Bike Week** (⊕ www.bikeweek.com) and its rallies, parties, and motorcycle parades.

MARCH

The entire month is dedicated to racing and boating activities, beginning with the **Banderas Bay Regatta** (☎ 322/297-2222 ⊕ www. banderasbayregatta.com), which starts in San Diego, California, and ends here with a great awards banquet. Throughout the month there are cocktail parties, charity events, receptions, seminars, additional races, and boat parades.

MAY

Begun in the early '90s, the five-day **Annual Sports Classic** (☎ 322/226-0404, Ext. 6038 [Veronica Alarcon at the Sheraton Buganvilias]) invites amateurs, pros, and semi-pros to compete in disc golf, basketball, softball, soccer, tennis, and an aerobics marathon. Most events take place at the Agustin Flores Contreras Stadium or Los Arcos Amphitheater.

NOVEMBER

The **Puerto Vallarta International Half Marathon** (⊕ www.maratonvallarta. com), held in early November, gets bigger each year, with nearly 1,000 participants in 2005, its third year. The **International Puerto Vallarta Sailfish and Marlin Tournament** (☎ 322/225-5467 ⊕ www. fishvallarta.com) celebrated its 50th anniversary in 2005. The entry fee is more than $1,000 per line, but the prizes and prestige of winning are great. Categories are dorado, tuna, marlin, and sailfish.

7

Golf

"Not a bad mango in the bunch" is how one golf aficionada described Puerto Vallarta's courses. From the Four Seasons Punta Mita to the Gran Bay at Barra de Navidad, the region is a close second to Los Cabos in variety of play at a range of prices. Well-known designers are represented, including Jack Nicklaus and Tim Weiskopf.

Logistics

Most of these courses offer first-class services including driving ranges and putting greens, lessons, clinics, pro shops, and clubhouses.

Courses

PUERTO VALLARTA Joe Finger designed the 18-hole course at **Marina Vallarta** (⊠ Paseo de la Marina s/n, Marina Vallarta ☎ 322/221-0545 or 322/221-0073); the $121 greens fee includes practice balls and a shared cart. It's the area's second-oldest course and is closest and most convenient for golfers staying in the Hotel Zone, Old Puerto Vallarta, and Marina Vallarta. Very flat, it's way more challenging than it looks, with an awful lot of water hazards. Speaking of hazards, the alligators have a way of blending into the scenery. They might surprise you, but they supposedly don't

★ bite. Some of the best views in the area belong to the aptly named **Vista Vallarta** (⊠ Circuito Universidad 653, Col. San Nicolás ☎ 322/290-0030 or 322/290-0040). The course has 18 holes designed by Jack Nicklaus and another 18 by Tom Weiskopf. It costs $163 to play the former and $153 on the latter, which are a few miles northwest of the Marina Vallarta area. A shared cart and tax are included.

NUEVO VALLARTA
TO BUCERÍAS

At the Paradise Village hotel and condo complex, **El Tigre** (⊠ Paseo de los Cocoteros 18, Nuevo Vallarta ☎ 322/297–0773, 866/843–5951 in U.S., 800/214–7758 in Canada ⊕ www.eltigregolf.com) is an 18-hole course with 12 water features. The greens fee of $130 includes a shared cart and practice balls but not 15% tax. Don't be surprised if you see a guy driving around with tigers in his truck: the course's namesake and mascot is the passion of the club's director. El Tigre has a fun island par 3. **Four Seasons Punta Mita** (⊠ Punta de Mita ☎ 329/291–6000 ⊕ www.fourseasons.com) was designed by Jack Nicklaus. Nonguests are permitted, but not *encouraged*, to play the 195-acre, par-72 course; advance reservations are essential. The club's claim to fame is that it has perhaps the only natural island green in golf. Drive your cart to it at low tide; otherwise hop aboard a special amphibious vessel (weather permitting) to cross the water. There are seven other oceanfront links, as well as an optional par 3, the resort's signature hole.

Designed by Percy Clifford in 1978, PV's original course, **Los Flamingos Country Club** (⊠ Carretera a Bucerías, Km 145, 12 km [8 mi] north of airport, Nuevo Vallarta ☎ 329/296–5006 ⊕ www.flamingosgolf.com. mx), has been totally renovated. The 18-hole course at the northern extremity of Nuevo Vallarta has new irrigation and sprinkler systems to maintain the rejuvenated greens. The greens fee is $130, including a shared cart and a bucket of balls. The $147 greens fee for the 18-hole course at **Mayan Palace** (⊠ Paseo de las Moras s/n, Fracc. Nautico Turistico, Nuevo Vallarta ☎ 322/227–0773 or 225–2969) includes a golf cart for each player.

COSTALEGRE
Fodor'sChoice

About two hours south of Vallarta on the Costalegre is the area's best course. At least six of the holes at **El Tamarindo** (⊠ Carretera Melaque–Puerto Vallarta, Careterra 200, Km 7.5, Cihuatlán ☎ 315/351–5032, Ext. 500 or 34) play along the ocean; some are cliffside holes with fabulous views, others go right down to the beach. On a slow day, golfers are encouraged at tee time to have a swim or a picnic on the beach during their round, or to play a hole a second time if they wish. Designed by David Fleming, the breathtaking course is the playground of birds, deer, and other wildlife. It's an awesome feeling to

> **WORD OF MOUTH**
>
> "El Tamarindo is a beautiful spot, perfect for getting away from it all. . . . If you golf or play tennis, you'll be in hog heaven." –Tansy

nail the course's most challenging hole, the 9th: a par-3 with a small green surrounded by bunkers. The greens fee is $205, including cart. Resort guests get priority for tee times; call up to a week ahead to check availability. **Isla Navidad** (⊠ Isla Navidad, Barra de Navidad ☎ 314/337–9006 or 800/996–3426 ⊕ www.islanavidad.com) must have the best variety of play in the area, with three 9-hole courses of different flavors: mountain, lagoon, and ocean. Designed by Robert VanHagge, the course is beautifully sculpted, with lovely contours. Greens fees are $80 (plus tax), carts are $30.

Horseback Riding

Most of the horse riding outfits are based on family ranches in the foothill towns of the Sierra like Las Palmas. Horses are permitted on the beach in smaller towns like Sayulita and San Francisco, but not in Vallarta proper, so expect to ride into the hills for sunset-viewing there.

Logistics

Outfitters pick you up either from the hotel or strategic locations north and south of town and return you to your hotel or to the pickup point. Short rides depart morning and afternoon, while longer rides are generally in the morning only, at least during winter hours of early sunset.

Ask at the beachfront restaurants of tiny towns like Yelapa, Quimixto, and Las Animas, south of PV, to hook up with horses for treks into the jungle. Horses are generally well cared for and some are exceptionally fit and frolicky.

Outfitters

Hacienda de Doña Engracia (✉ Carretera a las Palmas, K 10, La Desembocada ☎ 322/224–0410 ⊕ www.haciendadonaengracia.com) has, among other activities, a three-hour horseback excursion ($30). After the river has receded at the end of the wet season (this dry period usually lasts from late November through June), you ride one hour to a series of three hot springs, where you spend an hour before heading back, crossing a river mid-trip. In rainy season the tour through jungly hills is still impressive, but because one often can't cross the swollen streams, doesn't end at the hot springs. Some of the large stable of horses are of Arabian stock. At the hacienda, you can fish in the small artificial lake, do a tequila tasting, go mountain biking, or lunch at the restaurant. Most people arrive as part of a cruise-ship excursion or dune-buggy tour with Wild Vallarta (⇨ ATV Tours, *above*) or other adventure companies, but you can drive on your own as well.

★ **Rancho Charro** (☎ 322/224–0114 ⊕ www.ranchocharro.com.mx) provides transportation to and from your hotel for rides to rivers and waterfalls. Choices include three-hour ($47), five-hour ($60), and all-day rides ($100), and several multiday camping-riding combos. The friendly

★ folks at family-owned **Rancho Manolo** (✉ Highway 200, Km 12, at Mismaloya bridge, Mismaloya ☎ 322/228–0018 day, 322/222–3694 evening) take you into the mountains they know so well. The usual tour is to El Edén, the restaurant-and-river property where the movie *Predator* was filmed. The three-hour trip (one hour each way, with an hour for a quick meal or for splashing in the river) costs just $30.

The horses of **Rancho Ojo de Agua** (✉ Cerrada de Cardenal 227, Fracc. Aralias, Puerto Vallarta ☎ 322/224–0607) are part Mexican quarter horse and part thoroughbred; according to proud owner Mari González, the stock comes from the Mexican cavalry. The family-owned business conducts sunset and half-day horseback rides (three to five hours, $33–$53), some including lunch and time for a swim in a mountain stream. Also available is a full-day excursion into the Sierra Madre ($95).

Manuel, of **Rancho Manuel** (✉ Calle 33, Gringo Hill, Sayulita ☎ 322/132–7683) rents horses for riding on the beach or in the hills behind Sayulita. You can find him on the beach at San Pancho or Sayulita, or give him a call ahead to arrange. Though the trail rides at **Club de Polo Costa Careyes** (✉ Km 53.5, Carretera 200, Carretera a Barra de Navidad, El Careyes ☎ 315/351–0320 ⊕ www.mexicopolo.com) are expensive at $70 for 45 minutes to

> ### PICKUP POLO
>
> Rent a pony and join a game of polo at the **Club de Polo Costa Careyes** (✉ Km 53.5 Carretera 200, Carretera a Barra de Navidad, El Careyes ☎ 315/351–0320 ⊕ www.mexicopolo.com). The cost is $80 per game per player. Spectators are welcome, too, at no charge, to watch the various tournaments (mid-April–November). Ask about packages including accommodations, clinics (March and April only), and lessons.

an hour, you know you're getting an exceptional mount. Trips leave in early morning or around sunset. Tours are mid-November through mid-April only.

Kayaking

Except on very calm, glassy days, the open ocean is really too rough for enjoyable kayaking, and the few kayaking outfitters there mainly offer this activity in combination with snorkeling, dolphin watching, or boating excursions to area beaches. The best places for kayaking-and-birding combos are the mangroves, estuaries, large bays, and islands of the Costalegre, south of Puerto Vallarta.

Logistics

Many of the larger beachfront hotels—especially the all-inclusives—rent or loan sea kayaks to their guests. Double kayaks are easier on the arms than single kayaks. As the wind usually picks up in the afternoon, morning is generally the best time to paddle. Stick to coves if you want to avoid energy-draining chop and big waves. Kayaks range from $5 to $15 an hour or $10 to $40 per day.

Rent kayaks or take a half-day, full-day, or two-day paddling and birding tour with **Immersion Adventures** (✉ Entrada Camino a La Manzanilla, La Manzanilla ☎ 315/351–5341 ⊕ www.immersionadventures.com). Although the company has an office on the entrance road to La Manzanilla, it's best to book your excursions at least a week ahead of your arrival. Opportunities include trips to offshore islands Cocinas and Iglesias, the riparian environment of Ríos Purificación or Cuixmala, or five- to six-hour coastal forays with time for snorkeling. In addition to its other curricula, **Ecotours** (✉ Ignacio L. Vallarta 243, Col. E. Zapata ☎ 322/223–3130 or 322/222–6606 ⊕ www.ecotoursvallarta.com), in downtown Vallarta, has kayaking tours from Boca de Tomatlán. After paddling around a rocky point you end at tiny Playa Colomitos, where there's time for snorkeling and then a snack. You'll spend 1½ to 2 hours kayaking and though it's fun being on the water, the scenery is not exactly breathtaking. **Vallarta Adventures** (⊠Paseo de las Palmas 39–A, Nuevo Vallarta ☎ 322/297–1212, 888/303–2653 in U.S. and Canada ⊠ Edifício Marina Golf, Local 13–C, Calle Mástil, Marina Vallarta ☎ 322/221–0657 ⊕ www.vallarta-adventures.com) includes kayaking in its boat trip to Las Caletas, the company's private beach; the coastline here is fun to explore. The only other option is on dolphin-watching trips to Las Marietas Islands, where there are about five kayaks per boatload of up to 100 passengers, most of whom choose to snorkel.

Mountain Biking

Although the tropical climate makes it hot for biking, the Puerto Vallarta area is lovely and has challenging and varied terrain. Based in Puerto Vallarta, the major biking operators lead rides up river valleys, to Yelapa, and from the old mining town of San Sebastian (reached via plane; included in price), high in the Sierra, back to Vallarta. It's about 45 kilometers of downhill.

In the rainy season, showers are mainly in the late afternoon and evening, so bike tours can take place year-round. In summer and fall rivers and waterfalls are voluptuous and breathtaking. A popular ending point for rides into the foothills, they offer a place to rest, rinse off, and have a snack or meal. During the dry season, it's cooler and less humid—although still hot and humid. The very best months for biking are January through March: the weather is coolest and the vegetation, rivers, and waterfalls still reasonably lush after the end of the rainy season in October.

Logistics

PRICES Four- to five-hour rides average $45 to $70; Yelapa costs $115–$150. The ride down from San Sebastián, including one-way plane trip, is $165–$220. Rides of more than a half day include lunch, and all include helmet, gloves, and bikes.

Outfitters

Oscar del Díos of **Bike Mex** (⊠ Calle Guerrero 361, Centro ☎ 322/223–1834 or 322/223–1680) can tailor rides to your level of fitness and ability. He has a technical, single-track ride for the very advanced, local rides for beginners to advanced, and an all-day downhill from San Sebastian. Excursions include guide, gear (24-speed mountain bikes), and light breakfast and snacks. Multiday excursions can be arranged. A few streets behind Vallarta's cathedral, **Eco Ride** (⊠ Calle Miramar 382, Centro ☎ 322/222–7912 ⊕ www.ecoride.com) caters to intermediate and expert cyclists. Rides start at the shop and go up the Río Cuale, passing some hamlets along single tracks and dirt roads. A few rides include time at local swimming holes; the Yelapa ride—with two 10-km uphills and a 20-km downhill—returns by boat.

Family operation **Vallarta Bikes** (⊠ Franisco Villa 1442, Col. Los Sauces ☎ 322/293–1142 ⊕ www.vallartabikes.com) has custom tours of up to 10 days. More common, however, are set itineraries for beginner to advanced cyclists. A three- to four-hour beginner's ride to La Pileta is popular, as the departure point is near the town center and the destination a year-round swimming hole. This easy downhill includes lunch. The six-hour, 60-km tour to Yelapa is more physical, but the reward is lunch overlooking Yelapa's beautiful beach and returning by water taxi. Owner-guide Alejandro González leads groups whenever possible. He will certainly push you, but don't expect him to hold your hand.

Multisport Tours

Natura Tours (⊠ Carretera Aeropuerto, Km 5.5, Zona Hotelera 🏢🏢 322/224–0410) has nature-oriented excursions, including bass and deep-sea fishing, scuba diving, hiking, horseback riding, and biking. Two-and-a-half hour villa tours get you inside the garden walls of some attractive PV homes. Tours depart promptly at 11 AM (arrive by 10:30) from the Hotel Posada Río Cuale (Calle Aquiles Serdán 242) on Wednesday and Thursday mid-November through the end of April. The $30 fee benefits local charities.

Canadian expat Ray Calhoun and his wife Eva run **Tours Soltero** (⊠ Privada Las Cabañas 26, San Patricio Melaque 🏢 315/355–6777). They rent mountain bikes, snorkeling equipment, and boogie boards ($10 per day), and lead active tours from their base in San Patricio Melaque to neighboring beaches and towns.

> ### A CUT ABOVE
>
> With more than 10 years' experience, dozens of tours, and a staff of some 350, the well-respected **Vallarta Adventures** (⊠ Paseo de las Palmas 39–A, Nuevo Vallarta 🏢 322/297–1212, 888/303–2653 in U.S. and Canada ⊠ Edificio Marina Golf, Local 13–C, Calle Mástil, Marina Vallarta 🏢 322/221–0657 ⊕ www.vallarta-adventures.com) is the obvious choice for high-end hotel concierges and cruise-ship activity directors.

Typical tours are snorkeling in Tenacatita with boogie boarding at Boca de Iguana, 10–5, ($25) and a day trip to the state capital, Colima, which includes lunch and a stop at a typical hacienda cum museum ($48). Tours run any day, all year with a minimum of four customers.

Sailing

Although large Bahía de Banderas and towns to the north and south have lots of beautiful beaches to explore and wildlife to see, there are few sailing adventures for the public. Most boating companies don't want to rely on the wind to get to area beaches for the day's activities. The companies below are recommended for their true sailing skills and reliable vessels.

Logistics

For insurance reasons, companies or individuals here don't rent bareboat (uncrewed) yachts even to seasoned sailors. Those who want to crew the ship themselves can do semi-bareboat charters, where the captain comes along but allows the clients to sail the boat.

Outfitters

Veteran sailor Pat Henry directs **Coming About** (☎ 322/222–4119 ⊕ www.coming-about.com), a sailing school for women open November through May. After an introductory dinner, the nine-day course ($2,900 per person) is followed by four days of combined instruction and sail practice, two full days of sailing, and finally a three-day live-aboard cruise. Schedule permitting Coming About also gives a one-day introductory sailing lesson, including lunch. Cost is $475 whether it's one person or four the maximum. **Vallarta Adventures** (✉ Paseo de las Palmas 39–A, Nuevo Vallarta ☎ 322/297–1212, 888/303–2653 in U.S. and Canada ✉ Edificio Marina Golf, Local 13–C, Calle Mástil, Marina Vallarta ☎ 322/221–0657 ⊕ www.vallarta-adventures.com) has sunset group sails once or twice a week during high season for about $60 per person. To charter your own private sailboat with a captain, contact Andre Schwartz of **Casa Naval** (✉ Puerto Vallarta ☎ 044 322/100–4154 cell ⊕ www.casanaval.com). The captain–owner has a comfortable Beneteau Oceanis 390 called the *Dèjá-Vu Again,* a 39-foot vessel that accommodates eight for trips of four hours to several days.

Scuba Diving & Snorkeling

The ocean isn't nearly as clear as the Caribbean, but the warm, nutrient-rich water attracts a rich and varied community of sea creatures. Many of the larger resort hotels rent or loan snorkeling equipment and have introductory dive courses at their pools. The underwater preserve surrounding Los Arcos, a rock formation off Playa Mismaloya, is a popular spot for diving and snorkeling. The rocky bay at Quimixto, about 32 km (20 mi) south of PV and accessible only by boat, is a good snorkeling spot. *Pangeros* based in Boca and Yelapa can be hired to take you to spots off the tourist trail.

On the north side of things, Punta de Mita, about 80 km (50 mi) north of PV, has the Marietas Islands, with lava tubes and caves and at least 10 good places to snorkel and dive, including spots for advanced divers. El Morro Islands, with their big fish lurking in the underwater pinnacles and caves, are also suitable for experienced divers.

Logistics

June through September is the very best time for snorkeling and diving, although it's fine all year long. In summer, however, the water is not only its warmest and calmest but visibility is best—80 to 120 feet on a good day—and you can spot gigantic manta rays, several species of eel, sea turtles, and many species of colorful fish. In winter, although conditions are less favorable, some luck will yield orca and humpback whale sightings, an awesome experience.

Outfitters

For PADI- or NAUI-certification, equipment rentals, and one- or two-tank dives, contact **Chico's Dive Shop** (✉ Paseo Díaz Ordáz 772, Centro ☎ 322/222–1895 ✉ Mismaloya Beach, in front of Barceló La Jolla de Mismaloya, Mismaloya ☎ 322/228–0248 ⊕ www.chicos-diveshop.com). Trips to Los Arcos accommodate snorkelers ($18) as well as those who want a one- or two-tank dive ($59 and $89 respectively). From the Mismaloya shop, rent Jet Skis ($95 per hour), or underwater scooters ($35 per hour). Kayaks, mountain bikes, and fishing poles rent by the hour, day, or week ($10 per hour, $25 per day, $50 per week). In Nayarit, **CISBAB** (✉ Héroes de Nacozarí 152, Bucerías ☎ 329/298–2364 ⊕ www.vallartaundersea.com) teaches PADI dive courses; runs dive trips; and sells, rents, and repairs dive equipment.

Ecotours, an authorized equipment dealer, has English-speaking PADI dive masters. Two-tank dives run $75 to $90; longer trips to Cor-

> ## A NATURAL HIGH
>
> A balloon tour with **Wild Vallarta** (✉ Calle Cardenal 160, Col. Los Sauces ☎ 322/224–2118 or 322/225–6105 ⊕ www.wildpv.com) is one of the best ways to drink in Vallarta's magnificent scenery. During the 3½-hour tour with an experienced pilot, you soar above jungle and beaches, getting an excellent view of one of the world's most magnificent bays. The cost is $205 to be shared among six passengers (minimum)

beteña cost $120. All two-tank trips include lunch and gear. The PADI dive masters at **Pacific Scuba** (✉ Blvd. Francisco Medina Ascencio 2486, Zona Hotelera ☎ 322/209–0364 ⊕ www.pacificscuba.com.mx) teach courses, rent equipment, and arrange trips. A two-tank package to one of at least six sites (including Los Arcos, Marietas Islands, or Corbeteña) costs $75 to $100 and includes lunch and all gear. Three-day packages are available, too.

Tours with **Sociedad Cooperativa de Servicios Turísticos** (✉ Av. El Anclote 1, Manz. 17, Nuevo Corral del Risco ☎ 329/291–6298 ⊕ www.prodigyweb.net.mx/cooperativapuntamita) are a great deal if you have a group: two hours of snorkeling around the Marietas Islands, for up to eight people, costs just $85. **Vallarta Adventures** (✉ Paseo de las Palmas 39–A, Nuevo Vallarta ☎ 322/297–1212, 888/303–2653 in U.S. and Canada ✉ Edifício Marina Golf, Local 13-C, Calle Mástil, Marina Vallarta ☎ 322/221–0657 ⊕ www.vallarta-adventures.com) has daylong, two-tank tours of the Marietas Islands ($80) El Morro Islands ($100), El Corbeteña ($120) and other sites. The latter two are for advanced divers only and offered usually just once a week. Their expert PADI guides accommodate snorkelers as well as divers. They also have introductory dive classes for children and adults ($35), and open-water certification.

Surfing

The main surfing areas are in the north, in Nayarit State, including (from south to north) Destiladeras, Sayulita, and nearly a dozen breaks off Punta de Mita, where offshore breaks for intermediate and advanced surfers are best accessed by boat. The best spots for beginners are shore breaks like those at El Anclote and Sayulita; in the south, Barra de Navidad is also appropriate for beginners.

Logistics

SEASONS Waves are largest and most consistent between June and December; the water is also warmest during the rainy season (late June–October), averaging nearly 80°F July through September.

PRICES Surfboard rentals start at $5 an hour or $25 a day. Surfing trips run around $40 per hour, usually with a three- or four-hour minimum. Shops sell rash guards (no need for a full wet suit here), boogie boards, wax, and other necessities. For good info and links check out www.surf-mexico.com.

> ## WHEN TO CATCH A WAVE
>
> Locals have lots of folk wisdom about when to catch the best waves. Some say it's best right before a good rain, others believe it's when the tide is moving toward an extreme high or low.

Outfitters

On the beach at Sayulita is **Captain Pablo** (✉ Calle Las Gaviotas at beach, Sayulita ☎ 329/291–2070 early morning and evenings only), where you can rent equipment or take surfing lessons with Patricia: $25 should get you to your feet (board included). Surf tours, gear included, cost $160 for four hours (up to four surfers). You can take lessons from **Oscar's Rental** (✉ El Anclote beach, Punta de Mita ☎ 329/291–6284 ⊕ www.puntamita.com/oscarrentals.htm), which has a stand right on the beach. The cost is a bit steep: $80 for two hours of instruction. Surfboard rentals go for $8 an hour, $30 a day, or $150 per week. Oscar's also runs surfing trips for up to eight people that last an average of three hours. If you're not up to surfing, try a boogie board or a sea kayak, both of which rent for $10 a day.

Although there's not much surf at its beach, **San Pancho Surf Shop** (✉ Av. Tercer Mundo 37, San Francisco ☎ 311/258–4215) sells and rents boards ($5 per hour or $20 per day to rent) and other surfing equipment. Lessons ($30 per hour) are generally taught at Sayulita, 10 minutes south of town, where the shore break is gentle. The shop sells organic coffee as well as a small selection of bikinis, flip-flops, and board shorts. On the beach at Sayulita, **Sininen** (✉ Calle Delfín 4–S, Sayulita ☎ 329/291–3186 ⊕ www.sininen.com.mx) rents and sells surfboards and surf paraphernalia. In Barra look for **South Swell Surf Shop** (✉ Hotel La Alondra, Suite 2, Calle Sinaloa 16, Barra de Navidad ☎ 044 315/354–5497 cell) for all your ripping requirements.

Wildlife-Watching

Banderas Bay and the contiguous coast and inland areas are blessed with abundant species of birds and beasties. The range of habitats from riparian forests to offshore islands are home to a wide range of native and migratory birds, including about two dozen endemic species. Beyond birds, most of the wildlife spotting is marine: whales (late November through end of March), dolphins, marine turtles, and giant manta rays, among many other species.

Bird-Watching

Although there aren't a lot of dedicated birding operators here, this region is perfect for the pastime, as Vallarta has more than 350 species in a wide variety of habitats, including shoreline, rivers, marshes, lagoons, mangroves, and tropical and evergreen forests. In the mangroves, standouts are the great blue heron, mangrove cuckoo, and vireo. Ocean and shore birds include brown and blue-footed boobies and red-billed tropicbirds. Military macaws patrol the thorn forests and songbirds of all stripes fill the pine-oak forests with their melodies.

LOGISTICS Most people come on trips through birding clubs or organizations like those below, or hire a private birding guide. Outfitters charge $45–$60 for half-day tours and $100–125 for full-day tours.

OUTFITTERS **Ecotours** (✉ Ignacio L. Vallarta 243, Col. E. Zapata ☎ 322/223–3130 or 322/222–6606 ⊕ www.ecotoursvallarta.com) runs a six-hour tropical forest tour approximately four days per week for $63. Bring plenty of insect repellent, especially in the rainy months. Clients of **Immersion Adventures** (✉ Entrada Camino a La Manzanilla, La Manzanilla ☎ 315/351–5341 ⊕ www.immersionadventures.com) sneak up on their idols via kayak, accessing mangrove swamps and riparian environments as well as hiking along jungle trails. **Victor Emanuel Nature Tours** (☎ 512/328–5221, 800/328–8368 in U.S. and Canada ⊕ www.ventbird.com) has several yearly small-group birding tours of the Puerto Vallarta from Rancho Primavera, just south of PV proper.

Mark Stackhouse, of **Westwings Birding Tours** (⊕ www.westwings.com), divides his time evenly between the U.S. and San Blas, Nayarit. According to Mark, a 30-year birder, it's possible to see about 25% of the birds found throughout Mexico on day trips from a San Blas Hotel. Contact Mark with plenty of lead time to arrange private birding tours. **Wings** (☎ 520/320–9868, 888/293–6443 in U.S. and Canada ⊕ www.wingsbirds.com) leads several weeklong tours each year to the mangroves and tropical forest around San Blas.

Dolphin Encounters

Many folks find the idea of captive dolphins disturbing; others cherish the opportunity to interact with these intelligent creatures that communicate through body language as well as an audible code we humans have yet to decipher. Decide whether you support the idea of captive-dolphin encounters, and act accordingly. Listed below are operators with captive dolphin programs as well as one that has an open-ocean encounter. As these gregarious mammals are fond of bow-surfing, most bay-tripping boats will encounter dolphins as they motor along the bay, providing more opportunities to see dolphins as well as leaping manta rays and other sea life.

> **CAUTION**
>
> Several organizations, including Greenpeace, the Humane Society (U.S.), and the Whale and Dolphin Conservation Society have spoken out against captive dolphin encounters, asserting that some water parks get dolphins from restricted areas, and that the confined conditions at some parks put the dolphins' health at risk. Consider putting the $100-plus fee toward a snorkeling, whale-watching, or noncaptive dolphin encounter, where you can see marine life in its natural state.

LOGISTICS Dolphins are abundant in the bay year-round, though not 24/7. Dolphin encounters limit the number of humans per encounter, and usually allow just two visits a day, so call early in your stay to book.

OUTFITTERS For both the Dolphin Encounter ($69; 30 minutes in the water and the Dolphin Swim; ($99; 45 minutes in the water) with **Dolphin Discovery** (⊠ Sea Life Park, Carretera a Tepic, Km 155, Nuevo Vallarta ☎ 322/297–0724) you spend about 30 of the 45-minute experience in the water interacting with dolphins. In the Royal Dolphin Swim ($139), you still get only 30 minutes in the pool, but at a higher ratio of cetaceans to humans, you get more face time. Mexican-owned **Wildlife Connection** ★ (⊠ Calle Francia 140, Col. Versalles, Puerto Vallarta ☎ 322/225–3621 ⊕ www.wildlifeconnection.com) uses two-motor skiffs equipped with listening equipment to find pods of dolphins in the wild blue sea. You can then jump in the water to swim with these beautiful creatures in their own environment. The most common destination is around the Marietas Islands. The cost is $65 per person for a four-hour tour, including travel time.

Hiking

The coastal fringe and the hills behind Vallarta—with streams and rivers heading down from the mountains—are beautiful areas for exploring, but few tour operators have hiking and walking trips. If you plan an impromptu exploration, it's best to take along a local familiar with the area.

LOGISTICS Some of the biking tour operators (⇨ Biking, *above*) will lead hiking outings as well, if you ask.

OUTFITTERS **Ecotours** (⊠ Ignacio L. Vallarta 243, Col. E. Zapata ☎ 322/223–3130 or 322/222–6606 ⊕ www.ecotoursvallarta.com) leads a very short hike (about one hour total hiking) from Boca de Tomatlánto the beach at Colomitos, just around the point. A slightly longer tour of several hours takes you along a stream from El Nogalito village to a rocky, waterfall-fed pool for a dip. En route to either you'll see a small number of birds, butterflies, and tropical plants, although nothing to write home about. **Vallarta Adventures** (⊠ Paseo de las Palmas 39–A, Nuevo Vallarta ☎ 322/297–1212, 888/303–2653 in U.S. and Canada ⊠ Edifício Marina Golf, Local 13–C, Calle Mástil, Marina Vallarta ☎ 322/221–0657 ⊕ www.vallarta-adventures.com) has a tour combining rappelling and hiking with a partial canopy tour. Although hikes are generally led by knowledgeable naturalists, the emphasis is on physical activity rather than flora and fauna sightings.

Turtle-Watching & Repatriation

Mexico has seven of the eight sea marine turtle species in the world. Three of those species live in and around Banderas Bay. The most prevalent is the olive ridley, or *golfina*. The fastest growing and earliest to mature of the Pacific coast turtles, they are much more numerous than the Careyes and leatherbacks; the latter are the least frequently sighted. Researchers estimate there are 1 to 10 leatherbacks for every 1,000 olive ridleys in the Puerto Vallarta area. The following tour companies offer educational programs combined with hands-on activities.

After the female turtle creates a nest in the sand, the eggs incubate for approximately 60 days. The babies must bust out of eggs and earth on their own, and with luck they will head for the ocean under cover of night. Birds, crabs, and other wild animals are relentless predators. For every 1,000 baby turtles born, only one survives to adulthood. Fortunately the average nest holds several hundred eggs.

For every 1,000 baby turtles born, only one survives to adulthood.

LOGISTICS   Tours run from summer through late fall. Wear shoes or sandals that are comfortable for walking in the sand, bring a sweatshirt or light jacket, and plan to stay out late in the evening for most turtle repatriation programs, as that is when predators are less active. Most tours cost $45–$50 per person and last three to four hours.

OUTFITTERS   Stay out late with **Ecotours** (⊠ Ignacio L. Vallarta 243, Col. E. Zapata ☎ 322/223–3130 or 322/222–6606 ⊕ www.ecotoursvallarta.com), whose three-hour turtle tours end just after midnight. After rounding up participants from several pickup points (the farthest north is in Bucerías), you walk the beach searching for females depositing their eggs in the sand, and help remove these eggs for safekeeping. Whether or not you find egg-laying females, there are always little turtles for releasing to the wild at the end of the evening. Tours are Monday through Saturday. Trained biologists from **Wildlife Connection** (⊠ Calle Francia 140, Col. Versalles, Puerto Vallarta ☎ 322/225–3621 ⊕ www.wildlifeconnection.com) lead turtle repatriation programs. During the four-hour tours you'll drive ATVs to the beach to find and collect recently deposited eggs, if possible, and then blast over to Boca de Tomates Beach to liberate tiny turtles under the relative protection of darkness.

Whale Watching

Most of the boats on the bay, whether fishing boats or tour boats, also run whale-watching tours (December–mid-March). Some boats are equipped with hydrophones for listening to the whales' songs and carry trained marine biologists; others use the usual crew and simply look for signs of cetaceans. The species you're most likely to see are humpback and killer whales (a gray whale occasionally), false killer whales, and bottlenose, spinner, and pantropic spotted dolphins (yup, dolphins are whales, too.)

LOGISTICS   Whale-watching is only available December through mid-March. Prime breeding grounds are around the Marietas Islands. The larger boats leave from Marina Vallarta, but fishermen in villages like Corral del Risco, Mismaloya, Boca de Tomatlán, and even Yelapa and Las Animas can be hired for less formal, more intimate trips to look for whales. The larger boats are more likely to have radio equipment useful for communicating with others about the location of whale pods.

OUTFITTERS   **Ecotours** (⊠ Ignacio L. Vallarta 243, Col. E. Zapata ☎ 322/223–3130 or 322/222–6606 ⊕ www.ecotoursvallarta.com) operates excursions aboard boats with hydrophones. After a brief lecture about cetacean ecosystems, board a boat at Punta de Mita for a three-hour tour. Tours are daily in season (mid-December–mid-March) and cost $80. **Sociedad**

Cooperativa de Servicios Turísticos (✉ Av. El Anclote 1, Manz. 1 ,
Corral del Risco ☎ 329/291–6298 ⊕ www.prodigyweb.ne.
cooperativapuntamita) has whale-watching around the Marietas
lands ($85 for one to eight people). You search until whales are spot
ted, and then have a half-hour of viewing time before returning to dry
land.

Vallarta Adventures (✉ Paseo de las Palmas 39–A, Nuevo Vallarta ☎ 322/
297–1212, 888/303–2653 in U.S. and Canada ✉ Edifício Marina Golf,
Local 13–C, Calle Mástil, Marina Vallarta ☎ 322/221–0657 ⊕ www.
vallarta-adventures.com) has professional guides who assist you in spotting dolphins and whales as you snorkel, dive, or kayak around the Marietas Islands. Professional biologists at **Wildlife Connection** (✉ Calle
Francia 140, Col. Versalles, Puerto Vallarta ☎ 322/225–3621 ⊕ www.
wildlifeconnection.com) are dedicated to educating the public about area
wildlife; the outfit gives tours in season.

OTHER ADVENTURES

Cruises

Daytime bay cruises generally begin with a quick jaunt to Los Arcos Underwater Preserve, off Mismaloya Beach. There's about a half hour for
snorkeling or swimming—sometimes with legions of little jellyfish in addition to the turtles that feed on them. Cruises then proceed to Yelapa,
Quimixto, or Playa las Ánimas, or to Islas Marietas for whale-watching (in winter), snorkeling, swimming, and lunch. Horseback riding might
be available at an additional cost (about $15).

There are plenty of similar tours available; the following are among the
most popular and professional.

Logistics

Buy your ticket from licensed vendors at Parque Lázaro Cárdenas, just
north of the Cuale River, along the boardwalk at Los Muertos Beach,
and at sportfishing operators such as Master Baiters. Prices are somewhat fluid; like car salespeople, the ticket sellers give discounts or jack
up the price as they see fit. Full-day booze cruises cost about $45–$70
per person, including open bar, continental breakfast, lunch, snorkeling and/or kayaks. Dinner cruises cost $75–$80. Expect to pay a small
port fee (less than $2) at the maritime pier in addition to the cost of
the ticket.

Outfitters

Cruceros Princesa (✉ Terminal Marítima, Marina Vallarta ☎ 322/224–
4777) has sunset cruises, half-day snorkel tours to the Marietas, and
full-day trips to the beaches of southern Bahía de Banderas with snorkeling, beach time, and lunch; it has a reputation for being somewhat
flexible about the itineraries of its daytime tours. Daytime bay cruises
generally go to Los Arcos, Yelapa, Quimixto, or Playa las Ánimas, as
well as to Islas Marietas for whale-watching (in winter), snorkeling, swimming, and lunch. Most trips depart from the Terminal Marítima at

9 AM; they return around mid-afternoon and cost about $70. **Santamaría** (✉ Paseo de la Marina Sur 161, Interior 14, Las Condominiums, Marina Vallarta ☎ 322/221–2511 ⊕ www. ~iacruises.com) has two different full-day tours to Los Arcos and ~as with visits to either Quimixto or Yelapa. It also rents boats ~e parties. You can buy tickets from their office or booth vendors. A really and truly sailing vessel that has circumnavigated the world more than once, the *Marigalante* (✉ Paseo Diaz Ordaz 770, Centro ☎ 322/223–0309 or 322/223–1662 ⊕ www.marigalante.com.mx) has a pirate crew that keeps things hopping for preteens and even older kids with fun and games. The dinner cruise, with open bar and pre-Hispanic show, is geared for adults and has some bawdy pirate humor. Women who don't want to be "kidnapped" may prefer the day cruise or another operator.

★ **Vallarta Adventures** (✉ Paseo de las Palmas 39–A, Nuevo Vallarta ☎ 322/297–1212, 888/303–2653 in U.S. and Canada ✉ Edifício Marina Golf, Local 13-C, Calle Mástil, Marina Vallarta ☎ 322/221–0657 ⊕ www.vallarta-adventures.com) has day or evening cruises to Caletas Beach, its exclusive domain. Although the day cruise can accommodate 150 passengers, there's plenty of room to spread out: boulder-bordered coves, sandy beaches, hammocks in the shade, and jungle trails ensure that you won't feel like a cow about to be branded "tourist." The Caletas by Day cruise includes snorkeling, kayaking, yoga, hiking, and lunch. The Rhythms of the Night evening cruise includes dinner on the beach and a show at the amphitheater. Most folks love the show—men and women dressed as voluptuous natives do a modern dance to dramatic lighting and music. Kids under 10 are not allowed.

> **WORD OF MOUTH**
>
> "There is no electricity [on the Rhythms of the Night tour], so dinner and the trails are all lit by candles. Very cool and romantic. I would highly recommend this."
> –MichelleY

Water Park

Traditionally more popular with Mexican families than foreigners, **Sea Life Park** (Formerly Splash), has added dolphin encounters (⇨ *above*) to attract a wider audience. Kids love the place just as it was: they can still plummet down enormous waterslides, swim, and play on playground equipment and carnival rides. There are restaurants and bars as well as sea-lion shows. ✉ *Carretera a Tepic, Km 155, Nuevo Vallarta* ☎ *322/297-0724* 💲 *$12* ⊙ *Daily 10–6.*

Culture

Huichol artisan

WORD OF MOUTH

"We lucked out because it was a festival week—the Virgin of Guadalupe. There were processions every night which were clearly not aimed at tourists."

—epi

"The most culture you can find [in PV] is to become friendly with locals."

—pschatz

In the 1950s, Puerto Vallarta was like an extended family: everyone knew everyone else. Most of the inhabitants were from related families who had come down from the mountain mining towns after the turn of the century. People sat in front of their houses in the evening, chatting; the action was in the street. Until the explosion of outside interest, most of PV's intellectual and artistic life has centered around traditional Mexican culture, which is synonymous with the Catholic religion. With an increase in foreign and domestic visitors came a demand for entertainment that Puerto Vallarta has met with moderate success. Today there are plenty of bars and nightclubs, but less live theater and music than locals would like. The fine arts scene, however, is thriving. Local and foreign artists are established and respected painters and sculptors, represented by PV's finest galleries. High season is the time to see these artists at their best, especially on Wednesday evenings, when everyone in town turns out for artWalk.

ARCHITECTURE

La Iglesia de Nuestra Señora de Guadalupe (Church of Our Lady of Guadalupe) is dedicated to the patron saint of Mexico and of Puerto Vallarta. The holy mother's image, by Ignacio Ramírez, is the centerpiece of the cathedral's slender marble altarpiece. The brick bell tower is topped by a lacy-looking crown that replicates the one worn by Carlota, short-lived empress of Mexico. The wrought-iron crown toppled during an earth-

> **GET THE SCOOP**
>
> One of the best sources of information for upcoming events is *Bay Vallarta*, published twice a month. The free bilingual publication gets scooped up fast from hotels, restaurants, car rental agencies, and other places frequented by visitors.

quake that shook this area of the Pacific Coast in October 1995, but was soon replaced with a fiberglass version, supported, as was the original, by a squadron of stone angels. ⊠ *Calle Hidalgo, Centro* 🕾 *No phone* 🕑 *7:30 AM–8 PM.*

THE ARTS

Dance

Under the direction of Professor Carlos Enrique Barrios Limón at the Centro Cultural Cuale, **Grupo Folklorico Municipal Xiutla** (🕾 322/223–0095) is a talented troupe of folkloric dancers. During the group's career of more than a decade, the 250 young people have performed at various venues around PV as well as elsewhere in Mexico, Canada, the United States, and Europe. Performances are sporadic and announced through the usual channels (*Bay Vallarta*, flyers, etc.).

Noches Culturales Sergio Medina takes place the first Thursday of the month, between 8 and 9:30 PM, at the Centro Cultural Cuale (⇨ Cultural Centers, *above*).

Film

Biblioteca Los Mangos (✉ Av. Francisco Villa, Col. Los Mangos ☎ 322/224–9966) shows art films, musicals, and blockbusters. The current schedule is Friday at 7 PM and Saturday at 4 PM, but call to check show times; tickets are $1.50.

Free movies of various genres are shown at an outdoor theater Friday at 7 PM at **Cine en el Cuale** (✉ Centro Cultural Isla Río Cuale, east end of island, Río Cuale ☎ 322/223–0095).

PV's original extravaganza for movie buffs and movie stars alike is the **Festival Internacional de Cine en Puerto Vallarta** (☎ 322/223–2500 ⊕ cinefest.pv.udg.mx). Held during six days each April, the festival honors the best full-length feature film with a "golden iguana" award. Full-length, documentary, and short-subject films are shown around town at Cinema Versalles, Cinema CUC, Cinema Bahía, or under the stars at Los Arcos Amphitheater; flyers all over town advertise the movies, or contact the movie houses directly (⇨ Chapter 6). The public is invited to attend lectures and listen to discourses on local radio programs. In 2005, dozens of movies from Mexico, Argentina, Chile, Peru, Cuba, and elsewhere were shown.

In early November, the public is welcome to see movies of many genres, at reasonable prices, during the six-day **PV Film Festival of the Americas** (☎ 322/222–3593 or 322/222–3674 ⊕ www.puertovallartafilm.com). Film industry types come to hobnob and honor each other with awards for best director, picture, cinematographer, and actor.

> ## LIFESTYLES OF THE RICOS Y FAMOSOS
>
> Two-and-a-half-hour **villa tours** (☎ 322/222–5466) arranged by the International Friendship Club, gets you inside the garden walls of some inspiring PV homes. Tours depart promptly at 11 AM (arrive by 10:30) from the Hotel Posada Río Cuale (Calle Aquiles Serdán 242) on Wednesday and Thursday mid-November through the end of April. The $30 fee benefits local charities.

Fine Art

See Chapter 5 for art gallery descriptions and locations.

An artist of worldwide renown, **Evelyn Boren** (✉ Casa Bugambilla, Sayulita ☎ 329/291–3095) lives and works in Sayulita each winter. Represented by Galeria Café des Artistes and other Puerto Vallarta shops, Ms. Boren shares her colorful landscapes with the public each Wednesday afternoon between 2 and 5 December through April. Her house is on the beach just south of the plaza.

The late Manuel Lepe's 1981 mural depicting Puerto Vallarta as a fanciful seaside fishing and farming village is painted above the stairs on the second floor of the **Palácio Municipal** (✉ Av. Juárez, on Plaza de Armas, Centro ☎ 322/222–4565), PV's city hall. Lepe is known for his blissful, primitive-style scenes of the city, filled with smiling angels. This one is rather tired, and the naïf work has been surpassed by his devotees. Still, Lepe is considered the father of PV naïf, and the mural is worth a quick look. The interior hallways surrounding the government building's central plaza sometimes host photography or fine art exhibitions. The tourism office is on the first floor. The Palácio is open weekdays 9–5.

An annual event since 1996, **Old Town artWalk** (☎ 322/222–1982) has expanded to 18 galleries. The galleries stay open late, usually offering an appetizer or snack as well as wine, beer, or soft drinks. Browse paintings, jewelry, ceramics, glass, and folk art while hobnobbing with some of PV's most respected artists. If you don't have a map, pick one up from one of the perennially participating galleries, which include Galería Arte Latinoamericano, Galería Corona, Galería 8 y Más, Galería Pacífico, Galería Uno, Galería Vallarta, and Leonardo Galerías (➪ Chapter 5). ArtWalk is held 6 PM–10 PM, from the last week of October until mid- or late-April.

> ### FOLKLORIC DANCE
>
> *Zapateado*, the dancing characterized by rhythmical foot-stomping, is accompanied by *sones*, narrative, up-tempo mariachi songs written specifically for the dances. Anywhere between 200 and 300 sones are known to exist, but the best-known is the *Jarabe Tapatío* (Mexican Hat Dance), whose dance includes the emblematic move of the male dancer putting his sombrero on the ground as a sign of respect to his female companion.

Music

Under the direction of Professor Carlos Enrique Barrios Limón, the 21-piece **Orquestra Vallarta** (☎ 322/223–0095) consists of local residents and a few "stringers": foreigners who come to Vallarta in winter. They have no set schedule but often play at **Auditorio CECATI** (Centro de Capacitación Turística e Industrial ✉ Calle Hidalgo 300, Centro ☎ 322/222–4910). Tickets generally cost about $10 for adults, half that for kids.

Vallarta's *banda municipal* (☎ 322/223–2500) serenades its citizens Thursday and Sunday afternoons between 6 and 7, sometimes a bit later. Couples dance around the main plaza to *cumbias* (a distinctive style of popular Latin dance-music that originated in Colombia), emanating from the central kiosk. Everyone's welcome to join in, and most of the dancers are just regular folks, both visitors and vallartenses, having some fun. Some days, however, the band plays *danzon,* a complicated, stylized box-step that originated in Cuba and is best left to those who know the steps.

Theater

The small **Santa Barbara Theater** (✉ Olas Altas 351, Col. E. Zapata ☎ 322/223–2048) is the place to see English-language shows, mainly musicals, November through April. It's community theater, not high art, but the

On the Boardwalk

PUERTO VALLARTA'S MALECÓN is the Champs Elysee of PV—only shorter, warmer, and less expensive. Along the half-mile cement walkway bordering the sea, small groups of young studs check out their feminine counterparts, all in meticulously pulled-together casual clothes; cruise-ship passengers stretch their legs; and landlocked tourists take a walk before dinner. Even those who have lived here all their lives come out to watch the red sun sink into the gray-blue water beyond the bay.

Every night and weekend is a parade. Vendors sell *agua de tuba,* a refreshing coconut-palm-heart drink. Empanada, corn-on-the-cob, and fried banana stands congregate near the Friendship Fountain and its trio of leaping bronze dolphins. Peddlers sell helium balloons and cotton candy. Clowns, magicians, and musicians entertain in the Los Arcos amphitheater.

Some of PV's most endearing art pieces are not in galleries, but here *en pleine aire.* Stretching along the seawalk is a series of bronze sculptures that are constantly touched, photographed, and climbed on. These nonstop caresses give a bright bronze

luster to strategic body parts of "Neptune and the Nereid," a mermaid and her man. Higher up on its pedestal, Puerto Vallarta's well-known seahorse icon retains a more traditional (and dignified) patina.

The three mysterious figures that compose "In Search of Reason," by world-famous artist Sergio Bustamante, are just as otherworldly as the jewelry, painting, and statuettes sold in his three Vallarta shops. Look for the pillow-headed figures climbing a ladder to the sky. Across from Carlos O'Brien's restaurant, Ramiz Barquet's "Nostalgia" is an ode to the artist's reunion with the love of his life at this very spot. You can find more of Barquet's work at Galería Pacífico.

"Rotunda on the Sea," a wacky grouping of chair-people by Alejando Colunga, is a good spot to sit and watch the sea and the swirl of people enjoying life, although around sunset, others waiting their turn make it hard to linger.

✉ *Extending south from Calle 31 de Octubre to Los Arcos outdoor amphitheater and the town Sq.*

8

---

productions are fun. Dinner and a show is usually $25; tickets for the show alone run about $10.

Inexpensive or free musical and theatrical events are often presented at **Centro Universitario de la Costa** (CUC ✉ Carretera a Ixtapa, Km 2.5, Ixtapa, at outskirts of Ixtapa ☎ 322/226–2263). Performances include experimental and classical theater and other genres. Productions are in Spanish, but because they are very visual, they're enjoyable even if you don't speak the language. Check the principal newspapers *El Tribunal de la Bahia* and *Vallarta Opina* for upcoming events. Tickets are usually about $6.

FLIGHT OF THE VOLADORES

A relatively new phenomenon on the malecón are performances by *los voladores de Papantla*, the Papantla "flyers" near Los Arcos. Dressed in exquisite costumes of red velveteen pants decorated with sequins, mirrors, embroidery, and fringe, five men climb a 30-meter (98-foot) pole. Four of them dive from the top of the platform as the leader "speaks" to them from the pinnacle with fife and drum. Held by a rope tied to one foot, the men wing around the pole exactly 13 times before landing on the ground. The total number of revolutions adds up to the ritualistically significant number of 52. Native to Veracruz State, this traditional performance is held Thursday and Sunday evenings at 6 PM and 8 PM in low season, and every hour on the hour from 6 PM to 9 PM in high season (December through April).

CLASSES & WORKSHOPS

A good source of information for current classes is the bimonthly, free *Bay Vallarta,* which always lists a Web page or phone number for further information.

A formal environment for studying piano, guitar, dance, theater, and singing, among other disciplines, is **CECAO** (Centro de Capacitación Artística de Occidente, or Western Center for Artistic Study) (⊠ Guadalupe Sanchez 960, Centro ☎ 322/222–4937). Foreigners are welcome and most instructors speak English. Most classes are five days a week on a trimester schedule, and average about $4 per hour.

You can matriculate mid-session at the informal **Centro Cultural Río Cuale** (⊠ East end of Isla Río Cuale, Centro ☎ 322/223–0095 ⊕ www.culturavallarta.com) for classes like painting, drawing, and acting for children and for adults. Most of the instructors speak some English, others are fluent.

English-speaking artist Alicia Buena gives ceramics and painting classes for individuals or groups at **Terra Noble** (⊠ Av. Tulipanes 595, Fracc. Lomas de Terra Noble, Col. 5 de Diciembre ☎ 322/223–3530 ⊕ www.terranoble.com). The cost is about $50 for the 2–2½ hour class. To schedule, call Terra Noble at around 10 AM the day you want to take the class, or a few days in advance to secure a spot in the class.

MUSEUMS

Elizabeth Taylor's former home, **Casa Kimberley,** is connected to Richard Burton's former home across the street by the pink-and-white "love bridge" he had constructed. Both homes have been converted into a very lived-in bed-and-breakfast, but you can tour rooms not currently occupied as well as the common areas Monday through Saturday 9–6. Burton bought the 24,000-square-foot home for Taylor's 32nd birthday after filming *The Night of the Iguana,* shot in and around Mismaloya beach, south of town. Taylor owned the house for 26 years, and left most of her possessions behind (all on display) when she sold it. ⊠ *Calle Zaragoza 445, Centro* ☎☎ *322/222–1336* 🎫 *$8.*

Pre-Columbian figures and Indian artifacts are on display at the **Museo Arqueológico** (Archeological Museum). Most of the exhibits are labeled in English and Spanish. There's a general explanation of Western Pacific cultures and shaft tombs, and abbreviated but attractive exhibits of Aztatlan and Purepecha cultures and the Spanish conquest. ⊠ *Western tip of Isla Río Cuale, Centro* ☎ *No phone* 🎫 *By donation* ☉ *Mon.–Sat. 10–7.*

CULTURAL CENTERS

The **Centro Cultural Cuale** (⊠ East end of Isla Río Cuale, Aquiles Serdán 437, int. 38, Centro ☎ 322/223–0095) sells the work of local artists, has art and dance classes (⇨ Classes, *below*), and hosts cultural events. Cost of classes is nominal and cultural events are free. The free bimonthly *Bay Vallarta,* available at tourist-oriented shops, hotels, and restaurants, is the best source of information on current classes.

> **CULTURAL TOUR**
>
> **Puerto Vallarta Tours** (☎ 866/217-9704 ⊕ www.puertovallartatours.net) runs twice-weekly all-day guided bus tours from Puerto Vallarta to Tepic, Nayarit for sightseeing, shopping, and learning about the spiritually atuned culture of the Huichol Indians.

Biblioteca Los Mangos (⊠ Av. Francisco Villa, Col. Los Mangos ☎ 322/224–9966) has lots of reasonably priced art classes (⇨ Classes, *below*), and free or inexpensive monthly events, such as dance performances. Themed performances are scheduled around Day of the Dead, Christmas, Easter, and other holidays.

Philo's (⊠ Calle Delfin 15, La Cruz de Huanacaxtle ☎ 329/295–5068) is the unofficial cultural center and meeting place of La Cruz, north of Bucerís. It has free classes in yoga, Spanish, and English (tipping the teachers is customary) in the mornings.

FESTIVALS & EVENTS

Winter

February

The two-day **Festival de Música San Pancho** (San Pancho Music Festival ☎ 298/258–4135) is an amalgam of the area's best local musicians, talented snowbirds, and other foreigners. Some folks come down especially for the free jamboree, usually held over a weekend in mid-to-late February. Look for flyers around town that describe events and their venues. San Pancho is just north of Sayulita, in Nayarit State, about 50 minutes north of downtown Puerto Vallarta.

THREE KINGS DAY

El Día de los Santos Reyes (January 6) was the traditional day of gift-giving in Latin America until Santa Claus invaded from the North (or North Pole, depending on your beliefs). Although many families now give gifts on Christmas or Christmas Eve, Three Kings Day is still an important family celebration.	The children receive token "gifts of the Magi." Atole (a drink of finely ground rice or corn) or hot chocolate is served along with the *rosca de reyes*, a ring-shape cake. The person whose portion contains a tiny baby Jesus figurine must host a follow-up party on Candlemass, February 2.

Tours, hotel rooms, works of art, and dinner at participating restaurants are auctioned during the **Benefício Annual Para la Biblioteca Los Mangos,** a benefit to support the city's only public library. Contact Ricardo Murrieta (☎ 322/222–9966) for more information. *Charros* (cowboys) from all over Mexico compete in the **Campeonato Charro Nacional** (National Charro Championship ☎ 322/224–0001) at Mojoneras, between the airport and the central bus station. In addition to men's *suertes* (rope and riding tricks) and the *escaramuza* (female competitors), there are mariachis, a parade, dances, and exhibitions of charro-related art Thursday through Sunday. Admission is $5–$10.

November
The **Festival Gourmet International** is one of PV's biggest events (⇨ "Mexico's Gourmet Town," *in* Chapter 3). The **Puerto Vallarta Film Festival of the Americas** (⇨ Film, *above*) is a great opportunity to see indie films from around the globe.

March
Held for the first time in 2005, the **Perrotón** (Dog Show ☎ 322/223–2500) hopes to become an annual event. In addition to lectures there are contests (ugliest dog, dog and owner who most resemble each other, most beautiful dog, and exhibitions of agility and obedience).

Spring

April
The **International Film Festival of Puerto Vallarta** (⇨ Film, *above*) is a huge event that draws films from the Spanish-speaking world, and filmgoers from around the globe. Most of the events and ceremonies are for filmmakers, but the public can enjoy the art and blockbuster films shown during the weeklong event.

May
Las Fiestas de Mayo (May Festivals ☎ 322/223–2500) is a traditional three-week fair with fireworks and regional crafts and foods that is more popular with locals than visitors. Here in Jalisco, no such festival would be complete without *charreadas* (rodeos) and cockfights. Restaurants lower

PUBLIC HOLIDAYS

Post offices, government and private offices, and banks are closed on public holidays (ATMs are plentiful, however). On Labor Day even tourist-related businesses like restaurants may be closed, as they prefer to give all employees the day off with pay. Public holidays include:

January 1: Año Nuevo (New Year's Day)

February 5: Día de la Constitución (Constitution Day)

March 25: Aniversário de Benito Juárez (Juárez's Birthday)

May 1: Día del Trabajador (Labor Day)

September 15: Día de la Independencia (Independence Day)

November 20: Día de la Revolución Mexicana (Mexican Revolution Day)

their prices for two weeks at the beginning of low season during **Restaurant Week** (⇨ "Mexico's Gourmet Town," *in* Chapter 3), also known as the May Food Festival.

Summer

June
June 1 is **Dí de la Marina** (☎ 322/224–2352). Like other Mexican ports, PV celebrates Navy Day with free boat rides (inquire at the Terminal Marítima or the XII Zona Naval Militar, just to the south). Watch colorfully decorated boats depart from here to make offerings on the water to sailors lost at sea.

July and August
During school vacations, **children's events** (☎ 322/223–2500), like the release of baby marine turtles are scheduled to educate, entertain, and heighten awareness of ecological issues.

Barra de Navidad celebrates its patron saint, **San Antonio de Padua,** the week preceding July 13 with religious parades, mass, street parties, and fireworks. **Cristo de los Brazos Caídos** is honored August 30–September 1 in much the same way as Saint Anthony.

Fall

September
The **Celebration of Independence** is held on September 15 and 16, beginning with great throngs of people that gather in and around the main square on the evening of September 15 in preparation for the traditional *Grito de Dolores*. It translates as "Cry of Pain" but also references the town of Dolores Hidalgo, where the famous cry for freedom was uttered by priest Miguel Hidalgo. Late in the evening September 15 there are mariachis, speeches, and other demonstrations of national pride. On September 16, witness parades and more charros on horseback along the length of the boardwalk.

October 28–December 12

Puerto Vallarta's most important celebration of faith—and also one of the most elaborate spectacles of the year, religion notwithstanding—is **Fiestas de la Virgin of Guadalupe** (☎ 322/223–2500), designed to honor the Virgin of Guadalupe, the city's patron saint and the patroness of all Mexico. Exuberance fills the air as the end of October approaches and each participating business—be it hotel, restaurant, church congregation, or office supply store—organizes its own procession. The most elaborate ones include allegorical floats and giant papier-mâché *matachines,* or dolls (for lack of a better word), and culminate in their own private mass. Throughout the afternoon and evening, groups snake down Calle Juarez between Woolworth's and the Cathedral in Old Vallarta. Traffic is diverted, and the streets surrounding the church are a crush of devout ladies in black, curious visitors, and locals whose intermittent expressions of faith are lovingly expressed during this moving time of year.

Overnight
Excursions

Guadalajara

WORD OF MOUTH

"[D]owntown GDL puts you in the heart of a living, breathing Mexican city. . . . The maze of interlocking plazas, cathedrals, and major buildings which make up the Centro Histórico are a walker's and looker's mecca."

–ETee

"We would strongly recommend the San Blas jungle tour. Lots of fun and alligators."

–Gilles

www.fodors.com/forums

EXCURSIONS FROM PUERTO VALLARTA

TOP REASONS TO GO

★ **Alchemic atmosphere:** San Blas's basic but charismatic attractions—beaches, markets, churches, and boat trips—combine like magic for a destination that's greater than the sum of its parts.

★ **Highland rambles:** Drop-dead-gorgeous hills and river valleys from Talpa to San Sebastián get you out into nature and away from coastal humidity.

★ **Amazing photography:** In the mountain towns, even amateur photographers can capture excellent small-town and nature shots.

★ **Palatable history:** Soak up Mexican history and culture in churches, museums, and political murals.

★ **Getting the goods:** From megamalls to entire pre-Hispanic townships, Guadalajara has excellent housewares and handcrafts at great prices.

1 San Blas. Change happens slowly in San Blas, which has yet to experience a tourism boom. Cruise wide dirt streets on one-speed bikes, read books in the shade, dig your toes in the sand, and just enjoy life—one lazy day at a time. Blue mountains and green hills provide a beautiful backdrop.

Sand sculpture on the Beach

2 The Mountain Towns. Former mining and supply towns **Talpa, Mascota,** and tiny **San Sebastián** were isolated for centuries by narrow roads and dangerous drop-offs and remain postcards of the past. Soak up the small-town atmosphere and alpine air.

3 Greater Guadalajara. Home to cherished archetypes like mariachi, charrería (elegant "rodeos"), and tequila, Guadalajara is often called "the Mexican's Mexico." The metropolitan area includes former farming community **Zapopán,** and two districts known for crafts: **Tlaquepaque** and neighboring **Tonalá.** Outside the city are unique archaeological digs at **Teuchitlán,** lakeside retreat **Chapala,** artists' and expats' enclave **Ajijic,** and **Tequila,** famous for . . . do we even need to say it?

GETTING ORIENTED

About 156 km (95 mi) north of PV, mountain-backed San Blas has beaches and birding. Inland 340 km (211 mi) or so from PV, Jalisco capital Guadalajara (pop. 4 million) sits in the Atemajac Valley, circled by Sierra Madre peaks. Sleepy Sierra Madre towns Talpa, Mascota, and San Sebastián lie about halfway between PV and Guadalajara; each offers a glimpse of rural life from centuries long gone.

NAYARIT
JALISCO

San Cristóbal de la Barranca

Magdalena — 54

Toll

Tequila — 23

Antonio Escobedo — 15D — Amatitán

El Arenal — Zapopan — Ixtlahuacán del Río

Jesús Maria — Ahualuco ◆ **Teuchitlán** — Área de Protección de Flora y Fauna la Primavera — Guadalajara — 80D

70 — Ameca — Zapotlanejo

Tlaquepaque — Tonalá

Acatlán de Juárez — 54 — El Salto — 15D

Área de Protección de Flora y Fauna — 80 — Cocula — Ajijic — 44

Ayutla — Tecolotlán — Zacoalco de Torres — Jocotepec — Chapala

Lake Chapala

Tuxcueca

Juchitlán — Chiquilistlán

Unión de Tula — Amacueca

Sayula — 54D

El Grullo — 110

Autlan de Navarro — San Gabriel — Ciudad Guzman — Tamazula de Gordiano

Reserva de la Biosfera Sierra de Manantlán — Parque Nacional Nevado de Colima — Tuxpan

Atenquique — Tecalitlán

JALISCO COLIMA — 54

Queseria

Colima

↙ TO MANZANILLO, IXTAPA, ZIHUATANEJO

Tonalá Ceramics

EXCURSION PLANNER

Coming and Going

If you plan to visit both Puerto Vallarta and Guadalajara, consider flying into one and out of the other. It costs little more than a round-trip ticket to either city. To do the trip one-way, go by bus ($32–$37), as drop-off charges for rental cars are steep. (Leave extra time if you're flying the same day.) Half-hour charter flights from PV offer painless access to the mountain towns, but then you've no car for sightseeing. The bus from PV is a long trip, but drivers are experts at navigating mountain roads, which are often in disrepair. Access to Mascota and Talpa from Guadalajara is shorter, more direct, and fully paved. The challenging road from PV is often impassable in rainy season. Buses take you directly from PV to San Blas, or you can get off at nearby beaches, but a car is handier for exploring the coast. The mostly two-lane PV–San Blas road is curvy but otherwise fine.

■ TIP→ **Most small towns that don't have official stations sell gas from a home or store. Ask around before heading out on the highway low on gas.**

Driving Times from PV

San Blas	3–3½ hours
San Sebastián	2½–4 hours
Mascota	2½–3 hours
Talpa de Allende	3–3½ hours
Guadalajara	4½–5 hours

Day Trips versus Extended Stays

The San Blas area is best as an overnight unless you go with an organized tour (⇨ Tour Companies), though you could easily drive to Platanitos, south of San Blas, for a day at the beach.

If busing or driving to the mountain towns, plan to overnight unless you take the day tour with Vallarta Adventures. Alternately, you can fly on your own with **Aerotaxis de la Bahía** (☎ 322/221–1990) for a quick day trip or an overnight stay.

Guadalajara is too far to go for the day from Vallarta or San Blas, and at least two days is recommended.

How Much Can You Do?

What you can (physically) do and what you should do are very different things. To get the most out of your excursion from Puerto Vallarta, don't overdo it. It's a vacation—it's supposed to be fun, and possibly even relaxing! If you'll be in the Sayulita, San Francisco, and Chacala areas in Nayarit, it's easy to do an overnight jaunt up to San Blas, enjoying the myriad beaches and small towns as you travel up and back. Or make San Blas your base and explore from there.

You could also feasibly spend one night in San Blas and two in Guadalajara, about four hours driving and five hours by bus. For true nature and adventure junkies, two to three nights in the mountain towns gives you ample time to explore San Sebastián, Mascota, and Talpa as well as the surrounding countryside. You could spend one night in the mountains and continue to Guadalajara the next day, but keep in mind that a lot of driving is involved. To fully appreciate Guadalajara, plan to spend at least two nights.

Tour Companies

Eco San Blas Safari (☎ 322/222–1922) leads all-day tours ($100 per person) Tuesday and Thursday from PV to San Blas with a boat trip to La Tovara. It's a full day, but at least you're not driving. Contact the **Cámera de Comercio** (Chamber of Commerce ✉ Av. Vallarta 4095, Zona Minerva, Guadalajara ☎ 33/ 3121–0378 or 33/3122–7701) for information about the all-day tour aboard the **Tequila Train.** The cost is about $72, including lunch, mariachi sere- nades, and tequila.

Highly recommended **Vallarta Adventures** (✉ Edifício Marina Golf, Local 13–C, Calle Mástil, Marina Val- larta, Puerto Vallarta ☎ 322/297–1212 or 322/ 221–0657, 888/303–2653 in U.S. and Canada ⊕ www.vallarta-adventures.com) has daily, seven- hour jeep tours to San Sebastín ($70). It also runs air trips to San Sebastián on Tuesday and Thursday ($145) and to Mascota and Talpa on Wednesday and Sunday ($160). On Monday is a flight to and day tour of San Blas ($225), followed by land trips to several other Nayarit villages, including the island Mexitlán, possible homeland of the Aztec empire.

With a day's notice, **Viajes Panoramex** (✉ Av. Federal- ismo Sur 944, Centro Histórico, Guadalajara ☎ 33/ 3810–5057 or 33/3810–5109 ⊕ www.panoramex. com.mx) has tours to Tequila, Chapala and Ajijic, and the main sights of Guadalajara with time for shopping at Tlaquepaque at the end of the day.

While focusing mainly on vacation rentals, **Vista Travel Tours** (✉ Av. Olas Altas 250, Col. E. Zapata, Puerto Vallarta ☎ 866/256–2745 ⊕ www.vistatours.com) also leads all-day trips to San Blas with a tour of the city and a motorboat ride into the mangroves to see the local fauna and flora.

When to Go

With its springlike climate, Guadala- jara can be visited any time of year, though in winter pollution can cause raw throats, sore eyes, and sinus ir- ritation. Book well in advance to visit during the October Festival or other holidays. Because roads can be dangerous during summer rains, June through October aren't the best time to visit Mascota and the moun- tain towns by land.

San Blas and the coast begin to heat up in May; during the late June through October rainy season both the ambient and ocean temps are highest. Make hotel reservations far in advance for Christmas, Easter, and the San Blas Festival (February 3).

FESTIVALS & SPECIAL EVENTS

Guadalajara's major events include a May cultural festival; suburb Tlaquepaque celebrates itself during the June ceramics festival.

The International Mariachi and Tequila Festival, in September, teams mariachi bands with the philhar- monic orchestra.

Also in Guadalajara, the entire month of October is given up to mari- achis, *charreadas* (rodeos), soccer matches, and theater; the blessed Virgin of Zapopan is feted the week preceding October 12.

In the Sierra Madre, Talpa's equally admired icon brings the faithful en masse four times a year for street dances and mariachi serenades.

At the San Blas Festival (February 3), a statue of the town's patron saint gets a boat ride around the bay.

9

SAN BLAS & ENVIRONS

The cool thing about San Blas and the surrounding beaches—if you like this sort of thing—is that they're untouristy and authentic. Sure, there's an expat community, but it's miniscule compared to that of Puerto Vallarta. Parts of San Blas itself are deliciously disheveled, or should we say, ungentrified. The

> **CAUTION**
>
> The fierce biting *jejenes* (no-see-ums) of San Blas are legendary, but not everyone reacts to their sting.

lively square is a nice place to polish off an ice-cream cone and watch the world. If you're looking for organized activities and perfect English speakers, this isn't the place for you.

2–3 Days in San Blas & Environs

Most people come to the San Blas area for basic R&R, to enjoy the long beaches and seafood shanties. The town's sights can be seen in a day, but stay for a few days at least to catch up on your reading, visit the beaches, and savor the town as it deserves. La Tovara jungle cruise through the mangroves should not be missed.

LOGISTICS & TIPS To really go native, rent a bike from Wala Wala Restaurant, a half block up from the plaza on Calle Juárez, and cruise to your heart's content. To get to the beaches south of town, to Matanchén Bay, and to the village of Santa Cruz, take a bus (they usually leave on the hour) from the bus station behind the church on the main plaza. To come back, just stand by the side of the road and flag down a passing bus.

Buses depart in the morning and again in the afternoon for Puerto Vallarta, and on the hour for Tepic, Nayarit's state capital. To get to Platanitos Beach, about an hour south of San Blas, take the Puerto Vallarta bus; ■ TIP→ **always check the return schedule with the driver when taking an out-of-town bus.** A car is handy for more extensive explorations of the coast between Puerto Vallarta and around San Blas. Within San Blas, the streets are wide, traffic is almost nonexistent, and with the exception of the streets immediately surrounding the main plaza, parking is easy.

San Blas

Travelers come here looking for Old Mexico, or the "real Mexico," or the Mexico they remember from the 1960s. New Spains's first official Pacific port has experienced a long, slow slide into obscurity since losing out to better-equipped ports in the late 19th century. But there's something to be said for being a bit player rather than a superstar. Industrious but not overworked, residents of this drowsy seaside city hit the beaches on weekends and celebrate their good fortune during numerous saints' days and civic festivals. You can, too.

What to See

San Blas has a few fun places to visit, but don't expect to be bowled over.

Check out the chaste little **Templo de San Blas,** called *La Iglesia Vieja* (the Old Church) by residents, on the town's busy plaza. Look for the words to Henry Wadsworth Longfellow's poem "The Bells of San Blas," inscribed on a brass plaque. (The long-gone bells were actually at the church dedicated to the Virgin of the Rosary, on Cerro de San Basilio.) Browse for fruits or good photo-ops at the market, **Mer-**

> **BEHIND THE MUSIC**
>
> If you're a fan of the rock group Maná, it's interesting to note that the song "Muelle de San Blas" ("Wharf of San Blas") refers to a tiny dock and a few wooden posts hosting friendly looking pelicans, just south of the Aduana.

cado José María (⊠ Calle H. Battalón de San Blas, between Calles Sonora and Sinaloa), where you can take a load off at Chito's for a milk shake or fresh fruit juice.

The old **Aduana** (Customs House ⊠ Calle Juárez, near Calle del Puerto) has been partially restored and is now a cultural center with sporadic art or photography shows and theatrical productions.

For a bird's-eye view of town and the coast, hike or drive up Calle Juárez, the main drag, to **Cerro de San Basilio.** Cannons protect the ruined **Contaduría** (Counting House ⊠ Cerro de San Basilio), built during colonial times when San Blas was New Spain's first official port. Continuing down the road from the Contaduría brings you to **El Templo de la Virgen del Rosario.** Note the new floor in the otherwise ruined structure; the governor's daughter didn't want to soil the hem of her gown when she married here in 2005. A bit farther on, San Blas's little cemetery is backed by the sea and the mountains.

Where to Stay & Eat

$ ✕ **Casa del Canibal.** How does grilled chicken served with mashed potatoes and big hunks of steamed broccoli sound? Or a big Caesar salad with garlic toast? There's also beef stroganoff, penne primavera, and a few other international dishes. The small bar, more popular with gringos than with locals, closes down by 9 or 10 PM. ⊠ *Calle Juárez 53* ☏ *323/285–1412* ▭ *No credit cards* ☉ *No lunch; closed Mon., Tues., and July–Sept.*

$ ✕ **La Isla.** Shell lamps; pictures made entirely of scallops, bivalves, and starfish; shell-drenched chandeliers . . . every inch of wall space is decorated in different denizens of the sea. Service isn't particularly brisk (pretty much par for the course in laid-back San Blas), but the seafood, filet mignon, and fajitas are all quite good. Afterwards stroll over the main plaza a few blocks away. ⊠ *Calle Mercado s/n* ☏ *323/285–0407* ▭ *No credit cards* ☉ *Closed Mon.*

$$ ✕▤ **Hotel Garza Canela.** Opened decades ago by a family of dedicated bird-watchers, this meandering, three-story hotel with expansive grounds is the home base of choice for birding groups. Rooms have small balconies and polished limestone floors; junior suites have large whirlpool tubs. Betty Vasquez, who runs the French restaurant there, studied at Le Cordón Bleu in France; she prepares elegant and very tasty meals.

✉ *Calle Paredes 106 Sur, San Blas 63740* ☎ *323/285–0112 or 323/285–0480* ⊕ *www.garzacanela.com* ⬲ *44 rooms, 6 suites* ⌂ *Restaurant, fan, cable TV, pool, shop, meeting room, Internet room, free parking; no room phones* ▤ *AE, MC, V* ⬭ *EP.*

$ ⊞ **Hacienda Flamingos.** Built in 1882, this restored mansion-turned-hotel was once part of a large hacienda. The restoration is stunning: surrounding a pretty, plant-filled courtyard is a covered veranda of lovely floor tiles, with lazily rotating ceiling fans, antique furniture, and groupings of chairs for a casual conversation. Opening off the veranda, elegant rooms have also been restored to their original glory. It's amazingly lacking in guests given the low price. It's right across from the cultural center and near the market and town plaza. ✉ *Calle Juárez 105, San Blas 63740* ☎ *323/285–0485* ⧠ *669/985–1185 in Mazatlán* ⊕ *www.sanblas.com.mx* ⬲ *20 rooms* ⌂ *Fans, cable TV, pool, gym, laundry, free parking; no room phones* ▤ *MC, V* ⬭ *EP.*

¢ ⊞ **Casa Roxanna.** This is an attractive little village of cozy, very clean (and painted yearly) cottages with screened windows. Full kitchens with lots of pots and pans invite cooking; lovingly tended gardens surround the lodgings, the covered patio, and the sparkling, three-lane lap pool. If you love it, settle in a while; monthly rates are usually available. ✉ *Callejón El Rey 1, San Blas, 63740* ☎ *323/285–0573* ⊕ *www.casaroxanna.com* ⬲ *6 cottages* ⌂ *Fans, kitchens, refrigerators, cable TV, pool, laundry, free parking; no room phones* ▤ *No credit cards* ⬭ *EP.*

Outdoor Activities & Sports

BOAT TOUR A series of narrow waterways wends through the mangroves to **La To-**
★ **bara**, San Blas's most famous attraction. Turtles on logs, crocs that *look* like logs, birds, iguanas, and exotic orchids make this maze of mud-brown canals a magical place. Begin the tranquil ride ($10; four people minimum) at the El Conchal Bridge, at the entrance-exit to San Blas, or the village of Matanchén. Boats depart when there are enough customers, which isn't usually a problem. Either way you'll end up, after a 45-minute to 1-hour boat ride, at the freshwater pool fed by a natural spring. Rest at the snack shop overlooking the water or jump in using the rope swing, keeping an eye out for the allegedly benign resident croc. There's an optional trip to a crocodile farm.

ECOTOUR **Singayta** (✉ 8 km [5 mi] from San Blas on road to Tepic ☎ 323/282–7019 ⊕ www.singayta.com) is a typical Nayarit village that is attempting to support itself through simple and un-gimmicky ecotours. The basic tour includes a look around the town, where original adobe structures compete with more practical but less picturesque structures with corrugated tin roofs. Take a short guided hike through

> **BIRDER'S PARADISE**
>
> More than 500 species of birds settle in the San Blas area; 23 are endemic. Organize a birding tour through Hotel Garza Canela (⇨ *above*). In January, you can attend the **International Festival of Migratory Birds** (⊕ www.semarnat.gob.mx/nayarit/festival2006) for bird-watching tours and conferences with experts and fellow enthusiasts.

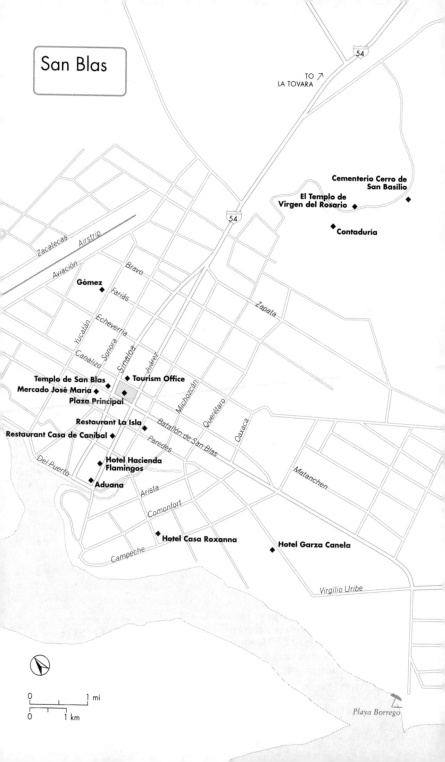

San Blas

54

TO ↗
LA TOVARA

54

Cementerio Cerro de San Basilio ◆

El Templo de Virgen del Rosario ◆

Contaduría ◆

Zacatecas

Airstrip

Aviación

Bravo

Gómez ◆

Farías

Zapata

Echeverría

Yucatán

Canalizo

Sonora

Sinaloa

Juárez

Templo de San Blas ◆   ◆ **Tourism Office**

Mercado José María ◆

Plaza Principal

Michoacán

Querétaro

Oaxaca

Restaurant La Isla ◆

Batallón de San Blas

Restaurant Casa de Canibal ◆

Paredes

Del Puerto

Hotel Hacienda Flamingos ◆

Matanchen

Aduana ◆

Arista

Comonfort

Hotel Casa Roxanna ◆

Hotel Garza Canela ◆

Campeche

Virgilio Uribe

0   1 mi

0   1 km

Playa Borrego

the surrounding jungle, and a boat ride around the estuary. Or rent mountain bikes ($5 per hour) to check out a broader area. This is primo birding territory. The easiest way to book a tour is to look for English-speaking Juan Bananas, who sells banana bread from a shop called Tumba de Yako (look for the sign on the unmarked road Av. Batallón de San Blas, en route to Playa Borrego). He will set up the visit and guide you there. Otherwise, call ahead to make a reservation.

The Beaches Near San Blas

Like San Blas itself, the surrounding beaches attract mostly local people and travelers fleeing glitzier resort scenes. Beaches here are almost uniformly long, flat, and walkable, with light brown sand, moderate to largish waves, and seriously bothersome no-see-ums, especially around sunrise and sunset (and during the waxing and waning moons). Almost as ubiquitous as these biting bugs are simple *ramadas* (open-sided, palm-thatch-roof eateries) on the beach whose owners don't mind if you hang out all day, jumping in the ocean and then back in your shaded hammock to continue devouring John Grisham or leafing through magazines. Order a cold lemonade or a beer, or have a meal of shrimp, fillet of fish, ceviche, or chips and guacamole. All these beaches are accessible by bus from San Blas's centrally located bus station.

You can walk or ride a bike to **Playa Borrego,** just 1 km (½ mi) south of town. Rent a surfboard at Mar y Sol Restaurant to attack the year-round shore break there, or stroll down to the southern end to admire the lovely estuary. About 6 km (4 mi) south of Playa Borrego, at the northern edge of Bahía de Matanchén, **Playa Las Islitas** used to be legendary among surfers for its long wave, but this has diminished in recent years; the beach is now suitable for swimming, body surfing, and boogie boarding. At the south end of the Matanchén Bay, **Playa Los Cocos and Playa Miramar** are both great for long walks and for hanging out at ramadas.

Adjacent to Miramar Beach is the well-kept fishing village of **Santa Cruz.** Take a walk on the beach or around the town; buy a soft drink, find the bakery and pick up some banana bread. Or, on a Saturday evening, head to the diminutive central plaza for the weekly dance. Beyond Matanchén Bay the road heads inland and reemerges about 8 km (5 mi) later at **Playa Platanitos,** a lovely little beach in a sheltered cove. Fisherman park their skiffs here, and simple shacks cook up the catch of the day.

Where to Stay & Eat

¢ ✕▦ **Casa Mañana.** Some of the pleasant rooms overlook the beach from a balcony or terrace, but most people stay here for easy access to the good burgers, guacamole, and seafood platter for two ($14) at the adjoining **El Alebrije** restaurant. The bar, with its cool, brick-floor interior open to the beach, is also popular. Other perks: the long beach, large pool, and hiking and other outdoor activities. ✉ *South*

> **BEST BEACH BITE**
>
> For a marvelous albeit simple barbecue fish feast, visit **Enramada Ruiz,** the best of the seafood shanties on Playa Platanitos.

end of Playa Los Cocos, 13 km (8 mi) south of San Blas ☎ *323/254–9090* ⊕ *www.casa-manana.com* ⤴ *26 rooms* △ *Restaurant, pool, beach, fishing, hiking, bar, free parking* ▤ *MC, V* ⍾ *EP.*

San Blas & Environs Essentials

TRANSPORTATION

BY AIR   If you *really* want to fly directly to San Blas from outside Mexico, you can—or at least, you can fly to Tepic (via Mexico City), 69 km (43 mi) from San Blas. But the majority of visitors going to PV start there, and road-trip up to San Blas. To get to San Blas from Tepic, Nayarit, head north on Highway 15D, then west on Highway 11. AeroCalifornia, Mexicana de Aviación, and Aeromexico do the Mexico City–Tepic route.

🏧 **AeroCalifornia** ☎ 800/237-6225 ⊕ www.aerocalifornia.com. **Aeromexico** ☎ 800/237-6639 in U.S. and Canada, 01800/021-4000 in Mexico ⊕ www.aeromexico.com. **Mexicana** ☎ 800/531-7921 in U.S, 866/281-3049 in Canada, 01800/509-8960 in Mexico ⊕ www.mexicana.com.

BY BUS   The bus station is less than 5 kilometers (a couple of miles) north of the PV airport; there are four daily departures for San Blas ($10; 3 hours). These buses generally don't stop, and they don't have bathrooms. Departure times vary throughout the year, but at this writing, there are no departures after 3 PM.

🏧 **Transportes Norte de Sonora** ☎ 323/285-0043 in San Blas, 322/290-0110 in Puerto Vallarta.

BY CAR   From Puerto Vallarta, abandon Highway 200 just past Las Varas in favor of the coast road (follow the sign toward Zacualpan). The distance of about 160 km (100 mi) takes 3½ hours.

From Guadalajara, take 15D (the toll road, about $20) or Carretera 15, the free road, to just north of Tepic. The toll road shaves a couple of hours driving time off the five-hour drive along the free highway, Carretera 15 (227 km [141 mi]). From either 15 or 15D, follow the "Miramar" turnoff for about 70 km (43 mi) to San Blas.

BY TAXI   A taxi from the Puerto Vallarta airport costs $50–$60; it's about $100 from Puerto Vallarta proper.

CONTACTS & RESOURCES

EMERGENCIES   🏧 Hotlines **Police** ☎ 323/285-0221.

🏧 Medical Center **Centro de Salud San Blas** ⊠ Calle H. Batallón at Calle Yucatán, San Blas ☎ 323/285-0232.

🏧 Late-Night Pharmacies **Farmacia Económica** ⊠ Calle H. Batallón at Calle Mercado, San Blas ☎ 323/285-0111.

EXCHANGE   🏧 **Banamex** ⊠ Calle Juárez 36, 1 block east of plaza, San Blas ☎ 323/
SERVICES   285-0031 ⊕ www.banamex.com.mx.

MAIL   🏧 Post Office **Correos** ⊠ Corner of Calles Echevarrí and Sonora, San Blas ☎ 323/285-0295.

VISITOR   In *la presidencia* (city hall), the Oficina de Turismo de San Blas attends
INFORMATION   to visitors daily 9–3, though it may close during slow periods. Look for

a booth with maps and info in the plaza across the street. The Web site **www.visitsanblas.com** is very helpful for planning.

🛈 Oficina de Turismo de San Blas ✉ Calles Canalizo and Sinaloa on main plaza San Blas ☎ 323/285-0221 or 323/285-0005.

THE MOUNTAIN TOWNS

A trip into the Sierra Madre is an excellent way to escape the coastal heat and the hordes of vacationers. The Spanish arrived to extract ore from these mountains at the end of the 16th century; after the Mexican Revolution the mines were largely abandoned in favor of richer veins. The isolation of these tiny towns has kept them old-fashioned.

The air is crisp and clean and scented of pine, the valley and mountain views are spectacular, and the highland towns earthy, unassuming, and charming. Whitewashed adobe homes radiate from town plazas where old gents remember youthful exploits. Saturday night boys and girls court each other alfresco while oom-pah bands entertain their parents from the bandstand. Although most of the hotels in the region have only basic amenities (continued work on the road from PV is encouraging entrepreneurs, however), the chill mountain air and kilos of blankets can produce a delicious night's sleep.

1-2 Days in the Mountain Towns

Vallarta Adventures (☎ 322/297-1212 ⊕ www.vallarta-adventures.com) has excellent day tours to either San Sebastián or to Mascota and Talpa. The small-plane ride provides a wonderful photo op and aerial introduction to the Sierra Madre.

If you're not joining an organized day tour, there are many possible itineraries, depending on whether you leave from PV or from Guadalajara, your tolerance for driving mountain roads, and desire to see lots or just relax and enjoy the tranquillity, mountain-and-valley views, and quaint lifestyle. Mascota is the largest town and makes a good base if you're returning to Guadalajara. From there, Lake Juanacatlán can be visited as a day trip, or you can overnight at the lodge there, which serves excellent food. Each of the three towns has hills to be climbed for excellent vistas and photos. Otherwise activities in each town are wandering the streets, visiting small museums and Catholic churches, tasting regional food and drinking in the mountain air and old-fashioned ambience. If starting from and returning to Puerto Vallarta, consider spending the first night in either Talpa or Mascota and the second in Mascota or, en route back to Vallarta, San Sebastián. Make sure you get where you're going before dark, as mountain roads are unlighted, narrow, and in many cases have sheer drop-offs.

LOGISTICS & TIPS From Guadalajara to Talpa or Mascota, it's a scenic drive along a paved but serpentine mountain road. The route to San Sebastián (from Mascota) is part paved, part dirt. It takes about 1¼ hours when in good condition. From Puerto Vallarta (on a good day), it's a 2-hour drive to San Sebastián, 2½ to Mascota, and about 3 to Talpa by car. The road is newly paved and 90% finished. The last 10% is being replaced by a suspen-

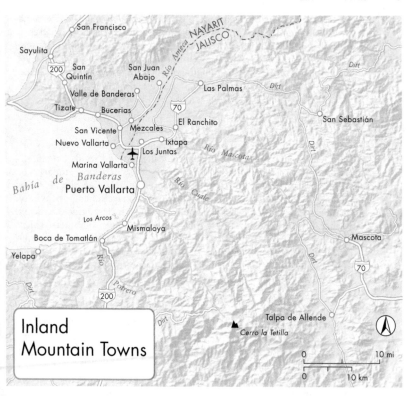

Inland
Mountain Towns

0   10 mi

0   10 km

9

sion bridge that is supposed be finished in early 2007. The last 8 km (5 mi) of the road to leading to San Sebastián and Mascota tends to get washed out in the rainy season, when it becomes a heart-stopping narrow dirt track with gullies and drop-offs. Lago Juanacatlán is an hour from Mascota on a rough one-lane road of dirt and rock.

San Sebastián

If, physically, there's about 80 treacherous km (50 mi) between Puerto Vallarta and San Sebastián, metaphorically they're as far apart as the Earth and the moon. Sleepy San Sebastián is the Mayberry of Mexico, but a little less lively. It's the kind of place where you feel weird walking past people without saying hello, even though you don't know them from Adam. The miners that built the town have long gone, and more recently, younger folks are drifting away in search of opportunity. Most of the 800 or so people who have stayed seem perfectly content with life as it is, although rat-race dropouts and entrepreneurs are making their way here along with (somewhat) improved roads.

What to See

The most interesting thing to see in San Sebastián is the town itself. Walk the cobblestone streets and handsome brick sidewalks, admiring the white-faced adobe structures surrounding the plaza. Take any side street and wander at will. Enjoy the enormous walnut trees lining the road into town, and diminutive peach trees peaking over garden walls. The reason to go to this cozy, lazy, beautiful town at 5,250 feet above sea level is to look inward, reflecting on life, or outward, greeting or chatting as best you can with those you meet. Look anywhere, in fact, except a laptop or if possible, a television screen. That's just missing the point.

San Sebastián has a few things to do, although none of them is the reason to visit. Stop in the *abarrotes* (general store) on the north side of the square for a beverage or a spool of thread; then head to directly behind it to **Iglesia de San Sebastián** a typically restored 1800s-era church that comes to life in the days preceding its saint's day, January 20. You're welcome any time at the **Casa Museo de Doña Conchita** (⊠ Calle Juarez 2 ☎ 322/297–2860 ☜ $1). The aged but affable lady loves to show visitors photos of her venerable family—which she traces back six generations. See bank notes from the mining days, bloomers, shirts made by hand by the lady for her many children, and other old memorabilia. If you speak Spanish, ask Dona Conchita to tell you about the ghosts that haunt her house, which is right on the square between the basketball court and *la presidencia,* or town hall.

Where to Stay & Eat

¢–$ ✕ **Fonda de Doña Lupita.** Typical food of the countryside—enchiladas, tamales, pozole, beefsteak with beans and tortillas, and so on—is served in an equally typical family home. The house has been enlarged to welcome guests, and the friendly owner does her part. Straw-bottom chairs are comfortable enough, and the oilcloths shiny and new. The small bar is at the back behind the large, open kitchen. It's open for breakfast, too. ⊠ *Calle Cuauhtemoc 89* ☎ *322/297–2803* ▤ *No credit cards.*

$$ ⬚ **La Galerita de San Sebastián.** A pair of displaced *tapatios* (Guadalajarans) have created a cluster of

> **WARM CUPPA CORN?**
>
> For an authentic experience, pop into any *fonda* or *lonchería* (simple eateries, the former usually in someone's home, the latter open for lunch only) for a typical *atole con piloncillo* (hot corn drink sweetened with unrefined brown sugar) and a simple meal. Some, like the **Fonda Doña Leo** (⊠ Calle Paso del Norte ☎ 322/297–2909), down the street from the basketball court, don't even have signs out front.

pretty cabins on their property about four blocks from the plaza. Lie on the comfortable tatami futon (in each room) for a nap, or to view satellite TV on the small computer screen. The double-sided fireplace heats the bedroom and adjoining sitting room. Bed coverings and matching drapes of earthy, muted colors are all good quality. This is the most modern and stylish place to stay in San Sebastián, and is geared to adults. ⊠ *Hacienda La Galera 62, Barrio La Otra Banda, San Sebastián 46990* ☎ *322/297–3040* ⊕ *www.lagalerita.com.mx* ⇆ *6 bungalows* ♨ *Dining room, refrigerator, Wi-Fi, pond, some free parking; no a/c, no room phones,* ▤ *No credit cards* ⦿ *EP.*

$ 🏠 **Hacienda Jalisco.** Come for the history (it was built not long after the War of Independence), the stone fireplaces and antiques in most of the cozy guest rooms, and the delightful meals (breakfast and dinner are included in the price) choreographed by expat Roberto Acord. Call a week ahead to reserve a room, or drop by to ask about horse rental or for a brief tour of the historical structure, much of it restored by the owner himself. It's lighted by lamps only; there's no electricity. ⊠ *Entrance to town, San Sebastián s/n 46990* ☎ *322/223–1695* ⊕ *www. haciendajalisco.com* ↙ *6 rooms* ⬧ *Restaurant, library; no a/c, no room phones, no room TVs* ⊟ *No credit cards* �‖⊙ *MAP.*

$ 🏠 **Real de San Sebastián.** Small rooms are dominated by snug king beds in curtained alcoves in this interesting B&B. It has a (somewhat cramped) shared main living space with a cushy plush couch facing a large-screen satellite TV, and more formal round tables where afternoon coffee or hot chocolate is served. Take coffee and rolls in bed before emerging for a full breakfast in the dining room. The manager, Margarito, is friendly and solicitous. ⊠ *Calle Zaragoza 41, San Sebastián 46990* ☎ *322/ 297–3223* ⊕ *www.sanSebastiándeloeste.com* ↙ *6 rooms* ⬧ *Restaurant; no a/c, no room phones, no room TVs* ⊟ *No credit cards* �‖⊙ *BP.*

Outdoor Activities & Sports

Local men can be hired for a truck ride up to **La Bufa,** a half-dome visible from the town square. One such man is **Obed Dueña** (☎ 322/297–2864), who charges about $30 for the trip. It's the same price if you ride with him or hike back. The truck will wait while you climb—about 15 minutes to the top—and enjoy the wonderful view of the town, surrounding valleys, and, on a clear day, Puerto Vallarta. San Sebastián was founded as a silver-and-gold mining town; ask the driver to stop for a quick visit to a mine en route. Or you can hike both ways; it takes most folks 2 to 2 ½ hours to reach the top, and half to two-thirds that time to return. Another great destination for a walk is **Hacienda Jalisco** (⇨ *above*), a 15–20 minute walk from San Sebastián's plaza; ask the owner to show you around the property.

Mascota

Mascota's cool but sunny climate is perfect for growing citrus, avocados, nuts, wheat, corn, and other crops. Fed by the Mascota and Ameca rivers and many springs and year-round streams, the blue–green hills and valleys surrounding town are lusciously forested; beyond them rise indigo mountains to form a painterly tableau. This former mining town and municipal seat is home to some 13,000 people. Its banks, shops, and a hospital serve surrounding villages. On its coat of arms are a

9

MASCOTA'S MARTYR

In 1927, during the anti-clerical Cristero movement, Mascota's young priest refused to abandon his post. Soldiers peeled the skin from his hands and feet before forcing him to walk to a large oak tree, where he was hanged. Mascota's hero, José María Robles was canonized in 2000 by Pope John Paul II.

pine tree, deer, and rattlesnake. The town's name derives from the Nahuatl words for deer and snake.

What to See

Mascota's pride is **La Iglesia de la Preciosa Sangre** (Church of the Precious Blood), started in 1909 but unfinished due to the revolution and the ensuing Cristero Revolt. Weddings, concerts, and plays are sometimes held here under the ruins of Gothic arches. Note the 3-D blood squirting from Jesus's wound in the neighboring seminary chapel. Walk around the **plaza,** where old gents share stories and kids chase balloons. Couples dance the stately *danzón* on Thursday and Saturday evenings as the band plays in the wrought-iron bandstand. The town produces *huaraches* (woven leather sandals), ceramics, saddles, and *raicilla,* a relative of tequila.

On one corner of the plaza is the town's white-spired **Iglesia de la Virgen de los Dolores.** The Virgin of Sorrow is feted on September 15, which segues into Mexican Independence Day on the 16th. A block beyond the other end of the plaza, the **Museo de Mascota** (⊠ Calle Morelos near Calle Allende) is worth a look. Open Monday through Saturday 10–2 and 4–8, the museum closes between 3 and 5. Around the corner from the Mascota Museum, the **Casa de la Cultura** (⊠ Calle Allende 115) has rotating exhibits of photography and art. It's open 10–2 and 4–7 Monday through Saturday.

Where to Stay & Eat

¢–$ ✕ **La Casa de Mi Abuela.** Everyone and his mother likes "Grandma's House," which is conveniently open all day (and evening), every day, starting at around 8 AM with breakfast. In addition to beans, rice, *carne asada,* and other recognizable Mexican food, there are backcountry recipes that are much less familiar to the average traveler. ⊠ *Calle Corona at Calle Zaragoza, Mascota* ☎ *No phone.*

$$–$$$ ▦ **Sierra Lago.** About an hour outside Mascota, this mountain lodge of knotty pine is a tranquil retreat for travelers weary of the city scene. Choose a comfortable cabin or a suite. Walk around the lovely lake, go for a sail or kayak, lie in the sun at the shore, or just read a book in the steamy hot tub. Go for the full meal plan, as there's nothing for miles and the cooking is excellent; the dining room has high ceilings and a huge stone fireplace. ⊠ *An hour north of Mascota, Lago Juanacatlán* ☎ *322/224–9350* ⊕ *www.sierralago.com* ⇨ *10 rooms, 6 suites, 7 cabins* ⌂ *Restaurant, some refrigerators, some cable TV, tennis, pool, hot tub, horseback riding, fishing, boating, mountain bikes, massage, bar, free parking; no room phones* ⊟ *MC, V* ⦿ *EP, AI.*

★ $ ▦ **Mesón de Santa Elena.** Beautiful rooms in this converted 19th-century house have lovely old tile floors, beige cotton drapes covering huge windows, rag-rolled walls, and wonderful tile sinks. The dining room has old-fashioned cupboards and there are dining tables inside and out on two patios festooned with flowers and large potted plants. Second-floor rooms have views of fields and mountains to the west. ⊠ *Hidalgo 155, Mascota* ☎ *388/386–0313* ⊕ *www.mesondesantaelena.com* ⇨ *10 rooms, 2 suites* ⌂ *Restaurant, cable TV, no a/c, no room phones, no room TVs* ⊟ *No credit cards* ⦿ *EP, BP, AI.*

Outdoor Activities & Sports

The beautiful countryside just outside town is ideal for hikes and drives. From Mascota's plaza you can walk up Calle Morelos out of town to **Cerro de la Cruz.** The hike to the summit takes about a half hour and rewards with great valley views. The newish **Presa Corinches,** a dam about 5 km (3 mi) south of town, has bass fishing, picnic spots (for cars and RVs), and a restaurant where locals go for fish feasts on holidays and weekend afternoons. To get to the dam, head east on Calle Juárez (a block south of the plaza) and follow the signs to the reservoir. Take a walk along the shore or set up a tent near the fringe of pine-oak forest coming down to meet the cool blue water, which is fine for swimming when the weather is warm. **Lago Juanacatlán** is a lovely lake in a volcanic crater at 7,000 feet above sea level. Nestled in the El Galope River valley, the pristine lake is surrounded by alpine woods, and the trip from Mascota past fields of flowers and self-sufficient *ranchos* is bucolic. Walk along the lakeshore or just enjoy it from the restaurant of the rusti-chich Sierra Lago lodge, where you can kayaks and small sailboats.

Shopping

Stores in town sell homemade preserves, locally grown coffee, raicilla (an alcoholic drink of undistilled agave), and sweets. A good place to shop for local product and produce is the **Mercado municipal** (⊠ Calle P. Sánchez, at Hidalgo, 1 block west of plaza).

Talpa de Allende

Another tranquil town surrounded by pine-oak forests, Talpa, as it's called, has just over 7,000 inhabitants but welcomes 4 million visitors a year. They come to pay homage or ask favors of the diminutive Virgen del Rosario de Talpa, Jalisco's most revered Virgin. Some people walk three days from Puerto Vallarta as penance or a sign of devotion; others come by car or truck but return annually to show their faith.

What to See

On the large town plaza, the **Basilica de Talpa** is the main show in town. The twin-spired limestone temple is Gothic with neoclassic elements. After visiting the diminutive, royally clad Virgin in her side chapel, stroll around the surrounding square. Shops and stalls sell sweets, miniature icons of the Virgin in every possible presentation, T-shirts, and other souvenirs. *Chicle* (gum) is harvested in the area, and you'll find small keepsakes in the shapes of shoes, flowers, and animals made of the (nonsticky) raw material.

> **HOLY CITY**
>
> During several major annual fiestas, the town swells with visitors. The Fiesta de la Candelaria culminates in Candlemass, February 2. The town's patron saint, St. Joseph, is honored March 19. May 12, September 10, September 19, and October 7 mark rituals devoted to the Virgin del Rosario de Talpa.

Where to Stay & Eat

$ ✕**Casa Grande.** This excellent steak house also serves grilled chicken and seafood. Under a roof but open on all sides and with an incredible view, it's highly recommended by visitors and locals. Lunch is served after 2 PM and the kitchen stays open until 10:30. ⊠ *Calle Juárez 53, Talpa de Allende* ☎ *388/385–0709* ▭ *No credit cards* ☉ *Closed Tues.*

¢ ✕▥ **Hacienda Jacarandas.** The charming, two-story building has high ceilings, wide corridors, and comfortable guest rooms with fine and folk art. Bougainvillea in shades of purple and pink climb up the cream-color exterior walls, and the rooftop terrace—with a terrific view—is a nice place to laze away a morning or afternoon, in the sun or under the covered portion. The 62-acre property has a small lake. ⊠ *Rancho Portrellos, just over bridge at southeast end of town, Talpa de Allende 48200* ☎ *333/447–7366* ▤ *388/385–0669* ⊕ *www.haciendajacarandas.com* ⋙ *6 rooms* ⌂ *Restaurant, pool, hot tub, library, bar* ▭ *No credit cards* ☉ *Closed Easter–June* ⦿⃒ *BP, MAP.*

Mountain Town Essentials

TRANSPORTATION

For an effortless excursion, go on a Vallarta Adventures day tour (⇨ Overnight Excursions Planner). For more flexibility or to spend the night in a cozy, no-frills hotel or a refurbished hacienda, fly on your own through Aerotaxis de la Bahía.

BY AIR Aerotaxis de la Bahia in PV has charter flights to all three towns. For three passengers the rate is 3,000 pesos (about $100 each); four to eight passengers pay 6,648 pesos ($637) split among them. ■ TIP➔ **The return flight is often free if you fly back with the pilot within two to three hours of arrival.**

🛈 **Aerotaxis de la Bahia** ☎ 322/221-1990.

BY BUS Weather permitting, ATM (Autotransportes Talpa–Mascota) buses depart from Vallarta's Parque Hidalgo (north side) at around 6 AM, stopping at La Estancia (11 km [7 mi] from San Sebastián), (5 hours), then Mascota (8 hours), and Talpa (10 hours). Buses also depart several times a day from Guadalajara's new bus station (Entronque carretera libre a Zapotlanejo, Modules 3 and 4). Note that the bus does not enter San Sebastín; you can usually find a cab or someone heading to town to get the rest of the way for under $5. You'll be dropped at the side of the road, where one or more local men usually is available to transport you to town.

🛈 **Autotransportes Talpa–Mascota** (ATM) ☎ 322/222-4816 in Puerto Vallarta, 388/386-0093 in Mascota, 388/385-0701 in Talpa, 33/3600-0588 or 33/3600-0098 in Guadalajara.

BY CAR Mascota is 190 relatively carefree km (120 mi; 3 hours) from Guadalajara on a paved, two-lane but circuitous highway; it's about the same distance to Talpa. From Puerto Vallarta it's about 80 km (50 mi; 2.5 hours to San Sebastián,) 1½ to Mascota, and an additional 30 minutes to Talpa.

BY TAXI Taxis are easily found near the main square in Talpa, Mascota, and San Sebastián.

CONTACTS & RESOURCES

EMERGENCIES For most problems in these small towns, seek assistance at the tourism office or *la presidencia* (the town hall). Medical services are available in Mascota's government-sponsored health clinic. If you get sick in Talpa or San Sebastín, ask for help at the pharmacy or town hall.

Pharmacies Farmacia Estrella ⊠ Calle 5 de Mayo, at Calle Ayuntamiento, Mascota ☎ 388/386-0285. **Farmacia del Oeste** ⊠ Calle Cuauhtemoc at Calle López Mateos, across from plaza, San Sebastián ☎ 322/297-2833. **Farmacia San Miguel** ⊠ Calle Independencia, at Calle Anahuac, across from Sq., Talpa ☎ 388/385-0085.

Medical Center Centro de Salud de Mascota ⊠ Calle Dávalos 70, Mascota ☎ 388/386-0174.

EXCHANGE SERVICES There are banks with ATM machines in Mascota and Talpa, but it's best to bring plenty of cash just in case; most businesses don't accept credit cards. San Sebastián has no bank, and businesses don't accept credit cards.

Bancomer ⊠ Calle Constitución at Calle Hidalgo, Mascota ☎ 388/386-0387. **Banco HSBC** ⊠ Calle Independencia, across from la presidencia [town hall], Talpa ☎ 388/385-0197.

INTERNET & MAIL Mail any postcards or packages from Puerto Vallarta or Guadalajara. Mascota has an Internet café.

Cyber Center ⊠ Calle Ayuntamiento, catercorner from plaza near Calle Constitución, Mascota.

VISITOR INFORMATION In small towns like these, the *presidencia* (town hall or mayor's office) is the place to get tourist information or to locate a specific service. Tourism offices are generally open weekdays 9–5, with a lunch closing around 1 (Mascota) or 3 (San Sebastián, Talpa), but hours tend to be flexible.

Oficina de Turismo de Mascota ⊠ La Presidencia (Town Hall), Calle Ayuntamiento, at Calle Constitución, facing plaza, Mascota ☎ 388/386-1179 or 388/386-00525. **Oficina de Turismo de San Sebastián** ⊠ Calle López Mateos, around corner from La Presidencia (Town Hall), San Sebastián ☎ 322/297-2938. **Oficina de Turismo de Talpa** ⊠ La Presidencia (Town Hall), Calle Independencia s/n, 2 blocks north of plaza, Talpa de Allende ☎ 388/385-0009 or 388/385-0287.

THE GUADALAJARA REGION

Guadalajara rests on a mile-high plain of the Sierra Madre Occidental, surrounded on three sides by rugged hills and on the fouth by the spectacular Oblatos Canyon. Mexico's second largest city has a population of 4 million and is the capital of Jalisco State. This cosmopolitan if traditional and quintessentially Mexican city offers a range of activities. Shop for handicrafts, housewares, and especially fine ceramics in smart shops or family-owned factories. Dress up for drinks, dinner, and dancing in smart Zona Minerva, in downtown Guadalajara, or put on your comfy walking shoes to visit satellite neighborhoods of indigenous origin. For shoppers and metropolis lovers, this is a great complement to a Puerto Vallarta vacation.

An hour's drive in just about any direction from Guadalajara will bring you out of the fray and into the countryside. Due south is Lake Chapala, Mexico's largest natural lake. Bordering it are several villages

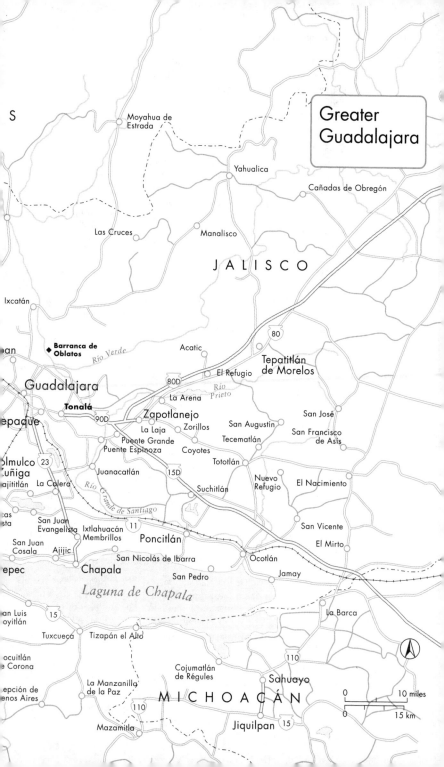

with large expat communities, including Chapala and Ajijic, a village of bougainvillea and cobblestone roads. Tequila, where the famous firewater is brewed, is northwest of Guadalajara. Teuchitlán, south of Tequila, has the Guachimontones ruins. The placid lakeside area makes for a weeklong (expats would say lifelong) getaway, while Tequila and Teuchitlán are great for day-trippers.

2–3 Days in the Guadalajara Region

The four primary municipalities of metropolitan Guadalajara are Guadalajara, Zapopan, Tlaquepaque, and Tonalá. With the exception of Zapopan, they can each be navigated on foot in a few hours, though each deserves at least half a day. Zapopan requires more time since it's a sprawling suburb with lots of shopping. Due west of Guadalajara's Centro Histórico, Zona Minerva is the place to go for great restaurants and after-dark action. Plan on a third day if you want to visit outlying areas like Lake Chapala and Teuchitlán.

On the morning of Day 1, visit historic Guadalajara, checking out the cathedral and other landmarks on the interconnecting plazas. Enormous Mercado Libertad (aka Mercado San Juan de Dios) is several long blocks east of Plaza Fundadores, or take the subway two blocks south of the cathedral on Avenida Juárez. If it's Sunday, see a charreada; otherwise head to Zapopan to see the basilica, the Huichol Museum, and the Art Museum of Zapopan, and spend 15 minutes at *la presidencia municipal* (city hall) to admire the leftist-themed mural inside. If you have more time, check out the market, two blocks west at Calles Eva Briseño and Hidalgo, and a couple of surrounding churches before grabbing a drink or a bite on Paseo Teopinztle, two blocks south. Freshen up at your hotel, then dine in downtown Guadalajara or the Zona Minerva.

Spend the second day shopping and visiting churches and museums in the old towns of Tonalá and in more compact, walkable Tlaquepaque. If you're here on Thursday or Sunday, don't miss the Tonalá crafts market, with its super deals. El Parián in Tlaquepaque is a great place to enjoy a mariachi serenade with a cool refreshment. Have Mexican food for lunch or dinner in one of Tlaquepaque's charming restaurants. If you don't want to shop, consider spending the day hiking in Barranca de Oblatos or visiting the playground, park, and gardens at Parque Azul. Arrive in the morning to avoid crowds; leave before dark.

If you've got three days in Guadalajara you'll have time to visit Tequila or Lake Chapala. It's a refreshing change to get out of the city and admire the relatively dry hills and valleys, noting the fields of blue agave that are Tequila's reason for being. Tequila is en route to San Blas and Puerto Vallarta. Lake Chapala and the towns on the shore work well as a day excursion if you have a car.

LOGISTICS & TIPS Allot a minimum of three hours for the Centro Histórico, longer if you really want to enjoy the sculptures and street scene. Mornings are generally the least crowded time of day, although the light is particularly beautiful in the afternoons when jugglers, street musicians, and other informal entertainers tend to emerge.

Beware of heavy traffic and *topes* (speed bumps). Traffic circles are common at busy intersections.

Tonalá's crafts market and Mercado Libertad are the region's top two marketplaces. Allot yourself plenty of time and energy to explore both. El Trocadero is a weekly antiques market at the north end of Avenida Chapultepec. Feel free to drive a hard bargain at all three.

Guadalajara

Metropolitan Guadalajara's sights are divided into four major areas: Guadalajara, Zapopan, Tlaquepaque, and Tonalá. Within Guadalajara are many districts and neighborhoods. Of most interest to visitors are the Centro Histórico (Historic District), a rather small section of town that's part of the larger downtown area (El Centro). Outside the Centro Histórico, Guadalajara resembles any large, rather contaminated city with gnarly traffic. On the west side are Zona Minerva, the most modern section of the city and the place to go for dining, dancing, shopping in large malls, and high-rise hotels. The Centro Histórico, Tlaquepaque, and Tonalá can each be navigated on foot in a few hours, though they deserve at least half a day. Zapopan's high-end hotels, bars, shops, and cafés are spread out, but historic Zapopan is reasonably compact. Likewise, Tonalá is a lot more spread out than more tourist-oriented, walkable Tlaquepaque.

City Tours

Take free, three-hour **artisan-studio walking tours** (☎ 33/3284–3092 or 33/3284–3093) given by the Tonalá Municipal Tourist Office. Tours depart daily (except Sunday and Thursday) at 10 AM from the **Casa de los Artesanos** (✉ Av. Tonalteca Sur 140, between Calles Matamoros and 16 de Septiembre, Tonala ☎ 33/3284–3092). Ten guests or more can request an English-speaking guide by prior arrangement.

Viajes Panoramex has a five-hour **historic and cultural tour** (☎ 33/ 3810–5057 or 33/3810–5109 ⊕ www.panoramex.com.mx) that ends up in Talquepaque for some shopping. You can hire a **horse-drawn carriage,** or *calandria* in front of the Museo Regional, the Mercado Libertad, or Parque San Francisco. It's about $15 for a shorter tour for up to five; $20 for an hour. Few drivers speak English. There are no reservations, just show up.

A free, 2½-hour **walking tour** (☎ 33/3616–9150 or 33/3615–1182 ⊕ www.vive.guadalajara.gob.mx) is given by the Guadalajara Municipal Tourism Office every weekend, starting at 10 AM at the Palacio Municipal Palace (English guide available with advance reservation only). Saturday evenings at 7 there's a 1½-hour tour accompanied by mariachis or minstrels.

What to See

EL CENTRO &   Guadalajara's historical center is a blend of modern and old buildings
THE CENTRO   connected by a series of large plazas radiating from the Cathedral.
HISTÓRICO   Many colonial-era structures were razed; others stand crumbling, as there's
no money for restoration. But overall there are many colonial- and

9

Republican-era buildings with impressive carved limestone facades, tiled steeples and domes, magnificent wooden doors, and wrought-iron grills. The surrounding parks, plazas, and fountains have Corinthian columns and a great sense of community.

For a taste of how the wealthy once lived, visit the **Casa-Museo López Portillo**, a mansion with a stunning collection of 17th- through 20th-century furniture and accessories. ⊠ *Calle Liceo 177, Centro Histórico* ☎ *33/3613–2411* ⊒ *Free* ⊙ *Tues.–Sat. 10–5, Sun. 10–3.*

★ Construction was begun in 1561 on the **Catedral**, a downtown focal point and an intriguing mélange of Baroque, Gothic, and other styles. Exquisite altarpieces line the walls. In a loft above the main entrance is a magnificent late-19th-century French organ. ⊠ *Av. Alcalde between Av. Hidalgo and Calle Morelos, Centro Histórico* ⊙ *Daily 8–7.*

Fodor'sChoice
★ Originally a shelter for the elderly and orphans, the neoclassical-style **Instituto Cultural Cabañas** has 106 rooms and 23 flower-filled patios that now house art exhibitions. Kids love the murals by Orozco, as well as his smaller paintings and cartoons and the labyrinthine compound in general. Large-scale theater, dance, and musical performances occasionally take place on a patio here. The Tolsá Chapel hosts more intimate events. ⊠ *Calle Cabañas 8, Centro Histórico* ☎ *33/3818–2800 Ext. 31016* ⊒ *$1; free Sun.* ⊙ *Tues.–Sat. 10:15–6, Sun. 10–2:45; occasionally closed for maintenance.*

★ Artifacts from prehistoric times through the Spanish conquest and an impressive collection of European and Mexican paintings make the **Museo Regional de Guadalajara**, a grand former seminary, worth a visit. ⊠ *Calle Liceo 60, Centro Histórico* ☎ *33/3614–9957* ⊒ *$3; free Sun.* ⊙ *Tues.–Sat. 9–5:30, Sun. 9–4:30.*

Popular **Parque Agua Azul** has playgrounds, caged birds, an orchid house, and acres of trees and grass crisscrossed by walking paths. There aren't many butterflies in the huge, geodesic butterfly sanctuary, but the semitropical garden inside still merits a visit. The **Museo de la Paleontología** (⊠ Av. Dr. R. Michel 520, Centro Histórico ☎ 33/3619–7043), on the park's east side, has plant and animal fossils as well as exhibits on the origin of the planet. Admission is 70¢, and the museum is open Tuesday through Saturday 10–6 and Sunday 11–6. (There's no museum entrance inside Agua Azul; you must walk to the park's north side.) ⊠ *Calz. Independencia Sur, between González Gallo and Las Palmas, south of Centro Histórico, El Centro* ☎ *33/3619–0332* ⊒ *40¢* ⊙ *Daily 10–6.*

North of El Centro, **Barranca de Oblatos** is a multipronged, 2,000-

---

HORSING AROUND

Calandrias (horse-drawn carriages) take in the sights of the Centro Histórico; it's $20 for a long tour and $15 for a short one. Tapatío Tour, an open-top, double-decker bus, loops Zona Rosa ($9; daily 10 AM–8 PM). Get on and off as much as you like to explore the sights. The bus departs from the Rotunda, a plaza on the Cathedral's north side.

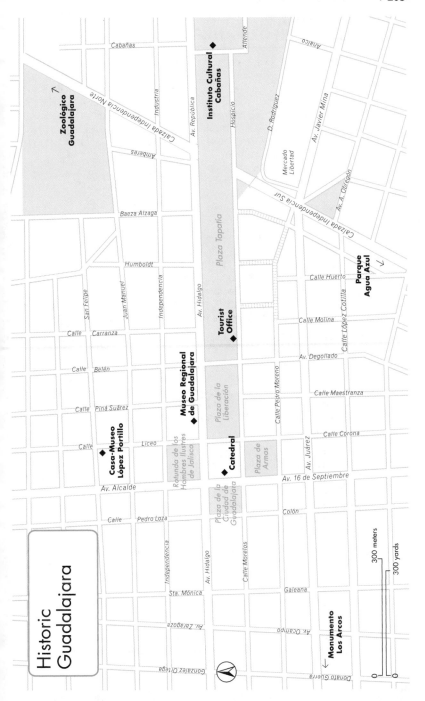

Historic
Guadalajara

Zoológico
Guadalajara

Instituto Cultural
Cabañas

Casa-Museo
López Portillo

Museo Regional
de Guadalajara

Tourist
Office

Catedral

Parque
Agua Azul

Monumento
Los Arcos

Plaza Tapatía

Plaza de la
Liberación

Plaza de
Armos

Plaza de la
Ciudad de
Guadalajata

Rotunda de los
Hombres Ilustres
de Jalisco

Mercado
Libertad

Calzada Independencia Norte

Calzada Independencia Sur

Cabañas

Allende

Hospicio

D. Rodríguez

Análco

Av. Javier Mina

Av. A. Obregón

Industria

Av. República

Amberes

Baeza Alzaga

Humboldt

San Felipe

Juan Manuel

Independencia

Av. Hidalgo

Calle Huerto

Calle López Cotilla

Calle Molina

Av. Degollado

Calle Maestranza

Calle Corona

Av. Juárez

Av. 16 de Septiembre

Colón

Calle Pedro Moreno

Calle Carranza

Calle Belén

Calle Piña Suárez

Liceo

Calle

Av. Alcalde

Calle Pedro Loza

Independencia

Av. Hidalgo

Calle Morelos

Sta. Mónica

Av. Zaragoza

Av. Ocampo

Galeana

Donato Guerra

González Ortega

300 meters

300 yards

LIVE PERFORMANCE

The State Band of Jalisco and the Municipal Band sometimes play at the bandstand on Tuesday around 6:30 PM. The internationally acclaimed **Ballet Folclórico of the University of Guadalajara** (☏ 33/3614–4773 or 33/3616–4991) performs traditional Mexican folkloric dances and music in the Teatro Degollado most Sundays at 10 AM; tickets are $3–$25. The state-funded **Orquesta Filarmónica de Jalisco** (Philharmonic Orchestra of Jalisco ☏ 33/3658–3812 or 33/3658–3819) performs pieces by Mexican composers mixed with standard orchestral fare. When in season (it varies), the OFJ performs Sunday at 12:30 PM and Friday at 8:30 PM; tickets are $5–$15.

Ask your concierge or the tourism office about other performances around town, or check the newspaper.

foot-deep ravine with hiking trails and the narrow Cascada Cola de Caballo (Horsetail Waterfall), named for its horsetail shape. A portion of the canyon complex, called Barranca de Huetitán (Huetitán Canyon), has a steep, winding, 5-km (3-mi) trail to the river below. The trails are less strenuous at the Barranca de Oblatos entrance.

🜨 The city's zoo, **Zoológico Guadalajara,** on the edge of the jagged Barranca de Huetitán, has more than 1,500 animals representing 360 species. There are two aviaries, a kids' zoo, and a herpetarium with 130 species of reptiles, amphibians, and fish. For 50¢ you can take a train tour of the grounds. Admission to the adjacent amusement park is $1.30. ⊠ *Paseo del Zoológico 600, off Calz. Independencia, Zona Huentitán, north of town near Barranca de Oblatos* ☏ *33/3674–4488 or 33/3674–3976* 🖅 *$3.50* ☉ *Wed.–Sun. 10–6.*

TLAQUEPAQUE   Another ancient pueblo that's gone upscale is crafts-crazy Tlaquepaque. Fabulous shopping for fine ceramics coupled with the attractive town's compact size make it appealing to Guadalajarans and visitors. Along its cobblestone streets are a wealth of mansions converted to shops and restaurants. B&Bs with jungly gardens, warming fires, and reasonable prices easily convince many travelers to make this their base.

Fodor'sChoice   On display at the **Museo del Premio Nacional de la Cerámica Pantaleon**
★   **Panduro** are prize-winning pieces from the museum's annual June ceramics competition. You can request an English-speaking guide at possibly the best collection of modern Mexican pottery anywhere. ⊠ *Calle Priciliano Sánchez at Calle Flórida, Tlaquepaque* ☏ *33/3639–5646, 33/3562–7036 Ext. 2007* 🖅 *Free* ☉ *Mon.–Sat. 10–6, Sun. 10–3.*

In a colonial mansion, the **Museo Regional de la Cerámica** has bilingual displays explaining common processes used by local ceramics artisans; presentation isn't always strong. ⊠ *Calle Independencia 237, Tlaquepaque* ☏ *33/3635–5404* 🖅 *Free* ☉ *Mon.–Sat. 10–6, Sun. 10–3.*

Continued on page 212

MARIACHI: BORN IN JALISCO

By Sean Mattson

It's 4 AM and you're sound asleep somewhere in Mexico. Suddenly you're jolted awake by trumpets blasting in rapid succession. Before you can mutter a groggy protest, ten men with booming voices break into song. Nearby, a woman stirs from her slumber. The man who brought her the serenade peeks toward her window from behind the lead singer's sombrero, hoping his sign of devotion is appreciated—and doesn't launch his girlfriend's father into a shoe-throwing fury.

At the heart of Mexican popular culture, mariachi is the music of love and heartache, of the daily travails of life, and nationalistic pride. This soundtrack of Mexican tradition was born in the same region as tequila, the Mexican hat dance, and *charrería* (Mexican rodeo), whose culture largely defines Mexican chivalry and machismo.

Today, mariachi bands are the life of the party. They perform at weddings, birthdays, public festivals, restaurants, and city plazas. The most famous bands perform across the globe. Guadalajara's annual mariachi festival draws mariachis from around the world.

The origin of the word *mariachi* is a source of some controversy. The legend is that it evolved from the French word *mariage* (marriage), stemming from the French occupation in the mid-1800s. But leading mariachi historians now debunk that myth, citing evidence that the word has its origins in the Nahuatl language of the Coca Indians.

THE RISE OF MARIACHI

Historians trace the roots of mariachi to Cocula, a small agricultural town south of Guadalajara. There, in the 17th century, Franciscan monks trained the local indigenous populations in the use of stringed instruments, teaching them the religious songs to help win their conversion.

The aristocracy, who preferred the more refined contemporary European music, held early mariachi groups in disdain. But by the late 19th century, mariachi had become enormously popular among peasants and indigenous people in Cocula, eventually spreading throughout southern Jalisco and into neighboring states.

MODERN MARIACHI INSTRUMENTS

Traditional mariachi groups consisted of two violins (the melody), and a vihuela and guitarrón (the harmony). Some long-gone groups used a *tambor* or drum, not used in modern mariachi. All members of the group shared singing responsibilities.

VIOLINS
Essential to any mariachi group

THE GUITARRÓN
A large-bellied bass guitar

TRUMPETS
Added to the traditional mariachi lineup in the 1930s when mariachis hit the big screen, at the insistence of a pioneer in Mexican radio and television

THE FOLK HARP
Longstanding mariachi instrument, used today by large ensembles and by some traditional troupes

GUITARS
The round-backed vihuela is smaller and higher-pitched than the standard guitar

5-string Vihuela   6-string guitar

In 1905, Mexican dictator Porfirio Díaz visited Cocula and was received with a performance of a mariachi group. Impressed with the performance, Diaz invited the group to Mexico City where, after a few years and a revolution, mariachi flourished. Over the next two decades, more groups followed to Mexico City. Mariachi groups gained wide popularity by the 1930s, when movie stars as Jorge Negrete and Pedro Infante began portraying mariachi musicians in their films.

MARIACHI STYLE

■ The mariachi *traje* (suit) consists of matching vest, *chaleco* (short jacket), and form-fitting pants, and a complementary *moño* (large bow tie). Simple *trajes* have soutache trim or embroidery; finer versions have suede patterns on the jacket with metal buttons down the pants legs. Trajes come in all colors, but formal costumes are black.

■ Sombreros made from pressed rabbit fur are the highest quality.

■ The modern mariachi's dress is an adaptation of *charro*, or Mexican cowboy, attire, first worn by the members of an early mariachi group led by Cirilo Marmolejo and adopted for Mexican movies of the 1930s–50s. A complete formal outfit can cost as much as US$3,000.

■ *Botonaduras* (decorative buttons on the pants legs) can be simple, or ornate, made of silver or gold. A brooch on the front of the jacket often matches the botonadura.

■ Black leather *botines* (half-boots) are standard mariachi footwear.

MARIACHI: BORN IN JALISCO

9

WHERE AND HOW TO HEAR MARIACHI

HIRE A MARIACHI GROUP

There may be no better way to thoroughly surprise (or embarrass) your significant other, or a more memorable way to pop the question, than with a mariachi serenade. Hiring a band is easy. Just go to Plaza de los Mariachis, beside Mercado Libertad in downtown Guadalajara. Pablo Garcia, whose Mariachi Atotonilco has been working the plaza for almost 40 years, says a serenade runs about 2,000 pesos, or just under US$200. Normal procedure is to negotiate price and either leave a deposit (ask for a business card and a receipt) and have the band meet you at a determined location, or, as Mexicans usually do, accompany the band to the unexpecting lady.

HIT THE INTERNATIONAL MARIACHI FESTIVAL

The last weekend of every August, some 700 mariachi groups from around the world descend upon Guadalajara for the annual International Mariachi Festival. Mexico's most famous mariachi groups—Mariachi Vargas de Tecalitlán, Mariachi los Camperos, and Mariachi de América—play huge concerts in Guadalajara's Degollado Theater, accompanied by the Jalisco Philharmonic Orchestra. The weeklong annual charro championship is held simultaneously, bringing together the nation's top cowboys and mariachis.

THE WORLD'S BEST MARIACHI BAND

At least, the world's most *famous* mariachi band, Mariachi Vargas de Tecalitlán was founded in 1897, when the norm was four-man groups with simple stringed instruments. Started by Gaspar Vargas in Tecalitlán, Jalisco, the mariachi troupe shot to fame in the 1930s after winning a regional mariachi contest, which earned them the favor of Mexican president Lázaro Cárdenas. The group quickly became an icon of Mexican cinema, performing in and recording music for films. Now in its fifth generation, Mariachi Vargas performs the world over and has recorded more than 50 albums, and music for more than 200 films.

The *gabán* (poncho) was worn traditionally for warmth

CATCH YEAR-ROUND PERFORMANCES

If you miss Guadalajara's mariachi festival you can still get your fill of high-quality mariachi performances on street corners, in city plazas, and at many restaurants. An estimated 150 mariachi groups are currently active in the City of Roses.

Restaurants, most notably Guadalajara's Casa Bariachi chain, hire mariachi groups, whose performance is generally included with your table (though tips won't be refused). On occasion, mariachis perform free nighttime concerts in Guadalajara's Plaza de Armas. Another venue, the Plaza de Mariachi, beside Guadalajara's landmark Mercado Libertad, is a longstanding attraction, albeit during the day—at night it's better known for crime than mariachi.

Tlaquepaque's El Parían, a former market turned series of bars around a tree-filled central patio, is a fantastic intimate setting for mariachi music. Between free performances in the central kiosk, you can request serenades at about $10 per song or negotiate deals for longer performances for your table.

ALL ABOARD THE TEQUILA TRAIN!

To experience the Jalisco quartet of traditions—mariachi, charreria, folkloric dance, and tequila—in one adventure, take the Tequila Express. It includes a train ride from Guadalajara through fields of blue agave to a tequila-making hacienda, live mariachi music, all the food and drink you can handle, and a charro and folkloric dance performance.

WORKING HARD FOR THE MONEY

It is becoming harder for mariachi groups to make a living at the trade. The increasing cost of living has made nighttime serenades, once a staple of a mariachi's diet of work, expensive ($200 and up) and out of the reach of many locals. Performers generally work day jobs to make ends meet.

THE COWBOY CONNECTION

Mariachi and Mexican rodeo, or *charreada* (Mexico's official sport), go together like hot dogs and baseball. Both charreada and mariachi music evolved in the western Mexican countryside, where daily ranching chores like branding bulls eventually took on a competitive edge. The first of Mexico's 800 charro associations was founded in Guadalajara in 1920, and to this day holds a two-hour rodeo every Sunday. Throughout the competition, mariachi music is heard from the stands, but the key mariachi performance is at the end of a competition when female riders perform synchronized moves, riding side-saddle in traditional ribboned and brightly colored western Mexican dresses.

MARIACHI: BORN IN JALISCO

9

ZAPOPAN   Expanding over the years, Guadalajara's population of almost 4 million now encompasses pre-Hispanic towns, such as Zapopan. The country's former corn-producing capital, Zapopan is now a wealthy enclave of modern hotels and malls. Beyond, some farming communities remain, but the central district is now home to two remarkable museums and one of Mexico's most revered religious icons.

The vast **Basílica de la Virgen de Zapopan,** with an ornate plateresque facade and *mudéjar* (Moorish) tile dome is home to Our Lady of Zapopan: a 10-inch-high, corn-paste statue venerated for miraculous healings and answered prayers. Every October 12, more than a million people pack the streets around the basilica for an all-night fiesta capped by an early-morning procession. Don't miss the adjoining **Huichol Museum,** which has Huichol art for sale. The adjacent **Museo de la Virgen** chronicles the Virgin of Zapopan's rise to fame. ⊠ *Av. Hidalgo at Calle Morelos, Zona Zapopan Norte* ☎ *33/3633–0141 or 33/3633–6614* 🖃 *Free* ☉ *Daily 10–8.*

Better known by its initials, MAZ, the **Museo de Arte de Zapopan** is Guadalajara's top contemporary art gallery. It regularly holds expositions of distinguished Latin American painters, photographers, and sculptors. ⊠ *Andador 20 de Noviembre 166, Zapopan* ☎ *33/3818–2200* 🖃 *$2 Tues.–Sat., $1 Sun.* ☉ *Tues., Wed., Fri., and weekends 10 AM–6 PM, Thurs. 10 AM–10 PM.*

★   The Huichol Indians are famed for their fierce independence, their use of peyote in religious ceremonies, and their exquisite bead and yarn mosaics (⇨ "The Art of the Huichol," *in* Chapter 5). At the **Museo Huichol Wixarica de Zapopan,** bilingual placards explain tribal history, and the museum exhibits many examples of the Huichols' unique artwork, some for sale. ⊠ *Av. Hidalgo, 152, Zona Zapopan Norte* ☎ *33/3636–4430* 🖃 *50¢* ☉ *Mon.–Sat. 9:30–5:30, Sun. 10–3.*

Where to Eat

Tapatíos love foreign food, but homegrown dishes won't ever lose their flavor. The trademark local dish is *torta ahogada,* literally a "drowned [pork] sandwich" soaked in tomato sauce and topped with onions and hot sauce. Other favorites are *carne en su jugo* (beef stew with bacon bits and beans), *birria* (hearty goat or lamb stew), and *pozole* (hominy and pork in tomato broth). Seafood is popular and is available in trendy restaurants as well as at stands. The best Mexican food is near the main attractions downtown. The most popular non-Mexican restaurants are scattered about western Guadalajara, in Zona Minerva.

Tlaquepaque

La Villa del Ensueño ◆

Museo Regional de la Cerámica ◆ *Florida*

Folklor Gastronómico ◆

Donato Guerra

Bus stop to return to El Centro Guadalajara ◆

Constitución

Augustín Parra Diseño Novohispano ◆

Cerámica Ken Edwards ◆

Morelos

Galería Sergio Bustamante ◆ Casa Fuerte ◆

Independencia

Museo del Premio Nacional de la Cerámica Panduro ◆

Bazar Hecht ◆ El Parián ◆

Juárez *Pantaleon*

El Abajeño ◆

Reforma

Quinta Don José ◆

Porvenir

0 ___ 350 meters
0 ___ 350 yards

La Casa del Retoño ◆

TO TONALÁ ↘

Santos Degollado

Casa de las Flores ◆

CENTRO HISTÓRICO
★ ¢–$$

✗ **La Fonda de San Miguel.** Located in a former convent, La Fonda is per-haps the Centro's most exceptional eatery. Innovative Mexican eats are presented in a soaring courtyard centered around a stone fountain and hung with a spectacular array of shining tin stars and folk art from Tlaque-paque and Tonalá. Relish the freshly made tortillas with the *molcajete,* a steaming stew of seafood or beef that comes in a three-legged stone mortar (the molcajete). ⊠ *Donato Guerra 25, Centro Histórico* ☎ *33/ 3613–0809 or 33/3613–0793* ▭ *AE, D, MC, V.*

¢–$
✗ **Birriería las 9 Esquinas.** Mexican families and tourists in the know come here for specialties like lamb *birría,* which are readied in full view in the vibrantly colored hacienda-style kitchen. The restaurant is on a plaza in one of Guadalajara's oldest districts, the Nine Corners, so-called for its intersecting streets. ⊠ *Colon 384, corner of Galeana, Centro Histórico* ☎ *33/3613–6260 or 33/3613–1081* ▭ *No credit cards.*

TLAQUEPAQUE
$–$$$

✗ **Casa Fuerte.** Relax with tasty Mexican dishes at the tables along the sidewalk or under the palms and by the fountain in the patio. Try the house specialty: chicken stuffed with *huitlacoche* (a corn fungus that's Mexico's answer to the truffle) and shrimp in tamarind sauce. Live mariachi or trio music accompanies lunch hours every day except Monday. ⊠ *Calle In-dependencia 224, Tlaquepaque* ☎ *33/3639–6481* ▭ *AE, MC, V.*

TONALÁ   ✕ **Restaurant Jalapeños.** Steaks are the specialty in this small, clean
¢–$ restaurant whose walls are adorned with brightly painted ceramic veg-
etables. The daily lunch special, with soup, main dish, drink, and dessert
is less than $5. ⊠ *Av. Madero 23, ½ block south of Plaza Principal, Tonalá*
☎ *33/3683–0344* ▤ *No credit cards.*

ZONA MINERVA   ✕ **El Sacromonte.** Come here for creative Mexican food, superior serv-
★ $–$$$ ice, and reasonable prices. You're surrounded by *artesanía* in the bright
dining area, and there's live music every afternoon and evening. Try a
juicy steak or *La Corona de Reina Isabel*—a crown of intertwined
shrimp in lobster sauce. ⊠ *Pedro Moreno 1398, Zona Minerva* ☎ *33/
3825–5447* ▤ *MC, V* ⌂ *Reservations essential* ☾ *No dinner Sun.*

★ $–$$ ✕ **La Trattoria.** Guadalajara's top Italian restaurant is a bustling family
place. The menu's highlights include spaghetti *frutti di mare* (with
seafood), *scaloppine alla Marsala* (beef medallions with Marsala and
mushrooms), and fresh garlic bread. All meals include a trip to the salad
bar. Make a reservation if you're eating after 8 PM. ⊠ *Av. Niños Héroes
3051, Zona Minerva* ☎ *33/3122–1817* ▤ *AE, MC, V.*

¢–$ ✕ **Karne Garibaldi.** Lightning service is made possible by the menu's sin-
gle item: *carne en su jugo,* a combination of finely diced beef and bacon
simmered in rich beef broth and served with grilled onions, tortillas, and
refried beans mixed with corn. Don't be put off by the somewhat gritty
area surrounding the restaurant. ⊠ *Calle Garibaldi 1306, Zona Minerva* ☎ *33/3826–1286* ▤ *AE, MC, V.*

★ ¢–$ ✕ **La Pianola Avenida México.** Signature piano music and a large, airy
courtyard in the back provide a soothing backdrop for you to sample
specialties from this restaurant's varied Mexican menu, including pozole and *chiles en nogada* (mild green chilies stuffed with a sweet meat
mixture draped in walnut sauce and decorated with pomegranate seeds).
⊠ *Av. México 3220, Zona Minerva* ☎ *33/3813–1385 or 33/3813–2412*
▤ *AE, MC, V.*

Where to Stay

Choosing a place to stay is a matter of location and price; tourists are
often drawn to the Centro Histórico, where colonial-style hotels are convenient to the historical and other sights, or to Tlaquepaque's genial B&Bs.
Businesspeople head for the Zona
Minerva, specifically around
Avenida López Mateos Sur, a 16-km
(10-mi) strip extending from the
Minerva Fountain to the Plaza del
Sol shopping center, where they can
take advantage of modern office
facilities and four-star comforts.

CENTRO   ▥ **Hotel de Mendoza.** This refined
HISTÓRICO   hotel with postcolonial architec-
★ $$ ture and hand-carved furniture is on
a relatively calm side street a block
from Teatro Degollado. Suites are
worth the extra cost: standard

> **WORD OF MOUTH**
>
> "Hotel Mendoza is first class, even
> if it's a little old. All that's worth
> doing in Guadalajara is within
> walking distance. The tip on suites
> is right on, though the 'senior'
> suite is just a large room with iron
> divider. The hotel dining room is
> good for breakfast and lunch, but
> you can get better dinners else-
> where."   –Jerry Holland

rooms are comfortable but small. Balconies overlook the courtyard pool from some rooms. ⊠ *Calle Venustiano Carranza 16, Centro Histórico, 44100* ☎ *33/3942–5151, 01800/361–2600 in Mexico* 📠 *33/3613–7310* ⊕ *www.demendoza.com.mx* 📞 *87 rooms, 17 suites* ♨ *Restaurant, pool, gym, meeting rooms, parking (fee)* ⊟ *AE, MC, V* ⑩ *EP.*

$–$$ 📺 **Hotel Cervantes.** All of the hotel's comfortable, carpeted rooms have sofa beds (as well as standard double beds) and are adorned with old-time photos; suites have terraces. Off the lobby is the hotel's relaxed restaurant with its scrumptious breakfast buffet. Several pastry shops and bookstores are nearby, and the Centro Histórico is a short walk away. ⊠ *Calle Priciliano Sánchez 442, Centro Histórico, 44100* ☎ *33/3613–6686 or 33/3613–6816* ⊕ *www.hotelcervantes.com.mx* 📞 *95 rooms, 5 suites* ♨ *Restaurant, pool, bar, laundry service, meeting rooms, free parking* ⊟ *AE, DC, MC, V* ⑩ *EP.*

$–$$ 📺 **Santiago de Compostela.** The more expensive rooms in this 19th-century building face the Parque San Francisco across the street, and have tall, narrow windows with iron balconies. For the most part the hotel has simple, modern accommodations, though the suites have Jacuzzis. From a fifth-floor terrace a pool looks onto Guadalajara's south side. ⊠ *Calle Colón 272, Centro Histórico, 44100* ☎ *33/3613–8880, 01800/365–5300 in Mexico* 📠 *33/3658–1925* 📞 *84 rooms, 8 suites* ♨ *Restaurant, pool, bar, shop* ⊟ *AE, DC, MC, V* ⑩ *EP.*

TLAQUEPAQUE 📺 **Quinta Don José.** This B&B is one block from Tlaquepaque's main
$–$$ plaza and shopping area. Natural lighting and room size vary, so look at a few before you choose one. Suites face the pool, and are spacious but a bit dark. There's remarkable tile work in the master suite. Hearty breakfasts are served in an inner courtyard; the inn's hosts are fonts of information, and aim to please. ⊠ *Av. Reforma 139, Tlaquepaque 45500* ☎ *33/3635–7522, 01800/700–2223 in Mexico, 866/629–3753 in U.S. and Canada* 📠 *33/3659–9315* ⊕ *www.quintadonjose.com* 📞 *8 rooms, 7 suites* ♨ *Some kitchenettes, pool, massage, bar, laundry service, Internet room, airport shuttle, free parking, no-smoking rooms* ⊟ *AE, MC, V* ⑩ *BP.*

$–$$ 📺 **La Villa del Ensueño.** Though it's a 10-minute walk from Tlaquepaque's center, this intimate B&B (fully renovated in 2005) is near the town's shops. The 19th-century hacienda has thick, white adobe walls, exposed-beam ceilings, and plants in huge unglazed pots. Smokers should request a room with private balcony, as smoking isn't allowed inside. ⊠ *Florida 305, Tlaquepaque 45500* ☎ *33/3635–8792, 800/220–8689 in U.S.* 📠 *33/3659–6152* ⊕ *www.villadelensueno.com* 📞 *14 rooms, 4 suites* ♨ *2 pools, bar, no-smoking rooms* ⊟ *AE, MC, V* ⑩ *BP.*

★ **$** 📺 **Casa de las Flores.** A favorite with those traveling for business as well as pleasure, this B&B is charismatic and inviting, with lovely art and wonderful food. Owners Stan and José, from the United States and Mexico, respectively, enjoy directing their guests to the best shops and markets for purchasing handicrafts. Guests meet and socialize by the fireplace in the large living room and out in the magical garden. ⊠ *Calle Santos Degollado 175, Tlaquepaque 45500* ☎ *33/3659–3186* ⊕ *www.casadelasflores.com* 📞 *7 rooms* ♨ *Laundry service, travel services,*

9

free parking; no a/c in some rooms, no TV in some rooms ⊟ *MC, V* ⧫ *BP.*

¢–$ ⊞ **La Casa del Retoño.** On a quiet street several blocks from the shopping district is this newer B&B. Smallish rooms are made of cinder block, but are clean and painted in cheerful hues. Rooms in the back overlook a large garden, while the ones upstairs have terraces. There's a small open-air reading area, and breakfast is served in the small courtyard. ⊠ *Matamoros 182, Tlaquepaque 45500* ☎ *33/3587–3989* ⧫ *33/3639–6510* ⊕ *www.lacasadelretono.com.mx* ⧫ *8 rooms, 1 suite* ⧫ *Fan, some kitchenettes, Internet room* ⊟ *AE, MC, V* ⧫ *CP.*

> ### JALISCO'S HOLY WAR
>
> When ultra right-wing president Plutarco Elías Calles effectively criminalized Catholicism in 1926, Jalisco-area Catholics launched an armed rebellion against the government. During the bitter *La Cristiada* war, many priests were executed. In recent years dozens of *Cristero* martyrs have been canonized by the Vatican, a great source of pride for Guadalajara's Catholics.

ZONA MINERVA

$$$$

Fodor's Choice

★

⊞ **Quinta Real.** Stone-and-brick walls, colonial arches, and objets d'art fill this luxury hotel's public areas. Suites are plush, though on the small side, with neocolonial-style furnishings, glass-top writing tables, and faux fireplaces. The hotel provides discount passes to a nearby Gold's Gym. ⊠ *Av. México 2727, at Av. López Mateos Norte, Zona Minerva, 44680* ☎ *33/3669–0600, 01800/362–1500 in Mexico* ⧫ *33/3669–0601* ⊕ *www.quintareal.com* ⧫ *76 suites* ⧫ *Restaurant, in-room data ports, pool, bar, babysitting, concierge, business services, meeting rooms, travel services, no-smoking rooms* ⊟ *AE, D, DC, MC, V* ⧫ *EP.*

$$$ ⊞ **Crowne Plaza Guadalajara.** Gardens encircling the pool add a bit of nature to this family-friendly hotel. A mix of antiques and reproductions fills the public spaces. Rooms have marble baths and natural lighting; those in the tower have city views. (Ask for a room near the back; those near the playground can be noisy.) Plaza Club room rates include a buffet breakfast. The top-floor restaurant is the only one in Guadalajara with a panoramic view. It's just down the street from the Plaza del Sol shopping center. ⊠ *Av. López Mateos Sur 2500, Zona Minerva, 45050* ☎ *33/3634–1034, 01800/365–5500 in Mexico, 800/980–6431 in U.S.* ⧫ *33/3631–9393* ⊕ *www.crowneroyal.com* ⧫ *197 rooms, 4 suites* ⧫ *3 restaurants, in-room data ports, Wi-Fi, golf privileges, pool, gym, hair salon, bar, shops, babysitting, playground, concierge floor, business services, car rental, kennel, free parking, no-smoking floor* ⊟ *AE, DC, MC, V* ⧫ *EP.*

$$–$$$ ⊞ **Fiesta Americana.** The dramatic glass facade of this high-rise faces the Minerva Fountain and Los Arcos monument. Four glass-enclosed elevators ascend dizzyingly above a 14-story atrium lobby to the enormous guest rooms, which have modern furnishings, marble bathrooms, and arresting views. The lobby bar has live music every night but Sunday. On the *piso ejecutivo* (executive floor), rooms come with breakfast, and there's a business center. Guests get discount passes to the neighboring gym. ⊠ *Av. Aurelio Aceves 225, Zona Minerva, 44100* ☎ *33/3818–1400,*

01800/504–5000 in Mexico 🖷 *33/3630–3725* ⊕ *www.fiestamericana. com* 🛏 *387 rooms, 4 suites* ⚅ *Restaurant, in-room data ports, gym, hair salon, bar, shops, babysitting, concierge, business services, meeting rooms, car rental, no-smoking floor* ⊟ *AE, DC, MC, V* ⑩ *EP.*

$$ 🖵 **Hotel Plaza Diana.** At this modest hotel two blocks from the Minerva Fountain the standard-size rooms have white walls and bright, patterned fabrics. One suite even has a sauna. Stay on the upper floors in the rear for the quietest rooms. ⊠ *Circunvalación Agustín Yáñez 2760, Zona Minerva, 44100* 🕾 *33/3540–9700, 01800/024–1001 in Mexico* 🖷 *33/ 3540–9715* ⊕ *www.hoteldiana.com.mx* 🛏 *136 rooms, 15 suites* ⚅ *Restaurant, bar, airport shuttle* ⊟ *AE, DC, MC, V* ⑩ *EP.*

Nightlife

With the exception of a few well-established night spots like La Maestranza, downtown Guadalajara is mostly asleep by 11 PM. The existing nightlife centers around Avenida Vallarta (Zona Minerva), favored by the well-to-do and under-thirty sets, or the Plaza del Sol. Bars in these spots open into the wee hours, usually closing by 3 AM. Dance clubs may charge a $15–$20 cover, which includes an open bar, on Wednesday and Saturday nights. Dress up for nightclubs; highly subjective admission policies hinge on who you know or how you look. The local music scene centers around Peña Cuicacalli and the Hard Rock Café.

For the latest listings, grab a *Público* newspaper on Friday and pull out the weekly *Ocio cultural* guide.

Guadalajara has a decent arts and culture scene. You can catch the University of Guadalajara's Ballet Folclórico on Sunday morning at Teatro Degollado. International exhibitions are sometimes shown at the Instituto Cultural Cabañas or the Arts Museum of Zapopan.

BARS **Cubilete** (⊠ General Río Seco 9, Centro Histórico 🕾 33/3613–2096) plays live tropical tunes Wednesday through Saturday after 10. Open since
★ 1921, **La Fuente** (⊠ Calle Pino Suarez, Centro Histórico 🕾 No phone) draws business types, intellectuals, and blue-collar workers, all seeking cheap drinks, animated conversation, and live music. Arrive early to avoid crowds, a din, and a thick carpet of cigarette smoke over the tables. Rock bands play at the bustling **Hard Rock Café** (⊠ Centro Magno, Av. Vallarta 2425, 1st fl., Zona Minerva 🕾 33/3818–1400) Wednesday through Sunday 8:30 PM–12:30 AM, and even later on Saturday.

For some local color, stop at **La Maestranza** (⊠ Calle Maestranza 179, Centro Histórico 🕾 33/3613–5878), a renovated 1940s cantina full of bullfighting memorabilia. After 9 PM Tuesday through Sunday, patrons cluster around the small stage at **La Peña Cuicacalli** (⊠ Av. Niños Héroes 1988, at Suarez traffic circle, Centro Histórico 🕾 No phone). There's *rock en español* on Tuesday and folk music from Mexico, Latin America, and Spain other nights.

DANCE CLUBS **Well-dressed professionals over 25 go to El Mito** (⊠ Centro Magno mall, Av. Vallarta 2425, 2nd fl., Zona Minerva 🕾 33/3615–7246); there's '70s and '80s music Wednesday, Friday, and Saturday 10 PM–4 AM.

ROOT FOR THE HOME TEAM

Futbol (soccer) is a national obsession. Guadalajara's two main teams nurse a healthy rivalry—as do their fans. Atlas appeals more to the middle and upper classes; working-class Tapatíos and students prefer Las Chivas. In fact the Chivas seem to be the working-class heroes of much of Mexico. Both teams play at Guadalajara's **Estadio Jalisco** (☎ 33/3637-0301) on weekends or Wednesday night January–May and July–December. Tickets are $5–$45.

Salón Veracruz (✉ Calle Manzano 486, behind Hotel Misión Carlton, Centro Histórico ☎ 33/3613–4422) is a spartan, old-style dance hall where a 15-piece band keeps hoofers moving to *cumbia*; merengue; and the waltzlike *danzón*. It's closed Monday and Tuesday. Dance to popular Latin and European music at **Tropigala** (✉ Av. López Mateos Sur 2188, Zona Minerva ☎ 33/3122–5553 or 33/3122–7903), across from the Plaza del Sol mall.

Sports & the Outdoors

BULLFIGHTS   *Corridas* (bullfights) are held Sunday at 4:30 from October to December at **Plaza Nuevo Progreso** (✉ Calle M. Pirineos 1930 and Calz. Independencia Norte, Zona Huentitán ☎ 33/3637–9982 or 33/3651–8506). Tickets are $8–$70; bleacher seats far from the action on the *sol* (sunny) side are much cheaper than more-comfortable up-close seats on the *sombra* (shady) side.

CHARREADAS   These "rodeos" of elegant equestrian maneuvers and rope tricks are the epitome of upper-class rural Mexican culture. Men in tight, elegant suits with wide-brimmed felt hats perform *suertes* in which they subdue young bulls or jump from one galloping horse to another in the *el paso de la muerte* (pass of death). Teams of women in flowing dresses perform audacious (yet less dangerous) synchronized movements on horseback. Mariachi or brass bands play between acts. Charreadas run year-round at the **Lienzo Charros de Jalisco** (✉ Av. Dr. R. Michel 577, Centro Histórico ☎ 33/3619–0315 or 33/3619–3232), next to Parque Agua Azul, Sunday at noon. Admission is $3–$5.

Shopping

Guadalajara is shopping central for people from all over Nayarit, Jalisco, and surrounding states. The labyrinthine Mercado Libertad is one of Latin America's largest markets; modern malls are gathering spots with restaurants and theaters. Tlaquepaque and Tonalá have the best Mexican art and handicrafts.

WHEELING & DEALING

To bargain effectively at markets and other informal venues, react skeptically (yet politely) or with mild disinterest to the first quoted price and see if you can get a lower offering. If not, offer as low as your conscience and intellect will allow and trade offers back and forth from there.

DEDICATED TO ITS CRAFT

LIKE TLAQUEPAQUE, neighboring **Tonalá** was in the crafts business long before the Spanish conquistadors arrived. Independent and industrious, less-touristy Tonalá remains dedicated to traditional pursuits: brilliant blown glass, polished brass housewares and gold jewelry, vibrant papier mâché statues and goofy piñatas. But it's the gracefully decorated, exquisitely stylized *petatillo*-style ceramics that's the town's best known handcraft. The distinctively Mexican earthenware: plates, pitchers, and even gourds are decorated with placid-looking birds and beasts and glazed in subtle tans and blues. Thursday and Sunday markets are the source of terrific bargains.

In Tlaquepaque, stroll along Independencia and Juárez streets for dozens of artsy shops. In less touristy Tonalá most shops and factories are spread out, with the exception of a concentration of shops on Avenida de los Tonaltecas, the main drag into town. On Thursday and Sunday, bargain-price merchandise is sold at a terrific street market there packed with vendors from 8 to 4.

CRAFTS & FOLK ARTS **La Casa de los Artesanos** (⊠ Av. de los Tonaltecas Sur 140, Tonalá ☎ 33/3284–3066) has pieces by Tonalá's most talented artisans. Prices are reasonable, and the staff will direct you to nearby studios. It's open weekdays 9–8 and Saturday 9–2. Antiquers come out of the woodwork every Sunday 10–5 to sell their antique European flatware and Mexican pottery at **El Trocadero** (⊠ Av. Mexico at Av. Chapultepec, Zona Minerva) market in the antiques district. Better known as Mercado San Juan de Dios, **Mercado Libertad** (⊠ Calz. Independencia Sur; use pedestrian bridge from Plaza Tapatía's south side, Centro Histórico) has shops that are organized thematically on three expansive floors. Be wary of fakes in the jewelry stores. Most shops are open Monday–Saturday 10–8, and 10–3 on Sunday.

Cramped **Tonalá crafts market** (⊠ Av. Tonaltecas, north of Av. Tonalá, Tonalá) is *the* place for Mexican arts and crafts. Vendors set up ceramics, carved wood, candles, glassware, furniture, metal crafts, and more each Thursday and Sunday (roughly 9–5). Look for *vajilla* (ceramic dining sets), but note that the more high-end ceramic offerings are at government-sponsored Casa de los Artesanos down the street.

MALLS Sprawling, tri-level **La Gran Plaza** (⊠ Av. Vallarta 3959, Zona Minerva ☎ 33/3122–3004) has nearly 330 shops and a big cinema. The food court is Guadalajara's best. Among the most memorable stores, **Eréndira Contis** (☎ 33/3123–1254),

> **CAUTION**
>
> Mercado Libertad has silver at great prices, but not everything that glitters there is certifiably silver. A safer, albeit pricier bet are the shops along Avenida República in downtown Guadalajara, where there are more than 400 jewelers.

9

on the top floor, has exceptional jewelry and modern Mexican art and crafts. Guadalajara's first mall, **Plaza del Sol** (⊠ Av. López Mateos Sur 2375, at Mariano Otero, Zona Minerva ☎ 33/3121–5950) has 270 commercial spaces scattered around an outdoor atrium and wacky sculpture-fountains by Alejandro Colunga. It's got everything the more modern malls have in a more low-key environment.

Tequila

56 km (35 mi) northwest of Guadalajara.

For an in-depth look at how Mexico's most famous liquor is derived from the spiny blue agave plant that grows in fields alongside the highway, stop by this tidy village. Head west from Guadalajara along Avenida Vallarta for about 25 minutes until you reach the toll road junction ("Puerto Vallarta Cuota"). Choose the toll road (faster, safer, and about $10) or the free road (*libre*) toward Puerto Vallarta. Or catch a bus to Tequila from the Antigua Central Camionera (Old Central Bus Station), northeast of the Parque Agua Azul on Avenida Dr. R. Michel, between Calle Los Angeles and Calle 5 de Febrero. Buses marked Amatitán–Tequila are easy to spot from the entrance on Calle Los Angeles.

■ TIP→ For more information about Jalisco's famous liquor, *see* "¡Tequila!" *in* Chapter 6.

What to See

The **Sauza Museum** (⊠ Calle Albino Rojas 22 ☎ 374/742–0247) has memorabilia from the Sauza family, a tequila-making dynasty second only to the Cuervos. The museum is open weekdays 10–2, and admission is $1.

Opened in 1795, the **José Cuervo Distillery** (⊠ Calle José Cuervo 73 ☎ 374/742–2442) is the world's oldest tequila distillery. Every day, 150 tons of agave hearts are processed into 74,000 liters of tequila here. Hard-hat tours are given daily every hour from 10 to 4. The tours at noon are normally in English, but English-speakers can be accommodated at other times. Admission is $6.50.

Teuchitlán

50 km (28 mi) west of Guadalajara.

For decades, residents in this sleepy village of sugarcane farmers had a name for the funny-looking mounds in the hills above town, but they never considered the Guachimontones to be more than a convenient source of rocks for local construction. Then in the early 1970s an American archaeologist asserted that the mounds were the remnants of a long-vanished, 2,000-year-old state. It took Phil Weigand nearly three decades to convince authorities in far-off Mexico City that he wasn't crazy. Before he was allowed to start excavating and restoring this monumental site in the late 1990s, plenty more houses and roads were produced with Guachimonton rock—and countless tombs were looted of priceless art.

The spot is most distinctive for its sophisticated concentric architecture—a circular pyramid surrounded by a ring of flat ground, surrounded by a series of smaller platforms arranged in a circle. The "Teuchitlán Tradition," as the concentric circle structures are called, is unique in world architecture. Weigand believes the formations suggest the existence of a pre-Hispanic state in the region, whereas it was previously held that only socially disorganized nomads inhabited the region at the time. Similar ruins are spread throughout the foothills of the extinct Tequila Volcano, but this is the biggest site yet detected.

To get to Teuchitlán from Guadalajara, drive west out along Avenida Vallarta for 25 minutes to the toll road junction to Puerto Vallarta: choose the free road 70 (*libre*) toward Vallarta. Head west along Route 15 for a couple of miles, then turn left onto Route 70 and continue until you reach the town of Tala. One-and-a-half kilometers (1 mi) past the sugar mill, turn right onto Route 27. Teuchitlán is 15 minutes from the last junction. The ruins are up a dirt road from town—just ask for directions when you arrive. There's a small museum off the main square. Plans to build greater infrastructure around the site continue. If you visit during the dry season you may score a look at a dig or restoration project.

Lake Chapala

Lake Chapala is Mexico's largest natural lake and just an hour's drive south of Guadalajara. Surrounded by jagged hills and serene towns, it is a favorite Tapatío getaway and a haven for thousands of North American retirees.

The area's main town, Chapala, is flooded with weekend visitors and the pier is packed shoulder-to-shoulder most Sundays. Neighboring Ajijic, 8 km (5 mi) west, has narrow cobblestone streets and vibrantly colored buildings. Its mild climate and gentle pace has attracted a large colony of English-speaking expats, including many artists.

Chapala

45 km (28 mi) south of Guadalajara.

9

When elitist president Porfirio Díaz bought a retreat in lakeside Chapala in 1904, his aristocratic pals followed suit. Today, some of these residences on the shore of Mexico's largest natural lake have been converted to cozy lodges, many geared to families. About an hour south of downtown Guadalajara, the diminutive but prosperous town is a retreat for the middle and upper classes, with restaurants (though not as many as you'd expect), shops, and cafés.

Three blocks north of the promenade, the plaza at the corner of López Cotilla is a relaxing spot to read a paper or succumb to sweets from surrounding shops. The Iglesia de San Francisco (built in 1528), easily recognized by its blue neon crosses on twin steeples, is two blocks south of the plaza.

On weekends the town is paralyzed by Mexican families who flock to the shores of the (for now, at least) rejuvenated lake. Vendors sell refreshments and souvenirs, while lakeside watering holes fill to capacity.

$–$$$$ ✕ **Mariscos Guicho's.** Bright orange walls and checkerboard tablecloths lend the best of the waterfront seafood joints an authentic Mexican flair. Dig into savory caviar tostadas, frogs' legs, garlic shrimp, and spicy seafood soup. ⊠ *Paseo Ramón Corona 20* ☎ *376/765–3232* ⊟ *No credit cards* ⊘ *Closed Tues.*

¢–$$$$ ✕ **Cozumel.** Ajijic residents regularly drive to Chapala on Wednesday and Friday for live mariachi music and well-prepared specials, which include a free cocktail and appetizers. Wednesday is chicken cordon bleu night; on other days, choose from seafood and international dishes. (You still get the free drink.) Reservations are essential for Friday and sometimes for Wednesday night. ⊠ *Paseo Corona 22–A* ☎ *376/765–4606* ⊟ *MC, V* ⊘ *Closed Mon.*

¢   ✕ **El Arbol del Café.** Expatriates cherish this modest café for its roasted-on-the-premises coffee, imported teas, and homemade cakes. Sip a decaffeinated cappuccino (rare in Mexico) and peruse the English-language papers. The café closes at 3 PM on weekdays and at 2 PM on Saturday. ⊠ *Av. Hidalgo 236* ☎ *376/765–3908* ⊟ *No credit cards* ⊘ *Closed Sun.*

$ ▥ **Hotel Villa Montecarlo.** The hotel's simple, clean rooms are in three-story contiguous units, all with patios or terraces. The grounds are enormous and well maintained, with several eating and play areas. One of the two swimming pools (the biggest in the area) is filled with natural thermal water. Popular with Mexican families, the hotel has frequent discounts and packages. ⊠ *Av. Hidalgo 296, about 1 km (½ mi) west of Av. Madero, 45900* ☎ *376/765–2216, 376/765–2120, or 376/765–2025* ◱ *46 rooms, 2 suites* ♻ *Restaurant, 2 tennis courts, 2 pools, bar, laundry service, free parking; no a/c* ⊟ *AE, MC, V.*

★ $ ▥ **Lake Chapala Inn.** Now that the lake is back to its original size (the 1990s saw it shrink to an unattractive shadow of its former self due to lack of rainfall and overuse of supplying rivers), this European-style inn is an especially appealing place to stay. Three of the four rooms in this restored mansion face the shore; all have high ceilings and white-washed oak furniture. Rates include an English-style breakfast (with a continental breakfast on Sunday). ⊠ *Paseo Ramón Corona 23, 45900* ☎ *376/765–4786* ⊟ *376/765–5174* ⊕ *www.mexonline.com/chapalainn.htm* ◱ *4 rooms* ♻ *Dining room, pool, library, laundry service; no a/c* ⊟ *No credit cards* ⋈ *BP.*

Ajijic
8 km (5 mi) west of Chapala.

Ajijic has narrow cobblestone streets, vibrantly colored buildings, and a gentle pace—with the exception of the very trafficky main highway through the town's southern end. The foreign influence is unmistakable: English is widely (though not exclusively) spoken and license plates come from far-flung places like British Columbia and Texas.

The Plaza Principal (aka El Jardín) is a tree- and flower-filled central square at the corner of Avenidas Colón and Hidalgo. In late November the plaza and its surrounding streets fill for the saint's nine-day fiesta of the town's patron, St. Andrew. From the plaza, walk down Calle Morelos (the continuation of Avenida Colón) toward the lake and peruse the boutiques on Ajijic's main shopping strip. (There are also many galleries and shops east of Morelos, on Avenida 16 de Septiembre and Calle Constitución.) Turn left onto Avenida 16 de Septiembre or Avenida Constitución for art galleries and studios. Northeast of the plaza, along the highway, activity centers around the soccer field, which doubles as a venue for bullfights and concerts.

HEALING WATERS

San Juan Cosalá, 2 km (1 mi) west of Ajijic, is known for its natural thermal-water spas along Lago de Chapala. The ☾ **Hotel Balneario San Juan Cosalá** (⊠ Calle La Paz Oriente 420, at Carretera Chapala-Jocotepec, Km 13 ☎ 387/761–0222 or 387/761–0302) has four large swimming pools and two wading pools; admission is $8. Weekends are crowded and loud.

WHERE TO STAY & EAT

$–$$ ✕ **Johanna's.** Come to this intimate bit of Bavaria on the lake for German cuisine like sausages and goose or duck pâté. Main dishes come with soup or salad, applesauce, and cooked red cabbage. For dessert indulge in plum strudel or blackberry-topped torte. ⊠ *Carretera Chapala-Jocotepec, Km 6.5* ☎ *376/766–0437* ▤ *No credit cards* ⊗ *Closed Mon.*

¢–$ ✕ **La Bodega de Ajijic.** Eat in a covered patio overlooking a grassy lawn and a small pool at this low-key restaurant. The menu has Italian and Mexican dishes, which are a bit small and overpriced. Still, service is friendly, and there's live music—ranging from Mexican pop and rock to jazz, guitar, and harp—most nights. ⊠ *Av. 16 de Septiembre 124* ☎ *376/766–1002* ▤ *MC, V.*

¢–$ ✕ **Salvador's.** An old mainstay that's showing its years, this cafeteria-like eatery is a popular expat hangout. There's a well-kept salad bar and specialties from both sides of the border. A pianist performs during the fabulous Sunday brunch as well as at lunch on Wednesday. On Friday people flock here for the fish-and-chips lunch special. ⊠ *Carretera Chapala-Jocotepec Oriente 58* ☎ *376/766–2301* ▤ *No credit cards.*

★ **$** ✕▥ **La Nueva Posada.** The well-kept gardens framed in bougainvillea define this inviting inn. Rooms are large, with carpets, high ceilings, and local crafts. Villas share a private courtyard and have tile kitchenettes. The bar has jazz or Caribbean music most evenings. Out in the garden restaurant ($–$$), strands of tiny white lights set the mood for an evening meal. ⊠ *Calle Donato Guerra 9* ⊙ *A.P. 30, 45920* ☎ *376/766–1344* 🖷 *376/766–1444* ⊕ *www.mexconnect.com/MEX/rest/nueva/posada.html* ⤳ *19 rooms, 4 villas* ⚖ *Restaurant, fans, pool, bar, laundry service* ▤ *MC, V* ⦿ *BP.*

$–$$ ▥ **Los Artistas.** Surrounded by an acre of splendid gardens, this spacious yet intimate inn has rooms with brightly painted walls and red-tile floors. Each has colorful handwoven Mexican bedspreads, wrought-iron or carved-wood bed frames, and fresh-cut flowers. Most rooms have patios shaded by bowers of blooming plants. There are no televisions or radios to spoil the tranquillity. ⊠ *Calle Constitución 105, 45920* ☎ *376/766–1027* 🖷 *376/766–1762* ⊕ *www.losartistas.com* ⤳ *7 rooms* ⚖ *Pool; no a/c* ▤ *No credit cards* ⦿ *BP.*

SPORTS & THE OUTDOORS

The **Rojas family** (⊠ Paseo Del Lago and Camino Real, 4 blocks east of Los Artistas B&B ☎ 376/766–4261) has been leading horseback trips

9

for more than 30 years. A ride along the lakeshore or in the surrounding hills costs around $7 an hour.

Guadalajara Essentials

TRANSPORTATION

BY AIR   Many major airlines fly nonstop from the U.S. to Guadalajara.

Aeropuerto Internacional Libertador Miguel Hidalgo is 16½ km (10 mi) south of Guadalajara, en route to Chapala. Autotransportaciones Aeropuerto operates a 24-hour taxi stand with service to any place in the Guadalajara area; buy tickets at the counters at the national and international exits. Some hotels also offer airport pickup shuttles; these need to be arranged in advance. Although flying from your hometown to Guadalajara, then back home from PV can be a good deal, flying round-trip to Guadalajara from PV is not. The bus is much cheaper, scenic, and efficient.

🛪 Airports **Aeropuerto Internacional Don Miguel Hidalgo y Costilla** (Aeropuerto Internacional de Guadalajara) ✉ Carretera Guadalajara-Chapala ☎ 33/3688-5248 or 33/3813-4002.

🛪 Airport Transfers **Autotransportaciones Aeropuerto** ☎ 33/3812-4278.

🛪 Carriers **Aeroméxico** ✉ Av. Vallarta 2440 ☎ 01800/021-4000 or 01800/021-4010 ⊕ www.aeromexico.com. **American Airlines** ✉ Av. Vallarta 2440 ☎ 33/3688-5394 or 01800/904-6000 ⊕ www.aa.com. **Continental** ✉ Hotel Presidente Intercontinental, Av. López Mateos Sur 3515 ☎ 33/3647-4251 or 01800/900-5000 ⊕ www.continental. com. **Delta Air Lines** ✉ Av. López Cotilla 1701 ☎ 33/3630-3530 ⊕ www.delta.com. **Mexicana** ✉ Av. Vallarta 2440 ☎ 33/3615-3227 or 01800/502-2000 ⊕ www.mexicana. com.

BY BUS   **Greyhound** (☎ 33/3647-5070 in Guadalajara, 01800/710-8819 toll-free in Mexico, 800/231-2222 in U.S., 800/661-8747 in Canada ⊕ www. greyhound.com). Luxury buses between Puerto Vallarta and Guadalajara take 4½ hours and cost $33–$37 on ETN or Estrella Blanca buses. With one wide seat on one side of the aisle and only two on the other, ETN is the most upscale line, and has about nine trips a day to and from Puerto Vallarta, except Sunday, with only one. Within Mexico, they accept advance reservations with a credit card. Estrella Blanca is an umbrella of different bus lines; many head straight for Guadalajara. ■ TIP➔ **Many bus lines do not accept credit cards.**

Guadalajara's Nueva Central Camionera (New Central Bus Station) is 10 km (6 mi) southeast of downtown.

Most city buses (35¢) run from every few minutes to every half hour between 6 AM and 9 PM; some run until 11 PM. ⚠ **The city's public transit buses are infamously fatal; drivers killed more than 100 pedestrians annually in the late 1990s before the government intervened. These poorly designed, noisy, noxious buses are still driven ruthlessly and cause at least a dozen deaths per year.**

Large mint-green Tur and red Cardinal buses are the safest, quickest, and least crowded and go to Zapopan, Tlaquepaque, and Tonalá for around 70¢. Wait for these along Avenida 16 de Septiembre.

Autotransportes Guadalajara–Chapala serves the lakeside towns from Guadalajara's new bus station (Central Camionera Nueva) and from the old bus station (Antigua Central Camionera); cost is around $4. It's 45 minutes to Chapala and another 15 minutes to Ajijic; there are departures every half hour from 6 AM to 9:30 PM. Make sure you ask for the *directo* (direct) as opposed to *clase segunda* (second-class) bus, which stops at every little pueblo en route.

🚌 Bus Lines **Autotransportes Guadalajara Chapala** ☎ 33/3619-5675. **ETN** ☎ 33/3600-0477 or 01800/360-4200 ⊕ www.etn.com.mx. **Estrella Blanca** ☎ 33/3679-0404.

🚌 Bus Stations **Antigua Central Camionera** ⊠ Av. Dr. R. Michel, between Calles Los Angeles and 5 de Febrero, northeast of Parque Agua Azul, Guadalajara. **Central Camionera Nueva** ⊠ Entronque Carretera Libre a Zapotlanejo Tlaquepaque.

BY CAR Metropolitan Guadalajara's traffic gets intense, especially at rush hour; parking can be scarce. Streets shoot off at diagonals from roundabouts (called *glorietas*), and on main arteries, turns (including U-turns and left turns) are usually made from right-side lateral roads (called *laterales*)— which can be confusing for drivers unfamiliar with big city traffic.

■ TIP→ Ubiquitous and inexpensive, taxis are the best way to go in Guadalajara.

From Guadalajara, it's most practical to get to Tlaquepaque by taxi (⇨ *below*); alternately take a bilingual, guided tour to focus on shopping and sightseeing.

BY SUBWAY Guadalajara's underground *tren ligero* (light train) system is clean, safe, and efficient. Trains run every 15 minutes from 6 AM to 11 PM; a token for one trip costs about 35¢.

BY TAXI Taxis are easily hailed on the street in the Centro Histórico, Zapopan, Tlaquepaque, and most other areas of Guadalajara. Many hotels have rate sheets showing the fare to major destinations and parts of town. Taxi is the best way to get to Tlaquepaque ($7–$8). To continue from Tlaquepaque to Tonalá, take a taxi from Avenida Río Nilo southeast directly into town and the intersection of Avenida de los Tonaltecas ($4; 5 minutes).

🚕 Taxi **Aguirre** ⊠ Calle Etopia 660, Centro Histórico, Guadalajara ☎ 33/3644-4818. **Taxi Express** ☎ 33/3637-4525. **Taxi Sitio Miverva no. 22** ☎ 33/3630-0050.

CAR RENTAL Although renting a car in Mexico is on the expensive side, deals are available because there are lots of international companies. Note that deals found on Internet sites often have hidden charges.

🚗 **Alamo** ⊠ Av. Niños Héroes 982, south of Centro Histórico, Guadalajara ☎ 33/3613-5531, 33/3613-5560, 33/3688-6630 at airport. **Avis** ⊠ Hilton, Av. de las Rosas 2933, Zona Cruz del Sur, Guadalajara ☎ 33/3671-3422, 33/3688-5656 at airport. **Budget** ⊠ Av. Niños Héroes 934, at Av. 16 de Septiembre, Centro Histórico, Guadalajara ☎ 33/3613-0027, 33/3613-0287, 33/3688-5216 at airport. **Dollar** ⊠ Av. Federalismo Sur 480, at Av. de la Paz, Centro Histórico, Guadalajara ☎ 33/3825-5080. **Hertz** ⊠ At the airport only ☎ 33/3688-5633.

CONTACTS & RESOURCES

EMERGENCIES Like any large Mexican city, Guadalajara has countless police troops with overlapping municipal, state, and federal jurisdictions. In an emergency, don't bother calling any one of them—it would only increase the possibility that no one will show up. Instead, call 066, a 911-type service that channels emergency situations to the correct agency. On the off chance that a call doesn't go through, stay calm and dial again. You can call the Red Cross at 065 for medical emergencies, especially automobile accidents. Call a police agency only if you need information on detainees or have a specific issue to address with a specific agency. Expect to get the runaround regardless.

Guadalajara has a number of expensive, private hospitals. In general, all have top-notch service and staff English-speaking doctors.

🚩 Emergency Services **Cruz Verde** (Green Cross municipal emergency medical service) ☎ 33/3614-5252 central dispatch, 33/3812-5143, 33/3812-0472. **Federal Highway Patrol** ☎ 33/3629-5082 or 33/3629-5085. **General Emergencies** ☎ 066, 065 for Red Cross ambulance. **Guadalajara City Police** ☎ 33/3668-0800, 33/3617-0770 for detainees. **Red Cross** ☎ 33/3614-5600 or 33/3614-2707. **Jalisco State Police and Civil Protection** ☎ 33/3675-3060 for natural disaster response unit.

🚩 Hospitals **Hospital del Carmen** ✉ Calle Tarascos 3435, Zona Minerva, Guadalajara ☎ 33/3813-1224 or 33/3813-0025. **Hospital México-Americano** ✉ Calle Colomos 2110, Centro Histórico, Guadalajara ☎ 33/3641-3141. **Hospital San Javier** ✉ Av. Pablo Casals 640, Col. Providencia, Zona Minerva, Guadalajara ☎ 33/3669-0222.

🚩 Pharmacies **Benavides** ✉ Calle Morelos 468, near el Palacio Municipal, Centro Histórico, Guadalajara ☎ 33/3613-6500 ✉ Av. Hidalgo 307-A, Centro Histórico, Guadalajara ☎ 33/3637-7280. **Farmacias Guadalajara** ✉ Av. Javier Mina 221, between Calle Cabañas and Vicente Guerrero, Centro Histórico, Guadalajara ☎ 33/3617-8555.

EXCHANGE SERVICES ATMs are the most convenient way to get cash, and offer the best exchange rates. There are several ATMs at the Guadalajara airport and at banks throughout metropolitan Guadalajara, Chapala, and elsewhere. You can also change U.S. dollars and traveler's checks at a *casa de cambio* in Guadalajara; there are dozens on Calle López Cotilla, east of Avenida 16 de Septiembre. They generally open weekdays 9–7 and Saturday 9–1.

INTERNET, MAIL & SHIPPING There are several decent Internet cafés in the heart of the Centro Histórico. The cost is usually $1.20 to $1.50 per hour, and most places charge in 15-minute increments. Compu-Flash, one block east of the Hotel Cervántes, opens weekdays 9:30 AM–10 PM and Saturday 9–8.

Note that the Mexican postal system is notoriously slow and unreliable; for important letters or packages, use an overnight service.

🚩 Internet Café **Compu-Flash** ✉ Calle Priciliano Sánchez 402, Centro Histórico, Guadalajara ☎ 33/3614-7165 🖷 33/3124-1072.

🚩 Overnight Shipping Services **Federal Express** ✉ Av. Washington 1129, Centro Histórico, Guadalajara ☎ 01800/900-1100 toll-free in Mexico. **DHL** ✉ Plaza del Sol, Local 20, in front of Banamex, Plaza del Sol, Guadalajara ☎ 33/3669-0214.

🚩 Post Offices **Correos** ✉ Av. Alcalde 500, Centro Histórico, Guadalajara ☎ 33/3614-4770.

VISITOR INFORMATION The Guadalajara branches of the Jalisco State Tourist Office are open on weekdays and weekends, though hours vary. Guadalajara Municipal Tourist Office has an outlet in front of the Palacio Municipal and kiosks at several spots: downtown in the Plaza Guadalajara, near Los Arcos monument on Avenida Vallarta east of the Minerva Fountain, in

Parque San Francisco, in front of the Instituto Cultural Cabañas, in front of Mercado Libertad, at Calle Vicente Guerrero 233 (closed weekends), and at the airport. Hours are generally Monday–Saturday 9–7.

The Tourist Board of Zapopan opens weekdays 9–7:30. They also have information on Tonalá and Tlaquepaque. The Tlaquepaque Municipal Tourist Office is open weekdays 9–3. The Tonalá Municipal Tourist Office is open weekdays 9–3. In Ajijic, the nonprofit Lake Chapala Society is open daily 10–2.

🏢 **Guadalajara Municipal Tourist Office** ⊠ Monumento Los Arcos, Av. Vallarta 2641, 1 block east of Minerva Fountain, Zona Minerva, Guadalajara ☎ 33/3616–9150 or 33/3615–1182 ⊕ www.vive.guadalajara.gob.mx. **Jalisco State Tourist Office** ⊠ Calle Morelos 102, in Plaza Tapatía, Centro Histórico ☎ 33/3668–1600, 01800/363–2200 toll-free in Mexico ⊕ http://visita.jalisco.gob.mx (Spanish only) ⊠ Palacio de Gobierno, Centro Histórico ☎ No phone ⊠ Calle Madero 407-A, 2nd fl., Chapala ☎☎ 376/765–3141. **Lake Chapala Society** ⊠ Av. 16 de Septiembre 16, Ajijic ☎ 376/766–1582. **Tlaquepaque Municipal Tourist Office** ⊠ Calle Morelos 288, Tlaquepaque ☎ 33/3562–7050 Ext. 2318, 2320, and 2321. **Tonalá Municipal Tourist Office** ⊠ Av. de los Tonaltecas Sur 140, in La Casa de los Artesanos, Tonalá ☎ 33/3284–3092 or 33/3284–3093. **Tourist Board of Zapopan** ⊠ Av. Vallarta 6503, Ciudad Granja, Zona Zapopan, Guadalajara ☎ 33/3110–0754 or 33/3110–0755 ⊕ www.zapopan.gob.mx.

Gay Puerto Vallarta

WORD OF MOUTH

"Puerto Vallarta is *the* gay destination in Mexico, sort of like a Mexican Ft. Lauderdale or Miami."

—MikeT

"[PV is] as quiet or as happening as you want it to be. You could stay close to town at a big resort hotel like the Westin (*very nice*), or you could stay at a hotel in town, near or even right on the gay beach."

—robertino

Puerto Vallarta is a gay old town. Men check each other out over drinks and suntan oil at Blue Chairs, dangle from parachutes above Los Muertos beach, buff themselves out at South Side gyms. Rainbow boys (and girls) sail south to their own private nude beach and then dance 'til morning in one of the city's oversexed discos. Mexico's most popular gay destination draws crowds of "Dorothy's friends" from both sides of the Río Grande, and from the Old World as well.

> **GET THE SCOOP**
>
> Gay Guide Vallarta (⊕ www.gayguidevallarta.com) is an excellent and occasionally opinionated source of info about gay-friendly and gay-owned hotels, restaurants, and nightlife. Equally informative is ⊕ www.vallartaundiscovered.com.

The Romantic Zone is the hub for rainbow bars and sophisticated, gay-friendly restaurants. Here, many foreigners have—after falling in love with Puerto Vallarta's beaches, jungly green mountains, and friendly people—relocated to PV to fulfill their ultimate fantasy in the form of bistro, bar, or B&B. International savvy (and backing) teamed up with Mexican sensibilities have produced a number of successful gay businesses.

Clubbing may be the favorite pastime in the Romantic Zone, but there's more than one way to cruise Vallarta. Gay boat tours keep the libations flowing throughout the day, horses head for the hills for birds'-eye views of the beach, and Paco's private beach club encourages a head-to-toe tan.

DAYTIME ACTIVITIES

PV has something for every energy level. You can chill on the beach, get active by joining gay-oriented horse-riding tours or sailing expeditions, or spend the day at a secluded, clothing-optional beach.

Beaches & Resorts

The undisputed yet unassuming king of daytime beach action is **Blue Chairs** (⊠ South end of Los Muertos Beach, Col. E. Zapata ☎ 322/222–5040 ⊕ www.bluechairs.com). Shaded by the bright azure umbrellas that distinguish the restaurant/bar/hotel, local boys from the 'hood mingle with asphalt cowboys from the Midwest. Waiters range from snarky queens to cherubic heteros. This is PV's most popular gay beach scene, a magnet for first-timers as well as those sneaking away from social obligations in Guadalajara.

If you're looking to get away from the hoi polloi, head to the beach called **Paco's Paradise** (⊠ 19 km [12 mi] south of PV ☎ 322/222–5040 ⊕ www.pacopaco.com), the g-spot of PV's gay beach scene. Sunbathing is *au naturel,* except when the tour boats pass and patrons are requested to cover their tails. A day pass ($10–$15) includes activities like volleyball, kayaking, and snorkeling, plus transportation to the resort from Boca de

Tomatlán (see Web site for *La Rosita* skiff schedule). The "landlubber cruise" departs from Paco Paco Fridays at 11 AM; $48 includes transportation, open bar, and food served on the beach. If you want to stay longer in this rainbow-tinted Shangri-La, book one of the unaffected accommodations—no electricity makes things downright romantic. Share the bunkhouse for $20 per person, or get a room for $75 (breakfast included with both). The resort is closed Monday and Tuesday.

TOTAL RELAXATION

If you must break a sweat on your vacation, the best way is while experiencing a *temazcal*, an ancient Indian sweat lodge ceremony at **Terra Noble** (✉ Av. Tulipanes 595, Fracc. Lomas de Terra Noble ☎ 322/222–5400 and 223-3530 ⊕ www.terranoble.com). The spa also has therapeutic massage, body treatments, facials, and healing therapies such as Reiki.

Cruises

Affiliated with Blue Chairs, **Diana's Tours** (☎ 322/222–5040, 866/514–7969 in U.S. ⊕ www.bluechairs.com) is a Thursday booze cruise popular with lesbians and gays. Go for the swimming, snorkeling, and lunch on the beach at Las Animas, or for the unlimited national brands of beer and mixed drinks. Most of the time is spent on the boat. It's easiest to reserve tickets ($75) online using PayPal; there's a $10 discount for booking more than two weeks in advance.

Paco Paco's (⇨ *above*) has a full-day party cruise. To book your own sailing cruise, contact **Rainbow Dancer** (☎ 322/299–0936 ⊕ www. rainbowdancer.com). It's a cut above the booze cruises, with charter and day trips available on the 52-foot sailboat.

Sports & the Outdoors

Horseback Riding

Four-hour, $40 tours with **Boana Tours** (✉ Torre Malibú, Carretera a Mismaloya ☎ 322/222–0999 ⊕ http://boana.net) includes round-trip transportation to its ranch outside the city, several hours on the horse, a snack, and drinks.

10

AFTER DARK

Puerto Vallarta's club scene may seem tame compared to that of San Francisco or New York, but it's Mexico's most notorious. Guys and dolls begin their nocturnal perambulations at martini and piano bars and chummy pubs before heading to late night drag-shows, dance clubs, and strip joints.

Bars

Lesbian-owned, lovingly run **Apaches** (✉ Olas Altas 439, Col. E. Zapata ☎ 322/222–4004) is Vallarta's original martini bar. The single row of sidewalk tables fills up soon after the 5 PM opening, as that's the start of the two-hour happy hour. Popular with straights, lesbians, and gay men warming up for later-evening activities, the narrow bar has added an equally slender adjoining bistro serving bar food and snacks.

In addition to its famous beach scene, **Blue Chairs** (⊠ South end of Los Muertos Beach, Col. E. Zapata ☎ 322/222–5040 ⊕ www.bluechairs.com) has a popular rooftop bar, **The Blue Moon,** which is the perfect place to watch the sun set. Nightly late-afternoon and evening entertainment ranges from "Blue Balls" Bingo to the biweekly drag show and the Saturday night "Blue Hombre Review." The place has good snacks, and a small swimming pool. Friday is karaoke night, beginning at 7 PM.

> ### KEEP 'EM COMING
>
> Not that we're encouraging massive alcohol consumption, but you can spend all night at "happy hour." Hit the first at 2 in the afternoon and rotate throughout gay bars and clubs until 4 AM the next day.

We've heard **Frida's** (⊠ Lázaro Cárdenas between Insurgentes and Aguacate, Col. E. Zapata ☎ No phone) described as "the gay Cheers of Mexico." It's a friendly neighborhood bar where you meet young and old, many Mexicans, fewer foreigners, and maybe even some straights. Show up a few times and everyone is sure to know your name.

As popular with straights as it is with PV's rainbow crowd, **Kit Kat** (⊠ Calle Púlpito 120, Col. E. Zapata ☎ 322/223–0093) has a huge list of fun martinis and other classy cocktails: two for one on Tuesday. The small space combines South Beach retro with a Zen-like simplicity. The food's not bad either, and they have drag shows at least two weekends a month in high season, at which times reservations are de rigueur.

The air is sometimes smoky in tightly sealed **Garbo** (⊠ Púlpito 142, Col. E. Zapata ☎ No phone), open daily 6 PM to 2 AM. The small, highly refrigerated piano and jazz bar has a nice varied menu of sophisticated drinks, good canned or live tunes, and waiters that regularly check on your welfare. On the downside, the beer is pricey, and mixed drinks even more so.

Charming **La Noche** (⊠ Lázaro Cárdenas 257, Col. E. Zapata ☎ 322/222–3364) has red walls and a huge, eye-catching chandelier. Gringo-owned, it attracts a crowd of 20- to 40-year-olds (a mix of foreigners and Mexicans), who bring their CDs to play: electronica and house are the favorites. Speaking of which, the house makes excellent cocktails, and not too expensive, either.

The Palm (⊠ Olas Altas 508, Col. E. Zapata ☎ 322/223–4818) is popular with straights for the cabaret shows and for its occasional theatrical performances, but it's primarily a gay bar. Remodeled in 2005, it has tables outside on the sidewalk (as do the two adjoining gay bars). The subtly lighted indoor space has deep pink walls; plastic flamingos lounge here and there. Gay performers of one genre or another—including Ida Slapter, who does a great Cher impression during her very funny drag show—perform most weekend nights, definitely in high season (December–Easter). It's closed Monday and Tuesday.

Dance & Strip Clubs

Billing itself as "The Study of Man," **Anthropology** (✉ Calle Morelos 101, near Calle Encino below Ignacio L. Vallarta street bridge, Centro ☎ 322/221–5013) has nightly strip shows beginning around 10:30 PM and yup, they take it all off. The management has no rules about customers, shall we say, "interacting" with the strippers during their nearly nonstop parades. There's a cover of about $5, and the club is open nightly. There's a late-night happy hour between 1 and 4 in the morning.

Vallarta's first gay disco, **Los Balcones** (✉ Av. Juárez 182 Altos, Centro ☎ No phone) was remodeled in 2004. It has a rooftop bar where smokers can puff away, and the fresh tunes emerging from the sound system are popular with the younger crowd. The club is named for the balconies that overlook the street scene below. The strippers are said to be among the town's best endowed. Cover charge is less than $4. Things are liveliest on weekend nights between midnight and 2 AM, although the club usually stays open until 3 or 4 AM. It's closed Monday.

> **TRAILBLAZER LIZ**
>
> According to a 2001 article in *Passport* magazine, many gay men moved to PV in actress Elizabeth Taylor's wake. After filming *The Night of the Iguana* in 1963, Ms. Taylor established a home here, and many of her gay friends from the movie crew followed suit.

Adjoining clubs **Club Paco Paco & the Ranch** (✉ Lázaro Cárdenas 257, Col. E. Zapata ☎ 322/222–3364) are the most popular dance clubs in town with both gays and lesbians. One cover charge gets you into both. The main draw isn't the high-school-auditorium decor but the crowd (nearly everyone ends up here); the female impersonators miming pop songs aren't too bad either. Back at the Ranch, strippers are the draw: policemen, firefighters, construction-worker-types baring . . . almost all. Paco Paco's biggest selling point is that it outlasts the other gay clubs: it opens at 1 in the afternoon and doesn't close until 6 in the morning. Admission is $4.

WHERE TO STAY

Gay hotels offer entertainment that allows you to party on-site without having to worry about getting "home" at the end of the night. In addition to the hotels listed here, which are the crème de la crème of Vallarta, hotels like El Emperador, overlooking Los Muertos beach, and Quinta María Cortes above Playa Conchas Chinas (⇨ Chapter 2) are gay-friendly.

$$$ 🛏 **Casa Cupula.** This multistory, up-to-date B&B has a variety of rooms and prices. It's just a 15-minute walk down to the beach and the Romantic Zone (but the return trip is uphill). Some of the guest rooms have wonderful views of the sea and of layers of houses up and down the surrounding hills—most have balconies. The suites have kitchenettes, washers, dryers, and a separate bedroom upstairs. All are classy, restrained,

WORK UP A SWEAT

There's more to a gay Vallarta vacation than drinking and dancing. Before baring your bod at the beach, burn off those extra calories at one of PV's many gyms. On the South Side, **Acqua Day Spa and Gym** (✉ Constitución 450 ☎ 322/223–5270) has a sauna and steam room in addition to free weights and machines, massage, body treatments, and more. Closed Sunday. Serious muscle men and women head for **Gold's Gym** (✉ Plaza Las Glorias, Zona Hotelera ☎ 322/226–3070) with aerobics, tai chi, yoga, and Pilates as well as a sauna, hot tub, and chiropractic center. For women only, **Total Fitness Gym** (✉ Calle Timón 1 at marina, Marina Vallarta ☎ 322/221–0770) is a sparkly clean gym with yoga, spinning, meditation, aerobics classes, and Pilates.

and distinctly masculine. The airy shared dining room-lounge is comfortable and welcoming; the rooftop terrace with seating and BBQ is lovely. Gays, lesbians, their dogs, and straight friends are welcome. ✉ *129 Callejon de la Igualdad, Col. Amapas, 48399* ☎ *322/223–2484, 866/261–3516 in U.S.* 🖷 *755/263–9261 in U.S.* ⊕ *www.casacupula.com* ➪ *8 rooms, 2 suites* ⟁ *Restaurant, room service, in-room safes, some in-room hot tubs, some kitchenettes, some microwaves, some refrigerators, some in-room DVDs, in-room data ports, Wi-Fi, 2 pools, massage, bar, library, laundry service, concierge, some free parking, some pets allowed; no kids under 18* ▤ *AE, MC, V* ☾ *Closed Aug. and Sept.* ⦿ *CP.*

$$–$$$ 🖾 **Blue Chairs.** Guys stay here not for the plain, if serviceable, rooms but for all that Blue Chairs offers and stands for. Horseback riding, drag and strip shows, theme nights, events, parties, booze cruises, and beach cruising all begin—and often end—right here. ✉ *Los Muertos Beach, Col. E. Zapata, 48380* ☎ *322/222–5040, 866/514–7969 from Canada and U.S.* ⊕ *www.bluechairs.com* ➪ *24 rooms, 16 suites* ⟁ *2 restaurants, cable TV, fans, some kitchenettes, pool, 3 bars, concierge, boating, shop* ▤ *AE, MC, V* ⦿ *EP.*

$$ 🖾 **Mercurio.** The rooms here are plain, but there's nonetheless much to be said for this small, motel-like place surrounding a swimming pool. First, it has a fabulous location—although not on the beach—in the heart of the Zona Romántica, PV's gay headquarters. The reasonable price leaves money left over for shopping and cruising. ✉ *Calle Francisco Rodriguez 168, Col. E. Zapata, 48380* ☎ *322/222–4793* 🖷 *322/222–1419* ⊕ *www.hotel-mercurio.com* ➪ *28 rooms* ⟁ *Fans, cable TV, in-room safes, some kitchenettes, Wi-Fi, pool, bar, massage, concierge, laundry service; no room phones* ▤ *AE, D, DC, MC, V* ⦿ *CP.*

$$ 🖾 **Villa David.** The public spaces and rooms here are showpieces, melding traditional, Mexican architecture with more modern elements and lots of tile. The owners take good care of their gay (male) guests, and don't allow straights or lesbians to book rooms. A trio of little pomeranians have the run of the place, but they're friendly. The clothing-optional guesthouse is securely tucked behind old walls in Gringo Gulch, a straight neighborhood made famous by Liz and Richard. Views of the town and bay are outstanding from the rooftop aerie, and some of the rooms have great views, too. ⊠ *Calle Galeana 348, Centro, 48300* ☎ *322/223–0315* ⊕ *www. villadavidpv.com* ⌁ *10 rooms* ⌂ *Pool, in-room DVDs, Wi-Fi, hot tub, Internet room* ☰ *MC, V* ⏃ *CP.*

HOTEL ALTERNATIVES

Gayguide Vallarta (⊕ www. gayguidevallarta.com) has lots of listings for long- and short-term condo rentals.

10

UNDERSTANDING
PUERTO VALLARTA

PV AT A GLANCE

HISTORY

CHRONOLOGY

GOVERNMENT
& ECONOMY

PEOPLE & SOCIETY

THE NATURAL WORLD

BOOKS & VIDEOS

SPANISH VOCABULARY

PV AT A GLANCE

Fast Facts

Nickname: Foreigners call it PV, or Vallarta, but it has no real nickname. A *vallartense* (person from Puerto Vallarta), however, is known as a *pata salada* (salty foot)
State: PV is in the state of Jalisco, whose capital is Guadalajara
Population: About 350,000
Population density: 142.03 people per square km
Population growth rate 1990–2000: 65.74%
Literacy rate: 95.78%
Religion: Catholic 90%; Protestant/ Evangelical 8.5%; other/no religion 1.5%
Type of government: Federal republic; municipality has a democratically elected city council and mayor
Language: Spanish is the official language and spoken by nearly everyone. Many people speak fluent to intermediate-level English ; the few people who speak indigenous languages are Cora- and Huichol-speaking people

from remote areas of Jalisco and Nayarit.

I was taken in by the bravado and the sounds of Mexico . . . not so much the music, but the spirit.
—Herb Alpert (musician)

In its male, in its public, its city aspect, Mexico is an arch-transvestite, a tragic buffoon. Dogs bark and babies cry when Mother Mexico walks abroad in the light of day. The policeman, the Marxist mayor— Mother Mexico doesn't even bother to shave her mustachios. Swords and rifles and spurs and bags of money chink and clatter beneath her skirts. A chain of martyred priests dangles from her waist, for she is an austere, pious lady. Ay, how much—clutching her jangling bosoms; spilling cigars— how much she has suffered.
—Richard Rodriguez

Geography & Environment

Latitude: 20°N (same as Cancún, Mexico; Port-au-Prince, Haiti; Khartoum, Sudan; Hanoi, Vietnam; Calcutta, India)
Longitude: 105° W (same as Regina, Saskatchewan; Denver, Colorado; El Paso, Texas)
Elevation: 40 m (131 feet) above sea level
Land area: 1,972,550 sq km (761,605 sq mi)

Terrain: River basin backed by Sierra Madre foothills
Natural hazards: Hurricanes, tidal surges causing inundation of beachfront properties
Environmental issues: Destruction of natural areas due to migration and tourism

Economy

Currency: Mexican Peso
Exchange rate: 10.71 pesos = $1
GDP per capita: $9,000 (for comparison, Mexico national average is $10,000, and U.S. national average is $41,800)
Workers receiving minimum wage or less: 9.5%
Major industries: Tourism, commerce, construction, agriculture

I believe Mexico should dedicate 100% of its oil revenues to developing human capital and technological development. None of us politicians should be able to touch that money.
                                    —Vicente Fox

Did You Know?

• Two of the four quadrants in Puerto Vallarta's official seal symbolize the tourism industry: a sailfish represents sportfishing; the hands welcome tourists.

• International law limits the production of tequila to specific regions of Mexico; most are in Jalisco (with specific regions also in Michoacán, Nayarit, Guanajuato, and Tamaulipas states).

• Puerto Vallarta's population between 2000 and 2005 almost doubled: from 184,728 to 350,000.

HISTORY

Pre-Columbian Mexico

The first nomadic hunters crossed the Bering Straight during the Late Pleistocene Era, some 30,000 or 40,000 years ago, fanning out and finding niches in the varied landscape of North America. In the hot and arid "Great Chichimeca," as the vast area that included the Sonora and Chihuahua deserts and the Great Plains of the United States was known, lived far-flung tribes whose circumstances favored a nomadic lifestyle. Even the unassailable Aztecs were unable to dominate this harsh wilderness and its resilient people.

Mesoamerica, the name given posthumously to the great civilizations of mainland Mexico, spanned as far south of the Great Chichimeca as Honduras and El Salvador. Here, trade routes were established, strategic alliances were formed through warfare or marriage, and enormous temples and palaces were erected on the backs of men, without the aid of beasts of burden or the wheel. Some cultures mysteriously disappeared, others were conquered but not absorbed.

It was in northern Mesoamerica that the continent's first major metropolis, Teotihuacán—which predated the Aztec capital of Tenochtitlán by more than half a century—was built. The gleaming city with beautifully decorated pyramids, palaces, homes, and administrative buildings covered miles and administered to some 175,000 souls; it was abandoned for unknown reasons around AD 700. On the Yucatán Peninsula, great and powerful Maya cities rose up, but like Teotihuacán were abandoned one by one, seemingly at the height of civilization.

During the rise and fall of these great cities, small, loosely organized bands of individuals occupied Mesoamerica's western Pacific coast. By 1200 BC, the culture that archaeologists call Capacha occupied river valleys north and south of what would later be named Bahía de Banderas. From well-positioned settlements, they planted gardens and took advantage of animal and mineral resources from the sea and the surrounding foothills.

These cultures—centered primarily in the present-day states of Nayarit, Jalisco, and Colima—built no large, permanent structures and left few clues about their society. Some of the most compelling evidence comes from artifacts found in tombs. Unlike their more advanced neighbors, the Pacific coast people housed these burial chambers not in magnificent pyramids but in the bottom of vertical shafts deep within the earth. Lifelike dog sculptures were sometimes left to help their deceased owners cross to the other side; servants, too, were buried with their masters for the same purpose. Realistically depicted figures involved in myriad rituals of daily and ceremonial life, most of them excavated only since the 1970s, have given more clues about pre-Hispanic civilizations of Western Mexico.

Only so much information can be gleaned, however, especially since the majority of tombs were looted before archaeological research began. North and south of Banderas Bay, the Aztatlán people seem to have established themselves primarily in river valleys between Tomatlán, in southern Jalisco, and northern Nayarit. In addition to creating utilitarian and ceremonial pottery, they appear to have been skilled in at least rudimentary metallurgy. Aside from the Purépecha of Michoacán, to whom the Aztatlán are related, no other Mesoamerican societies were skilled in making or using metal of any kind.

The Colonial Period

History favors those who write it, and the soldier-priest-scribe who documented the discovery of Banderas Bay in 1525 gave it a decidedly European spin. According to Padre Tello, four years after the Spanish demolished the Aztec capital at Tenochtitlán, about 100 Spanish troops met 10,000 to 20,000 Azatlán at Punta de Mita, the bay's northernmost point. Then, by Tello's fantastic account, the sun's sudden illumination of a Spanish battle standard (a large pennant) bearing the image of the Virgin of the Immaculate Conception caused the armed indigenous peoples to give up without a fight. When they lay their colorful battle flags at the feet of the Francisco Cortés de Buenaventura, the Spanish commander named the site Bahía de Banderas, or Bay of Flags.

Subsequent adventurers and explorers rediscovered and used the region around the bay, but it wasn't colonized until three centuries later. The name Bahía de Banderas is seen on maps from the 1600s, although whalers in the 1800s called it Humpback Bay, after their principal prey. Boats were built on the beach in today's Mismaloya for a missionary expedition to Baja California, and the long, deep bay was used as a pit stop on other long sailing voyages.

To a lesser extent, Banderas Bay was a place of refuge and refueling for pirates (or, as they were known to their patrons, privateers). Around the end of the 16th century, Sir Francis Drake laid in wait here for the Manila galleon—sailing south along the coast laden with silk, spices, and porcelain from the Orient. He sent the booty to his patron, Queen Elizabeth of England.

The Formative Years

Although adventurers made use of the area's magnificent bay, Puerto Vallarta's story started inland and made its way to the coast. Mining in the Sierra Madre del Sur wasn't as profitable as in Zacatecas and Guanajuato, but there was plenty of gold and silver to draw the Spaniards' attention. At the vanguard of Spanish exploration in 1530, the infamous conquistador Nuño Beltrán de Guzmán arrived in the region with a contingent of Spanish soldiers and indigenous allies.

During his tenure in Nueva Galicia (which included today's Jalisco, Zacatecas, and Durango states), de Guzmán siezed land that was settled by native peoples and parceled out *encomiendas* (huge grants of land) to lucky *encomendados* (landholders) in return for loyalty and favors to the Crown. The landholders were entitled to not only the land, but everything on it: the birds of the trees; beasts of the forest; and the unlucky indigenous people who lived there, who were consequently enslaved. Even by the day's standards, de Guzmán's behavior was so outrageous that by 1536 he had been stripped of authority and sent to prison.

In exchange for their forced labor, the native population received the "protection" of the encomendado, meaning food and shelter, which they had previously without any help from the Spanish. Abuse was inevitable, and many overworked natives died of famine. Epidemics of smallpox, diphtheria, scarlet fever, influenza, measles, and other imported diseases had a disastrous effect. The region's native population was reduced by about 90% within the first 100 years of Spanish occupation.

By the early 17th century, gold and silver were being mined throughout the region; there were bases of operation at San Sebastián del Oeste, Cuale, and Talpa. After the War for Independence (1810–21), Mexican entrepreneurs began to extract gold, silver, and zinc previously claimed by the Spanish. In the mid-1800s, the coast around today's Vallarta was under the jurisdiction of the mountain municipalities.

As in the rest of the country, independence from Spain brought little contentment to the average man and woman, who were as disenfranchised and poor as ever. A prime topic of the day among the moneyed elite was the growing conflict between Liberals and Conservatives. Liberals, like the lawyer Benito Juárez, favored curtailing the Church's vast power. When the Liberals prevailed and Juárez became Mexico's first indigenous president (he was a Zapotec from Oaxaca), a host of controversial reforms were enacted. Those regarding separation of church and state had immediate and lasting effects.

Settlers on the Bay

The power struggles of the first half of the 19th century had little real impact on relatively unpopulated coastal areas like Banderas Bay. In 1849, a few men from the tiny fishing hamlet of Yelapa camped out at the mouth of the Cuale River, in present-day Puerto Vallarta. A few years later, young Guadalupe Sánchez, his wife, and a few friends were the first official settlers. This entrepreneur made his money not through fishing or gold, but by importing salt, vital for extracting mineral from rock. From this small import business grew the tiny town called Las Peñas de Santa María de Guadalupe.

When silver prices dipped between the two World Wars, some of the mountain-based miners returned to their farming roots, relocating to the productive lands of the Ameca River basin (today, Nuevo Vallarta) at the southern border of Nayarit. The fecund land between the mountains and the bay produced ample corn crops, and the growing town of Las Peñas—renamed Puerto Vallarta in honor of a former Jalisco governor, became the seat of its own municipality in 1918.

Development came slowly to this isolated town. By the 1930s there was limited electricity; a small airstrip was built in the 1950s, when Mexicana Airlines initiated the first flights and electricity was finally available around the clock. Retaining the close-knit society and values brought down from the mining towns,

each family seemed to know the others' joys and failures. As small-town families do, they sat outside their adobe brick homes in the cool of the evening to discuss the latest gossip and the international news of the day.

The Modern Era

Honoring a promise made to the Mexican government by John F. Kennedy, President Richard Nixon flew into an improved PV airport in 1970 to sign a treaty settling boundary disputes surrounding the Rio Grande, meeting with his Mexican counterpart, Gustavo Díaz Ordaz. Upon asking for an armored car, he was cheerfully told that the convertible that had been arranged would do just fine. After riding parade-style along the roadway lined with cheering citizens and burros garlanded in flowers, the American leader is said to have asked why, if he was a Republican, the road was lined with donkeys. To which his host sensibly responded, "Well, where in the world would we get all those elephants?"

It took about 500 years for Puerto Vallarta to transition from discovery to major destination, but the city is making up for lost time. "When I was a child here, in the 1950s, Puerto Vallarta was like a big family," the town's official chronicler, Don Carlos Munguía, said. "When I married, in 1964, there were about 12,000 people." By the early '70s the population had jumped to 35,000 and continued to grow steadily, and then more than doubled between 2000 and 2005.

Today the city has some 350,000 people, a significant number of them expat Americans and Canadians who vacationed here and never left; many others are transplants for whom the tourism boom provided job opportunities. The metropolitan area has three universities and a vast marina harboring private yachts, tour boats, and the Mexican navy. In 2005 the cruise-ship harbor was expanded to accommodate three ships simultaneously; the overflow that still exists has to anchor offshore. While many folks lament the loss of the good old days before tourism took off, there's simply no turning back now. But some things haven't changed: Most *vallartenses* (residents native to Puerto Vallarta) are still intimately acquainted with their neighbors and the man or woman who owns the corner taco stand, which is likely to have been there for years, maybe even generations.

CHRONOLOGY

ca. 350 BC	Oldest evidence of civilization—a ceramic piece from Ixtapa (northwest of Puerto Vallarta inland from Nuevo Vallarta)—dates to this time
ca. 1100	Indigenous Aztatlán people dominate region from present-day Sinaloa to Colima states; creates first-known settlement in Vallarta area
1525	First Spanish–Indian confrontation in the region, at Punta de Mita. By Spanish accounts, 100 Spanish soldiers prevailed over tens of thousands armed native peoples. Bahía de Banderas (Bay of Flags) was named for the battle flags of the indigenous "army" that were (or so claimed the Spanish) thrown down in defeat
1587	Pirate Thomas Cavendish attacks Punta de Mita, looting pearls gathered from Mismaloya and the Marietas Islands
1664	Mismaloya serves as a shipyard for vessels bound for exploration and conquest of Baja California
1849	A few fishermen from Yelapa are said to have found excellent fishing around the mouth of the Cuale River, making them the first unofficial settlers
1851	Puerto Vallarta founded, under the name Las Peñas de Santa María de Guadalupe, by the salt merchant Guadalupe Sánchez
1918	The small but growing seaside town becomes county seat and is renamed Puerto Vallarta in honor of former Jalisco State governor Ignacio Luis Vallarta (1871–75)
1922	Yellow fever epidemic decimates the population, killing some 150 people
1925	Flood and landslides during a great storm form narrow Cuale Island in the middle of the Cuale River in downtown PV
1931	Puerto Vallarta gets electricity (7–10 PM only)
1951	Mexican reporters covering centennial celebrations—marked with a 21-gun naval salute and a wealthy wedding—capture the small town charm on film and in news reports, exposing this isolated coastal gem to their countrymen
1963	Hollywood film *Night of the Iguana,* directed by John Huston and starring Richard Burton and Ava Gardner, puts PV on the world map, due to the much-publicized affair between Burton and Elizabeth Taylor (who was not in the movie) during the filming here
1970	Vallarta builds a new airport, and improves the electrical and highway systems for Richard Nixon's official visit with President Díaz Ordaz
2000	Census reports the city's population as 159,080
2005	Population more than doubles from 2000, reaching 350,000

GOVERNMENT & ECONOMY

Government & Politics

Mexico is a federal republic with three branches of government—executive, judiciary, and legislative; the latter comprised by a senate and house of deputies (house of representatives). The basis for today's government is the 1917 Constitution, which, when ratified and implemented several years after that date, signaled the end of the Mexican Revolution.

The Revolution, at the dawn of the 20th century, was the combined, if disjointed, effort of various groups with almost polar opposite ideals and reasons for revolt. Campaigning under the slogan "No re-election!" the wealthy and influential northerner Francisco I. Madero's driving desire was to end the 33-year presidency/dictatorship of General Porfirio Diaz. Madero's goals were mainly ideological and intellectual. In the south, the poor, disenfranchised, and mainly indigenous population rallied around the charismatic Emiliano Zapata, who crusaded relentlessly for land reform in his native state of Morelos. Lack of cohesive leadership and goals made the revolt drag on for a decade, resulting in some 2 million deaths—including many civilians.

From the ashes of postwar chaos rose the political party known by its acronym, PRI (Partido Revolucionario Institucional). Adopting the green, red, and white of the Mexican flag, the Institutional Revolutionary Party quickly became the national party of Mexico.

As the decades rolled by, opposition parties were allowed in the legislature in small numbers, mainly to provide an illusion of legitimacy. Outgoing PRI presidents hand-selected their successors and left office with piles of the nation's cash and magnificent properties. And why not, as federal law protects ex-presidents from prosecution?

Modern presidents have been no exception to the pattern of corruption. Well-respected during his term, president (and Harvard-educated economist) Carlos Salinas de Gortari (term: 1988–94) increased his personal fortune while leaving Mexico in financial ruin. Mexico's economy had been on a downward spiral for decades, and Salinas's imprudent fiscal policies pushed the country to the breaking point (⇨ Economics).

Salinas's successor, Ernesto Zedillo Ponce de León (term: 1994–2000), was left to deal with a massive devaluation of the country's currency and the resulting across-the-board financial hardship for the Mexican people. Middle-class people awoke just weeks after the president's inauguration to find their salarys cut by 40% and their mortgages and car payments increased by roughly the same amount.

Although generally following the mandate of his political party, Zedillo did institute important changes. Instead of hand-selecting his successor in the time-honored tradition, the former banker and education minister established the first presidential primary election. This departure from the norm inspired cautious optimism in previously apathetic voters. Blatantly illegal election maneuvers like voter intimidation and ballot-box stuffing in the countryside were monitored and curtailed.

Despite these advances, most of the news during the Zedillo administration was negative and frustrating for the Mexican people. Popular presidential candidate Luis Donaldo Colosio was murdered in 1994. Fighting for social justice, the Zapatista Liberation Army (EZLN) staged a sudden and dramatic uprising in Chiapas State, while lesser rebellions threatened in Guerrero and Oaxaca. Mexico City mayor Cuauhtémoc Cárdenas lost the 1988 election due to obvious election fraud. No longer able to ignore the nation's financial, political, and social crises, Mexicans were finally fed up with the status quo during the Zedillo administration.

The election in 2000 of opposition-party candidate Vicente Fox Quesada, and the peaceful transition to power that followed, left the country in a state of shock: more than 70 years of one-party rule was over. Even the winning party, PAN (Partido de Acción Nacional, or National Action Party), could scarcely believe the results.

By his own account, President Vicente Fox has, since 2000, fallen far short of the promised 7% economic growth per year; however, his historic tenure of office has changed the country. He has enjoyed an approval rating averaging nearly 60% during his six-year term, and earned the admiration of his countrymen for his sincere interest in the working poor.

At this writing, the country is gearing up for election of a new president in July 2006. The front-runner is Andrés Manuel López Obrador, former mayor of Mexico City, representing the left-of-center PRD (Partido de la Revolución Democrática, or Party of Democratic Revolution). The populist firebrand is a huge hit with the poor. PAN's candidate Felipe Calderón is energy secretary to President Fox. Trailing at the polls is Roberto Madrazo, former president of the PRI party and ex-governor of Tabasco State. The main challenges to the new president will be expanding trade, creating jobs, and fighting drug trafficking and corruption.

Following the national template, Puerto Vallarta and Jalisco State have traditionally voted PRI, and the majority of legislators still represent the tri-color party, as does the mayor of Puerto Vallarta. The last two governors (since 1994) have belonged to the business-oriented PAN, including the incumbent, Francisco Javier Ramírez Acuña. Mirroring the national trend, greater transparency is seen in local and state politics.

Economy

January 2006 figures indicated the country's biggest trade surplus in nine years: $398 million. Record oil exports were reported in 2005 as well as increased auto exports, the latter mainly to the United States. The U.S. is far and away Mexico's largest trading partner, representing 87.6% of its trade as opposed to its second-most-important partner, Canada, with just 1.8%.

Trade statistics in the past had been significantly smaller. Traditionally inward-looking, the government party, PRI, was forced to expand Mexico's static and tightly controlled economy under President Miguel de la Madrid (1982–88) after a necessary but painful devaluation of the peso in 1982. Successor Carlos Salinas de Gortari continued to open the Mexican market, signing the North American Free Trade Agreement (NAFTA) with the United States and Canada in 1994.

However, Salinas and the PRI ignored the country's obvious signs of economic distress. Salinas's blatant corruption and failed economic programs left his successor, Ernesto Zedillo, with a 40% currency devaluation just weeks after taking office, followed by a bank bailout of more than $90 billion.

Zedillo's prudent economic policies slowly got the country back on track. And his handling of the opposition party's triumph in the 2000 presidential election—after 71 years of uninterrupted PRI rule—kept Mexico from erupting into political and economic chaos.

Today Mexico fluctuates between the largest and second-largest economy—and consistently has the highest per-capita income—in Latin America. Conversely, the unemployment rate, 3.7% at this writing, is the lowest in Latin America. In 2005 Mexico's inflation rate was 3.3%, the lowest in 36 years.

It's not all highs and glory, however. The 490,000 new jobs created during President Fox's administration is about one-tenth of what's needed to keep the country employed. Millions of Mexicans—including a significant number from Jalisco State—work illegally in the United States, where they might easily earn 10 times or more the minimum wage of their own country, which is less than US$5 a day. According to a July 2005 article in *The San Diego-Union Tribune,* remittances from these workers are Mexico's second-largest source of income, after oil. Nearly $20 billion is estimated to have been wired south of the border in 2005.

Another of Mexico's leading industries is tourism. Nearly 22 million international visitors came to Mexico in 2005, a 6.5% increase over the previous year. According to SECTUR, Mexico's Tourism Secretariat, these visitors left behind $11.8 billion in revenue, compared to $10.84 billion in 2004 and $9.46 billion in 2003. Hotel occupancy and the number of cruise-ship passengers continues to rise as well.

Tourism is the largest sector of Vallarta's economy, and Puerto Vallarta's tourism stats continue to climb. The cruise-ship terminal is being expanded, and the number of hotel rooms in Puerto Vallarta and Nayarit is rapidly increasing.

PEOPLE & SOCIETY

Ethnic Groups

The population of Puerto Vallarta is overwhelmingly of mixed native American and Spanish descent. According to the 2000 census, fewer than 1% of Jalisco residents speak an indigenous language. Compare that to nearby states: Michoacán with 3.6%, Guerrero with about 14% and Oaxaca, where more than a third of the inhabitants converse in a native language. Those indigenous people who do live in Jalisco State are small groups of Purépecha (also called Tarascans), in the south. The Purépecha were among the very few groups not conquered by the powerful Aztec nation that controlled much of Mesoamerica at the time of the Spanish conquest.

Although not large in number, the indigenous groups most associated with Nayarit and Jalisco states are the Cora and their relatives, the Huichol. Isolated in mountain and valley hamlets and individual *rancherías* (tiny farms) deep in the Sierra Madre, both have maintained to a large extent their own customs and culture. According to the CDI (Comisión Nacional Para el Desarrollo de los Pueblos Indígenas, or National Commission for the Development of Native Peoples), there are about 24,390 Cora in Durango, Zacatecas, and Nayarit states, and some 43,929 Huichol, mainly in Jalisco and Nayarit. Nearly 70% of the culturally related groups speak their native language and about half of the households have electricity.

In 1947 a group of prominent vallartenses was returning along twisty mountain roads from an excursion to Mexico City. When the driver lost control and the open-sided bus plunged toward the abyss, death seemed certain. But a large rock halted the bus's progress, and *"Los Favorecidos"* ("The Lucky Ones"), as they came to be known, returned to Puerto Vallarta virtually unharmed. Their untrammeled gestures of thanks to the town's patron saint, the Virgin of Guadalupe, set the precedent for this animated religious procession.

Today, all Puerto Vallartans consider themselves to be Los Favorecidos, and thus universally blessed. This optimism and good cheer are two vital components of the local persona. For those of us fortunate enough to visit—for a short vacation or half a year—that angelic magnetism is a big part of the pull.

Religion

Mexico is about 89% Catholic; Puerto Vallarta is 90% Catholic. The Catholic population is overwhelmingly dedicated to the Virgin of Guadalupe, the patron saint of Puerto Vallarta, and of Mexico. Most of the non-Catholic 10% of the population have been converted in the last 50 years to Protestant and Evangelical Christianity.

Despite its strong religious character, Mexico has strict anticlerical laws inaugurated by president Benito Juárez and codified in the 1917 Constitution, which still governs the country. Dozens of laws limit religious participation in civil life. A church wedding is not recognized, churches and church land are public property, and Mass may not be held in public. Ministers, priests, and nuns may not vote or wear their vestments in public.

It's no surprise that these and other strict laws outraged the Church and devout Catholics when the Constitution was ratified. The ensuing Cristero Revolt (1926–29) led to tens of thousands of deaths and the assassination of then-President Alvaro Obregón by a religious fanatic. The headquarters for the revolt was staunchly Catholic and traditionalist Guadalajara, the capital of Jalisco State.

Many of the religious laws are not strictly enforced, however. No one dared to deny charismatic John Paul II the right to hold open-air Masses when the hugely popular pope visited in the 1980s and '90s. And because of the need, foreign priests are permitted to work in Mexico despite a law that bans this.

Family, friends, and having a good time are central to Mexican life, and the Catholic liturgical calendar obliges with many excuses to party. In Puerto Vallarta the biggest fiesta of the year honors the Virgin of Guadalupe. Consecutive visions of *la virgen morena* (the dark-skinned virgin), as she is affectionately called, are said to have appeared to Juan Diego, a Chichimec peasant, soon after the Spanish conquest of Mexico. Asked by a bishop to provide proof of the Lady's visit (on Tepeyac Hill, north of present-day Mexico City), Juan Diego is said to have collected in his cloak a shower of roses that the apparition provided. During transport, however, the bundle of roses disappeared to be replaced by an image of the saint herself. Report of the supposed miracle greatly helped the invaders to convert the pantheistic native population.

The bishop, the Pope, and soon the majority of Mexicans were convinced of the miracle. The cloak, with the image still clearly visible, hangs above the altar in one of several important churches built at Tepeyac Hill, now called La Villa de Guadalupe. The site of the Virgin's reported 1531 visit was near a temple to the Aztec earth goddess Tonantzín.

The Feast Day of the Virgin of Guadalupe is Puerto Vallarta's most important religious holiday. During the weeks leading to the Mass held in her honor on December 12, area congregations, civic leaders, and businesses—including restaurants and hotels—join in colorful processions from their place of business to the downtown cathedral.

Dress

In deference to the tropical heat, vallartenses dress comfortably and casually, yet not indifferently. Young girls wear the latest fashions, with bellies—of all shapes and sizes—bared, while matrons favor comfortable, cool shifts and skirts. Men wear suits (with or without ties) or slacks and guayaberas. Businesswomen wear suits or classy outfits, panty hose, and high heels with elegant aplomb, always managing to look cool and crisp, while their north-of-the-border counterparts sport red faces, swollen ankles . . . and swoon at the mere mention of pantyhose.

Mexican men don't walk around shirtless except at the beach or pool, and women don a cover-up at least. While increasingly stylish and modern, Mexicans tend to dress modestly. It's only in the last generation or two that women have felt comfortable wearing bathing suits, and many—especially older women from smaller towns—still swim in shorts and T-shirts.

In downtown PV, cobblestone streets make walking in heels difficult, although Mexican women seem to pull it off. The addition of potholes and uneven sidewalks make sensible walking shoes or sandals preferable for most occasions. Popular on PV streets is the comfortable women's "San Miguel shoe," which comes in many styles and colors.

Etiquette

Mexicans are extremely polite people. The proverb "You catch more flies with honey than with vinegar" might have been invented here. Mexicans wait to be invited into a home, even by relatives. Business meetings begin with small talk and inquiries about family and mutual friends. Even phone conversations take a while to get to the point.

Ask a business acquaintance the name of the person who will be leading a meeting, and he might respond *"Su servidor"* (Your servant), referring to himself. Business letters often conclude "I remain your faithful servant."

Some of these formulaic phrases should be taken with a big grain of sea salt. When talking about his home, a Puerto Vallartan might say *"Your* home (meaning *his* home) is at 333 Juárez Street." This form of *"mi casa es su casa"* can be used equally with a great friend or a first-time acquaintance.

Resist the impulse to pay an unsolicited visit. Unspecific invitations to "come visit some time," which are, in most cases, made just to be polite, should be ignored unless a summons to a specific event is made.

Even when extremely annoyed or angry, Mexicans tend to maintain calm and decorum, using hyperbole or veiled sarcasm to display their displeasure. Foreign travelers throwing tantrums because of late tour buses or poor service must seem like creatures from another planet to Mexicans, who would usually endure most any inconvenience rather than create a scene.

This tendency of Mexicans to keep their thoughts to themselves can lead to frustration and confusion for foreigners. "When will the bus come?" a traveler might inquire regarding a bus that is 15 minutes late. *"Ahorita viene"* is the tour leader's inevitable answer. While the literal translation of this phrase is "It will be right here," the meaning in its cultural context is something like: "It will get here when it gets here. I have no control over the matter, but certainly cannot tell you that." Mexicans are experts at reading—and speaking—between the lines.

Language

The Mexican lexicon is full of examples of exceeding reticence and politeness. Some of these phrases leave other Spanish speakers rolling their eyes or rolling in the aisles with mirth. For example, instead of saying *"¿Cómo?"* ("What?") when something is not heard or understood, Mexicans say *"¿Mande?"*, an extremely old-fashioned, formal command meaning "Order me."

Most Mexicans use the terms *"Me da vergüenza"* and *"Me da pena"* interchangeably. To a Spaniard, the former means "I am embarrassed" or "I am ashamed"; the latter, "I'm in pain" or "It hurts me."

Another idiosyncrasy of Mexican Spanish is the use of the diminutive suffix *"–ita."* In Spain this word ending is mainly used to indicate a thing's small size or delicate

nature. In Mexico, this add-on is so common that words without it seem almost brusque, rude, or indicating lack of love or concern. Few people call their grandmother *abuela,* for example: *abuelita* (dear or little grandmother) is almost universal. One might ask for a *cervecita* instead of a *cerveza* to convey the desire not to impose on another person or put them out. A tour guide mentions that *propinitas* (small tips) are accepted when she is actually hoping for a big, fat tip. It's just another example of the national obsession with dancing delicately around life's baser truths and demands.

In his epic examination of the Mexican national character, *The Labyrinth of Solitude,* Nobel prize winning essayist Octavio Paz describes the Mexican like this: "His language is full of reticences, of metaphors and allusions, of unfinished phrases, while his silence is full of tints, folds, thunderheads, sudden rainbows, indecipherable threats." Which demonstrates that while the national tendency might be toward disguising true meanings, Mexican speech can be brilliant and filled with imagery.

The Magic of Mexico

To say that Mexico is a magical place means more than it's a place of great natural beauty and fabulous experiences. Cities like Catemaco, in Veracruz, have a reputation for their *brujos* and *brujas* (male and female witches, respectively) and herbal healers (*curanderos/ curanderas*). But Mexicans use these services even in modern Mexico City and Guadalajara, and tourist towns like Puerto Vallarta, although they don't always advertise it. Some might resort to using a curandera to reverse *mal de ojo,* the evil eye, thought to be responsible for a range of unpleasant symptoms, circumstances, disease, or even death.

A *limpia,* or cleansing, is the traditional cure for the evil eye. The healer usually passes a raw chicken or turkey egg over the sufferer to draw out the bad spirit. Green plants like basil, or branches from certain trees can also be used, drawing the greenery over the head, front, and back to decontaminate the victim. Prayer is an essential ingredient.

Some cures are of a more practical nature. Mexican herbalists, like their colleagues around the world, use tree bark, nuts, berries, roots, and leaves to treat everything from dandruff to cancer. Epazote, or wormseed, is a distinctly flavored plant whose leaves are used in cooking. As its English name implies, its medicinal task is to treat parasites.

Most folk wisdom seems to draw from both fact and, if not fiction, at least superstition. Breezes and winds are thought to produce a host of negative reactions: from colds and cramps to far more drastic ailments like paralysis. Some people prefer sweating in a car or bus to rolling down the window and being hit by the wind, especially since mixing hot and cold is something else to be avoided. Even worldly athletes may refuse a cold drink after a hot run. Sudden shock is thought by some to cause lasting problems.

Although it doesn't take a leap of faith to believe that herbal remedies cure disease and grandma's advice was right on, some of the stuff sold in shops is a bit "harder to swallow." It's difficult to imagine, for example, that the sky-blue potion in a pint-size bottle will bring you good luck, or the lilac-color one can stop people from gossiping about you. Those that double as floor polish seem especially suspect.

Whether magic and prophesy are real or imagined, they sometimes have concrete results. Spanish conquistador Hernán Cortés arrived on the east coast of present-day Mexico in 1519, which correlated to the year "One Reed" of the Aztec calendar. A few centuries prior to Cortés's arrival, the benevolent god-king Quetzalcoatl had, according to legend, departed the same coast on a raft of snakes, vowing to return in the year One Reed to reclaim his throne.

News of Cortés—a metal-wearing godman accompanied by strange creatures (horses and dogs) and carrying lightning (cannons and firearms)—traveled quickly to the Aztec capital. The Emperor Moctezuma was nervous about Quetzalcoatl's return and his reaction to the culture of war and sacrifice the Aztecs had created. In his desire to placate the returning god, Moctezuma ignored the advice of trusted advisers and literally opened the door for the complete destruction of the Aztec empire.

Machismo & La Malinche

Mexican machismo is a complicated concept fit for entire books of study. It's more than *piropos* (flirtatious or suggestive, and sometimes poetic, comments) or drinking beer for days at a time with the boys. According to essayist Octavio Paz (1914–98), the Mexican's machismo is in fact defensive rather than offensive: a kind of immunity to being hurt or humiliated by the outside world. Several great thinkers, including Paz, have suggested that this stoicism dates back to the Spanish conquest. Taking indigenous women as slaves or concubines, Spanish invaders left the girls' and women's husbands, fathers, and brothers outraged, yet powerless to intervene.

According to this psychological scenario, Mexican men take lovers in order to reject their wives before being snubbed themselves. Scorned and humiliated by her husband, a woman may then lavish her love and attention on her sons, who idolize their perfect mothers but grow up to emulate their fathers, perpetuating the cycle.

If the icon of the perfect woman is the Virgin Mary, the faithless woman who epitomizes female perfidy is La Malinche. Born Malinztín and christened Doña Marina by the Spanish, La Malinche was a real woman who played a fascinating role in the conquest of Mexico. As a young woman of possibly noble birth, Malinztín was sold into slavery and later given as a gift to the Spanish. She became a valued interpreter for Hernán Cortés thanks to her ability to speak three languages: her native Mayan tongue; Nahuatl, language of the Aztecs; and (later) Spanish. Her keen mind helped the Spanish strategize; as Cortés's mistress, she bore a son. Although it was her own people who originally sold her into slavery, La Malinche has become the national symbol for female infidelity and betrayal.

La Vida Loca

Living the good life in Mexico—specifically in and around Banderas Bay—seems to get easier year by year, but it's getting pricey as well. Americans and Canadians are by far the biggest groups of expats. In addition to those who have relocated to make Mexico their home, many more foreigners have part-time retirement or vacation homes here. Those who realized their dreams of moving to Mexico a decade or more ago are sitting pretty, as the cost of land and houses soars. A two-bedroom property in a gated community by the sea begins at around $350,000, and the cost is climbing. You could get more modest digs for several times less; at the upper end of the spectrum, the sky's the limit. Construction prices keep up, too, as builders realize how deep are the pockets of foreign investors.

The sheer number of foreigners living in Puerto Vallarta facilitates adventures that were much more taxing a decade or two ago, like building a home or finding an English-speaking realtor or lawyer. Contractors and shopkeepers are used to dealing with gringos; most speak good to excellent English. The town is rich with English-language publications and opportunities for foreigners to meet up for events or volunteer work.

THE NATURAL WORLD

Geography

On the same latitude as the Hawaiian Islands, Puerto Vallarta sits at the center point of C-shape Banderas Bay. Spurs from the Sierra Cacoma run down to the sea, forming a landscape of numerous valleys. This highly fractured mountain range is just one of many smaller ranges within the Sierra Madre—which runs south from the Rockies to South America. Sierra Cacoma sits at the juncture of several major systems: Sierra Madre Occidental and the Sierra Madre del Sur, which heads south toward Oaxaca State. Forming a distinct but related system is the volcanic or transversal volcanic axis that runs east to west across the country—and the globe. Comprising part of the so-called Ring of Fire, this transverse chain of mountains includes some of the world's most active volcanoes. Both Volcán de Fuego, southeast of Puerto Vallarta in Colima State, and the giant Popocateptl, near the Gulf of Mexico, are currently active. Visible from Puerto Vallarta are the more intimate Sierra Vallejo and the Sierra Caule ranges, to the north and south respectively.

Heading down to the sea from these abrupt and beautiful highlands are a number of important rivers, including the Ameca and the Mascota, which join forces not far from the coast at a place appropriately called Las Juntas (the joining). The Ameca is a large river whose mouth forms the boundary between Jalisco and Nayarit states. The valley floor is naturally boggy in some areas, but suitable for growing corn, sugarcane, and other crops elsewhere. The Cuale River empties into the ocean at Puerto Vallarta, dividing the city center in two. In addition to many rivers the area is blessed with seasonal and permanent streams and springs.

Banderas Bay, or Bahía de Banderas, is Mexico's largest bay, at 42 km (26 mi) tip to tip. The northern point, Punta de Mita, is in Nayarit state. Towns at the southern extreme of the bay, at Cabo Corrientes, are accessible only by boat or dirt roads. Cabo Corrientes (Cape Current) is named for the frequently strong offshore currents.The mountains backing the Costalegre are part of the Sierra Madre del Sur range. The hilly region of eroded plains has two main river systems: the San Nicolás and Cuitzmala.

Several hundred miles directly east of Banderas Bay, Guadalajara—capital of Jalisco State—occupies the west end of 5,400-foot Atemajac Valley, which is surrounded by mountains. Just south of Guadalajara, Lake Chapala is Mexico's largest natural lake. It is fed by the Lerma—Santiago system, which, crossing the mountains, feed other rivers and streams that eventually empty into the Pacific.

Flora

The western flanks of the Sierra Madre and foothills leading down to the sea are characterized by tropical deciduous forest. At the higher levels are expanses of pine-oak forest. Many species of pines thrive in these woods, mixed in with *encinos* and *robles,* two different categories of oak; within each are many separate species. Walnut trees and oyamel, a type of fir, are the mainstays of the lower arroyos, or river basins. Along the coastal fringe magnificent *huanacaxtle,* also called *parota* (in English, monkey pod or elephant ear tree), mingle with equally huge and impressive mango as well as kapok, cedar, tropical almond, tamarind, flamboyant, and willow. The brazilwood tree is resistant to insects and therefore ideal for making furniture. *Matapalo,* or strangler fig, are common in this landscape. As its name hints, these fast-growing trees embrace others in a death grip; once the matopalo is established, the host tree eventually dies.

Colima palms, known locally as *guaycoyul,* produce small round nuts smashed for oil or sometimes fed to domestic animals. Mango, avocado, citrus, and guava are found in the wild; these and a huge number of cultivated crops thrive in the region. Imported trees and bushes often seen surrounding homes and small farms include Indian laurel, bamboo, and bougainvillea.

The coastal fringe north of San Blas (in Nayarit) is surprisingly characterized by savannahs. Guinea grass makes fine animal fodder for horses and cows. Lanky coconut trees line roads and beaches. These have many uses and are sometimes planted in groves. The watery "milk" is a refreshing drink, and the meat of the coconut, although high in saturated fat, can be eaten or used in many types of candy. Another drink, *agua da tuba,* is made from the heart of the palm; the trunk is used in certain types of construction. Mangroves thrive in saltwater estuaries, providing an ecosystem for crabs and crustaceans as well as migratory and local birds.

South of Banderas Bay, thorn forest predominates along the coastal strip, backed by tropical deciduous forest. Leguminous trees like the tabachin, with its bright orange flowers, have long dangling seed pods used by indigenous people as rattles. Other prominent area residents are the acacias, hardy trees with fluffy puff-balls of light yellow blooms. Many species of cactus thrive in the dry forest, which is home to more than 1,100 species of vascular plants. The *nopal,* or prickly pear cactus abounds; local people remove the spines of the cactus pads and grill them, or use them in healthful salads. The fruit of the prickly pear, called *tuna,* is used to make a refreshing drink, *agua de tuna.* In this region, especially around Chamela and Cuixmala, about 16% of the plant species are endemic.

Fauna

Mammals in the area are few. Hunting, deforestation, and the encroachment of humans have diminished many once-abundant species. In the mountains far from humankind, endangered margay, jaguar, and ocelot hunt their prey, which includes spider monkeys, deer, and pec-

caries. More commonly seen in a wide range of habitats are skunks, raccoons, rabbits, and coyote. The coatimundi is an endearing little animal that lives in family groups, often near streambeds. Inquisitive and alert, they resemble tall, slender prairie dogs. Along with tanklike, slow-moving armadillo, the sandy-brown coatimundi is among the animals you're most likely to spot without venturing too deep within the forest. Local people call the coatimundi both *tejón* and *pisote,* and often keep them as pets.

Poisonous snakes in the area include the Mexican rattlesnake and the fer-de-lance. Locals call the latter *cuatro narices* (four noses) because it appears to have four nostrils. It's also called *nauyaca;* the bite of this viper can be deadly. There are more than a dozen species of coral snakes with bands of black, yellow, and red in different patterns. False corals imitate this color scheme to fool their predators, but unless you're an expert in the subject, it's probably best not to try to figure out which is which.

Of interest to most visitors are the region's birds and sea creatures both resident and migratory. The most famous of the migratory marine species is the humpback whale for which Banderas Bay was once named. Called *ballena jorobada,* or "hunchback" whale, these leviathans grow to 17 meters (51 feet) and weigh 40 to 50 tons and travel in pods, feeding on krill and tiny fish. During a given year the females in area waters may be either mating or giving birth. During their amazing annual migration of thousands of miles from the Bering Sea, the hardy creatures may lose some 10,000 pounds. Hunted nearly to extinction in the 1900s, humpbacks remain an endangered species.

A few Bryde whales make their way to Banderas Bay and other protected waters near the end of the humpback season, as do some killer whales (orca) and false killer whales. Bottlenose, spinner, and pantropic spotted dolphins are present pretty much year-round. These acrobats love to bow surf just under the water's surface and to leap into the air. Another spectacular leaper is the velvety-black manta ray, which can grow to 9 meters (30 feet) wide. Shy but lovely spotted eagle rays hover close to the ocean floor, where they feed on crustaceans and mollusks. Nutrient-rich Pacific waters provide sustenance for a wide range of other sea creatures as well. Among the most eye-catching are the graceful king angelfish and the iridescent bumphead parrotfish, striped Indo-Pacific sargeants and Moorish idols, and the funny-looking guinea fowl puffer and its close relative, the equally unusual black-blotched porcupine fish.

The varied landscape of Nayarit and Jalisco states provides a tapestry of habitats—shoreline, rivers, marshes, lagoons, and mangroves—for some 350 species of birds. In the mangroves, standouts are the great blue heron, mangrove cuckoo, and vireo. Ocean and shore birds include red-billed tropic birds as well as various species of heron, egret, gulls, and frigatebirds. Military macaws patrol the thorn forests and songbirds of all stripes live in the pine-oak forests. About 40% of the birds in the Costalegre region are migratory. Among the residents are the yellow-headed parrot and the Mexican wood nymph, both threatened species.

Environmental Issues

The biggest threat to the region is deforestation of the tropical dry forest. Slash-and-burn techniques are used to prepare virgin forest for agriculture and pasturing of animals. Like tropical forest everywhere, this practice has a very harmful and nonproductive effect, as the thin soil fails to produce after the mulch-producing trees and shrubs have been stripped.

Although the tropical dry forest (also called tropical thorn forest) has only been easily accessible to settlement since a coast highway opened in 1972, they are now being deforested due to the increasing tourism and human population. Controlled ecotourism offers a potential solution, although failed projects in the area have significantly altered or drained salt marshes and mangrove swamps.

Like similar ecosystems along Mexico's Pacific coast from southern Sonora to Chiapas, the dry forest is an extremely important ecosystem. It represents one of the richest in Mexico and also one with the highest level of endemism (plant and animal species found nowhere else). Several species of hardwood trees, including the Pacific coast mahogany and Mexican kingwood, are being over-harvested for use in the building trade. The former is endangered and the latter, threatened.

South of Puerto Vallarta in the Costalegre are two adjacent forest reserves that together form the 32,617-acre **Chamela–Cuixmala Biosphere Reserve.** Co-owned and managed by nonprofit agencies, private companies, and Mexico's National University, UNAM, the reserve protects nine major vegetation types, including the tropical dry forest, tropical deciduous, and semi-deciduous forests. A riparian environment is associated with the north bank of the Cuixmala River. Within the reserve there are approximately 72 species considered at risk for extinction including the American crocodile and several species of sea turtles.

Hojonay Biosphere Reserve was established by the Hojonay nonprofit organization to preserve the jaguar of the Sierra de Vallejo range and its habitat. The 157,060-acre reserve is in the foothills and mountains behind La Cruz de Huanacaxtle and San Francisco, in Nayarit State. At the present time there are no tours or casual access to either reserve, which serve as a buffer against development and a refuge for wildlife.

BOOKS & MOVIES

Books

Those interested in Mexican culture and society have a wealth of books from which to choose. *The Mexicans: A Personal Portrait of a People,* by Patrick Oster, is a brilliant nonfiction study of Mexican persona and personality. Like Patrick Oster, Alan Riding, author of *Distant Neighbors: A Portrait of the Mexicans,* was a journalist for many years in Mexico City whose insight, investigative journalism skills, and cogent writing skills produced an insightful look into the Mexican mind and culture.

Written by poet, essayist, and statesman Octavio Paz, *The Labyrinth of Solitude,* is classic, required reading for those who love Mexico or want to know it better. *The True Story of the Conquest of Mexico,* by Bernal Diaz de Castillo, is a fascinating account of the conquest by one of Cortés's own soldiers.

There are few recommended books specifically about Puerto Vallarta. These are available mainly in PV. *La Magia de Puerto Vallarta,* by Marilú Suárez–Murias, is a bilingual (English and Spanish) coffee-table book discussing beaches, history, people, and places of Puerto Vallarta. The information is interesting, but the photographs are terribly grainy. For a light-hearted look at life in PV through the eyes of an expat read *Puerto Vallarta on 49 Brain Cells a Day* and *Refried Brains,* both by Gil Gevins. Those interested in Huichol art and culture might read *People of the Peyote: Huichol Indian History, Religion and Survival,* by Stacy Shaefer and Peter Furst. If you can get past the first couple chapters, it's smoother sailing. Also by Stacy Shaefer is *To Think With a Good Heart: Wixarica Women, Weavers and Shamans.*

Movies

Night of the Iguana (1964), directed by John Huston, is the movie that alerted the world to Puerto Vallarta's existence. Set on the beach and bluffs of Mismaloya, the haunting movie with the jungle-beat soundtrack combines great directing with an excellent cast: Richard Burton as a cast-out preacher-turned-tour guide, Sue Lyons and Deborah Kerr as his clients, and Ava Gardner as the sexy but lonely proprietress of the group's idyllic Mexican getaway. There's no better mood-setter for a trip to Vallarta.

Like Water for Chocolate (Como Agua Para Chocolate) (1992) is a magic-realism glance into rural Mexico during the Mexican Revolution. This visual banquet will make your mouth water for the rose-petal quail and other recipes that the female lead, Tita, prepares. It's based on the novel of the same name by Laura Esquivel, which is equally wonderful. Academy Award winner *Treasure of the Sierra Madre* (1948), with Humphrey Bogart, is a classic with great mountain scenery. For more fantastic scenery and a great town fiesta, see *The Magnificent Seven,* (1960) starring Yul Brenner and Eli Wallach. Set in Mexico City with Pierce Bronson as a failing hit man, *The Matador* (2005) has some good scenes of the Camino Real in Mexico City, a great bullfighting sequence, and is a good drama.

SPANISH VOCABULARY

	English	Spanish	Pronunciation

Basics

Yes/no	Sí/no	see/no
Please	Por favor	pore fah-*vore*
May I?	¿Me permite?	may pair-*mee*-tay
Thank you (very much)	(Muchas) gracias	(*moo*-chas) grah-see-as
You're welcome	De nada	day *nah*-dah
Excuse me	Con permiso	con pair-*mee*-so
Pardon me/what did you say?	¿Como?/Mánde?	ko-mo/mahn-dey
Could you tell me?	¿Podría decirme?	po-*dree*-ah deh-*seer*-meh
I'm sorry	Lo siento	lo see-*en*-toe
Hello	Hola	*oh*-lah
Good morning!	¡Buenos días!	*bway*-nohs *dee*-ahs
Good afternoon!	¡Buenas tardes!	*bway*-nahs *tar*-dess
Good evening!	¡Buenas noches!	*bway*-nahs *no*-chess
Goodbye!	¡Adiós!/¡Hasta luego!	ah-dee-*ohss*/ ah-stah-*lwe*-go
Mr./Mrs.	Señor/Señora	sen-*yor*/sen-*yore*-ah
Miss	Señorita	sen-yo-*ree*-tah
Pleased to meet you	Mucho gusto	*moo*-cho *goose*-to
How are you?	¿Cómo está usted?	*ko*-mo es-*tah* oo-*sted*
Very well, thank you.	Muy bien, gracias.	*moo*-ee bee-en, grah-see-as
And you?	¿Y usted?	ee oos-*ted*
Hello (on the telephone)	Bueno	*bwen*-oh
I DON'T UNDERSTAND	*NO ENTIEDO*	*NO-EN-TEE-EN-DOE*

Numbers

1	un, uno	oon, *oo*-no
2	dos	dos
3	tres	trace
4	cuatro	*kwah*-tro
5	cinco	*sink*-oh
6	seis	sace
7	siete	see-*et*-ey
8	ocho	*o*-cho

9	nueve	new-*ev*-ay
10	diez	dee-*es*
11	once	*own*-sey
12	doce	*doe*-sey
13	trece	*tray*-sey
14	catorce	kah-*tor*-sey
15	quince	*keen*-sey
16	dieciséis	dee-es-ee-*sace*
17	diecisiete	dee-*es*-ee-see-*et*-ay
18	dieciocho	dee-*es*-ee-*o*-cho
19	diecinueve	*dee*-*es*-ee-new-*ev*-ay
20	veinte	*bain*-tay
21	veinte y uno/ veintiuno	*bain*-te-oo-no
30	treinta	*train*-tah
32	treinta y dos	train-tay-*dose*
40	cuarenta	kwah-*ren*-tah
43	cuarenta y tres	kwah-*ren*-tay-*trace*
50	cincuenta	seen-*kwen*-tah
54	cincuenta y cuatro	seen-*kwen*-tay *kwah*-tro
60	sesenta	sess-*en*-tah
65	sesenta y cinco	sess-*en*-tay *seen*-ko
70	setenta	set-*en*-tah
76	setenta y seis	set-*en*-tay *sace*
80	ochenta	oh-*chen*-tah
87	ochenta y siete	oh-*chen*-tay see-*yet*-ay
90	noventa	no-*ven*-tah
98	noventa y ocho	no-*ven*-tah *o*-cho
100	cien	see-*en*
101	ciento uno	see-en-toe *oo*-no
200	doscientos	doe-see-*en*-tohss
500	quinientos	keen-*yen*-tohss
700	setecientos	set-eh-see-*en*-tohss
900	novecientos	no-veh-see-*en*-tohss
1,000	mil	meel
2,000	dos mil	dose meel
1,000,000	un millón	oon meel-*yohn*

Colors

black	negro	*neh*-grow
blue	azul	ah-*sool*
brown	café	kah-*feh*
green	verde	*vair*-day
pink	rosa	*ro*-sah
purple	morado	mo-*rah*-doe
orange	naranja	na-*rahn*-hah
red	rojo	*roe*-hoe
white	blanco	*blahn*-koh
yellow	amarillo	ah-mah-*ree*-yoh

Days of the Week

Sunday	domingo	doe-*meen*-goh
Monday	lunes	*loo*-ness
Tuesday	martes	*mahr*-tess
Wednesday	miércoles	me-*air*-koh-less
Thursday	jueves	who-*ev*-ess
Friday	viernes	vee-*air*-ness
Saturday	sábado	*sah*-bah-doe

Months

January	enero	eh-*neh*-ro
February	febrero	feh-*brair*-oh
March	marzo	*mahr*-so
April	abril	ah-*breel*
May	mayo	*my*-oh
June	junio	*hoo*-nee-oh
July	julio	*who*-lee-yoh
August	agosto	ah-*ghost*-toe
September	septiembre	sep-tee-*em*-breh
October	octubre	oak-*too*-breh
November	noviembre	no-vee-*em*-breh
December	diciembre	dee-see-*em*-breh

Useful Phrases

Do you speak English?	¿Habla usted inglés?	*ah*-blah oos-*ted* in-*glehs*
I don't speak Spanish	No hablo español	no *ah*-blow es-pahn-*yol*

I don't understand (you)	No entiendo	no en-tee-*en*-doe
I understand (you)	Entiendo	en-tee-*en*-doe
I don't know	No sé	no *say*
I am from the United States/ British	Soy de los Estados Unidos/ inglés(a)	soy deh lohs ehs-*tah*-dohs oo-*nee*-dohs/ in-*glace*(ah)
What's your name?	¿Cómo se llama usted?	*koh*-mo say *yah*-mah oos-*ted*
My name is . . .	Me llamo . . .	may *yah*-moh
What time is it?	¿Qué hora es?	keh *o*-rah es
It is one, two, three . . . o'clock.	Es la una; son las dos, tres	es la *oo*-nah/sone lahs dose, trace
How?	¿Cómo?	*koh*-mo
When?	¿Cuándo?	*kwahn*-doe
This/Next week	Esta semana/ la semana que entra	*es*-tah seh-*mah*-nah/ lah say-*mah*-nah keh *en*-trah
This/Next month	Este mes/el próximo mes	*es*-tay mehs/el *proke*-see-mo mehs
This/Next year	Este año/el año que viene	*es*-tay *ahn*-yo/el *ahn*-yo keh vee-*yen*-ay
Yesterday/today/ tomorrow	Ayer/hoy/mañana	ah-*yair*/oy/mahn-*yah*-nah
This morning/ afternoon	Esta mañana/tarde	*es*-tah mahn-*yah*-nah/*tar*-day
Tonight	Esta noche	*es*-tah *no*-cheh
What?	¿Qué?	keh
What is this?	¿Qué es esto?	keh es *es*-toe
Why?	¿Por qué?	pore *keh*
Who?	¿Quién?	kee-*yen*
Where is . . . ?	¿Dónde está . . . ?	*dohn*-day es-*tah*
the train station?	la estación del tren?	la es-tah-see-*on* del *train*
the subway station?	la estación del Metro?	la es-ta-see-*on* del *meh*-tro
the bus stop?	la parada del autobús?	la pah-*rah*-dah del oh-toe-*boos*
the bank?	el banco?	el *bahn*-koh
the ATM?	el cajero automática?	el *kah*-hehr-oh oh-toe-*mah*-tee-kah
the . . . hotel?	el hotel . . . ?	el oh-*tel*
the store?	la tienda . . . ?	la tee-*en*-dah
the cashier?	la caja?	la *kah*-hah

the . . . museum?	el museo . . . ?	el moo-*seh*-oh
the hospital?	el hospital?	el ohss-pea-*tal*
the elevator?	el ascensor?	el ah-*sen*-sore
the bathroom?	el baño?	el *bahn*-yoh
Here/there	Aquí/allá	ah-*key*/ah-*yah*
Open/closed	Abierto/cerrado	ah-be-*er*-toe/ser-*ah*-doe
Left/right	Izquierda/derecha	iss-key-*er*-dah/dare-*eh*-chah
Straight ahead	Derecho	der-*eh*-choh
Is it near/far?	¿Está cerca/lejos?	es-*tah* sair-kah/*leh*-hoss
I'd like . . .	Quisiera . . .	kee-see-air-ah
a room	un cuarto/una habitación	oon *kwahr*-toe/*oo*-nah ah-bee-tah-see-*on*
the key	la llave	lah *yah*-vay
a newspaper	un periódico	oon pear-ee-*oh*-dee-koh
I'd like to buy . . .	Quisiera comprar . . .	kee-see-*air*-ah kohm-*prahr*
cigarettes	cigarrillo	ce-gar-*reel*-oh
matches	cerillos	ser-*ee*-ohs
a dictionary	un diccionario	oon deek-see-oh-*nah*-ree-oh
soap	jabón	hah-*bone*
a map	un mapa	oon *mah*-pah
a magazine	una revista	*oon*-ah reh-*veess*-tah
paper	papel	pah-*pel*
envelopes	sobres	*so*-brace
a postcard	una tarjeta postal	*oon*-ah tar-*het*-ah post-*ahl*
How much is it?	¿Cuánto cuesta?	*kwahn*-toe *kwes*-tah
Do you accept credit cards?	¿Aceptan tarjetas de crédito?	ah-*sehp*-than tahr-*heh*-tahs deh *creh*-dee-toh?
A little/a lot	Un poquito/mucho . . .	oon poh-*kee*-toe/*moo*-choh
More/less	Más/menos	mahss/*men*-ohss
Enough/too much/too little	Suficiente/demasiado/muy poco	soo-fee-see-*en*-tay/day-mah-see-*ah*-doe/moo-ee *poh*-koh
Telephone	Teléfono	tel-*ef*-oh-no
Telegram	Telegrama	teh-leh-*grah*-mah
I am ill/sick	Estoy enfermo(a)	es-*toy* en-*fair*-moh(ah)

Please call a doctor	Por favor llame un médico	pore fa-*vor ya*-may oon *med*-ee-koh
Help!	¡Auxilio! ¡Ayuda!	owk-*see*-lee-oh/ ah-*yoo*-dah
Fire!	¡Encendio!	en-*sen*-dee-oo
Caution!/Look out!	¡Cuidado!	kwee-*dah*-doh

On the Road

Highway	Carretera	car-ray-*ter*-ah
Causeway, paved highway	Calzada	cal-*za*-dah
Speed bump	Tope	*toh*-pay
Toll highway	Carretera de cuota	car-ray-*ter*-ha day dwoh-tah
Toll booth	Caseta	kah-*set*-ah
Route	Ruta	*roo*-tah
Road	Camino	cah-*mee*-no
Street	Calle	*cah*-yeh
Avenue	Avenida	ah-ven-*ee*-dah
Broad, tree-lined boulevard	Paseo	pah-*seh*-oh
Waterfront promenade	Malecón	mal-lay-*cone*
Wharf	Embarcadero	em-bar-cah-*day*-ro

In Town

Church	Templo/Iglesia	*tem*-plo/e-*gles*-se-*ah*
Cathedral	Catedral	cah-tay-*dral*
Neighborhood	Barrio	*bar*-re-o
Foreign exchange shop	Casa de cambio	*cas*-sah day *cam*-be-o
City hall	Ayuntamiento	ah-yoon-tah-mee *en*-toe
Main square	Zócalo	*zo*-cal-o
Traffic circle	Glorieta	glor-e-*ay*-tah
Market	Mercado (Spanish)/ Tianguis (Indian)	mer-*cah*-doe/ tee-*an*-geese
Inn	Posada	pos-*sah*-dah
Group taxi	Colectivo	co-lec-*tee*-vo
Mini-bus along fixed route	Pesero	pi-*seh*-ro

Dining Out

I'd like to reserve a table	Quisiera reservar una mesa.	kee-*syeh*-rah rreh-sehr-*vahr* oo-nah *meh*-sah
A bottle of . . .	Una botella de . . .	oo-nah bo-*tay*-yah deh
A cup of . . .	Una taza de . . .	oo-nah *tah*-sah deh
A glass of . . .	Un vaso de . . .	oon *vah*-so deh
Ashtray	Un cenicero	oon sen-ee-*seh*-roh
Bill/check	La cuenta	lah *kwen*-tah
Bread	El pan	el pahn
Breakfast	El desayuno	el day-sigh-*oon*-oh
Butter	La mantequilla	lah mahn-tay-*key*-yah
Cheers!	¡Salud!	sah-*lood*
Cocktail	Un aperitivo	oon ah-pair-ee-*tee*-voh
Mineral water	Agua mineral	*ah*-gwah mee-neh-*rahl*
Beer	Cerveza	sehr-*veh*-sah
Dinner	La cena	lah *seh*-nah
Dish	Un plato	oon *plah*-toe
Dish of the day	El platillo de hoy	el plah-*tee*-yo day oy
Enjoy!	¡Buen provecho!	bwen pro-*veh*-cho
Fixed-price menu	La comida corrida	lah koh-*me*-dah co-*ree*-dah
Is the tip included?	¿Está incluida la propina?	es-*tah* in-clue-*ee*-dah lah pro-*pea*-nah
Fork	El tenedor	el ten-eh-*door*
Knife	El cuchillo	el koo-*chee*-yo
Spoon	Una cuchara	oo-nah koo-*chah*-rah
Lunch	La comida	lah koh-*me*-dah
Menu	La carta	lah *cart*-ah
Napkin	La servilleta	lah sair-vee-*yet*-uh
Please give me	Por favor déme	pore fah-*vor* *day*-may
Pepper	La pimienta	lah pea-me-*en*-tah
Salt	La sal	lah sahl
Sugar	El azúcar	el ah-*sue*-car
Waiter!/Waitress!	¡Por favor Señor/Señorita!	pore fah-*vor* sen-*yor*/sen-yor-*ee*-tah

SMART TRAVEL TIPS

Addresses
Air Travel
Airports
Business Hours
Bus Travel
Cameras & Photography
Car Rental
Car Travel
Children in Puerto Vallarta
Computers on the Road
Consumer Protection
Cruise Travel
Customs & Duties
Disabilities & Accessibility
Discounts & Deals
Electricity
Embassies & Consulates
Emergencies
Etiquette & Behavior
Gay & Lesbian Travel
Health
Holidays
Internet, Mail & Shipping
Insurance
Language
Money Matters
Packing
Passports & Visas
Restrooms
Safety
Senior-Citizen Travel
Students in Mexico
Taxes
Taxis
Telephones
Time
Tipping
Tours & Packages
Travel Agencies
Visitor Information
Web Sites

Finding out about your destination before you leave home means you won't spend time organizing everyday minutiae once you've arrived. You'll be more streetwise when you hit the ground as well, better prepared to explore the aspects of Puerto Vallarta that drew you here in the first place. The organizations in this section can provide information to supplement this guide; contact them for up-to-the-minute details. Consult the Essentials sections in the Overnight Excursions chapter for facts about places beyond PV. Happy landings!

ADDRESSES

The Mexican method of numbering streets can be exasperatingly arbitrary. The fact that street numbers do not ascend in a logical fashion (i.e., the 100s on one block, the 200s on the next, and so on) drives even cab drivers crazy, not to mention the rest of us. Streets in districts outside El Centro generally have a theme to their names: names of planets, writers, musicians, countries, cities, or types of trees, for example. Many addresses have "s/n" for *sin número* (no number) after the street name. In small towns outside PV, references are often used in lieu of street names ("Across from the airport," for example).

Addresses are written with the street name first, followed by the street number (or "s/n"). A five-digit *código postal* (postal code) goes between the name of the city and the state.

SOME WORDS YOU SHOULD KNOW:

apartado (abbr. Apdo. or AP): post-office box

avenida (abbr. Av.): avenue

carretera: highway

colonia (abbr. Col.): neighborhood or district

fraccionamiento (abbr. Fracc.): subdivision

Th abbreviation for Jalisco is Jal.; Nayarit is Nay.

AIR TRAVEL

Major international carriers fly to Mexico City; from there you can fly to Puerto Vallarta, Guadalajara, or Manzanillo (to get to the Costalegre, south of PV).

Many airlines require that you reconfirm 48 hours ahead of the departure time for flights within Mexico.

FROM THE U.S.

There are nonstop and direct flights from a few U.S. cities. Flights with stopovers in Mexico City tend to take the entire day. If you plan to include Guadalajara in your itinerary, consider an open-jaw flight to Puerto Vallarta with the return from Guadalajara (or vice versa). There's almost no difference in price, especially when factoring in bus fare. Things change, but generally there are the greatest number of flights from Denver and Los Angeles, and sometimes San Francisco; www.latindiscountair.com, a subsidiary of cheapflights.com, quotes rates to Puerto Vallarta from different cities and on different airlines.

Nonstop flights are available from Los Angeles (Alaska Air, America West, AeroCalifornia), San Francisco (United), Seattle (Alaska Air), Phoenix (US Airways, Aero-California, America West), Tucson (Aero-California), Houston (Continental), Chicago (American), Dallas (American), St. Louis (American [seasonal]), Denver (Frontier Air, United), and Kansas City (Frontier Air).

You can fly to Manzanillo, just south of the Costalegre, via many airlines with a stop in Mexico City. AeroCalifornia has direct flights to Guadalajara and Manzanillo from Los Angeles, Phoenix, and Tucson. For more Guadalajara flight information, *see* Guadalajara Essentials *in* Chapter 9.

Flying times are about 2 hours 45 minutes from Houston, 3 hours from Los Angeles, 3½ hours from Denver, 4 hours from Chicago, and 8 hours from New York.

FROM CANADA

Air Canada has nonstop flights from Toronto, and connecting flights (via Toronto) from all major cities. The nonstop flight is 4½ hours. These flights are expensive, however, so you may save significant dollars by either flying to a U.S. city and connecting with a U.S. or Mexican carrier or taking a charter flight with Air Transat or Skyservice.

FROM THE U.K.

Consult a travel agent, or fly to Mexico City or to the U.S. and change planes there. Flight times are usually at least 15 hours with a layover.

FROM AUSTRALIA OR NEW ZEALAND

Consult a travel agent, who will probably send you first to Los Angeles, and then on to PV. Flying times vary widely, depending on the number of connections and the route, but the shortest travel time would be about 20 hours.

FROM ELSEWHERE IN MEXICO

The majority of national flights are via Mexico City. AeroCalafia flies 13-person Cessnas between Puerto Vallarta and Los Cabos with a stop in Mazatlán. It's easier and sometimes cheaper to buy tickets at travel agencies in Mexico. The flight from Mexico City to PV is about 1½ hours.

For flights within Mexico originating at Benito Juárez (Mexico City), arrive 1½ hours before the scheduled departure time; for flights originating at small airports, arrive 45 minutes before departure. You may need to arrive earlier if you're flying during peak air-traffic times, or during peak seasons.

Some airlines' toll-free numbers have an 001800 prefix—two zeroes before the "1"—rather than 01800, like most Mexican toll-free numbers. This is entirely correct: what it means is that your call is actually being routed to the United States and will be charged as an international call if you're calling from Mexico.

🚩 Major Airlines **AeroCalafia** ☎ 322/209-0378 in PV. **Aero California** ☎ 800/237-6225 in U.S., 01800/685-5500 in Mexico, 322/209-0643 in PV. **Aeroméxico** ☎ 800/237-6639 in U.S. and Canada, 01800/021-4010 in Mexico, 322/221-1204 in PV ⊕ www.aeromexico.com. **Air Canada** ☎ 800/361-5373 in Canada, 322/221-1212 in PV ⊕ www.aircanada.com. **Alaska Airlines** ☎ 800/252-7522 in U.S. and Canada, 001800/252-7522 in Mexico, 322/

221–2610 in PV ⊕ www.alaskaair.com. **America West** ☎ 800/235-9292 in U.S., 001800/235-9292 in Mexico, 322/221-1333 in PV ⊕ www.americawest.com. **American** ☎ 800/433-7300 in U.S. and Canada, 01800/433-7300 in Mexico, 322/221-1799 in PV ⊕ www.aa.com. **British Airways** ☎ 0845/773-3377 in U.K. ⊕ www.britishairways.com. **Continental** ☎ 800/523-3273 in U.S. and Canada, 01800/900-5000 in Mexico, 322/221-2212 in PV ⊕ www.continental.com. **Frontier** ☎ 800/432-1359 in U.S. **Mexicana** ☎ 800/531-7921 in U.S., 866/281-3049 in Canada, 01800/502-2000 in Mexico, 322/224-8900 in PV ⊕ www.mexicana.com. **Northwest** ☎ 800/225-2525 in U.S. and Canada, 01800/830-7400 in Mexico, 322/221-1655 in PV ⊕ www.nwa.com. **United** ☎ 800/864-8331 in U.S. and Canada, 01800/003-0777 in Mexico, 322/221-3264 in PV ⊕ www.united.com.

▐ Charter Airlines **Air Transat** ☎ 877/872-6728 or 514/636-3630 ⊕ www.airtransat.ca. **Skyservice Airlines** ☎ 416/679-8330, 888/571-0094 in Canada ⊕ www.skyserviceairlines.com.

▐ Domestic (Mexican) Airlines **AeroCalafia** ☎ 322/209-0378 in PV. **Aviacsa** ☎ 01800/711-6732, 55/482-8280 in Mexico City ⊕ www.aviacsa.com. **Azteca** ☎ 01800/229-8322, 322/221-2584 in PV. **Mexicana** ☎ 01800/502-2000, 55/5448-0990 in Mexico City, 322/224-8900, 322/221-1266 in PV.

AIRPORTS

The main gateway to the country, and where many PV-bound travelers change planes, is Mexico City's large, modern Aeropuerto Internacional Benito Juárez, infamous for pickpocketing, petty crime, and taxi scams; be careful with your possessions. Stopovers are usually lengthy, so use the time to exchange money for your ground transportation, or to buy last-minute gifts (although at high prices) on your way out of the country.

Puerto Vallarta's international airport is tiny by comparison and usually has just a few flights departing at a time. Aeropuerto Internacional Gustavo Díaz Ordáz is 7½ km (4½ mi) north of downtown Puerto Vallarta.

GROUND TRANSPORTATION

Vans provide transportation from the airport to PV hotels; there's a zone system with different prices for the Zona Hotelera Sur, downtown PV, and so on. Upon

leaving the luggage collection area, vendors shout for your attention. It's a confusing scene. Purchase the taxi vouchers sold at stands inside or just outside the terminal, but make sure to avoid the timeshare vendors, which trap you in their vans for a high-pressure sales pitch en route to your hotel. Before you purchase your ticket, look for a taxi-zone map (it should be posted on or by the ticket stand) and make sure your taxi ticket is properly zoned; if you need a ticket only to Zone 3, don't pay for a ticket to Zone 4 or 5. Don't leave your luggage unattended while making transportation arrangements. Taxis or vans to the Costalegre resorts between PV and Manzanillo are generally arranged through the resort. If not, taxis charge about $19 (200 pesos) an hour—more if you're traveling beyond Jalisco State lines.

▐ Airport Information **Aeropuerto Internacional Benito Juárez (MEX)** ✉ Mexico City ☎ 55/5571-3600. **Aeropuerto Internacional Gustavo Díaz Ordáz (PVR)** ✉ Carretera a Tepic, Km 7.5, Zona Aeropuerto ☎ 322/221-1298. **Aeropuerto Internacional Playa de Oro** (Aeropuerto Internacional de Manzanillo, ZLO) ✉ Carretera 200, Km 38, Manzanillo ☎ 314/333-1119.

BUSINESS HOURS

BANKS & PUBLIC OFFICES

Banks are generally open weekdays 9 to 3. In Puerto Vallarta most are open until 4, and some of the larger banks keep a few branches open Saturday from 9 or 10 to 1 or 2:30; however, the extended hours are often for deposits or check cashing only. HSBC is the one chain that stays open for longer hours; on weekdays they are open 8 to 7 and on Saturday from 8 to 3. Government offices are usually open to the public weekdays 9 to 3; along with banks and most private offices, they're closed on national holidays.

GAS STATIONS

Gas stations are normally open 7 AM–10 PM daily. Those near major thoroughfares stay open 24 hours, including most holidays.

PHARMACIES

Pharmacies are usually open daily 9 AM to 10 PM; on Sunday and in some small towns they may close several hours earlier. Puerto Vallarta has some 24-hour pharmacies: look for the big names such as Farmacias del Ahorro or Farmacia Guadalajara. In neighborhoods or smaller towns where there are no 24-hour drug stores, local pharmacies take turns staying open 24 hours so that there's usually at least one open on any given night—it's called the *farmacia de turno*. Information about late-night pharmacies is published in the daily newspaper, but the staff at your hotel should be able to help you find an all-night place.

SHOPS

Stores are generally open weekdays and Saturday from 9 or 10 AM to 2 or 3 PM; in resort areas, those stores geared to tourists may stay open until 9 or 10 at night, all day on Saturday; some are open on Sunday as well, but it's good to call ahead before making a special trip. Some more traditional shops close for a two-hour lunch break, roughly 2–4. Airport shops are open seven days a week.

BUS TRAVEL

ARRIVING & DEPARTING

Getting to Mexico by bus is no longer for just the adventurous or budget-conscious. In the past, bus travelers were required to change to Mexican vehicles at the border, and vice versa. Now, however, in an effort to bring more American visitors, the Mexican government has removed this obstacle, and more transborder bus tours are available. Buy a ticket for Guadalajara from any Greyhound station in the U.S. and you will transfer to a Mexico-bound bus in Phoenix or another city. Once across the border you will at some point transfer to a Mexican bus, but these are first-class and affiliated with Greyhound. Those that travel to Guadalajara are on the Mexican bus line Estrella Blanca. If you'll be leaving Mexico for points north of the border by bus, you can buy tickets from the Greyhound representative in Guadalajara. (There is no direct Greyhound service to or from PV.)

Within Mexico the bus network is extensive. PV's Central Camionero, or Central Bus Station, is 1 km (½ mi) north of the airport, halfway between Nuevo Vallarta and downtown Puerto Vallarta. Elite/Futura has first-class service to Acapulco, Mexico City, the U.S. border, and other destinations. ETN has the most luxurious service to Guadalajara, Mexico City, and many other destinations, with exclusively first-class buses that have roomy, totally reclining seats. Primera Plus, which has upgraded its fleet, connects PV with destinations throughout Mexico. Basic service, including some buses with marginal or no air-conditioning, is the norm on Transportes Cihuatlán, which connects the Bahía de Banderas and PV with southern Jalisco towns such as Barra de Navidad. Transporte del Pacifico is the economist's choice for destinations throughout the Pacific Coast.

CLASSES

First-class Mexican buses (known as *primera clase*) are generally timely and comfortable, air-conditioned coaches with bathrooms, movies, and reclining seats—sometimes with seat belts. Deluxe (*de lujo* or *ejecutivo*) buses offer the same and usually have refreshments (soft drinks, bottled water, and white-bread sandwiches). Second-class, or *segunda clase,* can be dilapidated "vintage" vehicles without air-conditioning, although they are sometimes fairly comfortable and with working air-conditioning.

A lower-class bus ride can be interesting if you're not in a hurry and want to experience local culture; these buses make frequent stops and keep less strictly to their timetables. Often they will wait until they fill up to leave, regardless of the scheduled time of departure. Fares are up to 15%–30% cheaper than first-class buses. The days of pigs and chickens among your busmates are largely in the past. Unless you're writing a novel or your memoir, there's no reason to ride a second-class bus if a first-class or better is available. Daytime trips are generally safer.

Bring snacks, socks, and a sweater—the air-conditioning on first-class buses is often set on high—and toilet paper, as restrooms might not have any. Smoking is prohibited on all buses.

There are several first-class and deluxe bus lines. Estrella Blanca goes from Mexico City to Puerto Vallarta as well as other destinations on the Pacific coast and the northern border. Primera Plus connects Mexico City with Manzanillo and Puerto Vallarta along with other central and western cities. TAP serves Mexico City, Puerto Vallarta, and Tepic before continuing north through Sinaloa and Sonora and to border cities like Tijuana (BCN) and Agua Prieta (Sonora). ETN is a deluxe line serving Mexico City and central Mexico, including Guadalajara, Puerto Vallarta, and the states of San Luis Potosi, Aguascalientes, Colima, and Michoacan. Transportes Cihuatlán has second-class buses connecting PV to the Costalegre, San Patricio–Melaque, and Barra de Navidad.

PAYING

Rates average 20–60 pesos ($2–$6) per hour of travel, depending on the level of luxury. For the most part, plan to pay in pesos, although most of the deluxe bus services have started accepting Visa and MasterCard.

RESERVATIONS

Tickets for first-class or better—unlike tickets for the other classes—can and should be reserved in advance. You can make reservations for many, though not all, of the first-class bus lines, through the UNO/Ticketbus central reservations agency. To travel by bus from the United States, you can buy tickets for destinations served by Estrella Blanca at Greyhound counters in San Diego, California, and Brownsville, Dallas, Houston, Laredo, and McAllen—all in Texas—and other gateway cities.

🚌 Bus Information **Central Camionero** ✉ Puerto Vallarta–Tepic Hwy., Km 9, Las Mojoneras ☎ 322/290-1008. **Estrella Blanca** ☎ 01800/507-5500 toll-free in Mexico, 322/290-1001 in Puerto Vallarta ⊕ www.estrellablanca.com.mx. **ETN** ☎ 01800/

800-0386 toll-free in Mexico, 322/290-0996, 322/290-0119 in PV ⊕ www.etn.com.mx. **Greyhound** ☎ 33/3647-5070 in Guadalajara, 01800/710-8819 toll-free in Mexico, 800/231-2222 in U.S., 800/661-8747 in Canada ⊕ www.greyhound.com. **Primera Plus** ☎ 322/290-0715 in PV. **Transportes Cihuatlán** ☎ 322/290-0994 in PV. **Transporte del Pacifico (TAP)** ☎ 322/290-0119, 322/290-0993 in PV.

GETTING AROUND

City buses (4.5 pesos) serve downtown, the Zona Hotelera Norte, and Marina Vallarta. Bus stops—marked by blue-and-white signs—are every two or three long blocks along the highway (Carretera Aeropuerto) and in downtown Puerto Vallarta. Buses to Playa Mismaloya and Boca de Tomatlán (55 pesos) run about every 15 minutes from the corner of Avenida Insurgentes and Basilio Badillo downtown.

Gray ATM buses serving Nuevo Vallarta and Bucerías (20 pesos), Punta de Mita (30 pesos), and Sayulita (50 pesos) depart from just two places: Plaza las Glorias, in front of the HSBC bank, and Wal-Mart, both of which are along Carretera Aeropuerto between downtown and the Zona Hotelera. It's rare for inspectors to check tickets, but just when you've let yours flutter to the floor, a figure of authority is bound to appear. So hang onto your ticket, and hang onto your hat: PV bus drivers race from one stoplight to the next in jarring, jerky bursts of speed.

There's no problem with theft on city buses aside from perhaps an occasional pickpocket that might be at work anywhere in the world.

CAMERAS & PHOTOGRAPHY

Majestic vistas and quaint cityscapes make Puerto Vallarta and environs a photographer's dream. Although Mexicans generally don't mind having picture-taking visitors in their midst, you should always **ask permission before taking pictures in churches or of individuals.** People who can really use the money may ask you for a *propina*, or tip, in which case 5 to 10 pesos is customary. Also, unless you're a spy, **don't snap pictures of military or**

high-security installations anywhere in the country. It's forbidden.

If you're bashful about approaching strangers, photograph people with whom you interact: your waiter, your desk clerk, the vendor selling you crafts. Even better, have a traveling companion or a passerby photograph you *with* them. Digital cameras make it possible to share the photo, at least for a moment, with your subject, and most people really enjoy seeing themselves in your camera. For the purpose of taking photos of indigenous people such as the Huichol, a tour is the way to go, as tour operators will have gained permission ahead of time for photographs to be taken.

To avoid the blurriness caused by shaky hands, get a minitripod—they're available in sizes as small as 6 inches. Buy a small beanbag to support your camera on uneven surfaces. If you plan to take photos on some of the region's many beaches, bring a skylight, 81B, 81C, or polarizing filter to minimize haze and light problems. If you're visiting forested areas, bring high-speed film or a digital camera to compensate for low light under the tree canopy and invest in a telephoto lens to photograph wildlife; standard zoom lenses in the 35–88 range won't capture enough detail.

Casual photographers should **consider using inexpensive disposable cameras** to reduce the risks inherent in traveling with sophisticated equipment. One-use cameras with panoramic or underwater functions are also nice supplements to a standard camera and its gear.

The *Kodak Guide to Shooting Great Travel Pictures* (available at bookstores everywhere) is loaded with tips.
🖪 Photo Help Kodak Information Center ☎ 800/242-2424 ⊕ www.kodak.com.

EQUIPMENT PRECAUTIONS

Don't pack film or equipment in checked luggage, where it is much more susceptible to damage. X-ray machines used to view checked luggage are extremely powerful and therefore are likely to ruin your film. Due to heightened airport security, most inspectors now refuse to hand check

cameras and bags of film, despite the fact that the latter becomes clouded after repeated exposure to airport X-ray machines. It's best to pack film in a lead bag in your carry-on luggage. If the X-ray machine can't penetrate the lead bag, the inspector will remove and check it by hand—this is what you wanted them to do in the first place. Always keep film, tape, and computer disks out of the sun. Carry an extra supply of batteries, and be prepared to turn on your camera, camcorder, or laptop to prove to airport security personnel that the device is real.

If you've got a digital camera, airport X-rays won't affect it. Petty theft can be a problem though, so **keep a close eye on your gear.**

FILM & DEVELOPING

Color print film—especially Kodak and Fuji brands—is fairly easy to find in Mexico, but black and white or slide film is not. If purchased in a major city, a roll of 36-exposure print film costs about the same as in the United States; the price is slightly higher in tourist spots and in more remote places. Advantix is available in Mexico, although developing may take one or two days. It's a good idea to pack more film and, for digital cameras, a larger memory card than you think you'll need. One-hour and overnight film developing is fairly common.

VIDEOS

Videotapes are good quality and are easy to find in urban areas. The local standard in Mexico is the same as in the United States: that is, all videos are NTSC (National Television Standards Committee). The best places to buy tapes are Sanborns restaurant-shops (they're all over the place), major pharmacies, photo shops, and at American outlet stores like Wal-Mart and Costco. A 120-minute tape costs about $3.

CAR RENTAL

When you think about renting a car, bear in mind that you will be sharing the road with local drivers whose customs and ideas of acceptable behavior are different than your own. Also, be prepared for different rules of the road and for challenging road conditions (*see* Road Conditions *in* Car Travel). Check on conditions before you rent, and do your best not to drive on desolate roads between cities at night.

Mexico manufactures Chrysler, Ford, General Motors, Honda, Nissan, and Volkswagen vehicles. With the exception of Volkswagen, you can get the same kind of midsize and luxury cars in Mexico that you can rent in the United States and Canada. Economy usually refers to a Volkswagen Beetle or a Chevy Aveo or Joy, which may or may not come with air-conditioning or automatic transmission.

It can really pay to shop around: in Puerto Vallarta, rates for a compact car with air-conditioning, manual transmission, and unlimited mileage range from $25 a day and $150 a week to $50 or even $60 a day and $300–$400 a week. Insurance averages $18 a day. While shopping for a good deal, **stick with the major companies** because they tend to be more reliable.

You can also hire a car with a driver (who generally doubles as a tour guide) through your hotel. The going rate is about $25 an hour within town, usually with a three-hour minimum. Limousine service runs about $65 an hour and up, with a three- to five-hour minimum. Rates for out-of-town trips are higher. **Negotiate a price beforehand** if you'll need the service for more than one day. If your hotel can't arrange limousine or car service, ask the concierge to refer you to a reliable *sitio* (cab stand).

🚗 Major Agencies **Alamo** ☎ 800/522-9696 ⊕ www.alamo.com. **Avis** ☎ 800/331-1084, 800/272-5871 in Canada, 0870/606-0100 in U.K., 02/9353-9000 in Australia, 09/526-2847 in New Zealand ⊕ www.avis.com. **Budget** ☎ 800/527-0700 ⊕ www.budget.com. **Hertz** ☎ 800/654-3001, 800/263-0600 in Canada, 0870/844-8844 in U.K., 02/9669-2444 in Australia, 09/256-8690 in New Zealand ⊕ www.hertz.com. **National Car Rental** ☎ 800/227-7368 ⊕ www.nationalcar.com.

CUTTING COSTS

Look into wholesalers, companies that don't own fleets but rent in bulk from those that do and often offer better rates than traditional car-rental operations.

Prices are best during off-peak periods. Rentals booked through wholesalers often must be paid for before you leave home.

🚗 Wholesalers **Auto Europe** ☎ 207/842-2000 or 800/223-5555 ⊕ www.autoeurope.com. **Kemwel** ☎ 877/820-0668 or 800/678-0678 ⊕ www.kemwel.com.

INSURANCE

When driving a rented car you are generally responsible for any damage to or loss of the vehicle. You also will be liable for any property damage or personal injury that you may cause while driving. Before you rent, see what coverage you already have under the terms of your personal auto-insurance policy and credit cards.

You could be jailed during investigations after an accident unless you have adequate liability and collision insurance. Some people are covered for collision by their own insurance or the credit card they use to rent the car, however it's imperative to know exactly what is covered before waiving the rental agency's coverage. Most Mexicans want to avoid dealing with the authorities, and after an accident might simply pull over, discuss things, arrive at an impromptu cash settlement on the spot if necessary, and continue on their way, rather than dealing with the authorities. Unfortunately, another common way to deal with the situation is for the driver at fault to simply get out of their car and run.

REQUIREMENTS & RESTRICTIONS

In Mexico the minimum driving age is 18, but most rental-car agencies have a minimum age requirement ranging from 21 to 25. Your own country's driver's license is perfectly acceptable.

SURCHARGES

Surcharges for additional drivers are around $5 per day plus tax. Children's car seats run about the same, but not all companies have them. Before you pick up a car in one city and leave it in another, ask about drop-off charges or one-way service fees, which can be substantial. Also inquire about early-return policies; some rental agencies charge extra if you return the car before the time specified in your contract while others give you a refund for the days not used. Note the tank's fuel level on your contract; to avoid a hefty refueling fee, return the car with the same tank level. If the tank was full, refill it just before you turn in the car, but be aware that gas stations near the rental outlet may overcharge.

CAR TRAVEL

It is absolutely essential that you **carry Mexican auto insurance for liability, even if you have full coverage for collision, damages, and theft** (⇨ Insurance). If you injure anyone in an accident, you could well be jailed—whether it was your fault or not—unless you have insurance.

ARRIVING & DEPARTING

PV is about 1,900 km (1,200 mi) south of Nogales, Arizona, at the U.S.–Mexico border, 354 km (220 mi) west of Guadalajara, 242 km (150 mi) north of Manzanillo, and 167 km (104 mi) south of Tepic.

If you enter Mexico with a car you must leave with it. Technically this rule applies even if your car gets totaled or dies some other horrible death, rendering it undrivable. In recent years the high rate of U.S. vehicles being sold illegally in Mexico has caused the Mexican government to enact stringent regulations on bringing cars into the country.

You must cross the border with the following documents: title or registration for your vehicle; a passport or a certified birth certificate; a major credit card (American Express, Diners Club, MasterCard, or Visa); and a valid driver's license with a photo. The title holder, driver, and credit-card owner must be one and the same—that is, if your spouse's name is on the title or registration of the car and yours isn't, you cannot be the one to bring the car into the country. For financed, leased, rental, or company cars you must bring a notarized letter of permission from the bank, lien holder, rental agency, or company. When you submit your paperwork at the border and pay the $27 charge on your credit card, you'll receive a car permit and a sticker to put on your vehicle, all valid for up to six months. Be sure to turn in the permit and the sticker at the border prior to their expiration date; otherwise you could incur high fines or even be barred from entering Mexico if you try to visit again. You can purchase insurance (⇨ Insurance, *below*) near border crossings on either the U.S. or Mexican side.

The fact that you drove in with a car is stamped on your tourist card or visa, which you must give to immigration authorities at departure. If an emergency arises and you must fly home, there are complicated customs procedures to face.

If you bring the car into the country you must be in the vehicle at all times when it is driven. You cannot lend it to another person.

GETTING AROUND

Driving in PV can be unpleasant, but the main problem is parking. From December through April—peak season—traffic clogs the narrow streets, and negotiating the steep hills in Old Vallarta (sometimes you have to drive in reverse to let another car pass) can be frightening. Avoid rush hour (7–9 AM and 6–8 PM) and when schools let out (2–3 PM). It's helpful to **travel with a companion and a good map.** Always lock your car, and never leave valuable items in the body of the car. The trunk is generally safe, although any thief can crack one open if he chooses.

Taxis and buses are the way to get around downtown; rent a car for days when you'll be sightseeing outside the city center. The trick to getting a good deal on a rental car is to book it before arriving in PV through Hertz and other international companies.

To get to the Costalegre from Puerto Vallarta, simply head south on Highway 200. It's about 2 ¼ hours to El Careyes Resort, a little more than halfway to Barra de Navidad; the latter is about 3½ to 4 hours to the south.

If you're heading to the Costalegre from Guadalajara, the most direct route is toll route 54D south; 2½ hours from the city you'll reach Colima; coastal Barra de Navidad is an additional hour and 45 minutes from there.

EMERGENCY SERVICES

To help motorists on major highways, the Mexican Tourism Ministry operates a fleet of more than 250 pickup trucks, known as the Angeles Verdes, or Green Angels, easily reachable by phone throughout Mexico by simply dialing 078. (If this number doesn't work—occasionally the case—call 01800/903–9200 toll-free.) The bilingual drivers provide mechanical help, first aid, radio-telephone communication, basic supplies and small parts, towing, tourist information, and protection. Services are free, and spare parts, fuel, and lubricants are provided at cost. Tips are always appreciated (figure a minimum of $5–$10 for big jobs and $3–$5 for minor repairs). The Green Angels patrol fixed sections of the major highways twice daily 8–8 (usually later on holiday weekends). If you break down, pull off the road as far as possible, lift the hood of your car, hail a passing vehicle, and ask the driver to notify the patrol. Most drivers will be quite helpful.

🚗 **Angeles Verdes** ☎ 078, 01800/903–9200 toll-free in Mexico.

GASOLINE

Pemex (the government petroleum monopoly) franchises all of Mexico's gas stations, which you'll find at most junctions and in cities and towns. Gas is measured in liters, and stations usually don't accept U.S. or Canadian credit cards or dollars, but this is beginning to change. Fuel prices tend to increase the farther you get from Mexico City and areas near the U.S. border. Overall, prices are slightly to moderately higher than in the United States. Premium unleaded gas (called *premium,* the red pump) and regular unleaded gas (*magna,* the green pump) are available nationwide, but it's still best to **fill up whenever you can and don't let your tank get below half full.** Fuel quality is generally lower than that in the United States and Europe, but it has improved enough so that your car will run acceptably. For general opening times, *see* Business Hours, *above.*

Gas-station attendants pump the gas and you may also wash your windshield and check your oil and tire air pressure. A 5- or 10-peso tip is customary, depending on the number of services rendered (including simply pumping the gas). **Keep a close eye on the gas meter** to make sure the attendant is starting it at "0" and that you're charged the correct price.

INSURANCE

You must carry Mexican auto insurance, at the very least liability as well coverage against physical damage to the vehicle and theft at your discretion, depending on what, if anything, your own auto insurance (or credit card, if you use it to rent a car) includes. It's sold by the day ($10 per day and up), and if your trip is shorter than your original estimate, some companies might issue a prorated refund for the unused time upon application after you exit the country. Mexican Insurance Professionals and Instant Mexico Auto Insurance are two of many online outfits that allow you to buy the insurance beforehand, but it's not absolutely necessary; if you're approaching the border at almost any U.S.–Mexico crossing, you'll be overwhelmed by essentially similar companies where you can buy the insurance on the spot. Sanborn's is a reliable company and has offices in almost every border town. If you're renting a car, there's no need to buy separate insurance; it will all be dealt with by the rental company.

🚗 **Instant Mexico Auto Insurance** ☎ 800/345–4701 in U.S. and Canada ⊕ www.instant-mex-auto-insur.com. **Mexico Insurance Professionals** ☎ 888/INS-4-MEX or 928/214–9750 in U.S. **Sanborn's Mexican Insurance** ☎ 800/222–0158 in U.S. and Canada ⊕ www.sanbornsinsurance.com.

PARKING

A circle with a diagonal line superimposed on the letter *E* (for *estacionamiento*) means "no parking." Illegally parked cars are usually either towed or have wheel blocks placed on the tires, which can require a trip to the traffic-police headquarters for payment of a fine. When in doubt, **park in a lot rather than on the street;** your car will probably be safer there anyway. Lots are plentiful, and fees are reasonable—as little as $4 for a whole day up to $1 or more an hour, depending on where you are. Sometimes you park your own car; more often, though, you hand the keys over to an attendant.

ROAD CONDITIONS

There are several well-kept toll roads heading into Mexico and out of major cities like Guadalajara—most of them four lanes wide. However, these *carreteras* (major highways) don't go too far into the countryside. (*Cuota* means toll road; *libre* means no toll, and such roads are often two lanes and not as smooth.) Some excellent roads have opened in the past decade or so, making car travel safer and faster. Those leading to, or in, Nayarit and Jalisco include highways connecting Nogales and Mazatlán; Guadalajara and Tepic; and Mexico City, Morelia, and Guadalajara. However, tolls as high as $40 one-way can make using these thoroughfares expensive.

In rural areas roads are sometimes poor; other times the two-lane, blacktop roads are perfectly fine and enjoyable to drive. **Be extra cautious during the rainy season,** when rock slides and potholes are a problem. **Watch out for animals,** especially untethered horses, cattle, and dogs, and to dangerous, unrailed curves. *Topes* (speed bumps) are ubiquitous; slow down when approaching a village and look for signs saying TOPES or VIBRADORES. Police officers often issue tickets to those speeding through populated areas.

Generally, driving times are longer than for comparable distances in the United States. Allow extra time for unforeseen occurrences as well as for traffic, particularly truck traffic.

ROAD MAPS

AAA publishes national road maps for Mexico, and Guía Roji publishes current city, regional, and national road maps. The latter are available in bookstores (or the book section in Sanborns), *papelerís,* and big supermarket chains for under $10. Maps of Mexico are also increasingly available in the U.S. and Canada and online at Web sites like www.

mexicomaps.com. Gas stations generally don't sell maps.

RULES OF THE ROAD

When you sign up for Mexican car insurance, you may receive a booklet on Mexican rules of the road. It really is a good idea to read it to avoid breaking laws that differ from those of your country. For instance: if an oncoming vehicle flicks its lights at you in daytime, slow down: it could mean trouble ahead; when approaching a narrow bridge, the first vehicle to flash its lights has right of way; right on red is not allowed; one-way traffic is indicated by an arrow; two-way, by a double-pointed arrow. (Other road signs follow the widespread system of international symbols.)

On the highway, using your left turn signal to turn left can be extremely dangerous. Mexican drivers—especially truck drivers with big rigs that block the view of the road ahead—use their left turn signal on the highway to signal the car behind that it's safe to pass. Conversely they rarely use their signal to actually make a turn. Foreigners signaling a left turn off the highway into a driveway or onto a side road have been killed by cars or trucks behind that mistook their turn signal for a signal to pass. To turn left from a highway when cars are behind you, it's best to pull over to the right and make the left turn when no cars are approaching, to avoid disaster.

Mileage and speed limits are given in kilometers: 100 kph and 80 kph (62 mph and 50 mph, respectively) are the most common maximums on the highway. A few of the toll roads allow 110 kph (68 mph). However, speed limits can change from curve to curve, so watch the signs carefully. In cities and small towns, observe the posted speed limits, which can be as low as 20 kph (12 mph).

Seat belts are required by law throughout Mexico.

Drunk driving laws are fairly harsh in Mexico, and if you're caught you may go to jail immediately. It's difficult to say what the blood-alcohol limit is since everyone we asked gave a different answer, which means each case is probably handled in a discretionary manner. The best way to avoid any problems is to simply not drink and drive.

If you're stopped for speeding, the officer is supposed to take your license and hold it until you pay the fine at the local police station. But the officer will usually prefer a *mordida* (small bribe). Just take out a couple hundred pesos, hold it out inquiringly (yet discreetly), and see if the problem goes away. Conversely, a few cops might resent the offer of a bribe, but it's still common practice.

If you decide to dispute a charge that seems preposterous, do so with a smile, and tell the officer that you would like to talk to the police captain when you get to the station. The officer usually will let you go rather than go to the station.

SAFETY ON THE ROAD

Never drive at night in remote and rural areas. *Bandidos* are one concern, but so are potholes, free-roaming animals, cars with no working lights, road-hogging trucks, and difficulty in getting assistance. It's best to use toll roads whenever possible; although costly, they're much safer.

Driving in Mexico can be nerve-wracking for novices, with people zigzagging in and out of lanes. Most drivers pay attention to signals and safety rules, but be vigilant. Drunk driving skyrockets on holiday weekends.

A police officer may pull you over for something you didn't do; unfortunately a common scam. **If you're pulled over for any reason, be polite**—displays of anger will only make matters worse. Although efforts are being made to fight corruption, it's still a fact of life in Mexico, and for many people, it's worth the $10 to $100 it costs to get their license back to be on their way quickly. (The amount requested varies depending on what the officer assumes you can pay—the year, make, and model of the car you drive being one determining factor.) Others persevere long enough to be let off with a warning only.

The key to success, in this case, is a combination of calm and patience.

CHILDREN IN PUERTO VALLARTA

Mexico has one of the strictest policies about children entering the country. **All children, including infants, must have proof of citizenship (a certified birth certificate) for travel to Mexico.** At some airports, notaries are available to notarize noncertified copies of birth certificates—but it's best to come prepared and not leave this to chance. Still, in a worst case scenario, ask an airline representative if the service is available. All children up to age 18 traveling with a single parent must also have a notarized letter from the other parent stating that the child has his or her permission to leave his or her home country. If the other parent is deceased or the child has only one legal parent, a notarized statement saying so must be obtained as proof. In addition, parents must now fill out a tourist card for each child over the age of 10 traveling with them.

If you are renting a car, don't forget to arrange for a car seat when you reserve. For general advice about traveling with children, consult *Fodor's FYI: Travel with Your Baby* (available in bookstores everywhere).

FOOD

Most restaurants in Puerto Vallarta are family-friendly—especially those whose name includes RESTAURANT FAMILIAR. Picky eaters and those wary of spices can usually stomach *pollo asado* or *carne asada* (grilled chicken or grilled beef). Other familiar choices are quesadillas, *tortas,* sandwiches made on a hard roll, usually with chicken, pork, or cheese, condiments, and a vegetable garnish, and *tacos de bistec,* tacos filled with grilled beef. The Sanborns and VIPS chain restaurants, though not rock-bottom cheap, usually have a good variety of recognizable, U.S.-style dishes. Most restaurants serve hamburgers, and Puerto Vallarta has American fast-food chains, plus mom-and-pop Mexican restaurants where things such as quesadillas, hot dogs, spaghetti with butter only (*spaghetti al burro*), and other kid-friendly dishes are available.

LODGING

Most hotels allow children under a certain age (usually 10 or 12) to stay in their parents' room at no extra charge, but some charge a percentage of the adult rate. In some hotels kids stay and eat for free. Very few charge for them as extra adults; but ask before you book. Major chain and luxury hotels tend to have the most child-friendly facilities and options, such as connecting family rooms, play areas, children's pools, and kids' clubs with special activities and outings. Extra beds and cribs are available and often free of charge; you can also arrange for a babysitter ($7–$20 an hour and up, usually with a three-hour minimum plus taxi fare home), though you'll need to specify if you'd like an English-speaking sitter. Some hotels only have children's programs during peak season. Confirm whether children's activities are included in the price or if there's an extra charge.

SIGHTS & ATTRACTIONS

Places that are especially appealing to children are indicated by a rubber-duckie icon (☺) in the margin.

SUPPLIES & EQUIPMENT

Baby formula, disposable diapers, baby food, and supplies such as bottles and lotions are widely available, especially in big pharmacies and supermarkets. You'll see such familiar powder formula brands as Similac, Nestlé's NAN, and Enfamil, with prices ranging from $7 (for 400 grams [14 ounces]) to $18–$25 (for 900 grams [31.5 ounces]). Premixed formula (*fórmula infantil*) isn't as common, but large stores often have Isomil ($2 for 236 ml, or just under 8 ounces). Fresh milk is readily available in both large and small groceries, as well as convenience stores. American disposable diaper brands such as Pampers and Huggies range from $5 for a package of 10 to $18 for 64. You'll often find disposable diapers (*pañales desechables*) at discounted prices, especially locally made brands.

COMPUTERS ON THE ROAD

Internet cafés have sprung up all over Puerto Vallarta and even small surrounding towns and villages, making e-mail by far the easiest way to get in touch with people back home. If you're bringing a laptop with you, check with the manufacturer's technical support line to see what service and/or repair affiliates they have in the areas you plan to visit. Carry a spare battery to save yourself the expense and headache of having to hunt down a replacement on the spot. Memory sticks and other accessories are usually more expensive in Mexico than in the U.S. or Europe, but available in megastores such as Sam's Club and Office Depot. The younger generation of Mexicans are computer savvy and there are some excellent repair wizards and technicians to help you with problems; many are bilingual.

CONSUMER PROTECTION

Whether you're shopping for gifts or purchasing travel services, **pay with a major credit card** whenever possible, so you can cancel payment or get reimbursed if there's a problem (and you can provide documentation). If you're doing business with a particular company for the first time, contact your local Better Business Bureau and the attorney general's offices in your state and (for U.S. businesses) the company's home state as well. Have any complaints been filed? Finally, if you're buying a package or tour, always consider travel insurance that includes default coverage(⇨ Insurance).

The Mexican consumer protection agency, the Procuraduría Federal del Consumidor (PROFECO), also helps foreigners, particularly with complaints about goods or services not received in the condition promised (it tries to negotiate settlements or refunds; the process does require written documentation, though). When calling its hotline, ask for *atención a extranjeros* to get an English-speaking staff member.

📋 BBBs **Council of Better Business Bureaus** ☎ 703/276-0100 ⊕ www.bbb.org. **Procuraduría Federal de Consumidor (PROFECO)** ☎ 55/5211-1723, 55/5625-6700 Ext. 1317 in Mexico City, 33/3616-7667, 33/3613-9672 in Guadalajara, 01800/

468-8722 toll-free in Mexico ⊕ www.profeco.gob.
mx.

CRUISE TRAVEL

Companies with cruises to the Pacific
Coast include Carnival, Cunard, Celebrity
Cruises, Holland America, Princess, Nor-
wegian, Royal Caribbean, and Royal
Olympia. Most depart from Los Angeles,
Long Beach, or San Diego and head to Los
Cabos or Mazatlán, Puerto Vallarta, Man-
zanillo, Ixtapa/Zihuatanejo, and/or Aca-
pulco; some trips originate in Vancouver
or San Francisco.

To learn how to plan, choose, and book a
cruise-ship voyage, consult *Fodor's FYI:
Plan & Enjoy Your Cruise* (available in
bookstores everywhere).

🚢 Cruise Lines **Carnival** 🕾 800/227-6482 in U.S.
and Canada ⊕ www.carnival.com. **Celebrity
Cruises** 🕾 800/433-3111 in U.S. and Canada
⊕ www.celebrity.com. **Cunard** 🕾 800/728-6273 in
U.S. and Canada ⊕ www.cunard.com. **Holland
America** 🕾 877/724-5425 in the U.S. and Canada
⊕ www.hollandamerica.com. **Norwegian** 🕾 800/
625-5306 in U.S. and Canada ⊕ www.ncl.com.
Princess 🕾 800/774-6237 in U.S. and Canada
⊕ www.princess.com. **Royal Caribbean International** 🕾 800/398-9819 in U.S. and Canada
⊕ www.royalcaribbean.com.

CUSTOMS & DUTIES

When shopping abroad, keep receipts for
all purchases. Upon reentering the country,
**be ready to show customs officials what
you've bought, with the receipts.** Pack purchases together in an easily accessible
place. (This really isn't necessary if everything totals less than the allowed limit for
your country of origin, but it's good to be
able to access these things if the inspector
wants to see them.) If you think a duty is
incorrect, appeal the assessment. If you
object to the way your clearance was handled, note the inspector's badge number. In
either case, first ask to see a supervisor. If
the problem isn't resolved, write to the appropriate authorities, beginning with the
port director at your point of entry.

IN AUSTRALIA

Australian residents who are 18 or older
may bring home A$900 worth of sou-
venirs and gifts (including jewelry), 250
cigarettes or 250 grams of cigars or other
tobacco products, and 2.25 liters of alcohol (including wine, beer, and spirits). Residents under 18 may bring back A$450
worth of goods. If any of these individual
allowances are exceeded, you must pay
duty for the entire amount (of the group of
products in which the allowance was exceeded). Members of the same family traveling together may pool their allowances.
Prohibited items include meat products.
Seeds, plants, and fruits need to be de-
clared upon arrival.

🚢 **Australian Customs Service** 🕾 02/6275-6666
or 1300/363263, 02/8334-7444 or 1800/020-504
quarantine-inquiry line ⊕ www.customs.gov.au.

IN CANADA

Canadian residents who have been out of
Canada for at least seven days may bring
in C$750 worth of goods duty-free. If
you've been away fewer than seven days
but more than 48 hours, the duty-free allowance drops to C$200. If your trip lasts
24 to 48 hours, the allowance is C$50; if
the goods are worth more than C$50, you
must pay full duty on all of the goods. You
may not pool allowances with family
members. Goods claimed under the C$750
exemption may follow you by mail; those
claimed under the lesser exemptions must
accompany you. Alcohol and tobacco
products may be included in the seven-day
and 48-hour exemptions but not in the 24-
hour exemption. If you meet the age requirements of the province or territory
through which you reenter Canada, you
may bring in, duty-free, 1.5 liters of wine
or 1.14 liters (40 imperial ounces) of
liquor *or* 24 12-ounce cans or bottles of
beer or ale. Also, if you meet the local age
requirement for tobacco products, you
may bring in, duty-free, 200 cigarettes, 50
cigars or cigarillos, and 200 grams of tobacco. You may have to pay a minimum
duty on tobacco products, regardless of
whether or not you exceed your personal
exemption. Check ahead of time with the
Canada Border Services Agency or the Department of Agriculture for policies regarding meat products, seeds, plants, and
fruits.

You may send an unlimited number of gifts (only one gift per recipient, however) worth up to C$60 each duty-free to Canada. Label the package UNSOLICITED GIFT—VALUE UNDER $60. Alcohol and to-bacco are excluded.

🔌 **Canada Border Services Agency** ☎ 800/461-9999 in Canada, 204/983-3500, 506/636-5064 ⊕ www.cbsa.gc.ca.

IN MEXICO

Upon entering Mexico, you'll be given a baggage declaration form and asked to itemize what you're bringing into the country. You are allowed to bring in 3 liters of spirits or wine for personal use; 400 cigarettes, 25 cigars, or 200 grams of tobacco; a reasonable amount of perfume for personal use; one video camera and one regular camera and 12 rolls of film for each; and gift items not to exceed a total of $300. If driving across the U.S. border, gift items must not exceed $50. You aren't allowed to bring firearms, ammunition, meat, vegetables, plants, fruit, or flowers into the country. You can bring in one of each of the following items without paying taxes: a cell phone, a beeper, a radio or tape recorder, a musical instrument, a lap-top computer, and portable copier or printer. Compact discs and/or audio cas-settes are limited to 20 total and DVDs to five.

Mexico also allows you to bring one cat or dog, if you have two things: 1) a pet health certificate signed by a registered veterinar-ian in the United States and issued not more than 72 hours before the animal en-ters Mexico; and 2) a pet vaccination cer-tificate showing that the animal has been treated (as applicable) for rabies, hepatitis, distemper, and leptospirosis. For more in-formation or information on bringing other animals or more than one type of animal, contact a Mexican consulate. Adu-ana Mexico (Mexican Customs) has a striking and informative Web site, though everything is in Spanish. You can also get customs information from the Mexican consulate, which has branches in many major American cities as well as border towns. To find the consulate nearest you, check the Ministry of Foreign Affairs Web

site, http://portal.sre.gob.mx/sre; go to the list of embassies, consulates, and delega-tions and choose the "Consulados de México en el Exterior" option.

🔌 **Aduana Mexico** ⊕ www.aduanas.sat.gob.mx. **Mexican Embassy in Australia** ✉ 14 Perth Ave., Yarralumla, ACT ☎ 02/6273-3963 or 6273-3905 ⊕ www.embassyofmexicoinaustralia.org. **Mexican Embassy in Canada** ✉ 45 O'Connor St., Suite 1000, Ottawa K1P 3M6 ☎ 513/233-8988 ⊕ www. embamexcan.com. **Mexican Consulate in New Zealand** ✉ 111 Customhouse Quay (level 8), Wellington ☎ 644/472-0555. **Mexican Embassy in the U.K.** ✉ 16 St. George St., Hanover Sq., London ☎ 20/7499-8586 ⊕ www.embamex.co.uk. **Mexi-can Embassy in the U.S.** ✉ 1911 Pennsylvania Ave. NW, Washington, DC, 20006 ☎ 202/728-1600 ⊕ www.embassyofmexico.org.

IN NEW ZEALAND

All homeward-bound residents may bring back NZ$700 worth of souvenirs and gifts; passengers may not pool their al-lowances, and children can claim only the concession on goods intended for their own use. For those 17 or older, the duty-free allowance also includes 4.5 liters of wine or beer; one 1,125-ml bottle of spir-its; and either 200 cigarettes, 250 grams of tobacco, 50 cigars, *or* a combination of the three up to 250 grams. Meat products, seeds, plants, and fruits must be declared upon arrival to the Agricultural Services Department.

🔌 **New Zealand Customs** ☎ 04/473-6099 or 0800/428-786 ⊕ www.customs.govt.nz.

IN THE U.K.

From countries outside the European Union, including Mexico, you may bring home, duty-free, 200 cigarettes, 50 cigars, 100 cigarillos, or 250 grams of tobacco; 1 liter of spirits or 2 liters of fortified or sparkling wine or liqueurs; 2 liters of still table wine; 60 ml of perfume; 250 ml of toilet water; plus £145 worth of other goods, including gifts and souvenirs. Pro-hibited items include meat and dairy prod-ucts, seeds, plants, and fruits.

🔌 **HM Customs and Excise** ☎ 0845/010-9000, 0208/929-0152 advice service, 0208/929-6731, 0208/910-3602 complaints ⊕ www.hmce.gov.uk.

IN THE U.S.

U.S. residents who have been out of the country for at least 48 hours may bring home, for personal use, $800 worth of foreign goods duty-free, as long as they haven't used the $800 allowance or any part of it in the past 30 days. This exemption may include 1 liter of alcohol (for travelers 21 and older), 200 cigarettes, and 100 non-Cuban cigars. Family members from the same household who are traveling together may pool their $800 personal exemptions. For fewer than 48 hours, the duty-free allowance drops to $200, which may include 50 cigarettes, 10 non-Cuban cigars, and 150 ml of alcohol (or 150 ml of perfume containing alcohol). The $200 allowance cannot be combined with other individuals' exemptions, and if you exceed it, the full value of all the goods will be taxed. Antiques, which U.S. Customs and Border Protection defines as objects more than 100 years old, enter duty-free, as do original works of art done entirely by hand, including paintings, drawings, and sculptures. This doesn't apply to folk art or handicrafts, which are in general dutiable.

You may also send packages home duty-free, with a limit of one parcel per addressee per day (except alcohol or tobacco products or perfume worth more than $5). You can mail up to $200 worth of goods for personal use; label the package PERSONAL USE and attach a list of its contents and their retail value. If the package contains your used personal belongings, mark it AMERICAN GOODS RETURNED to avoid paying duties. You may send up to $100 worth of goods as a gift; mark the package UNSOLICITED GIFT. Mailed items do not affect your duty-free allowance on your return.

For more about duties, restricted items, and other information about international travel, check out U.S. Customs and Border Protection's online brochure, *Know Before You Go*. You can also file complaints on the U.S. Customs and Border Protection Web site, listed below.

🖪 **U.S. Customs and Border Protection** ⊕ www. cbp.gov.

DISABILITIES & ACCESSIBILITY

The best way for people with disabilities to see Puerto Vallarta is to go with a tour company, although these are few and far between. Although Mexicans in general and Puerto Vallartans in particular are courteous and genuinely anxious to help those with mobility problems or other disabilities, accessiblity is extremely limited. Wheelchair ramps are practically nonexistent, and exploring towns and beaches involves uneven streets, multiple stairs, and steep or muddy paths. The Society for Accessible Travel & Hospitality (SATH) has general information about travel for people with disabilities.

TRAVEL AGENCIES

Varlo y Mar is a Mexican travel agency that addresses the needs of people with physical disabilities. You can also rent the company's van (making your own arrangements for a driver) for trips to nearby Costa Careyes.

🖪 **Varlo y Mar** ☎ 322/224-1868 in Puerto Vallarta ⊕ www.accesiblemexico.com.

DISCOUNTS & DEALS

Be a smart shopper and compare all your options before making decisions. A plane ticket bought with a promotional coupon from travel clubs, coupon books, and direct-mail offers or purchased on the Internet may not be cheaper than the least expensive fare from a discount ticket agency. And always keep in mind that what you get is just as important as what you save.

ELECTRICITY

For U.S. and Canadian travelers, electrical converters aren't necessary because Mexico operates on the 60-cycle, 120-volt system; however, many Mexican outlets have not been updated to accommodate three-prong and polarized plugs (those with one larger prong), so to be safe **bring an adapter.**

If your appliances are dual-voltage, you'll need only an adapter, too. Don't use 110-volt outlets marked FOR SHAVERS ONLY for high-wattage appliances such as blow-dryers. Most laptops operate equally well on 110 and 220 volts and so require only an adapter. Blackouts and brownouts—often lasting an hour or so—are fairly common everywhere, particularly during the rainy season, so bring a surge protector.

EMBASSIES & CONSULATES

◪ In Puerto Vallarta **Canadian Consul** ✉ Zaragoza 160, 2nd fl., Centro, Puerto Vallarta ☎ 322/222-5398. **United States Consul** ✉ Zaragoza 160, 2nd fl., Centro, Puerto Vallarta ☎ 322/222-0069.

◪ In Mexico City **British Embassy** ✉ Río Lerma 71, Col. Cuauhtémoc, Mexico City ☎ 55/5207-2089 or 5242-8500 ⊕ www.embajadabritanica.com.mx. **Canadian Embassy** ✉ Calle Schiller 529, Col. Polanco, Mexico City ☎ 55/5724-7900 ⊕ www. dfait-maeci.gc.ca/mexico-city/. **New Zealand Embassy** ✉ Jaime Balmes 8, 4th fl., Col. Los Morales Polanco, Mexico City ☎ 55/5283-9460. **U.S. Embassy** ✉ Paseo de la Reforma 305, Col. Cuauhtémoc, Mexico City ☎ 55/5080-2000 ⊕ www. usembassy-mexico.gov/emenu.html.

EMERGENCIES

In an emergency call ☎ 060 or ☎ 066. For roadside assistance contact the Angeles Verdes. If you get into a scrape with the law, you can call your nearest consulate (⇨ *above*); U.S. citizens can also call the Overseas Citizens Services Center in the United States. The Mexican Ministry of Tourism has Infotur, a 24-hour toll-free hotline. Two medical emergency evacuation services are Air Ambulance Network and Global Life Flight.

Cornerstone is the newest hospital in PV (opened 2004). It accepts various types of foreign health insurance and traveler's insurance and is American owned. The other recommended, privately owned hospital is Hospital San Javier Marina. Although most small towns have at least a clinic, there are no hospitals north or south of PV.

Both the Cornerstone and San Javier Marina hospitals have pharmacies that are open to the public.

◪ **Air Ambulance Network** ☎ 800/327-1966 in U.S. and Canada ⊕ www.airambulancenetwork. com. **Ambulance/Red Cross** ☎ 065 or 322/222-1533. **Angeles Verdes** ☎ 078 or 01800/903-9200 toll-free in Mexico. **General Emergency (Police,**

Transit, Fire) ☎ 060. **Global Life Flight** ☎ 01800/ 305-9400, 01800/361-1600 toll-free in Mexico, 888/ 554-9729 in U.S., 877/817-6843 in Canada ⊕ www. globallifeflight.com. **Infotur** ☎ 01800/903-9200 toll-free in Mexico.

U.S. Overseas Citizens Services Center ☎ 202/ 501-4444 ⊕ www.travel.state.gov.
◪ Late-Night Pharmacy **Farmacia CMQ** ✉ Calle Basilio Badillo 365 ☎ 322/222-2941.
◪ Hospitals **Cornerstone Hospital** ✉ Av. Los Tules 136, across from Plaza Caracol Zona Hotelera ☎ 322/224-9400 ⊕ www.hospitalcornerstone.com. **Hospital San Javier Marina** ✉ Blvd. Francisco M. Ascencio 2760, at María Montessori, Zona Hotelera Norte ☎ 322/226-1010.

ETIQUETTE & BEHAVIOR

In the United States and elsewhere in the world, being direct, efficient, and succinct is highly valued. But Mexican communication tends to be more subtle, and the American style is often perceived as curt and aggressive. Mexicans are extremely polite, so losing your temper over delays or complaining loudly will get you branded as rude and make people less inclined to help you.

Remember that things move at a slow pace here and that there's no stigma attached to being late; be gracious about this and other local customs and attitudes.

Learning basic phrases in Spanish such as *"por favor"* (please) and *"gracias"* (thank you) will make a big difference in how people respond to you. Also, being deferential to those who are older than you will earn you lots of points, as does addressing people as señor, señora, or señorita. Also, saying *"Desculpe"* before asking a question of someone is a polite way of saying "Excuse me" before launching into a request for information or directions. Similarly, asking *"¿Hable inglé?"* before embarking on said request is more polite than assuming every Mexican you meet speaks English.

In Puerto Vallarta, it is acceptable to wear shorts in houses of worship, but do avoid being blatantly immodest. Bathing suits and immodest clothing are also inappropriate for shopping and sightseeing in general. Although Mexican men do not generally wear shorts, even in extremely hot weather, this rule is generally ignored by both Mexican and foreign men on vacation here.

You'll probably notice that local friends, relatives, and significant others show a fair amount of physical affection with each other, but—if you're a foreigner—be more retiring with people you don't know well.

BUSINESS ETIQUETTE

Personal relationships always come first here, so developing rapport and trust is essential. A handshake and personal greeting is appropriate along with a friendly inquiry about family, especially if you have met the family. In established business relationships, do not be surprised if you're greeted with a kiss on the cheek or a hug. Always be respectful toward colleagues in public and keep confrontations private. Meetings may or may not start on time, but you should be patient. When invited to dinner at the home of a client or associate, bring a gift and be sure to send a thank-you note afterward. Your offers to pick up the tab at business lunches or dinners will be greatly appreciated but will probably be declined; as a guest in their country most Mexicans will want to treat you to the meal. Be prepared to exchange business cards, and feel free to offer yours first. Professional attire tends to be on the traditional side. Mexicans are extremely well-groomed, so you'll do well if you follow suit.

GAY & LESBIAN TRAVEL

Puerto Vallarta is Mexico's prime gay destination. In the Zona Romántica especially, mild displays of same-sex affection are common, and some gay-owned hotels, bars, restaurants, and beach clubs are no-holds-barred. These gay-oriented businesses are the place to ask about any blatantly anti-gay establishments in PV and beyond. In general, Mexican same-sex couples keep a low profile, and foreign same-sex couples should do the same. Outside the Zona Romántica, two men might have a hard time getting a *cama matrimonial* (double bed), especially in less sophisticated hotels, although for women this shouldn't be a problem.

Guadalajara is a huge but conservative city with a subdued gay scene.

🛈 Gay- & Lesbian-Friendly Travel Agencies Different Roads Travel ☎ 310/289-6000 or 800/429-8747 ✉ lgernert@tzell.com. Skylink Travel and Tour/Flying Dutchmen Travel ☎ 707/546-9888 or 800/225-5759, serving lesbian travelers.

HEALTH

DIVERS' ALERT

Do not fly within 24 hours of scuba diving.

FOOD & DRINK

A little *turista,* or traveler's diarrhea, is to be expected when you plop down in a foreign culture, but to minimize risks, avoid street stands; pass up *ceviche,* raw fish cured in lemon juice; and if you're not sure of a restaurant's standards, don't eat any raw vegetables that haven't been, or can't be, peeled (e.g., lettuce and raw chili peppers).

Drink only bottled water or, if it's not available, drink only water that has been boiled for at least 10 minutes (to ask for boiled water, say *"por favor, quiero que se hierva el agua para diez minutos"*), even when you're brushing your teeth. *Agua mineral* or *agua con gas* means mineral or carbonated water, and *agua purificada* means purified water. Hotels with water-purification systems will post signs to that effect in the rooms; even then, be wary.

Despite these warnings, keep in mind that Puerto Vallarta, Nuevo Vallarta, and the Costalegre have virtually no industry beyond tourism, and are unlikely to kill the geese that lay their golden egg. Some people choose to bend the rules about eating at street stands and fresh fruits and chopped lettuce or cabbage, as there's no guarantee that you won't get sick at a 5-star resort and have a delicious, healthful meal at a shack by the sea. If fish or seafood smells or tastes bad, send it back and ask for something different. **Don't fret about ice:** tourist-oriented hotels and restaurants, and even most of those geared toward the locals, used purified water for ice, drinks, and washing vegetables. Many alleged cases of food poisoning are due instead to hangovers or excessive drinking in the strong sun. But whenever you're in doubt, ask questions about the origins of food and water and if you feel unsure, err on the side of safety.

Mild cases of turista may respond to Imodium (known generically as loperamide), Lomotil, or Pepto-Bismol (not as strong), all of which you can buy over the counter; keep in mind, though, that these drugs can complicate more serious illnesses. You'll need to replace fluids, so drink plenty of purified water or tea; chamomile tea (*te de manzanilla*) is a good folk remedy, and it's readily available in restaurants throughout Mexico. In severe cases, rehydrate yourself with Gatorade or a salt-sugar solution (½ teaspoon salt and 4 tablespoons sugar per quart of water). If your fever and diarrhea last longer than a day or two, see a doctor—you may have picked up a parasite or disease that requires prescription medication.

PESTS

Mosquitoes are most prevalent during the rainy season, where it's best to be cautious and use mosquito repellent daily, even in the city; if you're in jungly or wet places and lack strong repellent, consider covering up well or going indoors at dusk (called the "mosquito hour" by locals).

An excellent brand of *repelente de insectos* (insect repellent) called Autan is readily available; do not use it on children under age two. Repellents that are not at least 10% DEET or picaridin are not effective here. If you're hiking in the jungle or boggy areas wear repellent and long pants and sleeves; if you're camping in the jungle, use a mosquito net and invest in a package of *espirales contra mosquitos*, mosquito coils, which are sold in *ferreterías* or *tlalpalerías* (hardware stores).

THE SUN

Caution is advised when venturing out in the Mexican sun. Sunbathers lulled by a slightly overcast sky or the sea breezes can be burned badly in just 20 minutes. To avoid overexposure, **use strong sunscreens, sit under a shade umbrella, and** **avoid the peak sun hours** of noon to 2 PM. Sunscreen, including many American brands, can be found in pharmacies, supermarkets, and resort gift shops.

MEDICAL PLANS

No one plans to get sick while traveling, but it happens, so consider signing up with a medical-assistance company. Members get doctor referrals, emergency evacuation or repatriation, hotlines for medical consultation, cash for emergencies, and other assistance. You can call International SOS Assistance's U.S.-based phone number collect from Mexico.

🚗 Medical-Assistance Companies **International SOS Assistance** ☎ 215/942-8000, 800/523-6586 in the U.S., 20/8762-8008 in U.K. ⊕ www.internationalsos.com.

OVER-THE-COUNTER REMEDIES

Farmacias (pharmacies) are the most convenient place for such common medicines as *aspirina* (aspirin) or *jarabe para la tos* (cough syrup). You'll be able to find many U.S. brands (e.g., Tylenol, Pepto-Bismol, etc.). There are pharmacies in all small towns and on practically every corner in larger cities. The Sanborns chain stores also have pharmacies.

SHOTS & MEDICATIONS

Consult your physician or local travel health clinic about inoculations recommended for your journey. Make sure polio and diphtheria–tetanus shots are up to date well before your trip. Hepatitis A and typhoid are transmitted through unclean food or water. Gamma-globulin shots prevent hepatitis; an inoculation is available for typhoid, although it's not 100% effective. If traveling in remote areas consider a series of chloroquine pills against malaria. There's no vaccine against dengue fever. Both malaria and dengue are transmitted through the bite of an infected mosquito, so preventing bites by covering up, using insect repellent with DEET, and burning mosquito coils are recommended in remote or infection-prone areas.

🚗 Health Warnings **National Centers for Disease Control and Prevention** (CDC) ☎ 877/394-8747 international travelers' health line, 800/311-3435 other inquiries, 404/498-1600 Division of Quarantine and international health information ⊕ www.cdc.gov/travel. **Travel Health Online** ⊕ www.tripprep.com. **World Health Organization** (WHO) ⊕ www.who.int.

HOLIDAYS

Banks and government offices close on January 1, February 5 (Constitution Day), March 21 (Benito Juárez's birthday), May 1 (Labor Day), September 16 (Independence Day), November 20 (Revolution Day), and December 25. They may also close on unofficial holidays, such as Day of the Dead (November 1–2), Virgin of Guadalupe Day (December 12), and during Holy Week (the days leading to Easter Sunday). Government offices usually have reduced hours and staff from Christmas through New Year's Day.

INSURANCE

The most useful travel-insurance plan is a comprehensive policy that includes coverage for trip cancellation and interruption, default, trip delay, and medical expenses (with a waiver for preexisting conditions).

Without insurance you'll lose all or most of your money if you cancel your trip, regardless of the reason. Default insurance covers you if your tour operator, airline, or cruise line goes out of business—the chances of which have been increasing. Trip-delay covers expenses that arise because of bad weather or mechanical delays. Study the fine print when comparing policies.

If you're traveling internationally, a key component of travel insurance is coverage for medical bills incurred if you get sick on the road. Such expenses aren't generally covered by Medicare or private policies. U.K. residents can buy a travel-insurance policy valid for most vacations taken during the year in which it's purchased (but check preexisting-condition coverage). British and Australian citizens need extra medical coverage when traveling overseas.

Always **buy travel policies directly from the insurance company**; if you buy them from a cruise line, airline, or tour operator that goes out of business you probably won't be covered for the agency or operator's default, a major risk. Before making any purchase, review your existing health and home-owner's policies to find what they cover away from home.

🚩 Travel Insurers In the U.S.: **Access America** ☎ 800/729-6021 ⊕ www.accessamerica.com. **Travel Guard International** ☎ 715/345-1041 or 800/826-4919 ⊕ www.travelguard.com.

🚩 In the U.K.: **Association of British Insurers** ☎ 020/7600-3333 ⊕ www.abi.org.uk. In Canada: **RBC Insurance** ☎ 800/565-3129 ⊕ www.rbcinsurance.com. In Australia: **Insurance Council of Australia** ☎ 02/9253-5100 ⊕ www.ica.com.au. In New Zealand: **Insurance Council of New Zealand** ☎ 04/472-5230 ⊕ www.icnz.org.nz.

INTERNET, MAIL & SHIPPING

For sending and receiving mail and packages, go to Mail Boxes Etc. At PV Café you can enjoy a sandwich or a salad and coffee while downloading digital photos, sending a fax, or surfing the Web (35 pesos per hour). At decidedly less-comfortable PV Net, which is open 24 hours a day, 365 days a year, you obtain an access code and use your minutes each time you visit; the cost for Internet access is 20 pesos per hour, offers monthly and weekly rates, and has a room at the back just for the kids. For laptop connections you can pay by the day, week, or month.

The Mexican postal system is notoriously slow and unreliable; **never send packages through the postal service** or expect to receive them, as they may be stolen. (For emergencies, use a courier service). If you're an American Express cardholder, you may be able to receive packages at a branch office, but check beforehand with customer service to find out if this client mail service is available at your destination.

Post offices (*oficinas de correos*) are found in even the smallest villages. International postal service is all airmail, but even so your letter will take anywhere from 10 days to six weeks to arrive. Service within Mexico can be equally slow.

POSTAL RATES

It costs 10.50 pesos (about 95¢) to send a postcard or letter weighing under 20 grams to the United States or Canada; it's 13 pesos ($1.17) to Europe and 14.50 pesos ($1.30) to Australia and New Zealand.

RECEIVING MAIL

To receive mail in Mexico, you can have it sent to your hotel or use *poste restante* at the post office. In the latter case, the address must include the words "a/c Lista de Correos" (general delivery), followed by the city, state, postal code, and country. To use this service, you must first register with the post office at which you wish to receive your mail. The post office posts and updates daily a list of names for whom mail has been received. Mail is generally held for 10 days, and a list of recipients is posted daily. Keep in mind that the mail service in Mexico is very slow, and it can take weeks for mail to arrive—presenting quite a timing crapshoot if you're hoping to send something to someone care of Lista de Correos. Holders of American Express cards or traveler's checks may be able to receive mail in care of the local American Express office; check with customer service beforehand to see whether the office at your destination will do so.
🖪 **American Express** ⊕ www.americanexpress.com/travel.

SHIPPING PARCELS

Federal Express, DHL, Estafeta, and United Parcel Service are available in major cities and many resort areas. These companies offer office or hotel pickup with 24-hour advance notice (sometimes less, depending on when you call) and are very reliable. FedEx's Web site is especially easy to navigate. From Puerto Vallarta to large U.S. cities, for example, the minimum charge is around $30 for an envelope weighing about ½ pound. Starting prices are higher for Australia, Canada, New Zealand, and the United Kingdom, and deliveries take longer. It's best to send all packages using one of these services.
🖪 **Mail Services Correos** ⊠ Calle Mina 188, El Centro ☎ 322/222-1888. **Mail Boxes Etc.** ⊠ Edificio Andrea Mar Local 7, Blvd. Francisco M. Ascencio, Zona Hotelera Norte, across from Hotel Los Tules ☎ 322/224-9434.

🖪 **Internet Cafés PV Café** ⊠ Calle Olas Altas 250, Olas Altas ☎ 322/222-0092. **PV Net** ⊠ Blvd. Francisco M. Ascencio 1692, across from Sheraton Buganvilias, Zona Hotelera Norte ☎ 322/223-1127.
🖪 **Shipping DHL** ⊠ Av. Federico M. Ascencio 1046, between Calle Sierra Rocosa and Av. De las Américas, Col. Olímpica ☎ 322/222-4720 or 322/222-4620 ⊕ www.dhl.com.

LANGUAGE

English is widely understood by most people employed in tourism, although less so in the less-developed areas. At the very least, shopkeepers in remote places will usually know numbers and basic phrases. Remember that regional accents vary (imagine trying to understand a Brit, French Canadian, Texan, and Aussie all in the same day). The average Mexican in and around Puerto Vallarta speaks good English, but speak slowly and avoid idiomatic expressions and slang.

As in most other foreign countries, knowing the mother tongue has a way of opening doors, so **learn some Spanish words and phrases.** Mexicans welcome even the most halting attempts to use their language. The exception to this rule are Mexicans who speak fluent English having a conversation with someone who wants to use his or her halting, high-school Spanish. This may work when you're seated at adjacent bar stools, but is less effective when there's a long line waiting for help at the front desk of your hotel.

For basic words and phrases, consult the glossary at the back of this book. For really subtle nuances, consult a native speaker. The *Random House Latin-American Spanish Dictionary* is a good reference. *Fodor's Spanish for Travelers* (available at bookstores everywhere) is another resource to get you *habla*-ing.

MONEY MATTERS

Prices in this book are quoted most often in U.S. dollars. We would prefer to list costs in pesos, but because the value of the currency fluctuates considerably, what costs 90 pesos today might cost 120 pesos in six months.

A stay in one of Puerto Vallarta's top hotels can cost more than $250, but if you aren't wedded to standard creature comforts you can spend as little as $50 a day on room, board, and local transportation. Lodgings are less expensive in the less-developed spots north and south of Puerto Vallarta as well as the charming but unsophisticated mountain towns like San Sebastián del Oeste.

You can get away with a tab of $50 for two at a wonderful restaurant (although it's also easy to pay much more). The good news is that there are hotels and eateries for every budget, and inexpensive doesn't necessarily mean bargain basement. This guide will clue you in to some excellent places to stay, eat, and play for extremely reasonable prices.

Prices throughout this guide are given for adults. Substantially reduced fees are almost always available for children, students, and senior citizens.For information on taxes, *see* Taxes.

ATMS

ATMs (*cajeros automáticos*) are widely available, with Cirrus and Plus the most frequently found networks. However, the transaction fees charged by your bank can be up to $5 a pop; before you leave home, **ask your bank about fees for withdrawing money in Mexico.**

Many Mexican ATMs cannot accept PINs with more than four digits. If yours is longer, **change your PIN to four digits before you leave home.** If your PIN is fine yet your transaction still can't be completed—a regular occurrence—chances are that the computer lines are busy or that the machine has run out of money or is being serviced. Don't give up.

For cash advances, plan to use Visa or MasterCard, as many Mexican ATMs don't accept American Express. Large banks with reliable ATMs include Banamex, HSBC, BBVA Bancomer, Santander Serfín, and Scotiabank Inverlat. (For information about avoiding ATM robberies, *see* Safety.)

🏧 Banks **Banamex** ✉ Calle Juárez, at Calle Zaragoza, Centro ☎ 322/226-6110 ✉ Plaza Marina,

Local 37 ☎ 322/221-0733 ✉ Calle Emiliano Zapata 48, Centro ☎ 322/224-8115 ✉ Paseo de los Cocoteros s/n, Paradise Plaza, Nuevo Vallarta ☎ 322/297-0688. **Banorte** ✉ Paseo Díaz Ordaz 690 at Calle L. Vicario, Centro ☎ 322/222-4040 ✉ Calle Olas Altas 246 at Calle Basilio Badillo E. Zapata ☎ 322/223-0481 ✉ Blvd. Francisco Medina Ascencio 500, Zona Hotelera Norte ☎ 322/224-9744.

CREDIT CARDS

Credit cards are accepted in Puerto Vallarta and major hotels and restaurants in outlying areas. Smaller, less expensive restaurants and shops, however, tend to take only cash. In general, credit cards aren't accepted in small towns and villages, except in some hotels. The most widely accepted cards are MasterCard and Visa.

When shopping, you can often get better prices if you pay with cash, particularly in small shops. But you'll receive wholesale exchange rates when you make purchases with credit cards. These exchange rates are usually better than those that banks give you for changing money. The decision to pay cash or to use a credit card might depend on whether the establishment in which you are making a purchase finds bargaining for prices acceptable, and whether you want the safety net of your card's purchase protection. To avoid fraud or errors, it's wise to **make sure that "pesos" is clearly marked on all credit-card receipts.**

Before you leave for Mexico, **contact your credit-card company to get lost-card phone numbers that work in Mexico;** the standard toll-free numbers often don't work abroad. Carry these numbers separately from your wallet so you'll have them if you need to call to report lost or stolen cards. American Express, MasterCard, and Visa note the international number for card-replacement calls on the back of their cards.

Throughout this guide, the following abbreviations are used: **AE**, American Express; **D**, Discover; **DC**, Diners Club; **MC**, MasterCard; and **V**, Visa.

CURRENCY

Mexican currency comes in denominations of 20-, 50-, 100-, 200-, and 500-peso bills. Coins come in denominations of 1, 2, 5, 10, and 20 pesos, and 10, 20, and 50 centavos. (Ten and 20-centavo coins are only rarely seen.) Many of the coins and bills are very similar, so check carefully.

U.S. dollar bills (but not coins) are widely accepted in tourist-oriented shops and restaurants in Puerto Vallarta. Pay in pesos where possible, however, for better prices. Virtually all hotel service personnel also accept dollars.

CURRENCY EXCHANGE

At this writing, the peso was fluctuating between 10.2 and 11 pesos to the U.S. dollar. Check with your bank or the financial pages of your local newspaper for current exchange rates. For quick, rough estimates of how much something costs in U.S. dollar terms, divide prices given in pesos by 10. For example, 50 pesos would be $5.

ATM transaction fees may be higher abroad than at home (⇨ ATMs), but ATM currency-exchange rates are the best because they're based on wholesale rates offered only by major banks. And if you take out a fair amount of cash per withdrawal, the transaction fee becomes less of a strike against the exchange rate (in percentage terms). However, most ATMs allow only up to $300 per transaction. Banks and *casas de cambio* (money-exchange bureaus) have the second-best exchange rates. The difference from one place to another is usually only a few centavos.

Most banks change money on weekdays only until 1 PM (though they stay open until 3 or later). Casas de cambio generally stay open until 6 and often operate on weekends; they usually have better rates and shorter lines. Some hotels exchange money, but they help themselves to a bigger commission than banks for providing you this convenience.

You can do well at most airport exchange booths, though not as well as at the ATM machines. You'll do even worse at bus stations, in hotels, in restaurants, or in stores.

When changing money, count your bills before leaving the window of the bank or casa de cambio, and don't accept any partially torn or taped-together notes: you won't be able to use them anywhere. (If you do end up with a torn bill, you can change it for a bill in good condition at any bank.) Also, many shop and restaurant owners are unable to make change for large bills. Enough of these encounters may compel you to request *billetes chicos* (small bills) when you exchange money.

🛈 Exchange Services **International Currency Express** ☎ 888/278-6628 ⊕ www.foreignmoney.com. **Travel Ex Currency Services** ☎ 800/287-7362 ⊕ www.travelex.com.

TRAVELER'S CHECKS

When traveling abroad meant having to move around with large wads of cash, traveler's checks were a godsend, because lost checks could be replaced, usually within 24 hours. But nowadays credit cards and ATM cards have all but eliminated the need for traveler's checks, and as a result fewer establishments than ever accept them in Mexico. If you do decide to use traveler's checks, buy them from American Express (some levels of cardholders might get them for free) or at a bank. You must always show a photo ID when cashing these checks.

PACKING

High-style sportswear, cotton slacks and walking shorts, and plenty of colorful sundresses are the palette of clothing you'll see in PV. Bring lightweight sportswear, bathing suits, and cover-ups for the beach. In addition to shorts, pack at least a pair or two of lightweight long pants. Men may want to bring a lightweight suit or slacks and blazers for fancier restaurants (although very few have dress codes). For women, dresses of cotton, linen, or other lightweight, breathable fabrics are recommended. Puerto Vallarta restaurants are extremely tolerant of casual dress, but it never hurts to exceed expectations.

The sun can be fierce; **bring a sun hat and sunscreen** for the beach and for sightseeing. You'll need a sweater or jacket to cope with hotel and restaurant air-conditioning, which can be glacial, and for occasional cool spells. A lightweight jacket is a necessity in winter, and pack an umbrella for summer rainstorms.

It's a good idea to bring along tissue packs in case you hit a place where the toilet paper has run out. You'll find familiar toiletries and hygiene products, as well as condoms, in shops in PV and in most rural areas.

It's good to pack a change of clothes and underwear, essential toiletries, and a bathing suit in your carry-on luggage, in case your other luggage is lost. In your carry-on luggage, pack an extra pair of eyeglasses or contact lenses and enough of any medication you take to last a few days longer than the entire trip. You may also ask your doctor to write a spare prescription using the drug's generic name, as brand names may vary from country to country. In luggage to be checked, never pack prescription drugs, valuables, or undeveloped film. To avoid customs and security delays, carry medications in their original packaging.

Check *Fodor's How to Pack* (available at online retailers and bookstores everywhere) for more tips.

PASSPORTS & VISAS

Citizens of the U.S., Canada, U.K., Australia, and New Zealand do not need a tourist visa to enter Mexico. Canadians, New Zealanders, Australians, and citizens of the United Kingdom must have a valid passport (valid for three months beyond your stay in Mexico). U.S. citizens must prove citizenship by presenting a valid passport or certified copy of a birth certificate (the latter must be accompanied by a government-issue photo ID). However, if at all possible, **bring a passport;** U.S. citizens have encountered problems once in Mexico without a passport.

A tourist card is required for all visitors to Mexico. If you're arriving by plane from the United States or Canada, the standard tourist card will be given to you on the plane. They're also available through travel agents and Mexican consulates, and

at the border if you're entering by land. You're given a portion of the form. Be sure to **keep track of your tourist card documentation throughout your trip: you will need it when you depart.** You'll be asked to hand it, your ticket, and your passport to airline representatives at the gate when boarding for departure. Visitors from other countries require a visa.

A tourist card costs about $20 (not to be confused with the airport departure tax). The fee is generally tacked onto the price of your airline ticket; if you enter by land or boat you'll have to pay the fee separately. You're exempt from the fee if you enter by sea and stay less than 72 hours, or by land and do not stray past the 26–30-km (16–18-mi) checkpoint into the country's interior.

Tourist cards and visas are valid from 30 to 180 days, at the discretion of the immigration officer at your point of entry (90 days for Australians). Americans, Canadians, New Zealanders, and the British may request up to 180 days for a tourist card or visa extension; Australians are allowed up to 90 days. The extension fee is about $20, and the process can easily take up an entire day. There's no guarantee that you'll get the extension you're requesting. **If you're planning an extended stay, plead with the immigration official for the maximum allowed days at the time of entry.** It will save you time and money later.

Minors traveling with one parent need notarized permission from the absent parent (⇨ Children in Mexico).

When traveling internationally, carry your passport even if you don't need one. Not only is it the best form of ID, but it's also being required more and more. As of December 31, 2005, for instance, Americans need a passport to re-enter the country from Bermuda, the Caribbean, and Panama. Such requirements also affect re-entry from Canada and Mexico by air and sea (as of December 31, 2006) and land (as of December 31, 2007). **Make two photocopies of the data page** (one for someone at home and another for you, carried separately from your passport). If you lose your passport, promptly call the nearest embassy or consulate and the local police.

U.S. passport applications for children under age 14 require consent from both parents or legal guardians; both parents must appear together to sign the application. If only one parent appears, he or she must submit a written statement from the other parent authorizing passport issuance for the child. A parent with sole authority must present evidence of it when applying; acceptable documentation includes the child's certified birth certificate listing only the applying parent, a court order specifically permitting this parent's travel with the child, or a death certificate for the nonapplying parent. Application forms and instructions are available on the Web site of the U.S. State Department's Bureau of Consular Affairs (⊕ travel.state.gov).

Mexican Embassies Worldwide Mexican Embassy ⊠ 14 Perth Ave., Yarralumla, ACT, Australia ☎ 02/6273-3963 or 6273-3905 ⊕ www. embassyofmexicoinaustralia.org ⊠ 45 O'Connor St., Suite 1000, Ottawa K1P 3M6 Canada ☎ 513/233-8988 ⊕ www.embamexcan.com ⊠ 16 St. George St., Hanover Sq., London, U.K. ☎ 20/7499-8586 ⊕ www.embamex.co.uk ⊠ 1911 Pennsylvania Ave. NW, Washington, DC 20006 U.S. ☎ 202/728-1600 ⊕ www.embassyofmexico.org.

Mexican Consulate Consulate of Mexico ⊠ 111 Customhouse Quay (level 8), Wellington, New Zealand ☎ 644/472-0555.

RESTROOMS

Expect to find clean flushing toilets, soap, cold running water, and toilet tissue at public restrooms in the major tourist destinations and at tourist attractions (although the latter is sometimes missing even in nice establishments). At many markets, bus stations, and the like you may have to pay a couple of pesos for the privilege of using a toilet that lacks a seat, toilet paper (keep tissues with you at all times), and possibly even running water. Gas stations have public bathrooms—some tidy and others not so tidy. You're better off popping into a restaurant, buying a little something, and using its restroom, which will probably be simple but clean and adequately equipped. Re-

member that unless otherwise indicated you should **put your used toilet paper in the wastebasket** next to the toilet; many plumbing systems in Mexico still can't handle accumulations of toilet paper.

SAFETY

Despite recent growth, PV retains a small-town attitude and crime is not as much of a problem here as in some other areas of Mexico. One of the most serious threats to your safety is local drivers. Although pedestrians have the right of way by law, drivers disregard it. And more often than not, drivers who hit pedestrians drive away as fast as they can without stopping, to avoid jail. Many Mexican drivers don't carry auto insurance, so you'll have to shoulder your own medical expenses. Pedestrians should be extremely cautious of all traffic, especially city bus drivers, who often drive with truly reckless abandon.

CRIME

Horror stories about highway assaults, pickpocketing, and bus robberies by armed bandits don't really apply to the area around Puerto Vallarta. Pickpocketing can be a problem even in sleepy Vallarta, and precaution is in order here as elsewhere. Store only enough money in your wallet or bag to cover the day's spending. And don't flash big wads of money or leave valuables like cameras unattended. Leave your passport and other valuables you don't need in your hotel's safe.

Bear in mind that reporting a crime to the police is often a frustrating experience unless you speak excellent Spanish and have a great deal of patience. If you're victimized, contact your local consulate or your embassy in Mexico City (⇨ Embassies & Consulates).

WOMEN IN MEXICO

If you're on your own, consider using only your first initial and last name when registering at your hotel. Solo travelers, or women traveling with other women rather than men, may be subjected to *piropos* (flirtatious compliments). Piropos are one thing, but more aggressive harassment is another. If the situation seems to be getting out of hand, don't hesitate to ask someone for help. If you express outrage, you should find no shortage of willing defenders.

If you carry a purse, choose one with a zipper and a thick strap that you can drape across your body; adjust the length so that the purse sits in front of you at or above hip level.

SENIOR-CITIZEN TRAVEL

To qualify for age-related discounts, mention your senior-citizen status up front when booking hotel reservations (not when checking out) and before you're seated in restaurants (not when paying the bill). Be sure to have identification on hand. When renting a car, ask about promotional car-rental discounts, which can be cheaper than senior-citizen rates.

Some facilities may recognize foreign-issued credentials (such as those from AARP), so make a habit of asking. It's not always enough to simply mention that you are a senior citizen.

🖪 Educational Programs **Elderhostel** ☎ 877/426-8056, 978/323-4141 international callers, 877/426-2167 TTY ⊕ www.elderhostel.org. **Interhostel** ☎ 603/862-1147 or 800/733-9753 ⊕ www.learn.unh.edu.

STUDENTS IN MEXICO

The ISIC student card or GO25 card can get you cut-rate plane tickets to Mexico at youth-oriented travel agencies. Within Mexico, many signs at tourist attractions will state that student discounts are only for Mexican students, but occasionally you'll get a discount by showing one of these cards. The Mundo Joven travel agency in Mexico City and other areas throughout the country sells ISIC and GO25 cards and offers good deals on plane tickets.

🖪 IDs & Services **Mundo Joven** ☎ 55/5661-3233 in Mexico City ⊕ www.mundojoven.com. **STA Travel** ☎ 212/627-3111, 800/777-0112 24-hr service center ⊕ www.sta.com. **Travel Cuts** ☎ 800/592-2887 in U.S., 416/979-2406, 866/246-9762 in Canada ⊕ www.travelcuts.com.

TAXES

Mexico charges an airport departure tax of US$18 or the peso equivalent for international and domestic flights. This tax is usually included in the price of your ticket, but check to be certain. Traveler's checks and credit cards aren't accepted at the airport as payment for this, but U.S. dollars are. Jalisco and Nayarit charge a 2% tax on accommodations, the funds from which are being used for tourism promotion.

VALUE-ADDED TAX

Puerto Vallarta and environs have a value-added tax of 15%, called IVA (*impuesto al valor agregado*). It's occasionally (and illegally) waived for cash purchases. Other taxes and charges apply for phone calls made from your hotel room.

TAXIS

Taxis in the Puerto Vallarta area aren't metered, and instead charge by zones. Always **establish the fare beforehand,** and count your change. Most of the larger hotels have rate sheets, and taxi drivers should produce them upon request. Tipping isn't necessary unless the driver helps you with your bags, in which case a few pesos are appropriate.

The minimum fare is 30 pesos (about $3), but if you don't ask, or your Spanish isn't great, you'll probably be overcharged. Negotiate a price in advance for out-of-town and hourly services as well; many drivers will start by asking how much you want to pay or how much others have charged you to get a sense of how street-smart you are. The usual hourly rate at press time is $19 (200 pesos) per hour. In all cases, if you are unsure of what a fare should be, ask your hotel's front-desk personnel or bell captain.

The ride from downtown to the airport or to Marina Vallarta costs $10, it's $19 to Nuevo Vallarta, and $21 to Bucerías. From downtown south to Mismaloya it's about $4 to the hotels of the Zona Hotelera Sur, $8 to Mismaloya, and $13 to Boca de Tomatlán. Cabs are plentiful, and you can easily hail one on the street. They aren't metered; be sure to agree on a fare before embarking. Radio Taxi PV provides 24-hour service.

⚠ Taxi Company **Radio Taxi PV** ☎ 322/225–0716.

TELEPHONES

AREA & COUNTRY CODES

The area code for PV (and the northern Costalegre) and Nuevo Vallarta is 322; San Francisco has both 311 and 329 area codes, otherwise between Bucerías and San Francisco it's 329. Lo De Marcos and Rincón de Guayabitos: 327. The Costalegre from around Rancho Cuixmala to San Patricio–Melaque and Barra de Navidad has a 315 area code.

The country code for Mexico is 52. When calling a Mexico number from abroad, dial any necessary international access code, then the country code and then all of the numbers listed for the entry.

DIRECTORY & OPERATOR ASSISTANCE

Directory assistance is 040 nationwide. For assistance in English, dial 090 first for an international operator; tell the operator in what city, state, and country you require directory assistance, and he or she will connect you.

INTERNATIONAL CALLS

To make an international call, dial 00 before the country code, area code, and number. The country code for the United States and Canada is 1, the United Kingdom 44, Australia 61, New Zealand 64, and South Africa 27.

LOCAL & LONG-DISTANCE CALLS

For local or long-distance calls, you can use either a standard public pay phone or a *caseta de larga distancia,* or long-distance telephone service (⇨ Phone Cards & Public Phones). To make a direct long-distance or local call from a caseta, tell the person on duty the number you'd like to call, and she or he will give you a rate and dial for you. Rates seem to vary widely, so shop around, but overall they're higher than those of pay phones, and more importantly, infrequently seen in the Vallarta area.

Using a prepaid phone card (⇨ Phone Cards & Public Phones) is by far the most convenient way to call long distance

within Mexico or abroad. Look for a phone 'booth' away from traffic noise; these phones are tucked behind three sides of plexiglass but street noise can make hearing difficult. If you're calling long distance within Mexico, dial 01 before the area code and number. For local calls, just dial the number; no other prefix is necessary. If calling abroad, buy the 100-peso card, the largest denomination available.

Sometimes you can make collect calls from casetas, and sometimes you cannot, depending on the individual operator and possibly your degree of visible desperation. Casetas will generally charge 50¢–$1.50 to place a collect call (some charge by the minute); it's usually better to call *por cobrar* (collect) from a pay phone.

LONG-DISTANCE SERVICES

AT&T, MCI, and Sprint access codes make calling long-distance relatively convenient, but you may find the local access number blocked in many hotel rooms. First ask the hotel operator to connect you. If the hotel operator balks, ask for an international operator, or dial the international operator yourself. One way to improve your odds of getting connected to your long-distance carrier is to travel with more than one company's calling card (a hotel may block Sprint, for example, but not MCI). If all else fails, call from a pay phone. If you're traveling for a longer period of time, consider renting a cell-phone from a local company.

⚠ Access Codes **AT&T Direct** ☎ 01800/288–2872 toll-free in Mexico. **MCI WorldPhone** ☎ 01800/674–7000 toll-free in Mexico. **Sprint International Access** ☎ 01800/234–0000 or 01800/877–8000 toll-free in Mexico.

PHONE CARDS & PUBLIC PHONES

Most pay phones only accept prepaid cards, called Ladatel cards, sold in 30-, 50-, or 100-peso denominations at newsstands, pharmacies, or grocery stores. These Ladatel phones are all over the place—on street corners, in bus stations, and so on. Older, coin-only pay phones are rarely encountered, those you do find are often broken or have poor connections. Still other phones have two unmarked slots, one for a Ladatel (a Spanish acronym for "long-distance direct dialing") card and the other for a credit card. These are primarily for Mexican bank cards, but some accept Visa or Master-Card, though *not* U.S. phone credit cards.

To use a Ladatel card, simply insert it in the appropriate slot with the computer chip insignia forward and right-side up, and dial. Credit is deleted from the card as you use it, and your balance is displayed on a small screen on the phone. You'll be charged about 1 peso per minute for local calls and more for long-distance and international calls. Most pay phones display a price list and dialing instructions.

A *caseta de larga distancia* is a long-distance/overseas telephone service usually operated out of a store such as a *papelería* (stationery store), pharmacy, restaurant, or other small business; look for the phone symbol on the door. Casetas may cost more to use than pay phones, but you tend to be shielded from street noise, as you get your own little cabin. They also have the benefit of not forcing you to buy a prepaid phone card with a specific denomination—you pay in cash according to the calls you make. The store employee places the call for you.

TOLL-FREE NUMBERS

Toll-free numbers in Mexico start with an 800 prefix. These numbers, however, are billed as local calls if you call one from a private phone. To reach them, you need to dial 01 before the number. In this guide, Mexico-only toll-free numbers appear as follows: 01800/123–4567. The toll-free numbers listed simply 800/123–4567 are U.S. or Canadian numbers, and generally work north of the border only (though some calling cards will allow you to dial them from Mexico, charging you minutes as for a toll call). Numbers listed as 001800/123–4567 are toll-free U.S. numbers; if you're calling from Mexico, you'll be charged for an international call.

TIME

Puerto Vallarta, Guadalajara, and the rest of Jalisco State fall into Central Standard Time (the same as Mexico City). Nayarit and other parts of the northwest coast are on Mountain Standard Time. Mexico switches to and from Daylight Savings Time on the same schedule as the United States.

The fact that the state of Nayarit (including Nuevo Vallarta and points north) are in a different time zone from Puerto Vallarta and points east and south leads to confusion. Businesses in Nuevo Vallarta and many tourism-related businesses in Bucerías run on Jalisco time since tourism in these towns has always been linked to that of Puerto Vallarta. Hotels in the two areas almost always run on Jalisco time to avoid having their clients miss planes when returning home. When asking the time, checking hours of operation, or making dinner reservations, double check whether the place runs on *hora de Jalisco* (Jalisco time) or *hora de Nayarit*.

TIPPING

When tipping, remember that the minimum wage is the equivalent of $4.50 a day and that, while many working in tourism sectors receive several times that amount or more, those at the lowest end of the spectrum earn very little. Porters in large hotels expect $1–$2 per bag and waiters and waitresses hope for 15% of the bill. Since their wages are low, they depend on tips. In these resort-oriented areas, U.S. dollars are as welcome as tips in pesos.

Naturally, larger tips are always welcome, but basic guidelines are: porters and bellhops, 10–20 pesos per bag at airports and hotels; maids, 10 pesos per night; waiters, 10%–15% of the bill, depending on service (make sure a service charge or gratuity hasn't already been added; most common in resorts); bartenders, 10%–15% of the bill, depending on service (and, perhaps, on how many drinks you've had); taxi drivers, 5–10 pesos if the driver helps you with your bags; cab drivers are not normally tipped, and it would be especially silly to tip when you've just finished negotiating for a reasonable fare. Tour guides and drivers, at least 50 pesos per half day; gas-station attendants, 3–5 pesos unless they check the oil, tires, etc., in which case tip more; parking attendants, 5–10 pesos, even if it's for valet parking at a theater or restaurant that charges for the service.

TOURS & PACKAGES

Don't confuse packages and guided tours. When you buy a package, you travel on your own, just as though you had planned the trip yourself. Fly/drive packages, which combine airfare and car rental, are often a good deal.

BUYER BEWARE

Each year consumers are stranded or lose their money when tour operators—even large ones with excellent reputations—go out of business. So check out the operator. Ask several travel agents about its reputation, and try to **book with a company that has a consumer-protection program.** (Look for information in the company's brochure.) In the United States, members of the United States Tour Operators Association are required to set aside funds (up to $1 million) to help eligible customers cover payments and travel arrangements in the event that the company defaults. It's also a good idea to choose a company that participates in the American Society of Travel Agents' Tour Operator Program; ASTA will act as mediator in any disputes between you and your tour operator.

Remember that the more your package or tour includes, the better you can predict the ultimate cost of your vacation. Make sure you know exactly what is covered, and beware of hidden costs. Are taxes, tips, and transfers included? Entertainment and excursions? These can add up.

🄵 Tour-Operator Recommendations **American Society of Travel Agents** (⇨ Travel Agencies). **CrossSphere–The Global Association for Packaged Travel** ☎ 859/226–4444 or 800/682–8886 ⊕ www.CrossSphere.com. **United States Tour Operators Association (USTOA)** ☎ 212/599–6599 ⊕ www.ustoa.com.

TRAVEL AGENCIES

A good travel agent puts your needs first. Look for an agency that has been in business at least five years, emphasizes customer service, and has someone on staff who specializes in your destination. In ad-

dition, **make sure the agency belongs to a professional trade organization.** The American Society of Travel Agents (ASTA) has more than 10,000 members in some 140 countries, enforces a strict code of ethics, and will step in to mediate agent-client disputes involving ASTA members. ASTA also maintains a directory of agents on its Web site; ASTA's TravelSense.org, a trip planning and travel advice site, can also help to locate a travel agent who caters to your needs.

🄵 Local Agent Referrals **American Society of Travel Agents (ASTA)** ☎ 703/739–2782, 800/965–2782 24-hr hotline ⊕ www.astanet.com or www.travelsense.org. **Association of British Travel Agents** ☎ 0901/201–5050 ⊕ www.abta.com. **Association of Canadian Travel Agencies** ☎ 613/237–3657 ⊕ www.acta.ca. **Australian Federation of Travel Agents** ☎ 02/9264–3299 or 1300/363–416 ⊕ www.afta.com.au. **Travel Agents' Association of New Zealand** ☎ 04/499–0104 ⊕ www.taanz.org.nz.

VISITOR INFORMATION

The Mexican Ministry of Tourism's Infotur is a 24-hour toll-free hotline. Learn more about foreign destinations by checking government-issued travel advisories and country information. For a broader picture, consider information from more than one country. The Mexico Tourism Board has branches in New York, Chicago, Los Angeles, Houston, Miami, Montréal, Toronto, Vancouver, and London.

For information before you visit, try the Puerto Vallarta Tourism Board & Convention and Visitors Bureau. You can also stop in for maps and other information once you're in town. Other convenient sources of information are the Municipal Tourist Office, right on the Plaza Principal. It's open weekdays 8–4. The friendly folks at the Jalisco State Tourism Office, open weekdays 9–5, are helpful with information about PV and destinations throughout the state, including mountain towns like Mascota and Talpán. For information about Nuevo Vallarta and southern Nayarit, contact the Nayarit State Tourism Office.

🄵 Tourist Information **Mexican Ministry of Tourism** ☎ Infotur: 800/446–3942 in U.S.,

01800/903-9200 in Mexico ⊕ www.sectur.gob.mx. **Mexico Tourism Board (U.K.)** ☎ 207/488-9392 ⊕ www.visitmexico.com. **Mexican Tourism Board (U.S. & Canada)** ☎ 800/446-3942 (44-MEXICO) in U.S. and Canada ⊕ www.visitmexico.com.

Puerto Vallarta Tourism Board & Convention and Visitors Bureau ⊠ Local 18 Planta Baja, Zona Comercial Hotel Canto del Sol Zona Hotelera, Las Glorias ☎ 322/224-1175, 888/384-6822 in U.S. ⊕ www. visitpuertovallarta.com. **Municipal Tourist Office** ⊠ Av. Independencia 123, Centro ☎ 322/223-2500 Ext. 131. **Jalisco State Tourism Office** ⊠ Plaza Marina shopping center, Local 144 & 146, Marina Vallarta ☎ 322/221-2676. **Nayarit State Tourism Office** ⊠ Paseo de los Cocoteros at Blvd. Nuevo Vallarta, between Gran Velas and Maribal hotels ☎ 322/297-0180.

🖪 Government Advisories **U.S. Department of State** ☎ 888/407-4747, 201/501-4444 from overseas ⊕ www.travel.state.gov. **Consular Affairs Bureau of Canada** ☎ 800/267-6788, 613/944-6788 from overseas ⊕ www.voyage.gc.ca. **U.K. Foreign and Commonwealth Office** ☎ 0845/850-2829 or 020/7008-1500 ⊕ www.fco.gov.uk/travel. **Australian Department of Foreign Affairs and Trade** ☎ 300/139-281 travel advisories, 02/6261-3305 Consular Travel Advice ⊕ www.smartraveller.gov.au. **New Zealand Ministry of Foreign Affairs and Trade** ☎ 04/439-8000 ⊕ www.mft.govt.nz.

VOLUNTEER & EDUCATIONAL TRAVEL

AmeriSpan (⇨ *below*) also places volunteers and interns in unpaid positions.

SPANISH-LANGUAGE STUDY

Attending a language institute is an ideal way not only to learn Mexican Spanish but also to acquaint yourself with the customs and the people. For total immersion, most schools offer boarding with a family, but there's generally flexibility in terms of the type of lodgings and the length of your stay.

AmeriSpan Unlimited, based in the United States, can arrange for language study and homestays. The Academia Hispano Americana offers a diploma for students who complete 20 weeks of Spanish-language study. Many programs offer courses in Latin American studies and culture, as well as language.

🖪 Language Institutes **Academia Hispano Americana** ☎ 415/152-0349 ⊕ www.ahaspeakspanish. com. **AmeriSpan Unlimited** ☎ 800/879-6640, 215/751-1100 in U.S. ⊕ www.amerispan.com. **Centro de Estudios para Extranjeros** ☎ 33/3616-4399 in Guadalajara, 322/223-2082 in PV ⊕ www.cepe. udg.mx.

WEB SITES

Do check out the World Wide Web when planning your trip. You'll find everything from weather forecasts to virtual tours. Be sure to visit Fodors.com (⊕ www.fodors. com), a complete travel-planning site. You can research prices and book plane tickets, hotel rooms, rental cars, vacation packages, see other traveler's reviews of area hotels, and more. In addition, you can post your pressing questions in the Travel Talk section. Other planning tools include a currency converter and weather reports, and there are loads of links to travel resources.

Several Mexican government Web sites have information about Puerto Vallarta and nearby resorts in English as well as Spanish. The Mexican Tourism Board's official page (⊕ www.visitmexico.com), has information about popular destinations (with 360-degree photos), activities, and festivals. The federal tourism ministry's site (⊕ www.sectorturismo.gob.mx) has general info about the tourism industry in Mexico. PV's official Web site is ⊕ www. visitpuertovallarta.com. The best of the private enterprise Web sites is ⊕ www. virtualvallarta.com,which has tons of good info and short articles about life in PV. For Buceriás information, go to ⊕ www. buceriasmexico.com. Heading to Punta de Mita? Check out ⊕ www.puntamita.com. For some info about the Costalegre, go to ⊕ www.costalegre.ca.

Excellent English-language sites for general history, travel information, facts, and news stories about Mexico are: the United States' Library of Congress well-organized Mexico pages (⊕ http://lcweb2.loc.gov/frd/cs/mxtoc.htmland ⊕ www.loc.gov/rr/international/hispanic/mexico/mexico. html); Mexico Online (⊕ www.mexonline. com); Mexico Connect (⊕ www.

mexconnect.com); the Mexico Channel (⊕ www.trace-sc.com); Mexican Wave (⊕ www.mexicanwave.com); and ⊕ www. eluniversal.com.mx, the online version of the newspaper *El Universal*, which has an English-language edition. The nonprofit site Ancient Mexico (⊕ www. ancientmexico.com) has information about Western Mexico as well as more comprehensive information about the Maya and Aztecs.

INDEX

A

Addresses, 264
Aduana, 187
Airports and transfers, 266
Air travel, 264–266
Guadalajara, 224
mountain towns, 198
San Blas and environs, 191
Ajijic, 222–224
Amber Sur Mer ✕, 86
Ana Liz 🖾, 38–39
Andale ✕🖾, 35, 64
Apartment rentals, 23
Aquiles Serdán, 105–106
Archie's Wok ✕, 75
Architecture, 172
Art galleries
Guadalajara, 212
Puerto Vallarta, 116–117, 130
Art in public spaces, 173–174
Arts, the, 172–176
ATMs, 284
ATV tours, 152–153

B

Baby supplies, 275
Bahía de Chamela, 107
Bahía de Jaltemba, 101
Bahía de los Angeles Locos, 107
Bahía de Navidad, 108
Balloon tours, 164
Banderas Bay
beaches, 97
dining, 67
lodging, 27
Banks, 266
Bar Above ✕, 79–80
Barceló La Jolla de Mismaloya 🖾, 24
Barcelona Tapas Bar ✕, 78
Barra de Navidad, 108
Barranca de Oblatos, 204, 206
Bars and pubs
Guadalajara, 217
Puerto Vallarta, 134–137, 142, 231–232
Basílica de la Virgen de Zapopan, 212
Basílica de Talpa, 197
Beaches, 93–95
Costalegre, 106–108
gay beaches, 230–231
North of Puerto Vallarta, 96–102

Puerto Vallarta, 95–98, 230–231
San Blas and environs, 190–191
shade from the sun, 99
South of Puerto Vallarta, 102–106
vendors at, 98
water-toy prices, 100
Bicycling, 161–162
Bird-watching, 165–166, 188
Birriería las 9 Esquinas ✕, 213
Blue Chairs 🖾, 234
Blue Chairs beach, 230
Blues clubs, 143, 146
Blue Shrimp ✕, 75
Boca Bento ✕, 66
Boca de Naranjo, 101
Boca de Tomatlán, 104
Books about Puerto Vallarta, 256
Bookstores, 117, 130
Brasil Nuevo Vallarta ✕, 89
Brasil Steakhouse ✕, 78
Bucerías, 99
Buenaventura 🖾, 31–32
Bullfights, 218
Bungalows Los Picos 🖾, 53, 55
Bungalows Tlaquepaque 🖾, 53
Business etiquette, 280
Business hours, 111, 266–267
Bus travel
Guadalajara, 224–225
Mexico, 267–268
mountain towns, 198
Puerto Vallarta, 268
San Blas and environs, 191

C

Cabo Corrientes, 105
Cafe del Mar ✕, 86
Café de Olla ✕, 72
Café des Artistes ✕, 65, 83
Cameras, 268–269
Canopy tours, 153–154
Car rentals, 269–271
Guadalajara, 225
Car travel, 271–274
emergency services, 272
Guadalajara, 225
Mexico, 271
mountain towns, 198
Puerto Vallarta, 271
road conditions, 273
rules of the road, 273–274

safety on the road, 274
San Blas and environs, 191
Casa Andrea 🖾, 35, 37
Casa Canta Rana 🖾, 51
Casa Cupula 🖾, 233–234
Casa de la Abuela ✕, 90
Casa de la Cultura, 196
Casa de las Flores 🖾, 215–216
Casa del Canibal ✕, 187
Casa Dulce Vida 🖾, 34
Casa Fuerte ✕, 213
Casa Grande ✕, 197–198
Casa Iguana Hotel de Mismaloya 🖾, 32
Casa Kimberley, 176–177
Casa Las Brisas 🖾, 39
CasaMagna Marriott 🖾, 30
Casa Mañana ✕🖾, 190–191
Casa Museo de Doña Conchita, 194
Casa-Museo López Portillo, 204
Casa Obelisco 🖾, 48, 50
Casa Roxanna 🖾, 188
Catedral, 204
Celebration of Independence, 179
Cenaduría Flor Morena ✕, 90
Ceramics artisans, 206
Ceramics shops, 118, 131
Cerro de San Basilio, 187
Chacala, 102
Chamela-Cuixmala Biosphere Reserve, 255
Chapala, 221–222
Charreadas, 218
Chayito's ✕, 88
Chez Elena ✕, 69
Children and travel, 274–275
Children's attractions, 275
adventures, 170
beaches, 99, 101, 104, 108
dining, 64, 70, 77, 79, 87
Guadalajara sites, 204, 206, 218, 223
lodging, 24, 30, 31, 48, 50, 53
shopping, 119, 120
Chiles ✕, 64
Choco Banana ✕, 79
Churches
Guadalajara, 204, 212
mountain towns, 194, 196, 197
Puerto Vallarta, 172
San Blas and environs, 187
Cigar shops, 117–118
Classes, 176, 177

Climate, *20*
Clothing shops, *118–120, 130*
Coconuts By the Sea ⊞, *59*
Coffee Cup (Col. C. Zapata) ✕, *64*
Coffee Cup (Marina Vallarta) ✕, *69*
Coffeehouses, *148–149*
Columba ✕, *89*
Computers, *275*
Consulates, *279*
Consumer protection, *275–276*
  shopping, *111, 114*
Costa Azul ⊞, *50–51*
Costalegre, *13*
  beaches, *106–108*
  dining, *90–91*
  forest reserves, *255*
  golf courses, *158–159*
  lodging, *55–60*
Cozumel ✕, *222*
Credit cards, *284*
Crime, *287*
Crowne Plaza Guadalajara ⊞, *216*
Cruises, *169–170, 231*
Cruise travel, *276*
Cueto's ✕, *75*
Cultural centers, *177*
Currency, *285*
Customs, *276–278*

D

Daiquiri Dick's ✕, *69, 82*
Dance, *172, 174, 206*
Dance clubs
  Guadalajara, *217*
  Puerto Vallarta, *146–147, 233*
Day trips. ⇨ *See* Excursions from Puerto Vallarta
Decameron ⊞, *51–52*
Destiladeras, *99*
Diarrhea, *280–281*
Dining, *16*
  agua de tuba drink, *89*
  American/casual restaurants, *64, 79, 90*
  Argentine restaurants, *79*
  barbecue restaurants, *64*
  breakfast spots, *75*
  cafés, *64–65, 79–80*
  with children, *64, 70, 77, 79, 87, 274–275*
  contemporary restaurants, *65, 80, 86*
  continental restaurants, *68, 86*
  Costalegre, *90–91*
  Cuban restaurants, *68*

delicatessens, *69*
dishes on area menus, *65, 84*
  with dogs, *72*
eclectic restaurants, *69–70, 86–87, 90*
festivals, *85*
fixed-price lunches, *71*
foodie hotspots, *62*
grocery stores, *114–115, 129*
Guadalajara, *212–214, 222, 223*
health concerns, *280–281*
Italian restaurants, *70–71*
meal plans, *23*
meal times, *62–63*
Mediterranean restaurants, *87*
Mexican restaurants, *71–72, 74–75, 87–88, 90*
mountain towns, *194, 196, 197–198*
North of Puerto Vallarta, *79–80, 86–89*
pan-Asian restaurants, *75*
price categories, *63*
Puerto Vallarta, *64–79*
reservations, *63*
roadside stands, *78*
San Blas and environs, *187–188, 190–191*
seafood restaurants, *75, 77–78, 89, 91*
Spanish restaurants, *78*
steak houses, *78, 89*
symbols related to, *10*
tacos, *74, 88*
time concerns, *80*
tipping, *290*
top restaurants and chefs, *82–83*
tortillas, *90*
vegetarian restaurants, *78–79, 89*
Disabilities and accessibility, *278*
Discounts and deals, *278*
Distilleries, *220*
Doctors, *279*
Dolphin encounters, *166–167*
Don Pedro's ✕, *86*
Dreams ⊞, *24*
Drunk driving laws, *273–274*
Dugarel Plays ✕, *89*
Dune-buggy tours, *152–153*
Duties, *276–278*

E

Ecotours, *188, 190*
Educational travel, *292*
El Anclote, *99*

El Andariego ✕, *71–72*
El Arbol del Café ✕, *222*
El Arrayán ✕, *72*
El Brujo ✕, *72*
El Campanario ✕, *74*
El Careyes Beach Resort ⊞, *45, 55–56*
El Centro, *12*
  dining, *73*
  lodging, *33*
  shopping, *112–113*
El Dorado ✕, *91*
Electricity, *278–279*
El Edén ✕, *77*
Eloísa ⊞, *37*
El Pescador ⊞, *34*
El Repollo Rojo ✕, *70*
El Sacromonte ✕, *214*
El Tamarindo Golf Resort ⊞, *58–59*
  spa facilities, *42*
El Templo de la Virgen del Rosario, *187*
Embassies, *279*
Emergencies, *279*
  Guadalajara, *226*
  mountain towns, *199*
  road service, *272*
  San Blas and environs, *191*
Emperador ⊞, *35*
Enramada Ruiz ✕, *190*
Etiquette and behavior, *249–250, 279–280*
Exchanging money, *285*
Excursions from Puerto Vallarta. ⇨ *Also* Guadalajara; Mountain towns; San Blas and environs
  driving times, *184*
  getting oriented, *182–183*
  tour companies, *185*
  transportation, *184*
  when to go, *185*

F

Famar ✕, *88*
Festival de Música San Pancho, *177*
Festivals and seasonal events, *85, 157, 177–180, 185, 197*
Fidensio's ✕, *70*
Fiesta Americana (Guadalajara) ⊞, *216–217*
Fiesta Americana (Puerto Vallarta) ⊞, *30–31*

Fiestas de la Virgin of Guadalupe, *180*
Film, *148, 173*
Films about Puerto Vallarta, *256*
Fishing, *154–156*
Folk art and crafts shops
Guadalajara, 219–220
Puerto Vallarta, 121, 124, 127, 130–131
Folkloric dance, *174*
Fonda de Doña Lupita ✕, *194*
Fonda Doña Leo ✕, *194*
Forest reserves, *255*
Four Seasons Resort 🖫, *39, 47*
Punta Mita Apuane Spa, 42

G

Gallo's Pizzeria ✕, *86*
Gasoline, *272*
Gas stations, *266*
Gaviota Vallarta 🖫, *37*
Gay Puerto Vallarta, *280*
daytime activities, 230–231
lodging, 233–235
nightlife, 231–233
Golf, *157–159*
Grand Bay Isla Navidad 🖫, *56*
Grand Velas 🖫, *44, 47*
Grocery stores, *114–115, 129*
Guadalajara, *183, 199–202*
contacts and resources, 225–227
dining, 212–214, 222, 223
emergencies, 226
excursions, 220–224
exploring, 203–206, 212
gay scene, 280
itineraries, 202–203
lodging, 214–217, 222, 223
nightlife, 217–218
outdoor activities and sports, 218, 223–224
shopping, 218–220
transportation, 224–225
visitor information, 226–227
Gyms, *234*

H

Hacienda Flamingos 🖫, *188*
Hacienda Jacarandas ✕🖫, *198*
Hacienda Jalisco 🖫, *195*
Hacienda San Angel 🖫, *24–25*
Hangover cures, *79*
Health concerns, *280–282*

Hiking, *167*
Hojonay Biosphere Reserve, *255*
Holidays, *179, 282*
Home furnishings shops, *127, 131*
Horseback riding
Ajijic, 223–224
Puerto Vallarta, 159–160, 231
Horse-drawn carriage rides, *204*
Hospitals, *279*
Hotel Balneario San Juan Cosalá 🖫, *223*
Hotel Cervantes 🖫, *215*
Hotel de Mendoza 🖫, *214–215*
Hotel Garza Canela ✕🖫, *187–188*
Hotelito Desconocido 🖫, *56, 58*
Hotel Molino de Agua 🖫, *32*
Hotel Plaza Diana 🖫, *217*
Hotel Villa Montecarlo 🖫, *222*
Huarache sandals, *129*
Huerta La Paz 🖫, *52–53*
Huichol Museum, *212*
Huichol woven and beaded art, *122–126*

I

Iglesia de la Virgen de los Dolores, *196*
Iglesia de San Sebastián, *194*
Inoculations, *281–282*
Insect hazards, *281*
Instituto Cultural Cabañas, *204*
Insurance
for car owners, 272
for car rentals, 270
medical plans, 281
travel insurance, 282
International Gourmet Festival, *85*
Internet cafés, *275, 282*
Guadalajara, 226
mountain towns, 199
Puerto Vallarta, 283
Isla del Coral, *101*
Isla Navidad, *108*
Islas Marietas, *99–100*
Itineraries, *18–19*

J

Jazz clubs, *143, 146*
Jewelry shops, *127–128*
Johanna's ✕, *223*

José Cuervo Distillery, *220*
Jumaica ✕, *78–79*

K

Kaiser Maximilian ✕, *68*
Karaoke bars, *136*
Karen's ✕, *86*
Karne Garibaldi ✕, *214*
Kayaking, *160–161*

L

La Bodega de Ajijic ✕, *223*
La Bodeguita del Medio ✕, *68*
La Casa del Café ✕, *88*
La Casa del Retoño 🖫, *216*
La Casa de Mi Abuela ✕, *196*
La Cruz de Huanacaxtle, *99*
La Fonda de San Miguel ✕, *213*
La Galerita de San Sebastián 🖫, *194*
La Iglesia de la Preciosa Sangre, *196*
La Iglesia de Nuestra Señora de Guadalupe, *172*
La Isla ✕, *187*
Lake Chapala, *221–224*
Lake Chapala Inn 🖫, *222*
Langostino's ✕, *77*
Language, *114, 250, 257–263, 283*
La Nueva Posada ✕🖫, *223*
La Ola Rica ✕, *80, 83, 86*
La Palapa ✕, *68*
La Paloma Oceanfront Retreat 🖫, *59*
La Peñita, *101*
La Pianola Avenida México ✕, *214*
La Piazzeta ✕, *70*
La Playita de Lindo Mar ✕, *69*
La Porteña ✕, *79*
Las Alamandas 🖫, *55*
Las Carmelitas ✕, *71*
Las Fiestas de Mayo, *178–179*
Las Villas 🖫, *60*
Las Villitas Club & Marina 🖫, *59*
La Taquiza ✕, *74*
La Terraza di Roma ✕, *70–71*
Latino music clubs, *142–143*
La Trattoria ✕, *214*
La Villa del Ensueño 🖫, *215*
Leather shops, *128–129*
Le Bistro ✕, *69*
Le Kliff ✕, *66*
Liquor shops, *129*
Lo de Marcos, *100*

Lodging, 16
alternatives, 23
boutique hotels, 23
chain hotels, 23
with children, 24, 30, 31, 48, 50, 53, 275
choosing a hotel, 22
Costalegre, 55–60
gay hotels, 233–235
Gran Turismo program, 22
Guadalajara, 214–217, 222, 223
meal plans, 23
mountain towns, 194–195, 196, 198
North of Puerto Vallarta, 39, 47–55
parking at hotels, 22
pillow menus, 50
price categories, 23
Puerto Vallarta, 24–39, 233–235
ratings, 23
San Blas and environs, 187–188, 190–191
symbols related to, 10
time-shares, 38, 48
tipping, 290
Los Alcatraces ✕, 71
Los Arcos, 104
Los Artistas 🏨, 223
Los Cuatro Vientos 🏨, 35
Los Xitomates ✕, 71

M

Mail and shipping, 282–283
Guadalajara, 226
mountain towns, 199
San Blas and environs, 191
Majahuitas 🏨, 25
Majahuitas beach, 104
Malecón, 175
Maps for driving, 273
Marco's Place Villas 🏨, 53
Mariachi music, 145, 207–211
Mariscos 8 Tostadas ✕, 77–78
Mariscos Guicho's ✕, 222
Marival 🏨, 47–48
Mark's Bar & Grill ✕, 80, 83
Mar Plata ✕, 87
Martini bars, 136–137
Martin's ✕, 90
Mascota, 195–197, 199
Maya ✕, 90
Medical insurance, 281
Medical services, 279
Memo's Pancake House ✕, 64

Mercurio 🏨, 234
Mesón de Santa Elena 🏨, 196
Mexican music, 144–145
Money matters, 283–285
Guadalajara, 225–226
mountain towns, 199
San Blas and environs, 191
Mosquitoes, 281
Mountain biking, 161–162
Mountain towns, 183, 192–199
contacts and resources, 199
transportation, 198
Movies about Puerto Vallarta, 256
Multisport tours, 162
Museo Arqueológico, 177
Museo de Arte de Zapopan, 212
Museo de la Paleontología, 204
Museo de la Virgen, 212
Museo del Premio Nacional de la Cerámica Pantaleon Panduro, 206
Museo de Mascota, 196
Museo Huichol Wixarica de Zapopan, 212
Museo Regional de Guadalajara, 204
Museo Regional de la Cerámica, 206
Museums
Guadalajara, 204, 206, 212, 220
mountain towns, 194, 196
Puerto Vallarta, 176–177
Music, classical, 174, 206
Music clubs, 142–143, 146
Music of Mexico, 144–145

N

Nightlife
bars and pubs, 134–137, 142, 217
coffeehouses, 148–149
dance clubs, 146–147, 217
film, 148
gay venues, 231–233
Guadalajara, 217–218
live music, 142–143, 146
Puerto Vallarta, 134–137, 142–149, 231–233
shows, 149
North of Puerto Vallarta, 13
beaches, 98–102
dining, 79–80, 86–89
golf courses, 158

lodging, 39, 47–55
shopping, 129–131
Nuevo Corral del Risco, 99

O

Outdoor activities and sports
gay activities, 231
Guadalajara, 218, 223–224
mountain towns, 195, 197
Puerto Vallarta, 152–169
San Blas and environs, 188, 190

P

Package deals, 291
Packing, 285–286
Paco's Paradise, 230–231
Page in the Sun ✕, 64–65
Palmeras 🏨, 55
Paradise Village 🏨, 48
Palenque Spa, 44
Parking, 272–273
Parque Agua Azul, 204
Passports, 286–287
Pepe's Tacos ✕, 74
Pharmacies, 267, 279, 281
Philo's ✕, 87
Photography, 268–269
Piano bars, 137
Pie in the Sky ✕, 80
Planeta Vegetariana ✕, 79
Playa Boca de Iguanas, 107–108
Playa Borrego, 190
Playa Camarones, 96
Playa Careyes, 107
Playa Chalacatepec, 106–107
Playa Conchas Chinas, 103
Playa Conchas Chinas 🏨, 32
Playa del Toro, 101
Playa El Salado, 96, 98
Playa Fidrieras, 101
Playa Garza Blanca, 103–104
Playa la Manzanilla (north), 99
Playa la Manzanilla (south), 108
Playa las Ánimas, 104
Playa las Glorias, 96, 98
Playa Las Islitas, 190
Playa las Minitas, 100–101
Playa Los Arcos 🏨, 34
Playa los Ayala, 101
Playa Los Cocos, 190
Playa los Muertos, 95–96
Playa los Tules, 96, 98
Playa los Venados, 101
Playa Miramar, 190
Playa Mismaloya, 104

Playa Mora, *107*
Playa Negrita, *107*
Playa Nuevo Vallarta, *98*
Playa Olas Altas, *96*
Playa Perula, *107*
Playa Platanitos, *190*
Playa Tenacatita, *107*
Playa Teopa, *107*
Polo, *160*
Porto Bello ✕, *70*
Posada de Roger ▥, *39*
Pottery shops, *118, 131*
Presidente InterContinental
  Puerto Vallarta Resort ▥,
  25
Price categories
dining, 63
lodging, 23
Public offices, *266*
Puerto Vallarta. ⇨ *Also*
  Banderas Bay; El Centro;
  Gay Puerto Vallarta; Zona
  Romántica
beaches, 95–98, 230–231
books and movies about, 256
bus travel, 268
car travel, 271
dining, 64–79
*facts and figures about,
  238–239*
getting oriented, 12–13
golf courses, 157–158
*government and economy,
  245–247*
history of, 17, 240–244
lodging, 24–39, 233–235
*natural environment,
  253–255*
*nightlife, 134–137, 142–149,
  231–233*
*outdoor activities and sports,
  152–169*
*people and society, 16,
  248–252*
*shopping, 112–113, 114–121,
  127–129*
taxis, 288–289
top experiences, 14–15
visitor information, 292
Punta de Mita, *99*
Punta Mita ▥, *51*
Punta Negra, *103*
Punta Serena ▥, *58*

Q
Quimixto, *104*
Quinta Don José ▥, *215*
Quinta María Cortez ▥, *31*
Quinta Real ▥, *216*

R
Rain Tree ✕, *87–88*
Rancho de Cuixmala ▥,
  59–60
Real de San Sebastián ▥,
  195
Restaurant Jalapeños ✕, *214*
Restaurant Week, *85*
Restrooms, *287*
Rincón de Guayabitos, *101*
Río ▥, *37–38*
River Cafe ✕, *66, 68*
Rock clubs, *143, 146*
Rodeos, *218*
Roots ✕, *89*
Rosita ▥, *34*

S
Safety, *287–288*
Sailing, *162–163*
Salvador's ✕, *223*
San Blas and environs, *182,
  186–192*
*contacts and resources,
  191–192*
transportation, 191
Sandrina's ✕, *87*
San Francisco, *100*
San Sebastián, *193–195, 199*
Santa Cruz, *190*
Santiago de Compostela ▥,
  215
Sauza Museum, *220*
Sayulita, *100*
Sayulita Café ✕, *88*
Scuba diving, *163–164*
Sea Life Park, *170*
Seamaster's ✕, *91*
Senior-citizen travel, *288*
Sheraton Buganvilias ▥,
  25–26
Shoe and handbag shops,
  128–129
Shopping
business hours, 111, 267
with children, 119, 120
consumer protection, 111, 114
department stores, 114
groceries, 114–115, 129
Guadalajara, 218–220
for huichol, 124
malls, 115, 130, 219
markets, 115
mountain towns, 197
*north and south of Puerto
  Vallarta, 129–131*
*Puerto Vallarta, 112–113,
  114–121, 127–129*
smart souvenirs, 110–111
Spanish vocabulary for, 114
*specialty stores, 116–121,
  127–129, 130–131*
tips for shoppers, 111
Shows, *149*
Sierra Lago ▥, *196*
Si Hay Olitas ✕, *88*
Silver items for sale, *128, 219*
Snorkeling, *102, 104,
  163–164*
Soccer, *218*
Sol Meliá Puerto Vallarta ▥,
  31
South of Puerto Vallarta, **13.**
  ⇨ *Also* Costalegre
beaches, 102–106
shopping, 129–131
Souvenirs, *110–111*
Spanish language, *114, 250,
  257–263, 283*
Spanish-language study, *292*
Spas, *41–46, 231*
Sports. ⇨ *See* Outdoor
  activities and sports
Sports bars, *142*
Stop-and-go bars, *135*
Strip clubs, *233*
Student travel, *288*
Sunbathing, *281*
Surfing, *102, 164–165*
Symbols, *10*

T
Taberna San Pascual ✕, *78*
Talavera-style pieces, *119*
Talpa de Allende, *197–198,
  199*
Tango lessons, *147*
Tapas del Mundo ✕, *87*
Taxes, *288*
Taxis
Guadalajara, 225
mountain towns, 198
Puerto Vallarta, 288–289
San Blas and environs, 191
Taylor, Elizabeth, *176–177,
  233*
Tehualmixtle, *106*
Telephones, *289–290*
Temazcal spas, *46, 231*
Templo de San Blas, *187*
Tennis, *26*
Tequila (drink), *138–141*
Tequila (town), *220*
Terra Noble spa, *43, 231*
Teuchitlán, *220–221*
Theater, *174–175*
Three Kings Day, *178*

Tía Catarina ✕ , 72, 74
Tile shops, 118, 131
Time, 80, 290
Time-shares, 38, 48
Tino's ✕ , 77
Tipping, 290–291
Tour operators, 185, 291
Travel agencies
for disabled travelers, 278
selecting an agent, 291
Traveler's checks, 285
Travel insurance, 282
Trio ✕ , 66, 82
Tropicana 🏨 , 35
Turtle-watching and
repatriation, 56, 101,
167–168
Tutifruti ✕ , 74–75

V

Vagabundo 🏨 , 60
Value-added tax, 288
Velas Vallarta 🏨 , 26
Videos, 269
Villa Amor 🏨 , 52
Villa Bella 🏨 , 50

Villa David 🏨 , 234–235
Villa rentals, 23
Villas Buena Vida 🏨 , 52
Villa tours, 173
Villa Varadero 🏨 , 53
Villa Vista Mágica, 51
Visas, 286–287
Visitor information,
291–292
Guadalajara, 226–227
mountain towns, 199
Puerto Vallarta, 292
San Blas and environs,
191–192
Vista Guayabitos ✕ , 88
Vitea ✕ , 66, 82
Vocabulary words, 114,
257–263

Voladores de Papantla, 176
Volunteer travel, 292

W

Water for drinking, 37,
280–281
Water parks, 170, 204

Water toys, 100
Weather information, 20
Web sites, 292–293
Westin Resort & Spa 🏨 , 26,
30, 45
Whale watching, 168–169
When to go, 20, 22, 185
Wildlife watching, 102,
165–169
Wine shops, 129
Women traveling alone,
287–288
Workshops, 176

Y

Yasmín 🏨 , 39
Yelapa, 104–105
Yoga classes, 52

Z

Zona Romántica, 12
dining, 76
lodging, 36
shopping, 112–113
Zoológico Guadalajara, 206

PHOTO CREDITS

Cover Photo, (Los Arcos amphitheater on the Malecon): *Karen Huntt/Corbis.* 5, *Eric Wessman/viestiphoto.com.* **Chapter 1: Experience Puerto Vallarta:** 11, *Danita Delimont/ Alamy.* 12, *Jane Onstott.* 13, *Mary Magruder/viestiphoto.com.* 14, *Walter Bibikow/ viestiphoto.com.* 15 (left), *Puerto Vallarta Tourism Board.* 15 (right), *Ken Welsh/age fotostock.* 16, *Ken Ross/viestiphoto.com.* 17 (left), *Ken Ross/viestiphoto.com.* 17 (right), *Walter Bibikow/viestiphoto.com.* 18, *Terrance Klassen/age fotostock.* 19 (left), *Walter Bibikow/viestiphoto.com.* 19 (right), *Puerto Vallarta Tourism Board.* 20, *Ken Ross/viesiphoto.com* **Chapter 2: Where to Stay:** 21, *El Tamarindo Golf Resort.* 40, *El Careyes Beach Resort.* 41 (left and right), *Four Seasons Resort, Punta Mita.* 42 (top), *Four Seasons Resort, Punta Mita.* 42 (bottom), *El Tamarindo Golf Resort.* 44, *Grand Velas.* 45 (top), *Ken Ross/viestiphoto.com.* 45 (bottom), *El Careyes Beach Resort.* 46, *Ken Ross/viiestiphoto.com.* **Chapter 3: Where to Eat:** 61, *Ken Ross/viestiphoto.com.* 81, *Lisa Candela.* 82 (all), *Ken Ross/viestiphoto.com.* 83 (top), *Jane Onstott.* 83 (center), *Mark's Restaurant.* 83 (bottom), *Ken Ross/viestiphoto.com.* 84 (top and bottom), *Ken Ross/viestiphoto.com.* 85, *Ken Ross/viestiphoto.com.* **Chapter 4: Beaches:** 93, *Corbis.* **Chapter 5: Shopping:** 109, *Ken Ross/viestiphoto.com.* 122, *Ken Ross/viestiphoto. com.* 123 (top), *Ken Ross/viestiphoto.com.* 123 (bottom), *Walter Bibikow/viestiphoto. com.* 124, *Ken Ross/viestiphoto.com.* 125 (top right), *Ken Ross/viestiphoto.com.* 125 (top left, bottom left and bottom right), *Jane Onstott.* 125 (center right), *José Zelaya Gallery: artedelpueblo.com.* 126 (top, bottom left, center left, bottom right), *Ken Ross/viestiphoto.com.* 126 (center right), *Jane Onstott.* **Chapter 6: After Dark:** 133, *Jeff Greenberg/Alamy.* 138, *Russell Gordon/viestiphoto.com.* 139 (all), *Russell Gordon/viestiphoto.com.* 140, *Ken Ross/viestiphoto.com.* 141 (top and bottom), *Ken Ross/viestiphoto.com.* 145, *David Sanger Photography/Alamy.* **Chapter 7: Adventure:** 151, *Bruce Herman/Mexico Tourism Board.* **Chapter 8: Culture:** 171, *Fide-*

I

MAPS
PG. 67-97-43   SEE PG 47

NOTES

IS MAYAN PALACE
ASSOCIATED
WITH
HAS GOOD GOLF
↓

NUEVO VALLARTA

~~NUEVO~~   MAYAN SEA GARDENS   HOTEL

ATTRACTION — ① CITY OF OLD VALLARTA IN P.V.
② MARINA VALLARTA & GOLF COURSES
AND   PG.'S 12

③ N.V. PG 13 PARADISE PLAZA MALL
HAS SOME RESTUARANTS

④ N.V. PG 13 PLAYA CHACALA BEACH +
SMALL TOWN CHARM SAN. FRANCISCO,
SAYULITA, PUNTA DE MITA.

⑤   PG 13 CLIFFSIDE HOTELS

PG 14   STROLL FAMOUS MALCON.
8 BLOCK SEA WALK, SUNSETS, MUSIC PK.

PG 14   CHART OF WHAT YOU WANT &
WHERE TO GET IT.

PG 15   SUNSETS

PG 16   P.V HAS GREAT FOOD!
VERY CLEAN STREETS & ENGLISH SPEAKING

PG 18   GREAT ITERNARIES —
PG 19   GOLF AT MAYAN PALACE

PG 23   SEE BOTTOM RIGHT SIDE OF PG.

PG 27 SEE HOTEL MAP
PG 29 SEE

NOTES

PG 37   ABOUT DRINKING WATER
PG 47 } WORD OR MOUTH (NUEVO)
PG 48 } POSSIBLE RESTAURANTS

PG 60   WHERE TO EAT STARTS
$$$ = OVER $25 $$$$ = 18 TO 25 $$ 12-17 $ 5-11
¢ = UNDER $5

PG 67   FOR FOOD IN NUEVO

PG 70   - MASHED POTATOES, GRAVY, CHICKEN
         & ITALIAN

PG 75   - BREAKFAST
PG 78 & 79   NUEVO   REST.
PG 82 & 83   - TOP REST. & CHEFS

PG 98 MAYAN PALACE SANDY BEACH
PG 99   WHALE WATCHING   ISLA MARIETAS

PG 102   BUSES TO SOUTH OF P.V.
     ALSO   BOAT TAXI'S (SEE CHAPTER 7)

PG 142   MUSICAL EVENTS IN BAY VALLARTA
     NEWSPAPER   2X PER A MONTH

PG 144   MUSIC (NORTEÑA

PG 149   SHOWS (MIRIACHI
          PLAYA LAS ARCOS

NOTES

VOCAB: 257

PG 156   WHALE   WATCHING   ISLAA MARIETTAS

PG 158   GOLF

P6 159   HORSEBACK RIDING   CHEAP

PG 168 + 169 WHALE WATCHING FROM MARINA V. LARGER BOATS
           SEE 169 GUARANTEE WHALE SIGHTINGS
                    ISLA   MARIETAS

PG 169, 170 - CRUISES, SOUTH OF PV
           OR   MARIETAS · MUST SEE

           NO CRUISES ON DIANA TOURS OR
              PACO PACO GAYS OR
           (THE BOAT RAIBOW DANCER
              GAY SECTION   PG 230)

PG 281   HEALTH

PGS 284 - 285   ATM, CREDIT CARD LOST
           NUMBERS IN MEXICO

PG 267   BUSES

PG 99   PUNTA DE MITA

ABOUT THE WRITER

Jane Onstott was primed for adventure travel in her late teens, when she wandered Central America for six months after being stood up at the Tegucigalpa airport up by an inattentive suitor. She has since survived a near plunge into a gorge in the highlands of Mexico, a knife-wielding robber in Madrid, and a financial shipwreck on one of the more remote Galapagos Islands. The last led to a position as director of communications and information at the Charles Darwin Research Station on the island of Santa Cruz, where she lectured on the ecology of Ecuador's unique Galapagos archipelago.

Before she turned 20, a six-month, total-immersion-Spanish course in rural Honduras paved the way for Jane's love of the language and of Hispanic culture. She studied for a year at la Universidad Complutense de Madrid, in Spain, and graduated in 1980 from San Diego State University with a B.A. in Spanish language and literature.

But at age 17 this adventurer's first foray outside the United States—Southern California's concrete jungle—was to a small village in the tropical forest just a few hours north of Puerto Vallarta. The stick-and-thatch house where she stayed has since been replaced by a more modern one of cement and bright stucco, but the warm hearts of its owners have changed little in the ensuing three decades. Mexico is Jane's favorite country, and Puerto Vallarta and the surrounding coast, one of her more frequent destinations, whether traveling for business or pleasure.

In the 1990s Jane spent several years studying painting, sculpting, and the fine art of loafing in Oaxaca—ancient capital of the Zapotec nation—where she was inspired by landscape, the people, and the culture. Today Jane continues to edit and write mainly about travel and mostly about Mexico, and to work part time leading tours to Baja California. She has a home in San Diego county, a short hop north of the border—and of the Tijuana airport.

Acknowledgments

Many people contributed to the writing of this book with their thoughtful advice, suggestions, support, and by divulging favorite restaurants they'd really prefer no one knew about. In particular, I'd like to express my appreciation to the Puerto Vallarta office of the Jalisco State tourism office, especially Ludwig Estrada Virgen and Alvaro Campos Langarica, for their unequivocal support. Georgina Rodríguez and Rubi Palacios of the Nayarit–Vallarta tourism office, and Alyson Cordova of INEGI also were fonts of useful data.

Mark McCoy, Pat Cordes, Victoria Pratt, Reto Josef Kade, Ray Calhoun, Dave Collins, Susan and Phil Pits, Dave Simmonds, Barbara and Memo Kirkwood, Susan Wiseman, Mercedes Gargollo Chavez, and Gloria Whiting provided much useful information about the region. I thank Wayland and Aruna Combe–Wright and Kevin Simpson for their insight into the Huichol culture and Darrique Barton for helping me to get acquainted with the gay culture. And here's to the friendly Mexican cabbies, a fabulous source of up-to-date information!

I thank my sister, Susan Humphrey, for her suggestions regarding murky writing, and my editor, Shannon Kelly, for pulling it all together.